Canadian Literature
at the Crossroads of
Language and Culture

Selected Essays by Barbara Godard

1987 – 2005

CANADIAN LITERATURE AT THE CROSSROADS OF LANGUAGE AND CULTURE

Edited by Smaro Kamboureli

NeWest Press

COPYRIGHT © BARBARA GODARD 2008

Library and Archives Canada Cataloguing in Publication

Godard, Barbara
Canadian literature at the crossroads of language and culture : selected essays by Barbara Godard, 1987 – 2005 / edited by Smaro Kamboureli.
Includes bibliographical references and index.
ISBN 978-1-897126-36-3
I. Canadian literature--History and criticism. 2. Canada--Civilization. 3. Canada--Intellectual life. 4. Culture in literature. I. Title.
PS8061.G62 2008   C810.9'3271   C2008-903934-3

Editor for the Board: Smaro Kamboureli
Cover and interior design: Natalie Olsen
Cover image: Marian Dale Scott, "Sans titre." Acrylique sur toile, 213 x 101.6 cm. Printed with permission from the Musée national des beaux-arts du Québec, collection 66.104. Photographer: Jean-Guy Kérouac
Proof and index: Carol Berger

 Canada Council for the Arts   Conseil des Arts du Canada   Canadian Heritage / Patrimoine canadien   Alberta Foundation for the Arts   edmonton arts council

NeWest Press acknowledges the support of the Canada Council for the Arts, the Alberta Foundation for the Arts, and the Edmonton Arts Council for our publishing program. We also acknowledge the financial support of the Government of Canada through the Book Publishing Industry Development Program (BPIDP).

NeWest Press would also like to thank TransCanada Institute for its contribution to the publication of this book.

trãnsCanâða
— INSTITUTE —

NEWEST PRESS

201 8540 109 Street
Edmonton, Alberta T6G 1E6
780 432 9427
newestpress.com

No bison were harmed in the making of this book.
We are committed to protecting the environment and to the responsible use of natural resources. This book is printed on 100% recycled, ancient forest-friendly paper.

1 2 3 4 5 11 10 09 08

printed and bound in Canada

Contents

11   Acknowledgements

13   Editor's Note by Smaro Kamboureli

17   The Critic, Institutional Culture, and Canadian Literature:
         Barbara Godard in Conversation with Smaro Kamboureli

53   Structuralism / Post-Structuralism:
         Language, Reality, and Canadian Literature (1987)

83   Critical Discourse in /on Quebec (1990)

109   The Politics of Representation:
         Some Native Canadian Women Writers (1990)

161   Deterritorializing Strategies:
         M. NourbeSe Philip as Caucasianist Ethnographer (2004)

175   Canadian? Literary? Theory? (1992)

201   Writing Between Cultures (1997)

235   Notes from the Cultural Field:
         Canadian Literature from Identity to Commodity (2000)

273   A Literature in the Making:
         Rewriting and the Dynamism of the Cultural Field (1999)

315   Relational Logics:
         Of Linguistic and Other Transactions in the Americas (2005)

359   Notes

381   Works Cited

403   Index

Acknowledgements

The essays in this collection were previously published in the following journals and volumes: "Structuralism/Post-Structuralism: Language, Reality, and Canadian Literature," *Future Indicative: Literary Theory and Canadian Literature*, ed. John Moss (Ottawa: U Ottawa P, 1987), 25–51, reproduced by permission of the University of Ottawa Press; "Critical Discourse in/on Quebec," *Studies on Canadian Literature: Essays Introductory and Critical*, ed. Arnold E. Davidson (New York: MLA, 1990), 271–95; "The Politics of Representation: Some Native Canadian Women Writers," *Canadian Literature* 124–25 (April 1990), 188–225; "Canadian? Literary? Theory?" *Open Letter* 8, 3 (April 1992), 5–27; "Writing Between Cultures," TTR 10, 1 (1997), 53–97; "Notes from the Cultural Field: Canadian Literature from Identity to Commodity," *Essays on Canadian Writing* 72 (2000), 209–47; "A Literature in the Making: Rewriting and the Dynamism of the Cultural Field: Quebec Women Writers in English Canada," is a translation by Barbara Godard of "Une littérature en devenir: la réécriture textuelle et le dynamisme du champ littéraire. Les écrivaines québécoises au Canada anglais," *Voix et images*, 24, 3 (72) (printemps 1999): 495–527; "Deterritorializing Strategies: M. NourbeSe Philip as Caucasianist Ethnographer," *Ebony, Ivory and Tea*, eds. Zbigniew Bialis and Krzysztof Kowalczyk-Twarowski (Katowice, Poland: Wydawnictwo Uniwersytetu Slaskiego, 2004), 228–42; and "Relational Logics: Of Linguistic and Other Transactions in the Americas," *Perspectivas Transnacionais/Perspectives Transnationales/Transnational Perspectives*, ed. Sandra R.G. Almeida (Belo Horizonte, Brazil: ABECAN, UFMG, 2005), 241–73.

Editor's Note

Canadian Literature at the Crossroads of Language and Culture gathers together for the first time a selection of essays by Barbara Godard — a selection because, in addition to being unequivocally one of the most influential critics in Canadian English and Quebec literatures, Godard is also one of the most prolific scholars in these fields. No single book could easily collect all of her published, let alone unpublished, work. So, though this volume is long, it includes only a small selection of her writings.

Deciding which of her essays to include was a real challenge. Known primarily as a Canadian literature specialist and a theorist, Godard has written about issues that range from aboriginal literature in Canada and Brazilian culture to feminist periodicals and translation, and has done so from similarly wide perspectives informed by structuralism, semiotics, comparative literature approaches, feminist theory, and poststructuralism, to mention only a few of the critical discourses and methods that she has been concerned with. Whether she writes through the impersonating trope of Cassandra or that of a critic who would rather be picking daisies on a sunny field than writing about the Bourdieusian cultural field, Godard has produced work that has never failed to advance our knowledge of Canadian literature. This editorial project, then, has been shaped by my desire for this volume to be at once cohesive and representative of the complexity and range of her critical and theoretical concerns. Reflecting the "wide net" within which she has always cast her writing, the nine essays here cover a span of about twenty years, from the late 1980s to mid 2000.

The essays have not been revised. Only typographical or other errors and inadvertent omissions in their original publication have been corrected and the essays' original documentation format changed and standardized. I consulted with Godard at every stage of this project's development. I wish to thank her for accepting my proposal to edit this volume and for working with me on some of the aspects of the editorial process.

My dialogue with Godard, "The Critic, Institutional Culture, and Canadian Literature," which appears here for the first time, took place at different stages, first as a recorded interview in her Toronto house in early December 2007 and subsequently through e-mail correspondence. The interview was designed to serve in lieu of the critical introduction I might have written to this volume.

When critics conduct interviews we tend to do so with literary authors as our interviewees, not fellow critics. As a result, what we come to know about critical thinkers relies mostly on their printed word about the material or other critics they engage with and rarely (if at all in the Canadian context) on their reflections about their own professional and critical development. I thought that an interview with Barbara Godard would help situate her in contexts that illuminate the conditions that have contributed both to the production of her own work and to the evolution of Canadian literature as a discipline. Not only does this interview illustrate the institutional, social, and cultural engagements that are at the heart of a humanist's profession, but it also performs the role of a cultural memory document. By revisiting the different stages of her academic career and the critical paths she has pursued, and thinking out loud about university culture, Godard also speaks here to the contingencies and materialities that pervade the critical and pedagogical acts at large.

I would like to thank my assistants Andrea K. Bennett and Robert Zacharias for their valuable assistance and dedication to this project. In the summer of 2006 Andrea scanned and collated over 800 pages of Godard's criticism so that I would be able to try out various configurations of material for this edited volume, while in 2008 Robert helped standardize the documentation format of the final manuscript. I also wish to acknowledge the meticulous transcription of my interview with Godard undertaken by my undergraduate students Phoebe Lusk and Jorgen (Zeke) Baker, as well as the help of my assistants Jennica Grimshaw and Derek Murray with some of the details of the manuscript's final preparation. Thanks are also due to Kathy Mezei for her help with clarifying some fact details in my interview with Godard.

The support provided by the Canada Research Chair program through my Chair in Critical Studies in Canadian Literature was instrumental in my being able to pursue the editing, production, and publication of this volume.

Smaro Kamboureli
Guelph, ON
May 2008

The Critic, Institutional Culture, and Canadian Literature:

Barbara Godard in Conversation with Smaro Kamboureli

SMARO KAMBOURELI: This interview, Barbara, is in lieu of a formal introduction to the volume of your selected essays. I thought that rather than having your essays introduced in the third person — by me — it would be interesting and useful for the reader to hear you talk about where your work is coming from, to get a sense of your trajectory as a critic. In some respects, the institutionalization of Canadian literature as we have come to know it started with your generation. You've been both a witness of and a participant in various kinds of initiatives that brought the teaching and critical study of Canadian literature into the mainstream, that contributed to the development of Canadian literature as a discipline. Above all, you've been a pathbreaker in many ways, not least of all the fact that your critical writing and various editorial projects introduced different critical tools and contexts through which to study Canadian literature. For example, you've been instrumental in introducing theory — semiotics, feminist theory, narratology, poststructuralism, translation theory, to give some obvious examples — into the Canadian literary and critical landscapes.

You've also been a key figure in generating a vibrant dialogue between anglophone Canadian literature and Quebec writers, especially women. All this, along with the fact that you've taught a large number of scholars over your long teaching career and inspired many through your writing, suggests that "Barbara Godard" is an institution in her own right. Mind you, not the kind of calcified institution that many of us these days feel compelled to question. Your work may reflect certain preoccupations, but it never quite returns to exactly the same ground. I'd like this interview to create a space for you to reflect on the critical paths that you have pursued, but also to think about the Canadian critical scene in general.

So let's start by talking about your education — I suspect most of your readers don't really know about or aren't really familiar with that — and then you can give us a sense of your intellectual trajectory and the contexts that have shaped your development as critic. You completed your postsecondary education in the early 1960s, right? Why Canadian literature at that point? Why French-Canadian literature? And why do a PhD in Bordeaux?

BARBARA GODARD: In my research this past year for a presentation on "Quebec, the National Question and Student Activism in the 1960s"[1] I have been investigating an event organized by some of my classmates at the University of Toronto, a demo in November 1963 with presentation of a brief to the Ontario government calling on it to recognize "le fait canadien-français." Digging in the University of Toronto Archives, I discovered a history of action on the Quebec question through the 1960s and I have made contact with former classmates as well as those involved later in the decade. What has been so uncanny is that I have crossed paths with them in very different circumstances during the intervening years. So what I thought was the trajectory of an individual, I now realize is that of a generation.

SK: That's not surprising, of course, and it relates to what I mentioned earlier, that the critical and professional shifts your career embodies have facilitated the shifts that have marked my generation of classmates.

BG: In this case, the people who were involved in organizing the demo and in the Canadien-Canadian Committee of the Student Administrative Council at the centre of the event and of activities concerning Quebec later in the 1960s have had a significant impact on politics and academic research and teaching more broadly as these concern French-English relations in particular, but also relations with aboriginal peoples. Many people active on the Canadien-Canadian Committee (Can-Can as it was jokingly called) have become journalists and academics in several disciplines. The most significant impact of this group seems to have been on French language rights in Ontario through the work of some of them on Ontario's Advisory Committee on Confederation (1965 – 1971). The organizers were in my fourth-year History course — my education was in English and History — a course in Quebec nationalism which I took with Ramsay Cook. I had only a vague memory of the demo and for several years had been trying to find out what happened in order to complete a detail in an autobiographical piece I had written. [2] I found the information in *The Varsity* the day I received news about the Global 60s conference.

So I was keen to give a presentation on the demo and to do further research into the history of the 1960s in Canada, about which so little has been written. In my hunt, I had read all the books on the student movement — most of them starting in 1965 with the baby boomers' arrival at university. I knew there was another earlier 1960s generation and movement which was very much involved with nationalism and internationalism in the anti-nuclear movement at the end of the Cold War era and the break-up of Europe's colonial empires. Many of us taking History had met in the 1950s, in the Model United Nations where high schools represented countries and students debated the international affairs of the day. Many of us had also met through the CUCND [Combined Universities Campaign for Nuclear Disarmament] which we had been introduced to through the Model UN and then continued with at university. The anti-nuclear movement was the major site of activism in the 1950s, one which also saw the beginning of feminist activism with the Voice of Women.

These movements had an international focus, but at the same time a nationalist one, since the protest against nuclear weapons involved opposition to US imposition of Bomarc missiles on Canadian soil. Also the 1950s and early 1960s were the years of liberation for many of Europe's colonies in Asia and Africa. The Algerian struggle had particular resonance in Quebec and through the FLQ [Front de libération du Québec] on English-Canadian students reading about a socialist liberation movement in the periodical *Parti pris*, started by writers and students connected to the Université de Montréal. A summer seminar of the World University Service in 1965 took Canadian students to newly liberated Algeria. One indication of the international perspective was the founding at U of T in the early 1960s of Canadian Volunteers Overseas, or CUSO [Canadian University Services Overseas] as it was later called. A number of people I knew in university were among the first group that went off to India. I've caught up with them later through the Shastri Indo-Canadian Institute. They became academics working on India or Black Canadian studies, pioneers in these fields. So students from the early 1960s have been very active in a number of social transformations through the period which influenced their later intellectual concerns.

sk: How did you come to study Canadian literature?

bg: In an era of liberation struggles, our generation saw parallels between Africa and Canada's situation as a political colony of England, and economic colony of the us, and a colonialist power within its borders in relations with Quebec and aboriginal peoples. The demands for independence in an era of anti-imperialism were voiced most forcefully in Quebec in the theoretical and creative writings of young activists. A concern about Canadian studies, especially in the field of literature, was also raised by Susan Jackel (who was in my year at the University of Toronto) protesting the absence of Canadian literature on the curriculum in the early 1960s in her reviews for *The Varsity*: the interest in Canadian writing was not mine alone, but that of a generation.[3] This was an argument — well, friendly conversation — I had with Philip Child, one of my professors [also a novelist and poet], over the fact that there were no Canadians and only one woman in the modern fiction course. So he gave us Sheila Watson's *The Double Hook* to read but it wasn't officially on the curriculum. Another professor, Gordon Roper, was preparing a section on nineteenth-century fiction for the *Literary History of Canada*, and Milton Wilson, who taught us Romantic poetry, was writing the poetry section.

They talked about this research outside of class and the books were all around in their offices. This split was characteristic of the discourse on Canadian literature in the period. The universities taught "the best that has been thought or written," that is, British literature, while the professors worked actively in the production of Canadian literature. Malcolm Ross, editor of the New Canadian Library series, turned out to be an important figure for me. I lamented to him that I had applied to graduate schools in the us to study nineteenth-century literature, but no longer wanted to do so. I wanted to study Canadian literature, and Quebec literature in particular in which I had become interested through a major paper for my history course on Jules-Paul Tardivel, a novelist, journalist, and separatist of the nineteenth century. Ross said, "Well, you must go to Montreal and work with Albert LeGrand," who had taught with Ross earlier at Queens. I had an OGS [Ontario Graduate Scholarship] to go to the U of T and had an interview with the graduate chair, but he wasn't very enthusiastic about my interest in Canadian literature.

So I went to the Université de Montréal where they'd revolutionized the curriculum. In 1962, students demanded they teach Quebec literature, so a certificate in Quebec literature (and English-Canadian, en français) had been established for the Licence. I was in the English department but you could take half your classes in the French department, so I was able to work comparatively across both programmes. I had two thesis supervisors: Philip Stratford, who arrived there in English the same year I did — I was his first student — and, because he hadn't yet done any work on comparative Canadian literature, I laid the groundwork for this new field; and Albert LeGrand from whom I learned a great deal as I was much closer to him and the French department in my theoretical interests. I worked with the concepts of Gaston Bachelard on the phenomenological imaginary and poetics of space linked to the sociological approach of Jean-Charles Falardeau to analyze literary form through a political lens in a thesis comparing the vertical French and horizontal English Montreal urban imaginaries. I applied for a Canada Council doctorate award, which I received. I was admitted to the U of T, but then Ross said, "Get out of here!"

sk: That's a clear and loud statement. What did it mean, that he didn't think the U of T was a good place at the time for the study of CanLit?

bg: Exactly.

sk: Was that the reason he too left the U of T?

bg: In part. He left the next year for Dalhousie, and Roper left for Trent, so there weren't many Canadianists there to work with. At that point they were planning a Comparative Literature programme at the Université de Montréal. Robert Escarpit, one of the founders of the International Association of Comparative Literature, came over to review the plans. I had the grant, so I registered at Bordeaux to work with Escarpit, thinking that I would transfer back to Montreal when the programme was established. Escarpit was one of the most renowned comparativists and interested in the sociology of literature, "le fait littéraire," or the workings of the literary institution in the material production and dissemination of texts.

sk: What took you to Paris and when did you go there?

bg: In Montreal I had done courses with Lucien Goldmann who came in the fall to give a seminar on the sociology of literature. He had just published *Pour une sociologie du roman*, a Marxist-structuralist analysis of ideology as manifested in the novel. When I was living in Paris from 1967, I went to his seminars at L'Ecole des hautes études pratiques, and then found my way into Roland Barthes' seminars there.

sk: What was the focus of your studies in Paris and Bordeaux?

bg: I was introduced to two types of sociology of literature, the structuralist one in Paris concerned with the politics of representation, and the more institutional analysis in Bordeaux. In both places, there was an emerging concern with communication theory. Barthes had just published an essay on the structuralist analysis of narrative in the new periodical *Communications*. Escarpit had started a research unit [Unité d'enseignement et recherché (uer)] where he was working not only on the modalities of movement of literary texts between cultures but also on visual culture, television especially.

sk: So your living in France had a lot to do with your exposure to theory?

bg: Well, that was when major debates were taking place in the turn from structuralism to post-structuralism. However, I had been interested in theory since high school when I pestered the teacher with questions about the theory of tragedy. And it had been a particular interest in my fourth year when we had no less than three courses in theory, one in the classical theorists read in translation, another in practical criticism of the New Critical variety of I.A. Richards and T.S. Eliot, and a third in the theorists from Sidney through Pater. I developed a particular interest in McLuhan's work that year — not on the curriculum. On the exam, I wrote about his theory of literature as communication in comparison with Wordsworth's emphasis on poetry's address to the common man. At the Université de Montréal I also took a compulsory course in literary theory which had a strongly Catholic cast with an emphasis on Aristotle, Aquinas, and Jacques Maritain. We also studied

C.S. Peirce's semiotics in relation to analyzing poetry. Just after I took his course in 1968, Barthes was taking the deconstructive turn — Derrida was part of the *Tel Quel* group with Barthes at the time. Like Foucault, Barthes was working on the author-function in the move from "work to text," or the displacement of the author as origin of meaning with the circulation of discourse determining the sayable.

With Goldmann I read Lukács on the novel and Balzac's *Les Chouans* on the failed peasant revolution, and with Barthes I read *Bouvard et Pécuchet* in relation to the failed revolution of 1848 — Flaubert's book about nothing — and the tautological nature of discourse as symptom of the implosion of the bourgeoisie. Both courses also engaged in reading the symptoms of yet another failed revolution in 1968, with the failure to go beyond the bourgeois revolution to total revolution. They introduced me to a way of reading texts as social discourse attentive to the politics of representation which was an important grounding in socio-semiotics and discourse analysis.

sk: Who were some of the other theorists at the time in Paris you studied with, or you were exposed to?

bg: I taught with Hélène Cixous. She was in the department where I was teaching at the Université de Paris viii, Vincennes, but at that point the feminist movement was really only starting. Cixous and Christine Brooke-Rose formed an independent uer on British Literature, while most of the professors and chargés de cours were in the larger uer in Anglo-américain — British and American civilization and American literature. Cixous was one of three professors appointed to establish the new university and select the other professors and she is still teaching at Paris viii, now at St. Denis. At the time, the splits between the young *gauchistes* assistants and the communist full professors dominated the debates in the uer Anglo-américain where I was based.

sk: What was going on at the time with psychoanalysis? Lacan must have already been a strong presence there.

bg: I think he was there that year. So were Foucault and Deleuze, who were involved with Cixous in the Groupe d'information sur les prisons. But I wasn't aware of the other units at Vincennes at the time except for Urban Studies, whose students came into my introductory classes in English. They were students at l'École des beaux-arts who wanted to study the social environment, not just the aesthetic aspect of built space, so had double-registered. We were too busy in our own unit, occupied with lengthy department meetings debating what English to teach. Vincennes was experimenting with teaching English to beginners at university. Should they be teaching people to understand English or Englishes? These students would more likely be going to international conferences and meetings than writing or teaching English. The discussions were endless.

sk: What an education! Quite amazing when you think of the latitude you had as a student, as a young academic, to explore and be exposed to different theories and approaches and different literary traditions rather than simply race through a prescribed programme, which is the case today. Not to mention that you found yourself in the midst of institutions trying to reconfigure themselves or start new programmes, and that you had the opportunity to witness the beginnings of what was to become so fundamental in rethinking all kinds of received assumptions. What did it feel like to be back in Canada? To want to teach Canadian literature?

bg: First of all, there was the question of where to go. I really wanted to go to Montreal and had interviews there but there were no jobs. Only York offered me something. So I arrived in the English department at York, team-teaching a second-year introductory course in Canadian literature with Frank Davey and Bill Gairdner, who had just come back from a year in Paris. He was hired to teach theory and modernism since in his dissertation he had used a variety of new theoretical approaches to Virginia Woolf's fiction, including Barthes from the angle of hermeneutics. Frank was restarting *Open Letter*, for which I translated some essays on writing and revolution by Quebec poets. So York was a place where there seemed to be people with compatible interests.

However, it turned out that my position was temporary, although they had written to me that it was a continuing position. At the first department meeting I found out there were four of us on one-year contracts. We probably wouldn't have moved back to Toronto had I known this in advance. While still in Paris I had put in a proposal for an interdisciplinary course in Canadian studies to the new Université de Paris xii, Créteil, where they'd advertised for an assistant professor.

Of course I hadn't been accepted for that, but they were prepared to hire me again to teach English as a second language. They were very interested in my letter and asked me to develop a proposal with a rationale on how such a course in Canadian studies might interest French students.

sk: So it's 1971, and you're back in Canada. How did you find the students at York and the overall academic climate? In terms of what you had brought back with you — your exposure to theory and possibilities of teaching in an interdisciplinary fashion — York must have been a quite different scene.

bg: I taught two sections in the Canadian literature course where I encountered some gifted students planning life as poets. At that time there was great student interest in Canadian literature. The biggest course in the department, it was taught in two separate courses of more than 150 students each.

sk: So Canadian literature was already a formal part of the curriculum at York at that time?

bg: Yes. Clara Thomas, the first person hired at York's Glendon College, was a Canadianist. She moved to the main campus in 1968 when the graduate programme started, and initiated a graduate course in Canadian. The first year there were six students, the next year twenty-two. At York, in the late 1960s and 1970s, Canadian literature was certainly the biggest field in graduate as well as undergraduate studies. Commonwealth, as it was called then, was also a vibrant field in which Clara taught along with other faculty members who had come to York in the 1960s from Africa. The convergence of their interests made York particularly open to the new literatures in English and to contemporary literature more generally with the number of poets teaching there — Irving Layton, Eli Mandel, Miriam Waddington, and Frank Davey, to name the best known.

sk: You have a great factual memory. This is important archival material.

bg: I've just finished organizing some of the history of Canadian literature and post-colonial studies at York that I prepared for a session on the politics of the academy a few years ago, at which time I interviewed some of the early members of the department. I was

25

interviewed recently by Michiel Horn, the university historian, who is working on a history for York's fiftieth anniversary [2009], which refreshed my memory. He alerted me to things I didn't know about the financial crisis at York during the 1970s. I knew that YUFA, the faculty union, was founded at that time. Things were so bad they were talking about firing tenured professors. In the end, I survived because someone hired into a tenure stream position to teach Canadian with only a Master's degree went off to do a PhD. So I took over a course on Modern Canadian Fiction, which I taught as a course in comparative literature, as modernism and postmodernism in Canadian and Quebec fiction until 1987.

SK: When did your annual contract become a tenure-track position?

BG: 1977 or 1978.

SK: You were starting your tenure-track career at the same time I was starting my grad studies at SUNY Binghamton.

BG: It was a very precarious period. The uncertainty alerted me to the workings of institutions which would later become the focus of my publications on the politics of the academy.[4]

SK: "Precarious" to say the least. Things may be, or appear to be, more regularized today, but it's instructive to be reminded of this kind of history — not only how recent the institutionalization of Canadian literature is, and how, despite its belatedness as a discipline, it's already under scrutiny, but also how we cannot take things for granted, how academic institutions operate. Let's try to move a little beyond the history of CanLit at York, which is of course also the history of your own beginnings in the profession. Are there any other turning points in terms of your research, but also in terms of the larger cultural, critical, theoretical scenes at the time, that you consider to be important in your development as a critic? In some respects, you still remain a comparativist but not in the traditional understanding of the term. How does your comparative work and your more intense focus on Canadian literature complement each other?

BG: In the 1970s I was teaching courses in comparative literature and the survey course in Canadian literature. As Gramsci notes, language — and culture, I would add — "cannot be anything but 'comparative,'" always positioned in relation to another temporal moment or geopolitical space and so considered not in terms of identity but of relationality within vectors of power. Thinking one literature or text in relation to another, thinking dialectically or intertextually, has been a key aspect of all my writing and teaching, informing the way I establish course syllabi as well as the topics I write on. In the literary translation I was doing at the time, and in the editing of translations for the Coach House translation series I ran with Frank Davey, such relational thinking for incommensurabilities or for convergences was at the heart of my writing practice. As well as the course in comparative Canadian and Quebec fiction, where I examined the differing responses to modernism, I was also teaching a course on the British and European Novel which examined the impact of French and Russian innovations in creating verbal representations of interiority on the advent of Modernism in English fiction.

sk: That was actually part of my own undergrad education in Greece — not a curriculum provided exclusively within the English department but courses in other departments such as the Classics, Modern Greek, French, German, and Slavic literatures, especially Russian, we were expected to take and to which we were exposed to through various events at the British Council, the Goethe Institute, the French Lycée, the Institute of Balkan Studies, and the American Information Centre that undergraduate students used to attend in droves. Those extracurricular events were certainly part and parcel of the Cold War policy and propaganda — especially the case with the American Information Centre. Still, the exposure we got through those events offered us a way of reading comparatively, of understanding literature and cultural traditions in terms that we would call today transnational.

bg: It is important to attend to the vectors of power in the relations between cultures at specific conjunctures which are often forgotten in the turn to the transnational. French and Russian fiction were received with suspicion by British critics in the nineteenth century. In the course on this fiction, I was able to draw on my work on Balzac and Flaubert when I did many of the lectures on the writers' theorization of the art of fiction. I was assigned to this course in order to help me get a tenure track position, by showing I could function like an ordinary "English" prof and not just an eccentric Canadianist. But this teaching

27

influenced my approach to the comparative Canadian course, as well as to the Canadian survey course for which I did the lectures on fiction and nineteenth-century authors, while Frank Davey lectured on the poets. We tried to highlight critical debate by sometimes both lecturing on the same topic from a different angle — the dialectic as lecture format. Theory was not central to that course. At the most lectures might frame a novel by Roch Carrier through Bakhtin's concept of the carnivalesque. However, the approaches were innovative and we published versions of many of our lectures.

Things changed in the early 1980s in part because the graduate English programme at York received a negative appraisal which provided an opportunity for rethinking English studies. The undergraduate programme was reorganized to provide three introductory streams: through the history of English literature, through genre, and through literary theory. Following my account of the course Introduction to Theory in the ACUTE [Association of Canadian University Teachers of English] theory newsletter,[5] that course became a model for many other English departments across the country. New fields of specialization were introduced into the graduate programme which broke with the traditional divisions by national literature and period to offer comprehensive examinations in the different genres and in Literary Theory and Women's Studies in Literature. My teaching shifted with the new curriculum about 1985.

SK: In what ways?

BG: To support the new orientation the department moved me out of Canadian to teach theory. I taught one of the first-year seminars introducing literature through theory, where we read a history of literature from [Sir Philip] Sidney to Wole Soyinka and Joy Kogawa and of theory from Plato to Gayatri Spivak. I was asked to teach every year the Canadian women writers course involving feminist theory, which I'd struggled earlier to get accepted as a special topics course. In the mid-1980s it was recognized as the department's contribution to the Women's Studies programme then formally established. I also developed a fourth-year course in Narratology. For the graduate programme I developed courses in Semiotics and French Feminist Theory, which were cross-listed with the programme in Social and Political Thought which I joined at that time, and a few years later with the graduate programme in Women's Studies, which I helped create.

sk: How did that teaching, especially in the context of these curricular shifts at York, influence your writing as a critic? You were already doing interdisciplinary work — and not only in the sense that comparative literature studies involves a certain kind of interdisciplinary perspective — before the notion of interdisciplinarity became, as it were, a household word. What were the issues and contexts that you were concerned with in those days?

bg: It was more the case that at last my teaching caught up with my writing. Since the 1970s I had been active in a number of publishing ventures and intellectual circles which provided both access to innovative thinking and opportunities to write. Feminist circles were especially important for me — the *Fireweed* collective in the literary sphere and the Toronto Area Women's Research Colloquium in the academic were the most rewarding. I served as French editorial link for the former and coordinator for a year of the latter, which brought together the pioneering Canadian feminists once a month to present their new research in an interdisciplinary forum. I was also on the working executive setting up the Women's Studies programme, in charge of a Brown Bag lunch speakers series and establishing links with feminists across the university. The research I had initiated in the 1970s on questions of language, orality, folklore, and magic realism from the perspective of narratological theory[6] was changed by my involvement in feminist dialogues.

I started to think through the same issues from a feminist perspective with essays on Isabella Valancy Crawford's literary fairy tales, read through a structuralist lens,[7] and on Sheila Watson's play with language in *The Double Hook*.[8] I was also writing about the emergence of new literary forms in the 1960s which questioned modernism and the new critical fictions emerging in the academy. I approached them comparatively, as with my essay on *La Barre du jour* and *Open Letter* for *Ellipse*.[9] Still, I had to struggle for four years to get a course on Canadian and Quebec women writers into the English curriculum as a special topics course.

sk: What do you think was the reason for that? Was your course ahead of its time or were there other institutional reasons?

BG: The department certainly didn't like the feminist emphasis and asked why there were no male authors on the booklist. On the other hand, there were people teaching women's writing in the graduate programme from the early 1970s — Lucille Herbert on Victorian women writers and Clara Thomas on nineteenth-century Canadian women writers. The undergraduate curriculum committee was really resistant. I was even sent to Glendon's English Department for a year to cool off, which made it possible for me to teach a course in Canadian and Quebec women in history and literature for their Multidisciplinary Studies when Jeannette Urbas, who had designed the course, got a permanent job at Seneca College at the last minute. It was a bilingual course with readings and essay writing in French.

SK: One of the things this history suggests is that your teaching and criticism at that time coincided with, in fact were directly related to, all kinds of developments and departmental tensions at York. Which of course shows the limits of academic agency but also how disciplines and area studies are shaped by institutional and administrative structures, the particular locations and circumstances that inform them. How about the larger scene of things, the scene beyond York? How or where would you situate yourself in that larger context at the time that we've been talking about, the 1970s and early 1980s?

BG: Beyond the English department and beyond York itself, I was involved in a number of Learned Societies and research groups which provided a sustained forum for my thinking. I went to the Learneds at McGill in 1972 and was present at the meetings that gave rise both to the Canadian Women's Studies Association [CWSA] and the Association for Canadian and Quebec Literatures [ACQL]. Margaret Eichler arrived with an issue of a newsletter that called for people to gather in a room one night, which brought together a network of feminist scholars who supported the journal as it grew into *Resources for Feminist Research/Documentation sur la recherche féministe* and much later formed the CWSA. ACQL was the result of another meeting. Robin Mathews gave a paper for ACUTE [10] that galvanized the audience who shared his concern about the absence of Canadian literature in the curriculum. The Symon Commission was just beginning its inquiry into the state of Canadian Studies and Mathews launched surveys to find out about the course offerings in English-Canadian literature, which were pretty dismal. Even ten years later, in a follow up to Symon's *To Know Ourselves: The Report of the Commission on Canadian Studies* [1975], the statistics were no better: Canadian literature represented only 12 per cent of the courses in English departments.

sk: This doesn't surprise me at all. In my first year at UVic [1987] I was shocked to discover that students majoring in English at a Canadian university could graduate without having taken a course in Canadian. What's more, the chair elected that year believed that Canadian literature should be taught only in the contexts of British or American literatures. And this was not because he wanted to promote a comparative perspective; instead, this attitude reflected the general sensibility at the time that Canadian literature hadn't come of age yet, had no academic caché. My first stance as a young, untenured female academic — with an accent to boot — was to present a motion that would make Canadian literature a compulsory credit.

The split you described about some of the faculty at the u of t, not teaching Canadian literature formally while promoting it outside of the curriculum, was symptomatic of a lot of things. The expansionist period of universities was almost over but they were still going through growing pains while dealing with the first wave of fiscal pressures. And there was an inferiority complex too — looking forward but still coming to terms with the colonial legacy, something that became apparent to me as a recent immigrant then, time and time again. For example, in English departments, Canadian doctoral degrees were looked down upon, and CanLit was still not taken seriously. Not only was it a discipline still in the process of becoming but it was also difficult for many authors ouside "central" Canada to get published, which was what led to the flourishing of a number of small presses, for example, in the West.

bg: Yes, that was the general perception in literature departments, that "CanLit is a soft option," a perception that hampered the expansion of course offerings. And there was a lack of books to teach with. Getting those books was a challenge. It was at that time that a group project to write a history of Canadian poetry and publish a series of volumes by Canadian poets had been turned down by the Canada Council. The grant applicants could not identify in advance which poets they would choose to republish because knowledge of the corpus of Canadian poetry was limited. Research was needed to find the poets' books. Uncertainty about the parameters of the project was one reason for the Council jury's rejection. Since the jury was composed primarily of specialists in British or French literature, who were not familiar with the body of Canadian writing, they didn't see the need for basic resources to launch this field of research and teaching. But the Records of Early English Drama [REED] and the Zola correspondence publication project, both based at the University of Toronto, had received millions. So access to research funding was a burning issue for Quebec literature specialists just as much as it was for English-Canadian specialists.

SK: And that was of course before SSHRC [Social Sciences and Humanities Research Council of Canada] was founded in 1977.

BG: Yes. That was in the early 1970s when the Canada Council supported academic research as well as the creative arts. Robin's paper generated a lot of excitement and a preliminary committee was set up to found the Association for Canadian and Quebec Literatures. ACQL's first formal meetings took place in 1974 at the Learneds in Toronto. Sandra Djwa was programme chair while I acted as local representative. However, I contributed to the programme by suggesting the topic — literary theory in Canada and Quebec — appropriate for a discipline-in-formation to reflect on its presuppositions. I also suggested names of people from Quebec who could represent different strands of criticism: David Hayne on historiography, Gérard Bessette with his Mauronian psychoanalysis, Jean-Charles Falardeau, whose sociological reading of a symbolics of space had been influential for my MA thesis. So my interests helped shape the deliberations. I was the programme chair the following year when the topic was drama, which attracted a great many people who went on to form the Association of Canadian Theatre History.

So I was very active in the early days of ACQL which was then a very lively organization, not just concerned with organizing an annual conference, but with stimulating research and especially lobbying the Canada Council and SSHRC for policies to support research on Canadian and Quebec literatures. I was also active in the Canadian Comparative Literature Association, participating in the conference of the International Association of Comparative Literature in Montreal and Ottawa in 1973, and in the annual conferences at which I regularly gave papers and served on the executive. With its emphasis on theory, Comparative Literature was the association with which I most closely identified, intellectually, at that time.

sk: It is almost forty years later but in some respects very little has changed. Or, rather, a lot has changed in how the research field is managed and is operating, but not necessarily for the better. But one thing is certain here, that you've been incredibly active, very involved in how the field of Canadian literature began to take shape both in terms of your writing, and the critical turning points it's produced, and in terms of how Canadian literature has come into its own. What you've outlined so far belongs to a very important archive, an archive that speaks to the power relations that remain operative today. One of the things that I find interesting in what you've just said is the double role institutionalization plays: on the one hand, established institutional structures, like those you've just referred to at York and the research paradigms in the 1970s, hierarchize the production of certain kinds of knowledge at the expense of other kinds of knowledge, while at the same time "new" operations come into play, like the movements to draw attention to and facilitate research on women's writing and Canadian literature.

But such movements too, movements that first enter the academic and pedagogical scenes as strategies of resistance, end up becoming institutions in their own right that we often find ourselves compelled to question, if not radicalize or dismantle altogether. The fact that many Canadianists today are concerned with how CanLit operates as an institution, never mind the relative brevity of its existence as a field, is an example of this. I guess the need to engage with institutional structures never goes away, and one reason for this seems to be the various epistemic and other changes that take place, that invite us to ask questions, sometimes the same questions, but do so in different ways.

bg: Certainly the need to engage with institutional structures persists. However, I think it important in the case of Canadian literature to insist on the brevity of its academic study. Many younger scholars are unaware of the history of the field. They are not helped by the absence of bibliographies of scholarship which has made much of the pioneering work invisible. The demise of publishing series of earlier texts has further

contributed to the relentless presentness of the field. And its internationalization has also encouraged a focus on the contemporary, when critics
abroad have limited access to library holdings and concentrate on the
most recent publications. There were struggles on many fronts to establish Canadian literature as a field in which people could do research.

A lot of my energy has gone to creating such institutional spaces for
intellectual work, Canadian literature in the 1970s, theory and especially feminism in the 1980s when it emerged as an academic field.
Maïr Verthuy did the first feminist critical work at APFUC [Association
des professeurs de français des universités canadiens] at the Learneds
in 1978 at Laval and APFUC established a feminist caucus which organized annual sessions in which I participated. There was also the second
Inter-American Women Writers' conference at the University of Ottawa
that same summer at which I was present. Founded by people working on Latino literature in the US, it expanded to include Canadian and
Quebec literatures, coordinated by Lorraine McMullen and Pat Smart,
with some papers published in the *University of Ottawa Review*. This event
launched a series of conferences. I gave one of the first presentations
on feminist criticism for ACQL at Halifax in 1981.

In Toronto there was the *Fireweed* collective in which I got involved
through the Landmarks conference, organized by members of the
Toronto women writers' groups in 1977. A lesson I learned from my
research in Canadian literary history was that the men self-published,
so women needed to start our own magazines. I was on the first *Fireweed* collective, an adjunct member, soliciting material from Quebec.
Betsy Warland, Gay Allison, Charlene Sheard, and Lynne Fernie were
the co-founders, supported by a fundraising group under Ayanna Black
which organized festivals and readings. So much of that activity has
been forgotten. We've been talking about doing something on this history of feminist cultural production. So much was happening in Toronto
alone — Women Writers in Dialogue, the Women's Cultural Building.

I helped to make links between groups: translating Nicole Brossard's
poetry for her reading with Adrienne Rich for Writers in Dialogue; writing on feminist issues for such theory and cultural studies journals as
Canadian Journal of Social and Political Theory and *Borderlines*; participating
in a small conference with American feminist critics, Caroline Heilbrun

and Sandra Gilbert, organized by Joan Coldwell at McMaster; organizing the Dialogue conference in 1981 which brought together Quebec and English-Canadian feminist writers and critics, and which established important connections that led to the formation of *Tessera* and the Women and Words conference in Vancouver in 1983. Mind you, not everything went smoothly. I hit an impasse with *Fireweed* because the things I was soliciting from Quebec embraced a new critical posture, a writing with the text rather than a meta-discourse, or magisterial critique on the text, which were not being accepted for publication. The different discourse emerging in Quebec in which I was interested had no appeal at the time in Toronto.

SK: Can you stop for a minute here and elaborate a bit more on that? Was the kind of resistance you found in *Fireweed* present in other venues as well? And what do you mean by "writing with the text"? Are you referring here to écriture feminine?

BG: I was feeling frustrated about the place of theory generally. However, it was not just a different theoretical lexicon that people were using but a very different set of cultural references. One of the people whose work was important for me was Suzanne Lamy, with whom I spent time at the Inter-American Women Writers' conference in Mexico in 1981. She was a co-founder of *Spirale*, a cultural journal in Montreal, a specialist in Surrealism, who in *d'elles* (1979) found innovative ways of writing in response to texts. *La Barre du jour* was publishing innovative writing in Quebec, especially in its feminist issues edited by Nicole Brossard, some of which I translated for *Room of One's Own* (1978). But it was difficult to get feminists in English Canada interested. It was partly out of frustration that I decided to run the Dialogue conference, to bring people together across the language barriers. I thought we needed a new periodical that would publish some of this writing. "Fiction-theory" was how we later called this kind of writing interwoven with another text, a reading-writing like that performed by Hélène Cixous with Clarice Lispector, heeding Luce Irigaray's insistence on contiguity and touch over the distancing gaze of the specular tradition with its subject/object binary.

SK: And was that what led to *Tessera*?

BG: Yes. The project had already been in the back of my mind before the conference. Kathy Mezei, on leaving in Ann Mandel's car, talked about it with Daphne Marlatt. Gail Scott joined the conversation in Montreal, where Kathy was on sabbatical.

sk: This is interesting. I remember the reference to the car ride. It was either Daphne who had mentioned this to me or I read about it in the *Tessera* folders in Daphne's archive at the National Library. I listened to the tapes and read the correspondence about the founding of *Tessera* around the time I was writing my "Beauty and the Beast" essay, [11] but you people didn't give me permission to quote from that material. I remember talking on the phone with you and Daphne about it. I was quite ticked off by that at the time. I remember listening to a tape, a conversation among the four of you, which sounded like a founding meeting — a strategic meeting — and I remember that I had some questions, that I didn't quite agree with some of your readings about certain critics and their role in or resistance to feminist discourse, and this was what I wanted to write about. But it was clearly a crucial dialogue that was meant to identify the various reasons for starting such a periodical and how to create a space for it. So I was very disappointed that you all decided you didn't want me quoting from it.

bg: Your request to publish material from the tapes launched a debate. None of us had heard the tape because Daphne had edited it for publication. So we didn't remember what we had said. Subsequently we all requested copies and decided that the discussions about the institution were still pertinent, but our work needed to be positioned differently. So we published *Collaboration in the Feminine: Writing on Women and Culture from* Tessera [1994] as a book. Permission is needed now to access material from the *Tessera* archives at York. I'd been talking to Daphne, who was in and out of the city passing through airports often in 1981. We seemed to do a lot of thinking over the telephone.

sk: There was no e-mail yet.

bg: Yes, letter writing and telephone exchanges. The only time we were all together was at Women and Words in July 1983, when we taped the dialogue that formed our introduction to the first issue, infiltrating *Room of One's Own*. So there were two conversations about starting a journal. Kathy and Daphne connected back in Vancouver in the spring of 1982 and the collective was formed then with the first issue appearing after considerable delay in January 1984. We had the radical idea of publishing as special issues of established journals. Guest editorships overcame funding problems, but generated others in following the timetables of the host journals. Funding was a problem more generally for feminist work and Canadian work.

sk: And for anything else that had to do with new discourses or was remotely related to theory. The journal *Signature,* which I founded virtually immediately after I got my job at UVic, along with Stephen Scobie and Evelyn Cobley, the only journal specifically devoted to theory in Canada at the time, never got support so we had to stop publishing after only a few issues [1988 – 92].

bg: Yes, and *Gynocritics* had difficulty with the Canadian Federation of the Humanities because of the bilingual aspect of the book.

Also, while the American reviewer, Sandra Gilbert, was very enthusiastic and saw the book as an extension of the recently published *New French Feminisms,* edited by Elaine Marks and Isabelle de Courtivron, the Canadian reviewer was negative about the use of terms like "intertextuality." It took about five years to get the project through cfh [Canadian Federation for the Humanities] — a long process. These were the kinds of institutional challenges to changing the critical discourse that took much time and energy to overcome. In hindsight, 1981 was an important year for change. Maïr Verthuy organized the first international feminist conference, Parlons-en/Talking Together, at Concordia's Simone de Beauvoir Institute in May of that year. At the Learneds, Pat Smart and Susan Jackel prepared a programme for acql focusing on alterity approached from different angles, feminism being the topic for the morning. There were hundreds of people in the audience, a challenging one. I remember the reaction to my paper, [12] the angry voices of the men. Nothing very radical, but it raised hackles. In the afternoon, alterity was addressed through papers on ethnicity. With acute [13] it was the Theory Group that later initiated questions of gender.

sk: Yes, I remember this. That was the time I started attending the Learneds, and the Theory Group, which was not quite part of acute's formal program. The Theory Group was extremely important for me for all kinds of reasons. In fact, it was important for my generation of young academics in general. Many of us were interested in theory but

37

encountered a lot of resistance in our home institutions, not to mention that there were very few people teaching theory in those days. When it comes to theory, mine is a self-taught generation. You studied it on your own or went, as I did, to the School of Theory and Criticism in the us.

It was in the context of the Theory Group that I first met people like Len Findlay and Norman Feltes, and perhaps you too — I can't recall when we first met. I remember vividly how enabling that rather small group of people was. That was the time, of course, that graduate students started becoming more visible at the Learneds, and it was crucially important to meet and listen to people like you and others who had a different sense of pedagogy, who practiced the profession in a self-reflexive fashion, not the usual top-down approach, and who made it possible for students like me to engage in those new discourses. In fact, I coordinated, along with Paul Hjartarson, one of the Theory Group's meetings. We had chosen Alice Jardine's *Gynesis*. I was still a doctoral student, and he was a postdoc, or perhaps he had already been hired at the University of Alberta.

BG: Eventually, in 1984, ACUTE held a session on feminism in the main programme at which Bina Freiwald and I read papers then too, to a crowd of hostile people. Fortunately, Norman [Feltes] was sitting in the front row, and he was always so supportive. At York, he made the space for my work possible with his advocacy of institutional change to introduce theory to the curriculum. I can remember his question to me, though I can't remember my answer.

SK: What was his question?

BG: It was the question of the cut, what was the implication of the cut. I was talking about intertextuality, stressing discontinuity over continuity, and how this creates an opening, a movement of thought, a shift in perspective, creating a new assemblage, bringing things together differently. It's a way of addressing crisis, of opening to adventure, in a narrative of fractures, gaps, relays, responding to concerns about repetition and closure. He asked me why I was emphasizing the cut. I can't remember what I said in response. But the focus on breaks and becomings has remained a constant thread weaving its way through my work since that time. So there were places I was able to pursue my work. More of these were outside English, however. A feminist discussion group in the French Department at the University of Toronto invited me to do a talk in 1985, and I stayed on as a member, participating in smaller reading groups with professors and students there. In a dean's seminar series on Cultural Studies at York in 1984, Ioan Davies invited me as a speaker and later included me in workshops bringing together people from Trent, OISE [Ontario Institute for Studies in Education], as well as Social and Political Thought. The Bakhtin Association was formed following a conference at Queen's in 1983: I gave a presentation there, as I think you did.

SK: Yes, I did. I presented an early draft of one of my dissertation chapters on the Canadian long poem that was very Bakhtinian in its approach. They had a special session for doctoral students. But I'd forgotten that that event was also the occasion for the formation of the Bakhtin Association. What I remember was going back home with a fat, loose package of papers on Bakhtin, with red covers, that were very influential on my thinking and which I still have. The Association had regular mail-outs that were very important in helping you keep up with research on Bakhtin.

BG: I attended later conferences in different countries. The same year, Constantin Boundas organized a mini-conference on Deleuze at York where he was guest teaching, which led many years later to a Deleuze association. In the interval I participated in Deleuze sessions Boundas organized at the International Association of Philosophy and Literature, among other places. Bahktin and Deleuze are thinkers of open and dynamic systems, attentive to the pragmatics or politics of any utterance or assemblage, which has made their work so compelling for me. Most important of these intellectual networks was the Toronto Semiotic Circle, of which I was an active member of the monthly Saturday gathering and participant in the International Summer Institute in Semiotic and Structuralist Studies [ISISSS]. In 1987, a year when courses focused on gender (Kaja Silverman, Teresa de Lauretis, Terry Threadgold) and ethnic diversity (Nebeeneta Dev Sen, Elliot Butler-Evans), I interpreted for Luce Irigaray's lectures and taught a seminar on translation and gender with a focus on her work.

SK: I don't recall courses at ISISSS specifically on ethnic diversity in 1987, but I do remember you on the stage at Emmanuel Hall sitting next to Irigaray and reading the translation, mediating the discussion. Those few years of ISISSS seminars, with Derrida, Greimas, Ricoeur, and others, and the seminar Foucault had given earlier, were very influential as they complemented what was happening theory-wise at Canadian universities then.

BG: Yes, this was a very exciting time with an explosion of interdisciplinary forums for conversation with the most innovative thinkers in philosophy and cultural practices which stimulated my teaching and writing, almost entirely focused on theory at that point. The following year, in 1988, my course on the Semiotics of Ethnicity in Canadian Literature had to be cancelled when an accident prevented me from travelling to the University of British Columbia. Through HOLIC [History of the Literary Institution of Canada], centred at the University of Alberta, some of these theoretical insights were brought to bear on Canadian literature approached through the comparative lens. However, the Polysystem theory embraced by the coordinators of this project, while a more compelling way of analyzing complex interrelations among literary phenomena than the sociology of literature of Barthes and Escarpit, nonetheless neglected the vectors of power operative as a dynamic force in any relation.

Moreover, this was a project emerging from Comparative Literature not English where many remained suspicious of the theoretical insights of a more politicized understanding of textuality. *Tessera* remained my anchor during this period, indeed became my daily preoccupation when I took over the role of managing editor, as we pushed further with the search for new ways of writing feminist theory. With hindsight, our tentative articulations of issues — the gendering of the critical institution, the crisis in representation, translation as a practice and paradigm for border writing, gender and narrative, the question of the subject — became key problematics in feminist theory and criticism. In English departments the struggle over the object and form of criticism persisted despite far reaching changes elsewhere in the academy.

SK: Yes, the late 1980s and early 1990s was a time of major cutbacks, hardly any jobs at all, but that was also the period when discourses of ethnicity and race and anti-racism became prominent, and there was, too, the major debate on cultural appropriation. Gender remained important, but now it was race and ethnicity that were vying for criti-cal attention and space, that called for curricular changes, that drew attention to the politics of representation — as much in the academic as in the cultural and social scenes.

BG: Certainly by the end of the 1980s gender was no longer the pri-mary way of signifying relations of power. The convulsions of many feminist cultural groups over issues of race were amplified in 1988 in the break-up of Women's Press and the challenge of Lee Maracle to Anne Cameron at the Feminist Book Fair in Montreal to "move over" and stop appropriating First Nations women's culture. By then, Makeda Silvera had founded Sister Vision Press to publish works by women of colour. Throughout the decade, race and ethnicity had been at the centre of struggles within the Toronto International Women's Day Committee.

Although the term "intersectionality" had not yet become current, the concept of theorizing the interlocking oppressions of race and class with gender had been central to feminist analysis since *Fireweed's* 1983 "Women of Colour" issue, edited by Himani Bannerji, Dionne Brand, and Makeda Silvera — poets, professors, and anti-racist activists. At the international Women's Studies conference organized by Maïr Verthuy at Concordia in 1981, a Black woman asked me why my presentation focused on works by white Canadian and Quebec women. At the time, only a couple of anthologies of Black women's poetry had been pub-lished by Williams-Wallace in the 1970s and there was no criticism of this work. I turned instead to investigate work by First Nations women. Although a first novel, Jeannette Armstrong's *Slash,* would not be pub-lished until 1985, there was an emerging body of life writing and retel-lings of traditional tales by First Nations women on which I wrote a paper for the 1983 conference of CRIAW [Canadian Research Institute for the Advancement of Women] focused on feminist challenges to knowledge. I argued that these cultural productions exceeded the conventional genres of English literature and had consequently been excluded from English department curricula. Later this became a much-reprinted CRIAW booklet and started me working on issues of race and ethnicity along with gender.

SK: Could you talk about your work on translation that was happen-ing at the same time?

BG: I started translating criminology essays for professors when I was a graduate student in Montreal in order to earn money. When Frank Davey revived *Open Letter* in 1972, I translated a series of essays by Quebec poets on writing and revolution. That year, following the enactment of the Official Languages Act in 1969, the Secretary of State established funding for literary translation through the Canada Council. In my temporary situation at York, I made a successful application to become the Translation Officer for the Council, but decided that I would rather translate for my living than hand out money to other translators. In this context, Coach House decided to start a translation series in 1973.

I was keen to increase the writing from Quebec available in English to use in my course on English-Canadian and Quebec fiction. Our focus initially was on the experimental fiction emerging in Quebec from Les Éditions du jour and Les Herbes rouges, especially, works that challenged the realism still dominant in English-Canadian novels. Reading and selecting the books for that series and supervising the translations kept me busy enough. But I also started to translate Antonine Maillet's *The Tale of Don L'Original*, winner of the 1972 Governor General's Award, a kind of magic realist take on the English-French conflict in Moncton at that time. I had to invent a synthetic language to render Maillet's innovative written version of Acadian oral speech. Hearing the novel on CBC's *Between the Covers* in 2004 was very exciting because Katherine Kilfoil read it as a score for a new dialect of English, as I had intended. Because of a deal negotiated between the Quebec publisher Leméac and Clarke Irwin to translate each other's books, my translation eventually came out in what turned out to be an aborted series. The Coach House series generated many more translations through 1985, with my Englishing of Nicole Brossard's *These Our Mothers* appearing in 1983.

Participating on the jury for the Canada Council [now Governor General's] Translation Prize launched me into writing about translation theory, at first through the annual translation review for the "Letters in Canada" section of the *University of Toronto Quarterly*. The first time I attended the meeting to select the prize-winning book, I was dumbfounded that my shortlist bore no relationship to anybody else's. The best translation was being determined on the placement of the commas in the English text, not on the challenges posed by the French text and the translator's creative response to them. This concept of value did not match my theory of translation, but I did not know how to argue my case. In the intervening year I set out to read everything I could on translation theory and found much to inspire me in the work of Henri Meschonnic and Antoine Berman, writing from a post-structuralist approach. This helped me clarify a difference between "domesticating" and "foreignizing" translation strategies, as Laurence Venuti would later adapt Berman's terminology, the "domesticating" strategy which had troubled me with its understanding that the translated text should be totally naturalized so that it appeared as if it had been written in English.

Since 1980, however, with my translation of Brossard's texts [*Lovhers*, started in 1981] and of Cécile Cloutier's poetry for an experiment in differences in translation strategies that included those of women and men translators, as well as of poet/non-poet translators, issues of gender had become paramount in my translation practice, especially when working with Brossard's texts which challenge patriarchal language. Translations of French feminist theory being published at the time did not always rise to the challenges of the linguistic play in the texts. Analyzing the gendered differences in the translation of texts and theorizing feminist translation strategies, my presentation to the inaugural session of the Canadian Association of Translation Studies, meeting in 1987 under the umbrella of the Canadian Comparative Literature Association, initiated a new problematic in Translation Studies in its concern with the dynamic interactions between hegemonic systems and subaltern subversions of them.[14]

As taken up in *Tessera* in its issue "Translating Women" (1989), such reflections on "womanhandling" the text in translation have been identified as a distinctive contribution of a "Canadian school of translation theory," which has introduced a new cultural paradigm of translation that exposes the political implications of intercultural transfer fundamental to any comparative activity. My involvement in translation theory, as with other facets of my work, has arisen from questions raised in the course of an activity which I then attempt to address through my teaching or writing — part of ongoing reflection on practice and participation in intellectual debates.

sk: You've talked about some of the history of Canadian literature as a field, especially in relation to your work, the kinds of difficulties that a critic who is a woman, a feminist woman, and interested in issues that didn't easily fit the curricular and research paradigms twenty-five, thirty or so years ago. The field, or more generally the Humanities, has been going through some major changes in the last few years, a few of them perhaps good, most of them decidedly problematic. What is your sense of where we're at now?

bg: The current situation is disheartening, with the accelerating corporatization of the university. Troubling in the current neo-liberal transformation of postsecondary education, with the withdrawal of government funding, is the commodification of knowledge along with a loss of collegiality and social commitment. "Research" funds are targeted to fields in which private intellectual property may be generated through the patenting and selling of commodities. Students have been turned into fee-paying clients who view a degree as a purchasable right. Universities may still serve as a subsidized testing service for private enterprise, but it is less in their 1960s function of producing "knowledgeable" graduates to expand the corporate state than in facilitating the proliferation of the corporate state's cybernetic systems among a compliant clientele. As the university transfers its archive outside itself into web-based data banks, it no longer carries out its traditional responsibility to generate knowledge and uphold justice, but has surrendered this "mission" to transnational capitalism which seeks to maintain its power. The extension of property rights over scientific and textual databases multiplies the risk of closing down the information commons and spaces for dissent. In a university where administrators measure success in the amount of dollars brought in through research grants and private-public partnerships, the Humanities and Social Sciences, whose professors measure success in the impact of their ideas on social progress, are increasingly marginalized. At York, these fields of critical knowledge are being starved for funds so as to establish faculties of Engineering and Medicine, with their bigger grants. In order to meet the conditions of Ontario's Superbuild grants, Arts admitted large numbers of students, swelling class sizes that are taught by part-timers and graduate students. The money, however, has financed new palaces for business and technology, including Fine Arts

44

in the latter category, all faculties with restricted enrolments. The situation for the Humanities is especially fraught as it is being squeezed out by the Social Sciences with better research funding possibilities.

Culture is vanishing from Women's Studies programmes. Some of us at York organized a panel on this disappearance for the Congress a couple of years ago: "A Big Divide?: Humanities and Social Sciences Together."[15] Things are changing in other countries too, as at the University of Galway, Ireland, where the Women's Studies programme is being moved to Political Science. No longer an epistemology of critique with a broad interdisciplinary approach inquiring into the production of knowledge, Women's Studies is becoming a more limited subfield of politics. This situation plays out the troubled relation of knowledge to power at the heart of the modern university. The responsibility to justice which Kant (1798) posited as central to the university was caught then in a conflict between royal power and pure reason which pitted the faculties closest to power, with their applied knowledges of theology, law, and medicine, against the "lower faculties" of the Humanities with their focus on history and critique. Today it is no longer possible to maintain this boundary between technicians, instruments of power trained in the university, and scholar-professors engaged in the free exercize of judgement in the service of truth when corporate power has appropriated this prerogative. Nor can the boundary be sustained within the scholar, in the split between the exercize of the technical functions of one's profession and the obligation as a citizen to make public use of one's reason to criticize the effects of these functions. With the emergence of new technologies, which extend the reach of corporate capital, the public sphere for such exercize of reason has been transformed so that media-savvy masters of the sound bite have displaced the public intellectual.

sk: And it's not only that the Humanities is not seen as being directly related to power, power in this case being also related to productivity and use-value, but also that the Humanities is often cast as a site of resistance, the reasons for which are invariably downplayed and diminished — the "culture of complaint" and all that.

bg: It's a matter of controlling literacy, too. The dumbing down of the Ontario school system under the neo-conservatives was designed to produce manipulable consumers by reducing support for students and minimizing the subject areas for challenging thought. Transformation in educational institutions has been engineered by changing policies of the Canadian state which aggressively, since the mid-1990s, have produced a general climate of insecurity by redistributing the wealth of citizens away from support for social institutions to build capital for the rich through tax concessions to corporations. Students now assume staggering debts in the hope of obtaining jobs which, with the casualization of labour, have become ever more elusive. Within the university, the increase in student enrolment is being managed with part-time positions, generalizing the insecurity among teachers and students alike. Consequently, there is a diminution in risk-taking to engage in the long and difficult tasks of learning. It is important to politicize these changes for they are not the inevitable new "reality." Protesting against the neo-liberal logic whose exploitative practices engender such insecurity, the interventionist tactics of a growing precarity movement show one way to politicize the issues while demonstrating alternate forms of social organization and solidarity.

The "cult" of San Precario, patron saint of flexible workers, is commemorated in processions through supermarkets, film festivals, and other sites of the temporary worker, on his name day, February 29, when he first appeared in Milan in 2004. San Precario's blessing has been invoked by Spanish and other European workers on EuroMayDay, the idea for the political day of action later migrating to Australia.[16] Parodic détournement of iconic images and rituals becomes *political* protest when linked to this annual demonstration to advance workers' rights. Acknowledging the pervasiveness of fear with the invocation of a saint, this movement minimizes the force of affect through laughter, all the while drawing on thick historical associations of benediction and resistance to create new forms of solidarity. The possibilities of such creativity for "transversal organization" facilitate the emergence of new collective forms of resistance to the informaticized "control society" with its digitalized "dividuals."[17]

sk: How do you think Canadian humanists could resist that? Or is resistance futile, as the Borg would have it?

bg: Well, it is important to guard against cynicism. Tackling the system may seem overwhelming but, if you start with small acts in harmony with the desired university, such everyday activism will ultimately have an impact on the system. A colleague in Social and Political Thought has been experimenting with practices of "slow reading" in his theory course, offered through Anthropology, in which he gets the students to reread the core texts.

sk: I'm all for that. Sign me up. I had a visiting fellow at TransCanada Institute this winter from Brazil, Sergio Bellei, who is writing a book about different kinds of literacy that engages with similar issues. He gave a wonderful talk that traced the history of reading from ancient times on, what the reading act entailed materially and otherwise — I guess we could call this the technology of reading — and he too addressed the value of slow reading. Can you talk a bit more about that, about your understanding of slow reading?

bg: The project reminds me of Barbara Johnson's advocacy of re-reading so as not always to read the same book. In other words, stop long enough with a text to let it change the way you think. However, it also acknowledges the challenge of reading new theoretical texts, emphasizing that learning takes time and effort. In the current issue of *Topia: Canadian Journal of Cultural Studies* (for which I have been Reviews Editor for ten years), there are a number of essays proposing ways of counteracting the corporatized university. Among them, my colleague Fuyuki Kurosawa calls for a revival of the intellectual worker as responsible citizen in his "manifesto" for a new generation in these "neoliberal times." Advocating an active response to the climate of insecurity, he proposes "intellectual risk taking" and "publicly engaged scholarly research" so as to invent alternatives to the prevailing "resigned quietism or instrumental careerism" (21 – 22).[18] Against the demands of instant electronic connectivity, a scholarly "practice of intellectual craftwork" (11) is necessary, a practice that acknowledges the arduous process of learning new things outside disciplinary bounds.

A return to engaged scholarship by a younger generation would offer hope to overcome what is most dismaying in the present university climate — the loss of collegiality and social commitment with the rise of careerism. However, it is difficult for contingent academic labour to take such risks in order to reclaim the university and to empower their students to aspire to a broader valuation of knowledge than as ticket to a middle-class job. It is crucial for professors to politicize the economic policies underpinning the instrumentalization of knowledge both without the university through their writing and within through their engagement in collegial self-governance in order to challenge its increasing bureaucratization. In an ideal world, university administrators would spend more energy in explaining to the public the need for more funding than they currently spend on fundraising in the corporate sector. Administrators must be held to account in order to promote academic planning responsive to the university's traditional commitment to social justice rather than to the interests of its board of directors.

sk: I agree, but it's not always easy to resist this already entrenched model of pedagogy and professional practice as individual students or individual teachers when everyone else is racing through knowledge material or trying to meet the four-year completion rate for doctoral programmes that ssHRC has helped introduce. I can honestly say that this is one of my worst dilemmas as a teacher. You want your students to do well, which means they have to compete — competing for grades, for awards, for grants, for professional visibility, for jobs, you name it — while at the same time you know that this is an insane process — counterproductive in many ways except insofar as it responds to the administrators' performance indicators and that it might get the students a job. Which is not to say that getting a job shouldn't be part of a graduate programme's goals, but all the emphasis on performance and the race we're on make a travesty of what we read, what we teach in the classroom, that knowledge is not just a product. And so, for example, reading lists for candidacy exams tend to eliminate all kinds of important material because there is no time to read it all, let alone reread it, but also because there is a tendency in some places to think that reading the so-called canon is by default a bad thing. The ethics of all this is terribly complex. How do you deal with this kind of problem? Can we deal with this debilitating situation effectively?

bg: It is hard to resist the industrial model of just-in-time production of students for a specific task. Nor is it easy to encourage students to take risks and move outside their specialization when the university emphasizes speed to completion over quality of intellectual work. Or to make the case to the administration for the time necessary for students to engage in serious work that advances knowledge through new theoretical approaches or thorough archival research. However, everyone is complaining now about the narrow topics of graduate students so something must be done to make them see the larger picture, how their own work is positioned politically within the institution. There are no certain academic jobs in Canada and never have been, but a dissertation that is a serious contribution to knowledge will not only be its own reward but generate unanticipated possibilities.

Increasingly in the last decade my writing has been directed to the politics of the academy, both in presentations within York in different forums and without in publications such as the collaborative project of Jan Newson and Claire Polster, *Academic Callings*, a volume from longtime activists addressed to a younger generation and the wider public. Within the university I have been involved on a number of committees, such as the Senate Committee on Research, where I argued against the majority of members from science disciplines for a qualitative approach to thinking about research in terms of its outreach ("social indicators"), not its costs in grants coming to the university. As a member of the Faculty of Graduate Studies Council, I questioned a new policy to shorten the time lines for acceptance of graduate dissertation topics along the model of the sciences', which would have been impossible for students in English to meet with the programme requirements for a second language and two comprehensive exams.

This started a debate among graduate programmes where my intervention on listserves explaining the issues led a number of faculty to criticize the legislation and several programmes to formally protest the new requirements. With the arrival of a new graduate dean, a historian, this policy was rescinded by Council which concurred with the dean's observation that English and History — and Philosophy, he might have added — take more time to complete because of the need to know the canon. The problem is compounded by the more limited high school curriculum which has had an impact on undergraduate curricula. We must not underestimate the agency of everyday activism, however, nor forget about the important third aspect of a faculty member's responsibilities — service.

sk: Absolutely. But the present conditions of academic labour — in part because of the ways in which universities are heavily managed today and in part because the publish-or-perish paradigm now goes hand in hand with the apply for grants or perish paradigm — often make it difficult for faculty to be as active as they ought or desire to be. How do you think these conditions affect the study of Canadian literature?

bg: Practicing "intellectual craftwork" would help to create an alternative academic culture to the treadmill of grants and "quantified output" with their instrumentalization of knowledge and discouragement of long-term research projects. Canadian literature and Canadian Studies more broadly are facing particular difficulties, as I outlined for the Japanese Association of Canadian Studies a couple of years ago. The situation today is much like that in the 1880s when Charles G.D. Roberts protested that there were many universities in Canada, but no Canadian universities. The introduction of Canadian literature courses was aided by the creation of Canadian Studies programmes following in the wake of the Symons' report, *To Know Ourselves*, initiated by the Association of Universities and Colleges of Canada, in response to an oecd [Organization for Economic Co-operation and Development] report on the inadequacies of the Canadian university system and as part of the Canadianization movement contesting American cultural and intellectual imperialism.

The tensions between knowledge and identity in the initial phases of Canadian Studies have ramified in the last three decades in view of the as yet incomplete promise of interdisciplinarity and the internal fractures in an era of global capitalism which have shifted education away from the formation of responsible citizens to the production of eager consumers. Canadian Studies never elaborated a distinctive methodology to deal with Canadian matters and, in the absence of such an intellectual project, many of the centres established in the 1970s either never developed or have been closed by universities, as has happened at York. We have returned to an earlier model, the study of Canada in discrete departments without the umbrella of an academic unit sheltering from disciplinary norms.

In an era of globalization, earlier arguments against Canadian Studies have become more compelling: knowledge cannot be particularized in national terms, not only because it is universal but because the nation itself no longer has stable boundaries within the transnationalism of its heterogeneous communities. Since fields for teaching at high school and university levels have persisted on a disciplinary basis, there is no economic rationale to support Canadian Studies' interdisciplinarity. Within the changing intellectual paradigms resulting from the corporatization of the university and the changing demographics of the Canadian [student] population, many universities are not replacing retiring Canadianists, but instead seeking specialists in the histories of the homelands of the new arrivals. Nor have younger scholars continued to support the academic networks such as ACQL which lobbied government agencies for research funds dedicated to Canadian literature projects.

The decline in focus on Canada is troubling, all the more so since the nation continues to be a significant horizon within which to produce and study culture, when national arts and research councils accord financial support to culture within their geopolitical boundaries. Presently, there is a renewed interest in cultural diplomacy as a possible result of UNESCO's efforts to ensure a future for linguistic and cultural diversity. Even the US government is taking interest in what may possibly be an exercize in nation branding to control their cultural image — and empire. And so many Americans are being hired again in English departments.

SK: Even for Canadian literature positions you mean?

BG: Not into Canadian positions. But the challenge of making a case for the importance of Canadian literature in a department dominated by non-Canadians returns us to the situation of fifty years ago. The ratio of Canadian literature courses at York is now well below 12 per cent. As a colleague said, she came to a recent graduate programme retreat because she suspected that with the movement towards transnationalism there would be no place left in the curriculum for Canadian theatre.

SK: How does this state of affairs relate to your immediate or future research and writing plans?

BG: Critical turning points in culture and in theoretical paradigms always offer a rich field for analysis. Undoubtedly, the transformations currently underway will continue to attract my attention. However, questions of history predominate at the moment, from my collaborative work on modernist women poets about to be published to work on the vibrant feminist culture of the 1970s and 1980s and study on the effects of translation in the 1960s. Our conversation may be a prelude to more such projects on institutional history.

Structuralism / Post-Structuralism:

Language, Reality, and Canadian Literature

My dilemma is that of Scheherazade, for I speak under the threat of forced closure. Like hers, mine is an endless tale, the saga of the "new new criticism" of Canadian literature. Such is the evolving nature of my subject that, even as I speak, it slips away from me. The thread of my narrative will be unravelled when I stop. Presenting their post-structuralist readings of Canadian literature, other critics will add new episodes to chapters or introduce new characters and new points of view. Such is the fate of a historical narrative about a contemporary phenomenon. Endings are elusive and beginnings ...

Without an ending, how can one begin? For in fixing the period, the last word constructs meaning. It defines the contours of an event, determines its possible structure and significance by confirming a beginning, then carves out a plot which assigns to incidents their position as complicating middle or irrelevant digression and so establishes hierarchies. My narrative is a quest for the origins of a discourse, the post-structuralist discourse in Canada, a movement back beyond the beginning to seek out the source of its meanings. Yet this beginning leads always to other beginnings in other countries and other literatures, in other discourses, indefinitely — moving to the vanishing point. Consequently, any selection of a point to begin is inevitably teleological, the "source meanings" appearing rather to be the goal towards which all other meanings are steadily moving. Interpretation, it must be remembered, takes place after, not before, the fact which it naturalizes by turning what is into what must be. To escape from the charnel house of the historian's plot, one could follow Scheherazade and take up the art of the fragment. These days, one would be in the company of many, for archeology is a flourishing critical activity. How it came to be so is the thread of my narrative.

Although organized under the sign of the future indicative, the present collection constitutes a period to my narrative and authorizes me to write in the past tense. It validates my text by demonstrating the vitality of Canadian post-structuralist criticism which has long been invisible. In this, my text is in intertextual relation with the conference on Post-Structuralism in Canada which took place at the University of Ottawa in 1984. On that occasion, criticism of English-Canadian literature was a present absence in a paper by Stan Fogel entitled "Why Michel Foucault does not like Canadian Literature" (Conference on Post-Structuralism in Canada, u of Ottawa, May 1984). [1]

Fogel's paper is a castigation of Canadian novelists for not writing postmodernist, meta-fictional narratives like those of Barth and Pynchon. Foucault's name, waved like a red flag, is virtually the only acknowledgement of deconstruction in the text. The attack is extended to include Canadian criticism which, unlike contemporary American criticism, shows no evidence of non-mimetic and anti-referential perspectives on the medium of prose fiction. Fogel does not go on to suggest that the absence of meta-fictional writing is only a mirage, produced by critics' blurred vision, and to reveal the inadequacy of the existing theoretical models for the analysis of the fiction in question, though this is an avenue which could be (and has been) fruitfully pursued. Indeed, his own paper is a perpetuation of the problem, building up a false opposition by overlooking the most experimental Canadian postmodernists. Turning aside from an exploration of the silences of the critical texts so as to decentre them and produce knowledge of contemporary critical practices, Fogel effaces contradiction as he elaborates on the essential conservatism underlying Canadian aversion to speculative fiction. [2]

That there is a divergence in the directions of contemporary American and Canadian criticism should not be quite so surprising. "New Criticism" never held sway in Canada as it did in the United States, where it presented the major challenge to Romantic expressive theories that privilege the author as guarantor of meaning by focusing attention instead on the formal properties of the text understood to be a "simulacrum ... an experience rather than any mere statement about experience" (Brooks 173). In the absence of any studies on the subject, the specificity of a Canadian critical tradition remains elusive. That it exists is undeniable, given its impact in shaping the "new new criticism." While the debate surrounding the death of the subject is being waged in English Canada, as elsewhere, between phenomenology and structuralism, its evolution in timing and configuration is unique. For the appearance of these two critical theories on the Canadian scene has been nearly simultaneous with the arrival of semiotics, deconstruction, and feminism. Forty years of European critical theory have been absorbed in ten brief years, resulting in hybrids which the respective grandparents, French and German philosophy and Saussurian linguistics, would have difficulty recognizing. For this reason, any study of contemporary Canadian literary theory is an exercise in comparative literature. When read for the silences and gaps, for the unexpected swerves and twists which occur when divergent cultures come into contact, this "new new criticism" testifies to an ongoing dialectic between tradition and imported innovation.

Caught in a crisis of paradigms, in turn part of a more global shift in *episteme*, to use Michel Foucault's term, the modernist "analytico-referential" class of discourse [3] is being replaced by a discourse that has as reference its own elaboration and thematizes the act of enunciation, that is, its production, reproduction, and reception. In an era when writing has become epistemological, Canadian critics are responding to the Zeitgeist by questioning "thematic" criticism, based on a positivistic theory of ordinary language. Research is becoming theoretical rather than practical, turning upon its own presuppositions, upon the structure of the model itself. This exploration of the model arises from the discovery that a methodology does more than reveal: it actually creates the object of study. Lived reality varies as a function of the choice we make of it or of the model through which we see it. For some, this period of metacritical reflection has resulted in new models. To discover them, one must leave aside the telescope fixed on distant shores to take up a refracting lens more appropriate for the examination of grafts and mutations. What one discovers, in mutant forms, is an initial development of structuralism, a pervasive presence of phenomenology and an enthusiastic movement to post-structuralism — deconstruction, semiotics, feminism, *Rezeptionsästhetik*, etc. — as the grounds for textual meaning have variously been located in the author, the text, the reader, and now the context. All participate in a larger critical project to "configure difference," to wrestle with the Canadian "plus."

To begin, to begin ...

My starting point is 1974. The late 1960s and 1970s were a critical moment in the evolution of the discipline of Canadian literature when it was first institutionalized within the academic community, through the development of courses in Canadian literature at the undergraduate and graduate levels and the hiring of scholars to teach them who were the first generation of specialists trained in Canadian literature. Their entry into academia challenged the Great Tradition on which a previous generation of critics had exercised their Leavisite practical criticism in an effort to morally revitalize an impersonal order on the Eliot model, preeminently British and authoritarian. This "rise of Canadian"[4] manifested itself in a rupture with the discipline of English as demonstrated in the founding of the Association for Canadian and Quebec Literatures. The first meeting of this organization took place at the Learned Societies in 1974. Significantly, this was the occasion for the first examination of the state of literary theory in Canada and Quebec.[5]

Taken as a whole, the papers of that conference celebrate the rise of the reader and the plurality of meaning. However, only the textual traces of this event have marked the evolving critical debate. While papers were read on psychoanalytic criticism of the school of Charles Mauron, on sociological and phenomenological criticism,[6] only one paper has been singled out as the rallying point in the critical debate, Frank Davey's "Surviving the Paraphrase."

Davey calls for a criticism which would turn the critic's attention to "literature as language, and on writing as writing" (1983, 12). Grouping together the work of Northrop Frye, Margaret Atwood, Douglas Jones, and John Moss, he denounces the prevailing mode of "referential," "thematic" criticism for its tendency to paraphrase, reducing literature to an adjunct of cultural studies approached through the mirror metaphor of poor sociology. In this, the guarantor of meaning and truth is the author's experience of the world, not grounded in textuality. Davey's judgement builds on the work of other poet-critics, notably Louis Dudek, whose denunciation of academics for failing to deal with literature *qua* literature may be overheard in Davey's insistence on the "technical concerns and achievements of their peers" (8). Academic critics (read referential, realistic critics), limited here to the "small Fryes," have turned aside from the autonomous world of literature to coin metaphors as "formulae for Canadianism." Camouflaged here is the voice of Eli Mandel who has written: "as soon as we add the word *Canadian* to criticism, we move the object of our concern into a particular space and time, a geographical and historical context, where what might normally remain simply an element of background — the sociology of literature — becomes the foreground" (1971, 3). Behind all of them, we catch faint echoes of the American New Critics' advocacy of the verbal icon, the poem conceived as self-enclosed object, mysteriously intact in its own being, each of its parts folded in on the other in a complex organic unity which cannot be paraphrased. The poem becomes a spatial figure rather than a temporal process. Rescuing the text from author and reader goes hand in hand with disentangling it from any social or historical context. Like the American New Critics, Davey is uncertain whether to locate meaning in language or in human experience. From "The Heresy of the Paraphrase" to "Surviving the Paraphrase" is but a short step.

Davey also quarrels with thematic critics over a view of literature that fails to grant the autonomy of the artist and the text. System lying behind and taking precedence over it is attacked in the name of process, system being characterized as conservatism, crystallization, objectivity, stability, while process is a chaos of contingency, accidental encounters, subjectivity. This "phenomenology" offers an alternative to the evaluative and normative criticism that Davey associates with "thematic" critics. "The phenomenological critic could study how this experience (of colonial, of regional writing) is projected by the form of the writing, could participate in the consciousness of the artist as it is betrayed by his syntax, imagery, and diction; ultimately the critic could give the reader a portrait of each writer's psychological world" (11).

At this point some of the characteristic features of contemporary Canadian criticism may be noted, notably an idiosyncratic use of terminology and the clash of critical ideologies, frequently self-contradictory. Davey's cryptic description bears marked resemblance to the project of Gaston Bachelard whom he quotes in support of an attack on thematic criticism (9). This is a radical swerve in light of the term "thematic" usually applied to the Bachelardian mode of phenomenology. Moreover, in reintroducing the author's world as guarantor of meaning of the text, Davey turns his back on the more radical aspect of his challenge to referentiality in which he advocates "analytic criticism" of "the formal characteristics of Canadian writing, into style, structure, vocabulary, literary form and syntax" (10), an emphasis on text and language that would lead to the death of the author.

A further paradox occurs when, as a third alternative to "thematics," Davey argues for a thorough application of archetypal criticism to Canadian literature. Here, he seemingly overcomes his antipathy to describing literature as a self-contained system — Frye's special contribution to English-language criticism — which his new critical valorizing of the discrete text would seem to preclude. Perceptively, Davey puts his finger on what Eli Mandel has called Frye's "schizophrenia," how when Frye puts on his tuque to write the "Conclusion" for the *Literary History of Canada* an inversion occurs. The theory of modes is laid aside: what constitutes Canadian literature is new as content, not as form. The resulting split between semantic and syntactic levels continues to characterize the Canadian critical scene as new waves of structuralism advance.

Of the alternatives Davey recommends, phenomenology is the one most frequently connected with his name.[7] And the pages of *Open Letter*, the magazine he edits, have been open to phenomenological criticism, whether in the form of theoretical essays like Leslie Mundwiler's "Heidegger and Poetry," or of extended documentaries on the participatory reading of contributors.[8] George Bowering's numerous interviews with writers also emphasize the intersubjectivity of the process of reading, I and you meeting in the work. The "conversation" Heidegger developed from Hölderlin occurs in the oral mode of Charles Olson. This mode of participatory reading that accompanies the poetics of openness to the surrounding field and kinetic poetry as process, which the Tish generation adapted from Olson, was formulated by Eli Mandel. Advocating a critical fiction that is direct, emotional, spontaneous, personal, conversational, Mandel posits a critic as "savage" who "does not want to judge but to participate in, to become one with the work of literature … Criticism must risk the excesses of subjectivity and sentimentality if it is going to become human once more and if it is going to bring us closer to the unsolved mystery at the heart of our best perceptions" (1966, 71 – 72).[9]

However, later critics taking up Davey's call for a new mode of Canadian criticism have focused on his advocacy of formal "analytic criticism," with its attention to "structure." Russell Brown, Michael Dixon, and Barry Cameron (142) interpret this latter term differently as they argue that Frye and the other "thematic" critics are in fact structuralists. Where Davey denounces, they support Atwood's search "for a single unifying symbol" (Davey 1983, 9), inherited from "a concept central to all (Frye's) writing" (Dixon and Cameron 142), namely, the autonomy of literary forms whose meaning is derived from their situation within a literary system. These are basic presuppositions of structuralist activity, for the critic works with a corpus which is a closed homogeneous system of signs, related in terms of resemblances and differences wherein the value of each term results solely from the simultaneous presence of others. Atomic empiricism is replaced by a "unified field" approach in which isolated elements in the system are never absolute (Merrell 70 – 71). Acknowledgement of Frye's structuralist affinities has come from several sources. Jonathan Culler praises Frye's typology of characters for uniting rigour of model and individual variance (236). Tzvetan Todorov too has lauded Frye's advocacy of "poetics"; however, he attacks his model for its lack of logical categories (1970, 7 – 26).

Indeed, in *The Anatomy of Criticism*, Frye does not bracket the content of the texts he examines to focus solely on differential relations. He does not deny that texts have meaning, but he insists that their final meaning is inward, centripetal. Literature is formal, not instrumental (74). In this book, he sets out to provide a system of classification of modes, symbols, myths, and genres which facilitates the making of distinctions and comparisons across historical periods, emphasizing the intertextual element of intelligibility. The "archetypes" or recurring images and symbols that connect one text with another are ritual patterns found in societies remote from each other. Their recurrence is based not in historical fact, but in human desire, representing the deepest wishes and anxieties of humanity (104 – 106, 109). The modes and myths of literature are transhistorical, collapsing history to sameness, or cyclical repetition of the same themes. There is a parallel between Frye's "myths" and those of structuralist anthropologist Claude Lévi-Strauss who wrote of mythological analysis that it can claim to show "not how men think in myths, but how myths operate in men's minds without their being aware of the fact" (12).

Returning to this element of Frye's critical theory in a later article, Barry Cameron expands on his advocacy of structuralism:

> Somewhat like Frye, I suppose, I believe that the narrative structures or informing myths of literature are not merely recurring structures of poetry, drama and novels, but also construct human imagination and memory, thus constitutive not only of literature, but of society and the human mind as well. (1980 – 1981, 26)

Cameron aims to rescue Frye's structuralism by exposing its incompleteness. While he supports Frye's emphasis on the creative imagination as a source of energy and form, he challenges Frye's statement that the writer is not "a passive force, ... merely an agent" through whom the system speaks, but an "active inventor of the world" who through his choices, his explorations of "the possibilities of art" (1980 – 1981, 27), dislocates and invents the conventions of language. As Cameron points out, Frye's structuralism stumbles on the question of language. Like the New Critics, Frye fails to assume the full implications of his attempt to decentre the human subject by centring all on the text or the literary system and to accept the full public and conventional nature of meaning towards which his theories are moving. For them all, language remains transparent, referential, untouched by the Saussurian theory of language as a system of signs that function "not through their intrinsic value but through their relative position" (1980 – 1981, 118). Despite the arbitrary nature of the individual sign, the differential network of signs as a whole is not arbitrary. Meaning, intelligibility, cannot be produced in isolation but only by a group. The implications of Saussure's thesis are that language is a social fact.

Cameron elaborates on the implications of considering literature as a signifying practice, stating that life, reality, and history exist only as discourse. We invent ourselves through language. All expressed forms of reality, though they have a status different from fiction, are fictions nonetheless. When we talk or write, we fictionalize. When we talk or write about works of art, we refictionalize them. Moving beyond Frye's position, Cameron advances the thesis of classic structuralism that language is the basic modelling system of our culture, and that study of all signifying practices would follow the example of linguistics in its mapping out of binary oppositions and networks of differences synchronically. For what he accepts, and Frye does not, is that reality is not reflected by language but produced by it. In this belief that reality and our experience of it are discontinuous with each other lies the death of the correspondence theory of knowledge. Classic structuralism brackets off the content of literary works and concentrates entirely on formal relations. Frye's structuralism does not, for the archetypes, which are his universals, are significant images of a longing for "the peaceable kingdom." As many commentators have pointed out, there is a tension in his ontology between energy as the will to technology and energy as the will to utopia. On the one hand, Frye's taxonomy — a method adapted from dated approaches to the physical sciences, a scientization of literary criticism — participates in a movement to decentre the subject, to disrupt the belief that the poem like the person has a vital essence. In another sense his theory is just one more displaced version of theology. Frye's fundamental Christian humanism affirms the powers of the "larger human brain" and "improved binoculars"[10] to revitalize creative energy. The energy of the imagination materialized in literature allows an escape into apocalyptic time from its alienation in the modern hell of technological society. In this, Frye's critical project shares certain "red tory" assumptions (Cook 33: "tory touch in liberalism") with the critical practices it would supplant. The assumption of a pastoral myth as the basis of all social visions is the key to Frye's social and political vision as it is to American New Criticism, produced within the Agrarian movement of the American south. Energy in the creative use of language is at the heart of Leavis and Eliot's Great Tradition which seeks to overcome the deadly abstraction and alienation of modern technological society (Eagleton 36 – 47). For all, literature becomes a way of escaping the bondage of history.

At first glance, Cameron's advocacy of classic structuralism marks a radical change. For in recognizing that literature is constructed like any other product of language, he demystifies literature. Moreover, the recognition that meaning is not natural but a way of interpreting the world in function of the languages one has at one's disposal contains the seeds of a social and historical theory of meaning. But whereas classic structuralism recognizes that the codes transmitting the message are socially produced, it affirms that the deep laws governing the working of systems are culturally invariable. Cameron joins Frye and Lévi-Strauss in rooting these universal structures in the larger human brain.

Objections to structuralism are directed to the ontological foundations. Its engagement with universals in synchronic analyses of a total system, simultaneous with itself, is based on an intellectual construction, the consequence of comparisons made by someone standing outside, presuming objectivity. The attack on synchronic analysis is waged by phenomenologists in the name of a diachronic approach which rests on the lived experience of the speaker, participant in a community. The static system of structuralism, it is argued, continues within an outdated Newtonian world which spatialized time, while the diachronic approach better represents the position of contemporary relativistic science (Merrell 85). Phenomenologists, as we have seen, assert the importance of time and the world we live in. Central to this is the concept of intentionality, purified of its psychological origins, Heidegger's *Dasein*, being-there, Merleau-Ponty's "in the thereness of the world." Because we are part of the world's there-ness, our intending of the world's constituents is possible. To intend an object is to intend ourselves. The phenomenological endeavour becomes a process of inseparable self-and-world recognition, achieved through the "epoché" or bracketing of the commonsense acceptance of the world around us. "The world is rediscovered 'in me' as the permanent horizon of all my cogitones and as a dimension in relation to which I am constantly situating myself" (Merleau-Ponty 69). The human being is not a static entity but a process whereby meaning comes into being. For Heidegger, the human being is the temporal horizon within which things of the world appear and come "to be" in time and history and in language, the very realm in which it unfolds. In the name of this processual hermeneutic Davey challenges Frye.

Although Heidegger's hermeneutic or existential phenomenology has been more historical than Husserl's transcendental phenomenology, it did not overthrow the metaphysical element in phenomenology. For it continued to bracket the actual historical context of a literary work and its author. Marxist criticism has argued for the importance of this context in the analysis of literature (Jameson 1972 and 1981). Within a Canadian literary tradition, the challenge to the metaphysics of presence came not from the poet phenomenologists but from feminists.

For feminists, Frye is a four-letter word. In a polemical critique of Frye's theory, Priscilla Galloway attacks his totalizing system and universals on the grounds that they are founded in the experience of only half of humanity. Armed with statistics that show his exclusion of female writers, Galloway challenges the purported objectivity of *The Anatomy of Criticism*. "One categorizes," she writes, "in the light of one's own overriding vision of reality" (23). The impact of feminist scholarship has been to show that gender is a fundamental organizing category of human experience and of the creation of knowledge. Women and men have different perceptions of experiences within the same event. The male perspective, though, has dominated fields of knowledge, marking them all as patriarchal discourse. Since this inequality between the sexes is a *social* construct, it is a subject for study in the Humanities. Arguing for the inclusion of lived experience in literature and the act of reading, Galloway's critique overlaps that of the phenomenologists. However, it moves the disagreement onto new terrain by exposing the ideology implicit in the conditions of production and readership of the text. Reading for ideological implications and revealing gaps and self-contradictions, the critical activity advocated by post-structuralism, is an avenue Galloway does not pursue. She turns instead to the construction of an alternate canon that would include Canadians and women, revealing thus the dual impetus of feminist criticism, deconstructive and reconstructive.

The metacritical moment in the theoretical debate on the directions the "new new criticism" was to take in Canada was brief — from 1974 to 1977. From it, we can grasp the lines of development of Canadian criticism of the past decade. Generalized analyses of critical theory of the type produced in the United States and England by Jonathan Culler and Terry Eagleton have not been part of the Canadian scene. Critics have been less interested in the grammars or deep structures of narrative than they have in readings of texts. Few have followed Frye's lead in the study of poetics, and their attempt to bracket what is Canadian (as one tries to isolate "poeticity") asserts no claim to scientifically verifiable and refutable hypotheses, nor does it limit itself to the study of "Canadian forms of language and language alone."[11] Structuralist focus on system is also muted by Frye's attention to variables, resulting in the study of a single text, on the model of American New Criticism. Reading activities and focus on the process of reading are stimulated by the pervasive presence of phenomenology. While Frye's work is contemporaneous with the period of classic structuralism in France, phenomenology emerges two decades after its heyday in the Geneva school to become the challenger, reversing the path of the evolution of criticism in Europe. This historical configuration has favoured the emergence of post-structuralism, which might also be termed post-Saussurianism in that it introduces to Canadian criticism the concept of literature as a signifying practice, central to classic structuralism. A further particularity of the Canadian critical scene is the division that has emerged between poetry and fiction. This is not founded on the celebrated distinction of Roman Jakobson between the metaphoric nature of poetic language and the metonymic character of prose. Indeed, Jakobson's identification of poetic language as that "promoting the palpability of signs" (356), a definition that linked poetics and linguistics, has had only minimal impact on the study of Canadian poetry.[12] On the contrary, structuralism remained the domain of "academic" critics interested in narratology, while critic-practitioners of poetry opted for phenomenology. Briefly, now I shall consider the critical practice that has emerged in the last decade out of this debate.

⸬

Patterns of selection are significant in any movement of theory from one cultural context to another. Not all facets of a particular school are imported: absences here are as important as presences in revealing presuppositions. With its emphasis on universals, high structuralism is appealing to many because of the dream of unity it holds forth in an over-specialized world, but Canadian critics have resisted a politics that is blind to the experience of the human subject. Structuralism's scientific claims to identify elements and the law-like relations between them have been modified by attention to the particular, the local. Lévi-Strauss's recourse to mathematical models, the "théorie d'ensemble" or set theory of the Tel Quel Group, and Greimas' search for the model of narrative in a single algorithm that would describe its possible combinations and permutations, are divested of their mathematical rigour when their methodology is applied by Canadian critics. Later developments in narratology like those of Tzvetan Todorov and Gérard Genette, which have paid attention to the individual work of art, have been more compelling models of textual analysis. Most attractive of all has been a third direction in structuralism, one that has moved closer to phenomenology to consider the question of the competence of the reader, emphasizing the act of reading through the isolation of the decoding operations occurring within it. The distinction between these types of structuralist activity may be thought of as one between structuralism and semiology as Saussure first described them, structuralism being concerned to establish the system of cultural conventions, semiology or the science of signs — semiotics as it is more commonly called today — concentrating on the analysis of the system.

Only the two latter modes of structuralist criticism are to be found in the corpus of Canadian criticism. The swerve is most evident, moreover, in the field of narratology where the development of a narrative grammar in an initial step is supplemented (and called into question) by a subsequent hermeneutical act, implying the referentiality of language, as in the single Canadian extended example of narratology, Grazia Merler's *Mavis Gallant: Narrative Patterns and Devices* (1978).[13] This is inspired by the work of Greimas that starts with binary oppositions, given anthropomorphic shape, through which purely logical or conceptual oppositions become "actants" in a situation allowing them to develop into a story. Greimas identifies the basic number of actants in a narrative sequence as two and the basic actions as disjunction and conjunction, separation and union, struggle and reconciliation. He then goes on to explore the triadic nature of the narrative sequence — a descriptive utterance, a modal utterance, and a transitive utterance — and to develop a lexicon of narrative syntagms or principles of construction to complete a grammar of narrative of three different types: performative, contractual, and disjunctional.

Merler's model eliminates this triadic structure, focusing exclusively on the oppositional nature of the sequence. She avoids what has been a major problem for her predecessors, the large narrative unit, by arguing that all Gallant's fiction reveals the same characteristics, her longer fictions being composed of many short stories. With the help of diagrams presenting her conclusions in schematic form, Merler dissects each story, then articulates a model of the Gallant story, somewhat reluctantly imposing this final "logical" order. "Although five different situations can be circumscribed, the two prevailing motifs (adult-child and man-woman) could probably be reduced further to a single situation, the adult-child confrontation, provided of course that adult and child are understood figuratively as well as literally" (70). The double reference to figurative and literal at this point is revealing. Not only has Merler not made the fundamental distinction between story and discourse in approaching these texts, she has not emptied the plots of their semantic content. Moreover, she fails to carry out a further reduction of these situations to a common motif of the power struggle, fundamental to the basic action of the narrative sequence in disjunction and conjunction. Instead, she declares them to be psychological projections of the author. The basic assumptions of this work are at odds with the method of differential analysis undertaken: the humanist subject in the guise of the author reasserts itself in the midst of a supposedly decentred text. Merler's book is illustrative of English-Canadian structuralism which refuses to focus exclusively on the text.

Nowhere mentioned in these studies are Tzvetan Todorov and Gérard Genette, whose spirit is nonetheless everywhere present. For in their criticism is to be found a concern for discovering the structures and conventions of literary discourse combined with an ability to provide rich interpretations of individual texts, illustrating the aim of "complementarité" between theory and criticism advocated by Genette (12). Instead of focusing on the rigid separation of the text and the author, which had become a critical battlefield, Genette reframes these, suggesting the need of naive criticism to escape from its impasses through theory and a corresponding renewal of "metacriticism" through the practical criticism of specific texts. He orients his work to illuminate the literariness of the literary text, isolating the elements that transcend it in organizing it: questions of stylistics, semiology, genre studies, discourse analysis, narratology. Extending structuralist concerns into areas of traditional literary interest, into genre theory and rhetoric especially, Genette and Todorov show how theory illuminates interpretation. Simultaneously, they demonstrate the way in which literature is a human institution, a mode of signification.

The movement towards post-structuralist concerns with signifying practices is prefigured in the work on reading by Todorov and other semioticians (Eco 1965, 1979). In his concluding essay to *The Poetics of Prose*, Todorov instructs us "How to Read." This is a rejection of structuralist typologies in order to show how functions are realized in words and how these then are perceived. This new definition of structuralist activity as "reading" works against form/content divisions. In "reading," a "grammatical form is made contiguous with a certain theme of the text." But more significantly, this acceptance of the "pertinence of language is to subject the text if not to an extratextuality, at least to a pretextuality" (240). In the essay, Todorov briefly describes some of the modes of intratextuality (figuration) and intertextuality (plagiarism). Intertextuality is a term developed from Bakhtin, a Marxist/Formalist critic of Saussure, for whom language is always inherently "dialogic": it can be grasped only in terms of its inevitable orientation towards another. As Todorov summarizes: "All literary discourse senses, more or less intensely, its auditor, reader, critic, and reflects his potential objections, appreciations, points of view" (245). The literary phenomenon is no longer located exclusively in the text, but in the interaction of text and reader, a shift in the locus of activity to the reception end of the act of enunciation where it approaches the concerns of the phenomenologist with the dialogue between reader and author. However, the semiotician remains more interested in seizing the text synchronically as an object in space to develop typologies of reading or in charting the work of a heuristic abstraction, the "superreader," as s/he manifests a great familiarity with the literary codes. Part of an interpretive group with a highly developed knowledge of literature, s/he is able to recognize pastiches, inversions, and allusions to other literary texts — intertextuality — and so activate or produce the meaning of a text.

Textual production is a subject about which Michael Riffaterre has written extensively. According to his definition, intertextuality is limited to a linguistic phenomenon that is the matrix of a spiralling text. The text in question is generally a literary text. Intertextuality, however, may be unbounded, imbricated within social and historical texts, in the definition advanced by Bakhtin. This involves a shift from the Saussurian emphasis on language as system, "langue," to the neglected "parole," the point of linguistic production, the speaking, writing, and reading of concrete social individuals, that is, a shift from "language" to "discourse."

For Bakhtin, the sign is not neutral but a site of struggle and contradiction. Language is not a monolithic system, but is caught up in specific social relationships that are part of broader political, ideological, and economic systems. In Bakhtin's theory of language are the seeds of a materialist theory of consciousness, perceived like language to be both within and without the subject. The text as intertextuality, as ideologem — with the introduction of this concept, the limits of structuralism have been transgressed in the recognition of the active (not fixed) nature of the sign and the ideological grounding of all language. With the advent of theories of reading, the doors are opened to post-structuralism's questioning of power and authority through its attempts to undo all binary, hierarchical relationships. In practice, however, semiotic analyses of reading stop short of this point, adopting a synchronic approach rather than focusing on the actual process of reading and literature as a social practice.

Analyses of reading have proliferated in English Canada. Intertextuality has become something of a buzz word, as it is preface to discussions of the clichés of Leonard Cohen (Hutcheon 1982), of women's writing (Godard 1983b), and of MacLennan's *The Watch that Ends the Night* (Blodgett 1978, 280).

MacLennan's novel has also been the object of a late structuralist study of reading by Stephen Bonnycastle which draws on the work of Roland Barthes. From establishing the system of cultural conventions in *Mythologies*, Barthes moved in *The Pleasure of the Text* to the anarchistic bliss of the reader of the writable text. Bonnycastle develops a typology of reading from this, then applies it to MacLennan's *The Watch that Ends the Night*. In *The Pleasure of the Text*, Barthes expands on his earlier distinction between readable and writable texts, rephrasing them as texts of pleasure and texts of bliss, the former involving the reader as consumer, the latter the reader as *producer* of meaning. Bonnycastle considers Barthes' work as freeing the reader by placing the emphasis on his experience. Working from hints in two pages of Barthes' texts, he establishes a typology of four different kinds of reading experience: hysterical, paranoid, fetishist, obsessional.

The first is "like hallucinating" (77) and the form it takes must be credible. It is the most "natural" way to read, certainly the most adolescent
response, one in which the character is thought to be a living being. As
well as reading for "reality," one can read the novel as allegory of another
story, "for the development of Canada or the Canadian consciousness." A
third interpretive strategy is to search for archetypal patterns. Bonnycastle
uses the typology to effect a critique of the presuppositions of previous
critics of MacLennan's work, placing Alec Lucas's reading within the allegorical category and George Woodcock's in the archetypal. While his aim
is to argue for a plurality of readings and strategies, he condemns these
critical readings for their reliance on value judgements. He then proceeds
to offer a fourth reading of the text, one that would seek out what Barthes
terms the "empty" structures of the text, those free of ideology. And it is
here in the structuralist body of his paper, that Bonnycastle's enterprise
runs aground on the same shoals as other Canadian structuralist projects: the structures he describes are aesthetic not logical ones, being the
"consciousness of George Stewart ... and the recurrence throughout the
book of passages of lyrical beauty describing either natural scenes or urban
landscape" (80). Discussion of these aspects of the novel provides illuminating excursions into the history of ideas and the concept of nature in
Spinoza and Wordsworth. These have not become "empty" structures. In
its critique of the ideological positions of criticism on MacLennan's work,
the metacritical section of this essay adumbrates the concerns of post-
structuralist theory. However, in its failure to foreground language as an
autonomous system or as a field of ideological contention, the essay is,
properly speaking, pre-Saussurian. For in it, language remains transparent, capable of supporting a second order of words, despite the vision of
readings proliferating in a labyrinth of metacriticism challenging metacriticism that Bonnycastle's typology presents.

Before pursuing the post-structuralist view of language as a limitless
web of constantly interchanging and circulating elements, which disrupts the classic structuralist concept of language as a clearly demar-
cated structure containing symmetrical units of signifiers and signifieds,

it is necessary to consider the critical practice of phenomenology in more detail. For while semiotics has been the successor to structuralism in Canada, deconstruction has been the sequel to phenomenology. Such a trajectory is not self-evident from the presuppositions of the two schools, for deconstruction is as much a challenge to the metaphysics of presence in phenomenology as in structuralism and earlier liberal humanist criticism. The connection is made through American poetry. J. Hillis Miller, once a member of the "New Geneva School" of phenomenology, and Paul de Man, now both members of the "Yale School," are responsible for the Americanization of Derrida.

In English Canada, the work of the "New Geneva School," more particularly that of Georges Poulet, has had considerable impact on the theory of Eli Mandel and the empathetic readings of *Open Letter* contributors. Beginning in the late 1930s, these Swiss critics explored the active process of reading, "vibrating phenomenologically," abandoning the empirical self and finding a faculty for identification and participation. Phenomenology shares with structuralism its activity of bracketing the commonsense world in order to carry out its critical operations. But whereas structuralism engages in a double operation of bracketing, of the object and the human subject, in order to locate the "deep structure" of which the literary text is a copy, phenomenology brackets off the real object alone. The goal of "la critique interne" is to penetrate the inner space of an author's consciousness. In his four-volume study, *Études sur le temps humain* [Studies in Human Time] (1949), Poulet has presented a view of literature as the history of human consciousness. Through a close reading of a text, he tries to discover the experiential patterns of the author's life-world, to empathize with the author's creative impulse, a joining of two moments in time, that of author and reader in dialogue, so as to locate the originating moment in the evolution of the literary work:

Criticism cannot be contented with thinking a thought. It must work its way farther back, from image to image to feelings. It must reach the act by which the mind ... unites itself to an object to invent itself as subject (1954, n.p.; my translation).

For Poulet, the critic as reader accumulates and documents his impressions, working on the "most primitive level" where a current "flows from mind to mind." As he writes,

> To identify with the work means here for the critic to
> undergo the same experiences, beginning with the most
> elementary. On the level of indistinct thought, of sensations,
> emotions, images, and obsessions of preconscious life, it is
> possible for the critic to repeat within himself, that life of
> which the work affords a first version, inexhaustively reveal-
> ing and suggestive. (1973, 111)

Poulet is interested in the imagery of writers, especially in their temporal imagery, a concern he shares with other Geneva critics and with
Gaston Bachelard, whose work focuses on the "reverberations" of the
material image, the contact between author and reader. In *The Poetics
of Space* Bachelard investigates the phenomenology of the imagination,
locating images of harmony, exploring them for their potential happiness, encouraging dialogue between poet and reader (xii).

This approach is concerned with the "deep structures" of the mind
which can be found in recurring themes and patterns of imagery;
in apprehending these we are grasping the way the writer "lived"
his world, the relation between himself as subject and the world as
object. The "world" of the literary work is not an objective reality, but
reality organized and experienced by a subject. Much interest in this
criticism of consciousness, or "thematic" criticism, has been shown
in Quebec where numerous studies have been carried out upon the
way an author experiences space.[14] Two English-Canadian studies have
focused upon images of time in contemporary writing. Both Robert
Lecker and Ofelia Cohn-Sfetcu specifically state that their aim is to
challenge what they perceive as a dominant preoccupation with space
in criticism of Canadian literature. The view of Canadian literature as
centred on a "garrison mentality" has resulted in Canadian literature
"being treated in terms of binary oppositions or as a complex grouping of polarities" (Lecker 1979, 1). Of the two, "To Live in Abundance
of Life" (Cohn-Sfetcu) is more clearly an example of existentialist criticism in the mode of Poulet. An initial difference from Lecker's thesis is
to be found in Cohn-Sfetcu's abolition of generic categories to distinguish between texts. Concluding that these Canadian authors affirm
the expansion of human intellectual and imaginative grasp of reality,

providing a rich psychological continuum to overcome the difficulties of mechanized or discontinuous objective time,[15] Cohn-Sfetcu focuses her analysis on their depiction of consciousness. In this her procedure is very different from Lecker's analysis of plot. As she explains: "The aesthetics of formal structure of works have only a supportive role in relation to the organizing consciousness. Structural symmetries and ambiguities are of little interest in the present discussion" (29). Cohn-Sfetcu diverges also from Poulet's approach in that she does not extend her reflections on human time to philosophical or historical works, opting instead for a view of literature as an autonomous system of words as advanced by Northrop Frye. However, literature is not a static system for Cohn-Sfetcu as it is for Frye, but one that encourages active involvement. Critics of consciousness, she reminds us, "look upon literature as an act, not an object" (29). Recognizing that this mode of criticism is "a humanistic revival" (29), she celebrates the humane values of the writers selected, informing us that they were chosen for very subjective reasons, "because I enjoyed reading their works and writing about them." As she says, this is a valid presupposition in a study about subjectivity (37).

Certainly the subject is more present in the criticism of consciousness than in any other contemporary critical approach, even those indebted to phenomenology. This "thematic" criticism is by no means the last fling of phenomenology, however, for feminist theory has drawn on it extensively, not surprisingly, given the pioneering role of Simone de Beauvoir's existentialist feminist critique which first introduced the concepts of difference and social construction to feminist debate. But contemporary feminism (at least in academic circles) is grounded in theories of textuality. This is especially true of the theories of reading being developed by Canadian feminists, whether these take the form of the rhetorical figure of "parallax," central to the formation of a feminist interpretive community, advanced by Lorraine Weir in "Toward a Feminist Hermeneutics," or of the discussion of the impact of the literary institution and the economy of the book in Louise Forsyth's theorizing.[16]

Nor is criticism of consciousness the last word in phenomenology. A more recent theoretical development has occurred with the advent of

72

the aesthetics of reception. It too has more complex and sophisticated models of the interactions between author, text, and reader, especially in the work of Linda Hutcheon.

Drawing on the theory of Wolfgang Iser and the "Constance School" of the aesthetics of reception, who focus attention on the two poles of the artistic work, the artistic and the aesthetic, both sending and "realizing" or receiving activities in the communication of the message, to insist that the work of art is identical with neither but lies between the two (1980, 274), Hutcheon describes the "game of the imagination" in which reader and author participate. "The reader must work to decipher the text as hard as the writer did to cipher it, with the result that the stress of the work is displaced from the communication of a message to the inciting to produce meaning as well as order" (1980, 143). Hutcheon's analysis is directed equally to describing the codes, in a semiotic approach, and to outlining the processes of realization or activation engaged in by the reader in the decoding operation, a phenomenological approach. The process of "recreation" comes into play when the "act of reading becomes creative, interpretive, one that partakes of the experience of writing itself," and is a cooperative activity which ultimately takes the form of writing.

Developing a typology of intertextual figures, Hutcheon argues that textual figures may be encoded in a text but cannot be decoded and actualized without a reader. In the self-reflexive texts that Hutcheon analyses, the games with the reader are foregrounded, critical, and creative acts meeting in the text itself, so avoiding some of the heuristic fictions necessary in other approaches. The phenomenological circle finds a new form here in the composite identity "The Reader, The Writer, The Critic." Moving from the text to the reader as source of meaning and authority, Hutcheon's combination of structuralism and phenomenology plays out the characteristic post-structuralist gesture of refusing binary authority. This formulation is quite close to the critical fictions of Barthes' post-structuralist phase.

Hutcheon's many demonstrations of the extent to which Canadian works are paradigms of reading provide additional evidence of the importance of Canadian writers as phenomenological critics. However, her underlining the primacy of *writing* in the Derridean manner, as the

marking or trace of an activity, moves beyond the orality of the conversation (criticism as performance, with its contingent implication of vision
as continuous with the world it represents and language as continuous
with vision), and beyond the other phenomenological criticism we have
examined. In her position, the necessity for making a metaphorical link
with the bracketed world has been overcome.

::

The name of Derrida at last, you sigh. But in conjunction with phenomenological criticism? How can that be when the deconstructionist position is linked with a critique of phenomenology and structuralism in
the name of a more radical *epoché*, an abandonment of a metaphysics of
presence for a posture of perpetual undecidability or *différance*? The leap
from phenomenology to deconstruction has been made by a number
of poets as part of a North American phenomenon.

Now identified with American deconstruction, Hillis Miller and
Joseph Riddell were pioneers of American phenomenological criticism
in studies of American poets. Miller's *Poets of Reality* (1969) and Riddell's *The Inverted Bell: Modernism and the Counterpoetics of William Carlos
Williams* (1974) assert that poetry is the hermeneutic circle of writing-
active reading-writing. In his more recent "Decentring the Image: the
Project of an American Verse" (1979), Riddell shows how American
poets respond to a double sense of tradition, their project "to make it
new" adding something to a tradition but also repeating in language ·
some moment of pure origin. The Imagists and Black Mountain poets,
according to Riddell, were at the centre of this interest. Parallels may
be found between Olson's "Projective Verse" and the deconstruction
of Derrida. Although the attempted phenomenological suspension is
invoked in this question of origins, Riddell would suggest that Olson
implies there is no inaugural creative act. No Adam mythically names
the world. Babel reigns. The beginning is selection. The ever-expanding
unit called the field (or poem), a space of relations, cannot be centred
and this play dissolves the referential function of the sign, decentring,
deconstructing, in the beginning again. The impact of Olson on contemporary Canadian poetry has been such that one can confidently

assert that the project of Canadian poets has also been to "make it new." In "Unearthing Language," a conversation with Shirley Neuman and Rudy Wiebe, and in "Unhiding the Hidden," Robert Kroetsch extends this perspective to all of Canadian writing:

> In his talking — in the language of the novel — he and Wiebe decreate the literary tradition that binds us into not speaking the truth. Wiebe and Harlow and Godfrey, like Grove before them, have a marvellous ability to keep the language clumsy, brutal, unbeautiful, vital, charged. Atwood makes a fine Canadian prose style of the run-on sentence. Davies distrusts any sentence that loses its connection to his newspaperman's background. But Wiebe is determined to destroy the sentence itself back to sense, back to its ground. He says in his dedication that he "unearthed" the story. He recognizes the problem of language. (1983, 20 – 21)

In conclusion, Kroetsch equates this process to the discovery of truth in the Heideggerian manner of "dis-closing, un-covering." It is through such a *via negativa* that Kroetsch enters into deconstructionist dissemination. From the desire for "truth," an absolute presence — albeit as total negation — and evidence of mimetic intent expressed in this article, his criticism shifts to the elaborate games and complex interweaving, the emphasis on process and continual decentring of *Labyrinths of Voice* (Neuman and Wilson 1982). Against the primacy of voice, of conversation, of phonocentrism, conveyed in that title, must be weighed Derrida's emphasis on writing, on the graph, and the attention given to the material signifier in Kroetsch's punning wordplay in such critical essays as "For Play and Entrance," and "The Exploding Porcupine," in which he retraces the undecidability of other Canadian writers. Deconstructionist project as postmodern aesthetic.[17]

A similar shift is visible in the criticism of Steve McCaffery between phenomenological analyses of reading a comic strip (1973) and the agon with "The Death of the Subject" (1977). Derrida's own strategy of decentring, his conscious attempt to make written discourse reflect its inherent unreliability through a highly ambiguous style, characterized by the infinite play of signifiers, is for McCaffery both a legitimization of his concrete poetry and a model for criticism that will be deferral of meaning, ceaseless movement of interpretation. Interjecting poems by several authors into his essay in a style that resists the tendency of writing to crystallize into set meanings and so reinforce the myth of absolute meaning, McCaffery expands on the ideas of Derrida:

> Jacques Derrida (the sign as diacritical ... reference ... difference ... the metaphysics of absence) ... Language-centred writing involves a major alteration in textual roles: of the socially defined functions of writer and reader as productive and consumptive poles respectively of a commodital axis. What it offers is the alternative sense of reader and writer as equal and simultaneous participants within a language product ... With the removal of grammatical conditioners as dictates of a single reading, language enters the domain of its own inwardness, the conventional centrifugality of signification is reversed and the sign turns inward through the absence of grammar to a pure lexemic presence.
>
> Seen as such, then, the text is a critique of language achieved by way of deconstruction of a grammatical context ... We are among isolated meanings, absolute potencies and graphic events. (1977, 61 – 63)

In contrast to Kroetsch, McCaffery's is not applied criticism. The issue he explores here is a crucial one, for the deconstruction of metaphysics by an appeal to figurative language contains its own impasse: the poet and critic can only carry out this enterprise with an analytical tool that is itself apt to become another metaphysic in turn. The danger of idealism, of an appeal to a metalanguage, is real should the dismantling of linguistic assumptions not be carried out through rhetorical analysis, suggests Hillis Miller. It can only be avoided "by recognition of the linguistic moment in its counter-momentum against idealism or against logocentric metaphysics. By linguistic moment, I mean the moment in a work of literature when its own medium is put in question" (248 – 49). Indeed, there are some who would suggest that deconstruction has not avoided that impasse even by adopting this strategy. The study of tropes and etymologies, for the aporia, self-contradictions, gaps, swerves in a text, is a reading operation similar to that of the New Critic. While he was preoccupied with irony, the deconstructionist settles on ambiguity, and potentially a metaphysics of negativity. This hint of continuity offers one possible explanation for American interest in deconstruction.[18]

In crossing the Atlantic to the United States, deconstruction lost its political edge. The work of the so-called Yale school has suggested that all language is metaphor, working by tropes and figures, that is, by substitution of one set of signs for another, hence "groundless," with no *literal* meaning. All forms of writing are figurative and ambiguous, but literature is the form in which the undecidability is most evident. This process of language undermining its own meaning, in a dizzying and undecipherable see-saw between "literal" and figurative mean- ing, becomes a new way of defining literature. Literature being about the operation of deconstruction, the critic's job is to retrace the way in which texts come to contradict their own systems of logic.

Canadian deconstructionist criticism, of which there is an increas- ing amount, is generally a retracing to expose this "dissemination" of writing in specific texts by fastening on to their impasses of meaning, the points at which they contradict all logic and system. Kroetsch's criticism led the way in this regard, as exemplified in "The Exploding Porcupine: Violence of Form in English-Canadian Fiction," a study of undecidability in the fiction of Michael Ondaatje and Audrey Thomas, written for the conference on Violence and the Canadian Novel (1981). Kroetsch's interest in deconstruction has not gone unnoticed by critics and has led to deconstructionist retracings of his literary and critical fictions by E.D. Blodgett and Shirley Neuman (1984).[19] More recently, in *bpNichol: What History Teaches*, Stephen Scobie carries out a deconstruc- tionist retracing of Nichol's work focusing on its heterogeneity, self- contradiction, and *différance*. Scobie draws a parallel between Barthes' praise of self-contradiction in *The Pleasure of the Text* and a 1968 text by Nichol, *Little Boy Lost Meets Mother Tongue*:

> Language does not exist on just one level it exists on many.
> and rather than trying to find the one *true* level you must

become fluent in all of them ... two truths can exist side by
side without contradicting each other. it is our desperate
search for the final answer that drives us to the grave. the
final answer is a Fallacy. the final answer is, quite simply,
that there is none. there is only the truth co-existing simultaneously with other truths, each with other truths, each
with their own laws which make them true. (20)

Following Nichol's writing through its deployment of Steinian devices
of repetition that introduce deferral, and other deconstructive gestures,
Scobie concludes that Nichol collaborates in the death of the author by
handing over control of *The Martyrology* to the reader who must make
her way through the maze or labyrinth of chains of ideas.

If Nichol's deconstruction, as Scobie sees it, is aesthetic, since the poem
turns inward on itself, unravelling its own history and basic materials,
this does not mean that Canadian deconstruction has lost the political
bite characteristic of its European roots. On the contrary, the contemporary popularity of deconstruction in this country is attributable to
deconstruction's project to dismantle first principles embedded in systems of meaning to show them to be products of a particular system,
rather than what supports the system from without. Feminist criticism
has been particularly searching in its exposure of the meaning system
of male-dominated society. In this, woman as sign is what is not man,
what he has expelled or repressed beyond himself. Yet she is an essential reminder of what he is, and the undermining of binary systems of
opposition. Feminist deconstruction has been concerned to point out the
way in which binary oppositions are a way of seeing typical of ideology.
Feminisms' various subversive strategies have been designed to unravel
these oppositions by showing how they collapse in on themselves in the
name of a difference which is relational, labyrinthean, web-like, rather
than hierarchical (Godard 1981). Another series of oppositions deconstructed to reveal antitheses secretly inhering one within the other is
that centred on colony and imperial centre. For deconstruction has reac-
tivated interest in isolating the characteristics of a Canadian discourse
in a colonial space, colony now perceived to be that which is banished to
the margins from where it returns to disrupt the established discourse

in the English language. Help unravelling the thread in this labyrinth comes from other theorists of deconstruction, notably Gilles Deleuze and Michel Foucault.

"The Canadian Discourse as the Discourse of the Other" is the title of a paper which suggests that Canadian literature is a deterritorialized literature. At the centre of its concerns is the Other — women, natives, and immigrants — to produce a hybrid, "littérature mineure," an a-signifying language, in which cultural difference is difference encoded within language itself (Godard 1987b). It draws on the concepts of Gilles Deleuze for whom binary oppositions are embedded in ideology to underline the political implications of marginality (1975). The hybridization and dissemination occurring within the Canadian literary discourse, as the writing of these minorities is included, are themselves emblematic of the place of Canadian literature within world literature: the rise of the repressed, dislocating and undermining the logic of the literary systems of the Anglo-American world, produces a limit to writing.

Paul Hjartarson suggests as much in the opening lines of his "The Fiction of Progress: Notes on the Composition of *The Master of the Mill*" which draws on the theory of Michel Foucault:

> Literary criticism traces the figure of our desire. Our repeated desire as critics of Canadian literature has been to de/sire, to discover our own identity, what in *Patterns of Isolation* John Moss, for example, terms "our emergence as a national being" (7) and thereby release ourselves from our literary and cultural precursors ... We desire a tradition to displace tradition. (1)

Hjartarson finds in our/his "fascination with documents, longing for authoritative biographies, descriptive bibliographies, and definitive editions another act of exorcism by repetition, another form of our desire to de/sire" (5). Repetition, as Gilles Deleuze has instructed us, is always and only difference. There is always a change in context created by the act of repetition itself. Repetition, as Harold Bloom has asserted, is the swerve or tessera, the discontinuous within continuity. The preoccupation with documents in the search for origins and essences will lead to an undoing,

79

as Hjartarson quoting Foucault concludes. For in such "genealogy" the critic will be led not to the founding moment of something, but rather to the accidents of the journey, to heterogeneity that disturbs and disperses any origin. Fidelity to documents will lead us to an undoing not only of the "great tradition," but of the concept of tradition itself. In the paper, Hjartarson works with the half-dozen or so manuscript fragments of Grove's novel in what becomes an increasingly dense web of beginnings for *The Master of the Mill*, these in turn examined within the traces of Grove/Greve's life. In conclusion, the paper turns to the symbol of the wheel of progress, image of self-contradiction, the point at which the book and the paper self-destruct: "the senator, throughout his life, fought consciously against the logic of the mill while unconsciously he promoted it" (qtd. in Hjartarson 29). The essay too is caught in this turning wheel, protesting against tracing lines of continuity and progression while filling these in. It spins endlessly, even as this endless turning is what makes forward movement possible. Like *The Master of the Mill*, the essay is undone in its doing, its fragmentary form and documentary impulse both disrupting and inscribing continuity.

If Michel Foucault's concept of "genealogy" has been key to the decentring of tradition and the foregrounding of the historical dimension in textual production, his concept of *epistemé* to describe discursive formations has encouraged Canadian critics to extend their deconstruction beyond the limits of literature to explore the historical intertext of literary works, as in Magdalene Redekop's "Authority and the Margins of Escape in *Brébeuf and His Brethren*." She demonstrates the self-contradictions at work in Pratt's "Brébeuf" when Catholic beliefs clash with Protestant theology. There is growing interest in this historical intertext, as the title of Linda Hutcheon's paper promises, but the Derridean interest in the clash between rhetoric as tropes and rhetoric as performative words to be interrogated in a ceaseless movement of interpretation has so far proved more engaging. The primacy of literacy is unchallenged (as with the Yale school). Cultural studies is a field yet to be cultivated by literary scholars who have left this edge (limit) to sociologists and political theorists of the *Borderlines* school.[20]

Oscillation, undecidability, this is one form for the paradoxical clash of scepticism and idealism to take. Another is that of Bakhtinian carnival. In the work of Bakhtin, the challenge of openness and scepticism is directed at the closed forms of ideology. According to his theory, the novel is the descendant of the carnival tradition which parodies and travesties the forms of dominant culture. Carnival is the place of resistance to church and state in classical and mediaeval Europe. In the carnival, the fool puts on the king's crown, the king dons the fool's cap, in a perpetual process of inversion. Down and up are continually changing places, in what is the prime feast of change and becoming. Bakhtin extends this concept of the dialogic novel to the work of Dostoevsky. More recently, critics have begun to apply it to modern literature. Robert Kroetsch extends its implications to North American literature which he sees as an uncrowning of European authority. However, within this process, the Americans with their un-tea party Revolution have been more active participants. Canadian writers like Susanna Moodie and Haliburton have maintained their distance from the carnival spectacle, refusing to become involved as participants in this performance without a stage in which actors and audience are confounded. However, in concluding his essay in the words of his character Johnny Backstrom, from his speech on death as "coming," Kroetsch implies the relevance of Bakhtin's theories to a study of contemporary Canadian writing.

Like that of Foucault, the appropriation of Bakhtin focuses critical debate on questions of authority and tradition whose established limits and logic are undermined by the marginal carnival rabble, in this case Canadians resisting imperial power in the Anglo-American axis. Bakhtin's theory has been invoked in such a context to describe the fiction of Robertson Davies (a remnant of the Celtic diaspora) (Godard 1984–1985). It has also been used to account for the disrupting of conventions in Jack Hodgins' fiction, carnival celebrations of the marginalized featuring prominently in the work of this Western novelist, resisting the hegemonic pull of Ontario sobriety (Thurston). Smaro Kamboureli has applied Bakhtin's theory to the Canadian long poem which she describes as a novelized genre.[21]

Bakhtin's theory of the novel provides a model for oscillation and process within the framework of an ideological challenge, and thus simultaneously embraces scepticism and idealism. While this may merely be the most recent stopping place in a dizzying change of critical fashions, it also rephrases the paradox which is at the heart of contemporary Canadian criticism, as I have attempted to illustrate, and roots it in discourse. Since Bakhtin becomes a point of reference for those like Kroetsch who have worked through Derrida's theory, it also implies that reading deconstructively in Canada is ultimately a political practice.

::

Throughout the decade, critical theory in Canada has been on a see-saw between support for zero-degree writing — "minus Canadian" — and advocacy of contextually bound writing. This Canadian "plus" is all meaningful in the present conjuncture preoccupied with figures of difference. To be a Canadian, as to be a woman, is to inhabit a colonial space from which one perceives discourse as a form of power and desire. The insights of structuralism and semiotics focus attention on language and the structuring of the message; phenomenology, especially reception theory, is concerned with the effect of these devices at the point where the message is received, while deconstruction, and above all feminism, teach much about the analyses of "interested" theories and arguments. That all these theories are themselves imported with their carpet bags stuffed with ideological positions is yet another paradox: a new colonization to free oneself from colonial status. As I have tried to show in my critique of presuppositions and analysis of the logic and ideology of these various textual strategies advocated by Canadian critics, there is nonetheless a perverse logic at work in the pattern of borrowing, one that foregrounds the Canadian "plus." Through its recombinant genetics, this new new critical theory seeks to unmask power and to focus on the study of "Canadian forms of language and language alone."[22] And it borrows freely from or subverts to its own end the dominant critical theories of the North Atlantic triangle.

If a wide net has been cast in this essay, it is a web of holes held together with a string. This thread will soon be unravelled by other deconstructions of its presuppositions and by the appearance of yet new critical theories on the scene.

CRITICAL DISCOURSE IN/ON QUEBEC

What narrative to relate? This is a fundamental question to be addressed by the literary critic faced with a vast body of material, a pluralistic critical scene, a border/line position both inside and outside the critical institution in question, and the limitations of the form imposed by the present venue. Narrative will inevitably emerge, for, as Lyotard has suggested, narrative is the preeminent mode in the formulation of customary knowledge (19).[1] Although opposed to scientific knowledge in that it is not sceptical, its truths having no recourse to argumentation and proof, narrative knowledge is not separate from scientific knowledge. Indeed, the "return of the narrative in the non-narrative" (27) is a part of the language game of science.[2] A scientist communicating a "discovery" relates a quest narrative or epic about the research. Narratives — of speculation or of emancipation — are modes of legitimation, statements of truth whose own legitimation is effected in the very act of transmission, through "performativity" (41). With the upsurge in technologies and techniques, however, these "grand narratives" of unification have lost their credibility (37). Instead of the coherence of the historical discourse of modernism, described by Jean-Pierre Roux as "seek[ing] the intelligible in the play of temporalities and the flow of a narrative deliberately constructed, intrigue, sequence and progress, the three rules on which has flowered modernist dramaturgy" (qtd. in Perron 84), we are confronted with the contesting narrative of delegitimation, characterized by its ruptures and dis/placements, its interrogation of the narrating instance, in which the narrator is cut off from the narratee and the story being told — in short, "the investigative language game" of the "postmodern world" (Lyotard 41). The choice of narrative mode in which to frame this story of contemporary Quebec critical discourse is of crucial importance, for narratives "formulate prescriptions that have the status of norms. They therefore exercise their competence not only with respect to denotative utterances concerning what is true, but also prescribe utterances with pretentions to justice" (31).

83

In selecting a narrative to frame this discourse of scientific knowledge, a critical discourse on critical discourses, the freedom of the critic is already limited. As Lyotard points out, an institution imposes constraints that "function to filter discursive potentials, interrupting possible connections in the communication network: there are things that should not be said. They also privilege certain classes of statements (sometimes only one) whose predominance characterizes the discourse of the particular institution: there are things that should be said, and there are ways of saying them" (17). Jacques Dubois has defined literature as an institution on three levels, as "autonomous organization, as socializing system, and as ideological apparatus" (1978, 34). A tendency of this institution, according to Bourdieu, is for criticism "to take as its task not the production of instruments of appropriation ever more imperative for the work in function as it is distanced from the public, but to supply a 'creative' interpretation for the use of its 'creators'" (1971, 56 – 57). The limits the institution imposes on potential language "moves" are never established once and for all, nor are they universal, but are themselves "the stakes and provisional results of language strategies, within the institution and without" (Lyotard 17). In the present discursive instance, in which the institutional boundaries are compounded by linguistic frontiers and national borderlines — English-Canadian-based narrator of Quebec critical discourse to a United States narratee — the institutional limits are multiplied and fractured. Which narrative to choose? The narrative of intelligibility emanating from the École des hautes études pratiques in Paris, where, in developing a "structural anthropology" (Perron 83) for Quebec literature, numerous Quebec critics have located a discursive formation in the writing of Roland Barthes, Julia Kristeva, Gérard Genette, and other structuralists? Or should I choose the new discursive practice in the form of discontinuous, delegitimating narratives, which challenge the master narratives and legitimate post-structural knowledges along the model of English-Canadian critics who, like their peers in the United States, have made steps to the École normale superieure, where presides the archdeconstructionist Jacques Derrida (Godard 1984a and "Structuralism/Post-structuralism")?

Plus ça change, plus ça reste pareil. A glance at the trajectory of literary criticism in Quebec since the 1950s would seem to bear out the truth of this venerable adage, forcefully reiterated in such classic Quebec novels as Louis Hémon's *Maria Chapdelaine* and Félix-Antoine Savard's *Menaud, Maître-draveur*, that nothing ever will or ever should change in the province of Quebec. The notion is suggested also by Robert Giroux:

> To judge by recent theoretical discourses on Quebec poetry — think of the numerous articles signed P. Haeck, C. Beausoleil, F. Charron, N. Bros-sard, to name the best known from *La Barre du jour, Dérives, Hobo Québec, Les Herbes rouges,* etc. — it seems that the movement begun towards the end of the sixties to displace the question of literature from an ideological level to a level of so-called scientific knowledge, it seems this movement is in the process of being reversed. After the difficult and loaded descriptive techniques of those proponents of a linguistic and logical perspective — "formalist" — on the subject of the analysis of poetic texts, we are witnessing a return to contemplation, to the real poetic text as an object for aesthetic consumption, to writing as the lived experience of gifted individuals, to reading as a ludic practice which is exclusive and incommunicable. (Giroux and Dame 29)

Giroux points out that the structuralist enterprise, focusing on the function of codes in the production of meaning and on cultural conventions, has given way in the 1980s under discursive subversion and deconstructive virtuosity to a focus on subjectivity.

A rapid scan of the horizon would confirm this reversal. Jean Éthier-Blais is once more writing a literary chronicle for *Le Devoir* after fostering academic criticism during his tenure at McGill University. Whether his current reviews will have the impact of his earlier work is a moot point. Published in the three-volume collection *Signets*, this criticism is typical of that practiced in Quebec periodicals before the development of academic criticism. Aesthetic values are of secondary interest: literary criticism is above all a criticism of life, a search for humane and spiritual values (Marcotte 345). French-Canadian literature is an "important sociological phenomenon in our lives," because it leads us to recognition of ourselves. Writers "describe us as we are" and "without fear of losing ourselves, we can plunge into [their works'] mirror" (Éthier-Blais *Signets* 2: 20, 5). Another sign of a return is the flourishing interest in the sociology of literature and the literary institution, as exemplified in issues of *Études francaises* (1984) and *Sociologies et sociétés* (1985) that mapped the terrain of contemporary sociological theories of literature and culture (*Sociologies, Sociologie critique*). Other signals of change were the innumerable publications of the research groups at the University of Sherbrooke and University of Laval that studied the institutionalization of literature in Quebec — for instance, *Structure, idéologie et reception du roman québécois de 1940 à 1960*, edited by Jacques Michon; Joseph Bonenfant's *À l'ombre de Desrochers*; and Maurice Lemire's *L'institution littéraire*. Exploring the teaching, publishing, and reception of Quebec literature, its relationship to government and the press, collective studies like Lise Gauvin and Jean-Marie Klinkenberg's *Trajectoires* testified to the vitality and range of interest in the literary fact. But sociology of literature was already the major critical narrative on Quebec literature in the early 1960s, when the literature was first being institutionalized, as manifest in the collaborative venture *Littérature et société canadienne-française*, edited by Fernand Dumont and Jean-Charles Falardeau, and in the Marxist criticism of *Parti Pris* (1963 – 68). While studies from the 1980s belong to what André Belleau has called "'professional' sociocritique," this continuum suggests a "traditional 'sociocritique,' a sort of general sociologizing discourse practiced forever by journalists, writers, professors, who tend to consider each important work that appears as a moment, successful or not, in a literary evolution inseparable from national and political evolution," the two series, to use Russian formalist terms, considered to be in an isochronic relationship (1983, 302, 300). The nationalist issue has in fact remained the touchstone for literary evaluation since the nineteenth century.

Additional evidence of an eternal return is to be found in a 1987 review of critical studies of Quebec literature, Agnes Whitfield's "La modernité." In answer to the question of how to link the seeming incongruities of Roger Chamberland's phenomenological study of the poetry of Claude Gauvreau, Marie-Andrée Beaudet's intertextual reading of Langevin, and *À double sens*, a dialogue between Hugues Corriveau and Normand de Bellefeuille on the current views on modernity, Whitfield picks up the thread of modernism.[3] Had she focused on the theories implicit in these studies rather than on their content as common denominator, she too might have heralded the return of the subject and a personal, though not impressionistic, criticism in the exchange between the two poet-critics, who question the limits of formalism with regard to what modernity has excluded — that is, with regard to the concepts of the author, style, and meaning. Corriveau and de Bellefeuille confront the impossibility of excluding writers' anthromorphologic relation to their own words. Corriveau especially argues for the rehabilitation of neglected concepts, notably *l'émotion* (158 – 59). Chamberland's study, too, is premised on the subjectivity of the author and the critic. Adopting the approach of the Geneva school, especially the criticism of Jean Starobinski, Chamberland's phenomenological reading of Gauvreau is grounded in a constant movement between the literary work and the consciousness of the reader, to outline the transformations that occur in the theme of the gaze. Drawing also on the work of Maurice Blanchot, he connects the gaze to the theme of eroticism and the metaphysical and aesthetic dimensions of the poet's "exploréen" language. Intended not as future-oriented critique of the positivism of formalism and structuralism, Chamberland's focus on the subjectivity of writer and reader, like Corriveau and de Bellefeuille's text, hearkens back to the heyday of phenomenology in the 1960s, when thematic criticism of space and time dominated the literary scene. Along with criticism of the themes of Anne Hébert's world by Lucille Roy, and Maurice Emond's explorations of the poet's symbolic universe, which listen attentively and trace the meanders of images and themes to uncover a vibrant, dynamic world of her imagination, Chamberland's study testifies to the continuing presence of phenomenology on the Quebec scene.

The reader's subjectivity is also a concern in Beaudet's book on Langevin. For Beaudet, too, criticism is conceived as an encounter between "the sensibility and the experience of the reader" and the "trajectory of the creator" (1985, 6). But in answer to questions about transformations of style, Beaudet offers explanations grounded not in the authorial function but in the text understood in its global sense — in this case, in the intertextual relations with the *roman du terroir*. Drawing on the work of Russian formalists and French structuralists, Beaudet argues with Maurice Blanchot that the work develops in complicity with the "literary space" that contains it and is contained by it, and with Julia

Kristeva that literature is born of literature, that every text is a "mosaic" of quotations, textuality being the absorption of texts by other texts, or intertextuality (16). Here is a clear enunciation of the preeminence of text over author or reader in the production of meaning. The battle of the subject has occurred in Quebec, as elsewhere, between phenomenology and structuralism, as the focus of critical activity has shifted from author to text to reader as locus of meaning. Whatever reinscription of the subject may be taking place on the Quebec critical scene, the text has not been entirely excluded from the discourse. Indeed, the lessons of structuralism have been well learned. To a much greater degree than in English Canada, Quebec critics acknowledge the structuring force of language in the constitution of knowledge, a characteristic trait of post-Saussurean discourses. Contemporary Quebec criticism is indeed poststructuralist. Subjectivity is not grounded in the humanist understanding of the subject as a free agent but as constructed and positioned within discourse(s) whose codes are legitimated by social institutions.

Rather than reading this article teleologically — as I have been in the footsteps of Giroux, looking for a narrative thread like that of the romance quest for becoming or of the epic of discovery, focusing on the moment of mythic return, to describe the development of contemporary Quebec criticism — I could read it as a grid or field of lines and forces, metaphorically an emblem of the pluralistic nature of critical theory in Quebec. For like Whitfield's, my reading of these three books together is happenstance. My narrative would no longer emphasize historical continuity and privilege these three texts as metonymies of successive phases of Quebec criticism since 1960: thematic, structuralist, poststructuralist. Instead, it would read these texts as a play of competing discourses framed in a disjunctive narrative that would challenge the totalizing and homogenizing claims of all narratives. Instead of giving oneself up to the pleasure of reading (which implies a pleasure in discussing the text based on familiarity with the "message" of the text or the author), one becomes implicated in the negative operation of language, seeing irony in the ephemeral meanings crystallized in the face of the writer's death drive, as described by Kristeva. To follow Giroux:

> It is no longer a question of recalling the structures of language

or a group of theoretical concepts and textual manipulations: finished with preexistent models, codes, cultural conventions, the text as an object to construct as an object of knowledge; make way for the individuality, the originality of the text, for discursive subversion, for the virtuosity of deconstruction. Too bad for unreadability, theoretical contradictions, umbilical metadiscourse. (Giroux and Dame 29–30)

A sarcastic dismissal of deconstruction's unfixing of the transcendental signifier and decentering of the subject in the free play of meaning, Giroux's statement is representative of a certain disjuncture between writing and criticism in Quebec, the deconstructive moment in the former confronting the formalist-structuralist practices of the latter. But then, as the discourse analysis of Lyotard and Foucault has shown us, the free play of signifiers is an illusion. The institution — through the authorial function or the critical function, in the case of critical fictions — fixes and defines meaning. The prescribed narrative on the Quebec critical scene probes the discourses authorized by the academy to expose their hidden assumptions and ideologies. While many critical discourses proliferate in books of criticism, not all are equally privileged by the literary institution itself, as evidenced in the reviewing patterns of *Lettres québécoises* and, more significantly, of *Voix et images*, two periodicals devoted exclusively to Quebec literature.

In isolating the hegemonic discourses in Quebec criticism, I shall make use of Raymond Williams's concepts of dominant, residual, and emergent discourses (121–27). Inevitably, since the 1960s, the dominant discourse of one moment has become the residual of another in the dialectics of genre, antigenre, and renewal of genre. This model, in which residual may form the grounds for emergent discourse, avoids the teleology and singularity of the historical narrative and the aleatory processes of the deconstructive challenge to narrative and representation. In this exploration, one must re/construct the critical dynamics of the early 1960s, to establish the residual humanist discourse against which the new academic institutional criticism of sociological and phenomenological persuasions emerged. The trajectory of one critic, André Brochu, whose career coincides with the development of the critical academy in

Quebec, is grounded in the Marxist sociocritique of *Parti pris*, later turning to the structuralist and semiotic approaches that came to dominate in the universities. Here, though, I shall explore only the emergent critical discourses, notably discourse analysis and feminism that draw on semiotics to analyze ideological signifying practices. To speak of these as emergent in the light of the recent deaths of the two most eminent practitioners, André Belleau and Suzanne Lamy, seems to be a logical contradiction worthy of the most assiduous deconstructivist critic. In this case, I write in the future perfect, in the promise of works in progress.

As in English Canada, the history of critical discourse in Quebec is for the most part a history of literary criticism and not of poetics. No literary theorist of the stature of Northrop Frye has emerged in Quebec. Quebec critics have followed the theoretical modes of France with more or less precipitation, selectively, it should be noted. Critical fashions in the United States have gone unnoticed by Quebec critics, especially the passage of New Criticism. Nor, despite translations of works by Northrop Frye and Marshall McLuhan, has Anglo-Canadian theory had a significant impact. Eclectic critics like Gilles Marcotte reveal a knowledge of their theory (Brochu and Marcotte) but do not apply it in their critical analyses of individual texts. Significantly, a body of literary theory has emerged in Quebec, especially in the field of feminist theory, through the work of creative writers like Nicole Brossard and Madeleine Ouellette-Michalska, whose deconstructive dismantlings of the master discourses of Western society — Freudianism, Marxism, and structuralism — have provided a highly innovative theory combining the theoretical concerns of French and United States feminism. Brossard has coined the term *fiction/theory* for her work, breaking down the boundaries between these two discourses in her theorization of gender, which has served as a model for other Quebec avant-garde writers associated with the periodical *La Nouvelle barre du jour*. Their "exploréen" fictions have initiated poststructuralist theory, continuing a line of writing as rupture that began with the emergence of the *nouveau roman* in 1964, "a brusque mutation" that led Jean Marcel, summing up the critical production of the year, to deplore the absence of what was most exciting and original in France, "la nouvelle critique," despite the vitality and variety of the year's criticism (23).

While structuralism is positioned in this narrative as a moment of rupture and discontinuity in which a dominant humanist focus on the subject and meaning is challenged, another narrative, one of continuity, would emerge, if we paid strict attention to dates. Just when structuralist analyses of texts began appearing in the 1970s, a counter-challenge was launched. Earlier, in Europe, Bakhtin criticized the Saussurean model for its failure to deal with the speech act and diachronic analysis: in Quebec, in the early 1970s, Belleau launched his critique of structuralism and positivism in the name of Bakhtin's theories of dialogism and the carnivalesque. Writing in the Marxist periodical *Stratégie* in 1974 on "littérature et politique," where he discusses the complex interrelationships of poetics and politics, Belleau acknowledges his debt to Marxist concepts of culture, especially those of "totality, multiplicity, becoming, etc." — "critical concepts, favouring the multivocal over the univocal and rejecting any fragmented, mutilated, or alienated vision of man" (1986, 75). Although Belleau foregrounds his adhesion to Theodor Adorno's view that literature is not "integrable," is not effective, and serves at most to prepare an intellectual and psychological terrain pertinent to the emergence of certain social changes, the reader recognizes in Belleau's language the concepts of Bakhtin — heteroglossia, polyphony, multivoiced discourse — that elsewhere Belleau sees as characteristics of Quebec culture.

Criticism may now be perceived as a genre with its own dialectics peculiar to its established taxonomies: genre, antigenre, renewal of genre. Belleau's role in launching Quebec criticism back into its perennial concern with the sociology of literature is primarily that of theoretician. As voice of an emergent critical discourse, Belleau holds a contradictory position. In that the majority of his critical production occurs in the form of brief, familiar essays that have appeared, for the most part, in nonacademic periodicals, Belleau is a direct inheritor of the impressionist criticism dominant in Quebec until the 1960s. Indeed, Belleau began as a general cultural critic advocating the engagement of intellectuals in social change (1961, 695), moving into academe in mid-career, when the academy became the central legitimating institution of that criticism. But *Le romancier fictif*, his study of the emergence of a genre of fiction, the novel about the novelist, as well as his discussion of the literary and social codes working in Quebec literature ("La démarche") indicates that Belleau has thoroughly absorbed structuralist theory. He uses it as a *bricoleur*, however, as heuristic device, his final aim being not merely the description of the rules of the literary artifact but the elucidation of its social meaning. Plus, not minus, Quebec.

Thoroughly dialectalized, Belleau's advocacy of the study of literature as a signifying practice, focusing on an exploration of the instance of enunciation with recognition of the heterogeneity of the discourses working the text and of the operation of the literary institution in shaping these discourses, accommodates the residual quest for the specificity of Quebec literature and classification of the *homo Québécensis* to the dominant structuralist paradigm, metonymy of a new critical discourse. Following these currents, Quebec critics such as Maroussia Hajdukowski-Ahmed and Joseph Bonenfant are turning their attention to the prevalence of the carnivalesque, to the exploration of dialogism and research in literary pragmatics, and to the study of the literary institution, the "code of codes," according to Belleau, which, presiding over the choice of codes as "obligatory mediation," intervenes between the mass of discourses composing the social discourse and the literary text, reorienting this heterogeneous linguistic material to the ends of the literary success of the text (1986, 188 – 89). Belleau recognizes the complexity of the mediation intervening in this intertextuality; his concept of the sociology of literature bears little resemblance to the sociology of the 1960s, which he has so vociferously attacked (1983).

As godfather to the new ideological criticism, Belleau has waged war on the positivism of the Quebec literary institution. "Literologist" is how he described himself in 1979 in an academic institution obsessively focused on result-oriented research (1986, 91). A change has taken place in the preceding decade so that the situation that existed when he began to teach at the university in 1970 (when the titles "Professor of literature, Journalist, Frenchman, Intellectual, Poet were interchangeable") has been transformed into one in which the professor is a "specialist in texts," engaged in a limited activity whose technicity is adapted from the social sciences (91). In this context, Belleau joins in the quarrel of *la nouvelle critique*, which opposes Barthes to Picard on the question of semiotics versus literary history. Railing against "an ingenuous semiotics which conceives literary works like musical cigarette boxes and believes in their [textual] closure," Belleau protests the irony that nobody in Quebec was doing real literary history before the vogue for semiotics (93). Developing the polemic in a later essay, Belleau denounces the unwillingness of literature departments to examine their own epistemological presuppositions, which he categorizes as "naively positivist" (1986, 212). The objects of their research they take as natural, not as "constructed." The hidden presuppositions of the reigning positivist and scientistic ideology are camouflaged by a more immediate pressure, that of electronic communications. The arrival of the computer coincides with the discovery, by the Quebec Ministry of Education, of Jakobson's linguistic theories with their model of the communicative act. The result, he fulminates, is the substitution of the word *emitter* for the word *writer* in the educational world (1986, 214). The death of the subject, the rise of the author function. Belleau concludes that theory is inevitably technicist and produces the same "anaesthetizing" effect as technology. The "logic of the informational machine" (1986, 215) is manifest in the proliferation of linguistic and semiotic theory in the educational institution. Elsewhere, exploring the ambiguous relations between mass culture and literary institution, he observes that confusion between mass culture and popular culture is knowingly fostered by a literary institution (publishers' catalogs and bookstores) that tends "increasingly to model itself on engineer-salesmen of standardized or prefabricated cultural products" (1986, 152).

Belleau's critique of the Quebec literary institution is formulated in the terms of the Frankfurt school's advocacy of a critical culture that alone grounds an "authentic art." This stance is mediated by the work of Fredric Jameson, whose analysis of postmodernism as evidence of consumer culture, not its critical negation, Belleau adopts in attacking the mechanized mass culture of late-capitalist, postmodern Quebec (1986, 200). In opposition to the positivist semiotics and narratology à la Gérard Genette, Mieke Bal, and Gerald Prince, practiced in Quebec by critics like Jean Fisette, Pierre Hébert, Patrick Imbert, and Janet Paterson, Belleau advances the example of Bakhtin in *Esthétique et théorie du roman* as the basis for a new, critical narratology where the "grotesque body" would be everywhere (1986, 201). It is not the carnival as semantic content that is key to Bakhtin's theory, Belleau contends, but the car-nivalesque or dialogic — that is, "what concerns the 'reproduction' and 'the aesthetic transfiguration' (in Bakhtin's words) of the heterogeneity of interacting discourses'" (1986, 94–95). In short, the type of artistic discourse called a novel, grounded in this concept of carnival, has as its concern not the life of society but the life of the enunciation (1986, 197). Carnivalization implies three registers of simultaneous oppositions: the binary oppositions (head-bottom, life-death, etc.) in popular culture; the double-voiced discourse of the popular carnivalesque culture in oppo-sition to the singular discourse of the "official" culture; and the textual transposition of the first two carnival systems (1986, 196). The question of the carnivalesque cannot be separated from that of "poetics through-out history" (199). In its efforts to describe the roles of the narrator as a function of the observation of properly discursive phenomena, nar-ratology on the Bakhtinian model moves beyond the positivist illusion of current narratology, which limits its analysis of the signification of texts solely to linguistic characteristics: "time, mood, aspect and voice" (1986, 202). Belleau does not carry out this textual analysis, though he made a start on such a project — a critical description and reading of a transtextual phenomenon, an attempt at "sociotextual analysis" — in *Le romancier fictif*. His aim of linking the social meaning of the novels with their context involves a consideration of "society" not as an essence but as a "text" (1980, 17). In this, he isolates the ideology of the text, the ide-ology in the aesthetic codes that mediate the relationship of the text to the social discourse. Belleau's discussion of the carnivalesque is para-doxically presented as theory — paradoxical because theory is offered as a textual strategy in opposition to theory denounced as "technicist"! One may read Belleau's critique as the traditional Marxist emphasis on the relationship between base and superstructures and the privileging of diachronic over synchronic analysis.

Although most critics engaged in the sociology of literature have chosen to focus on the literary institution, a study of the manifesto by Jeanne Demers and Line McMurray, *L'enjeu du manifeste/Le manifeste en jeu*, indicates that interest in the ideology of the text has not been eclipsed by attention to the legitimating instances of discourse. In fact, as the authors conclude, the manifesto is the ideology of the text carried to the ultimate: it is "the commentary of the institution," its way of speaking aloud about what happens silently within the institution (155). The manifesto makes precisely manifest the institutional character of literature — that is, its dimension as social practice, with its own sphere of activities as well as a number of codified relations to other aspects of social life. The literary manifesto may range along the scale between action and written text. The manifesto is a "bomb" strategically placed within the system of literary history, as Wlad Godzich describes it in his introduction to *L'enjeu* (1986, 7), underlining the role of the manifesto in the crisis and renewal of literary genres and movements.

This inseparability of text and discourse corresponds to the definition of the literary institution according to Giroux and Lemelin: "The institution is the inseparability of the body and the text, the undecidability of a boundary between the two and between the course of development and the discourse or between the story and the narration; [an] institution whose becoming-constitution is assured by the discipline" (8–9). In order to approach literature — "the process of reading, literature is nothing else but the spectacle of literature" (8) — it is not enough to add a sociology to an aesthetics, or a sociology to semiotics to come up with a sociosemiotics. For to do so would be to accept the closure of the text, to take the literary corpus as a given not to be questioned, to support a view that poetry has aesthetic or linguistic specificity when textual semiotics has shown that literature shares its special features with other systems, linguistic, symbolic, and social. What is needed to replace structuralist poetics with their focus on synchrony and the bounded text, Giroux and Lemelin suggest, is a "non-sociological theory of the social," "a generalized pragmatics" that will be a pragmatics of the perlocutory as well as of the illocutory and a focus on the complete instance of enunciation, on the reception as well as the production of texts. The concept of the institution itself is the necessary sociohistoric theory that "breaks with the logic and dialectic of production as (re)creation or (re) solution of literature by writing" (8). It understands literature to be the process of reading and institutional mechanisms. Reading makes writers — not the inverse. The process of reading distinguishes writers who sometimes write very little from nonwriters who often write a great deal, literary writers from scribblers who are not literary (9). Consequently,

in this collective study, the focus is on the institutional aspects of reading, on those facets of literary activity that link the institution and the
discipline of literary studies — namely, publishing, promotion, teaching,
research, labelling, and distribution. Jean-Marc Lemelin offers a number
of narratives of pragmatics — on the text, on its publishing, its promotion, on teaching, and on distribution — and a history of the discipline
of literary studies in Quebec, focusing on the intellectual and scientific
fields in relation to the literary, the relationship between the university
and other agents of diffusion — periodicals, presses — areas of struggle
for knowledge and power (Giroux and Lemelin). The collection opens
with a study by Robert Giroux on the social and economic status of the
writer — the ideological representation of the writer, the legal fiction of
the writer, and the figure of the writer in the public imagination. There
is clearly a difference in approach in these studies from that in studies by
Belleau and by Demers and McMurray. Whereas Demers, McMurray, and
Belleau are text-oriented, with "text" understood in its enlarged Derridean sense, in which there is no "hors-texte," no extratextual dimension,
or in the Bakhtinian sense of the dialogic (where text and reception are
dialectized), Giroux and Lemelin focus exclusively on reception. Meaning is created by the receiver of the text as shaped by social codes.

This distinction is introduced by Jacques Michon in his contribution
to the Quebec-Belgium dialogue on the institution when he contrasts
the outmoded "sociology of the work" with the new "sociology of literature." Whereas the former considered literature as an expression or
reflection of the social conscience, the latter studies literary conventions
and the way they function. Rejecting broad-ranging studies of society,
class, and ideology, this new sociology focuses on the "mechanisms of
mediation" through which the social constraints are translated into literary terms, mechanisms of production, and reception — namely, publishers, periodicals, criticism, prizes, all the apparatuses that keep the
literary institution going and that "participate in reading, at least by
strategies of orientation and recognition" (Michon 1985, 117). Quoting in
these final words the sociologist Jacques Dubois, Michon acknowledges
the eminence grise of this Montreal-Brussels encounter. Whereas the
Québécois in the 1960s headed to Paris to do a doctorate in semiotics,
aspiring critics in the 1980s rushed to Belgium to learn how to analyze

the literary institution. Dubois is not the only influence on the new sociology of literature. In outlining his method for studying Quebec avant-garde periodicals and the questions he planned to ask of them — questions regarding the relative numbers of university and religiously funded periodicals, the place they accorded Quebec literature, the fraction of intellectuals they represented, the ideological positions implied by their aesthetics, and their interaction as the avant-garde — Michon accepts Dubois's distinction of the avant-garde as that group which introduces the idea of crisis into the literary institution. He also grounds his analysis in Pierre Bourdieu's definition of the avant-garde as a "production for producers elaborated in a restricted circle that contests the dominant cultural legitimacy by admitting new categories of aesthetic perception" (1985, 118). The combination of Dubois's institutional analysis and Bourdieu's theory of the market in symbolic goods has generated a number of Quebec studies of literary production and reception.

Through a close analysis of the educational reforms of the 1960s — changes in exams, programmes, essay themes — Joseph Melançon demonstrates the increasing role of the teaching of Quebec literature in the production of the consumer goods that are literary texts, resulting in an increase from 233 in 1971 to 791 in 1981 with no change in the quality of texts or in financial support for their writing or publication (Gauvin and Klinkenberg 190). This flourishing situation coexists with the problematic identified by Lise Gauvin in her essay, in which Quebec literature is threatened with appropriation and assimilation by the Canadian literary institution as exemplified in the Appelbaum-Hébert report, which fails to name Quebec culture as a distinct entity and pairs its most famous authors with Anglo-Canadians in a list of celebrated "Canadian" writers (Gauvin and Klinkenberg 30). Healthy or threatened with extinction? Facts in support of either conclusion are garnered in these studies of the institution from government documents, publishers' accounts — a series of texts not hitherto read intertextually with experimental fiction.

While there has been a proliferation of institutional analyses in the 1980s, they build on data accumulated over the years. Melançon's work on Quebec pedagogy began in the late 1970s in collaboration with the Institut supérieur des sciences humaines at Laval University in a research group on Quebec literature coordinated by Fernand Dumont. This group cosponsored a conference on literature and ideologies in Quebec in which the institution was first scrutinized. Many of the same participants returned to Laval for another conference on the institution in 1985. This conference covered the customary terrain of institutional analysis: the double allegiance of Quebec literature, the infrastructure of publishing and prizes, the problem of the avant-garde, as well as the requisite reflections on the concept of the institution. New there, however, were explorations on the role of translation in Quebec theatre by Annie Brisset and a study of regionalism in Quebec literature by Antoine Sirois outlining the objectives of the Association des auteurs des Cantons de l'Est, organized in 1977 to defend the literary interests and make known the productions of writers of this region. What both these writers establish is the complexity and diversity of the literary institution in Quebec — not monolithic in its French purity and Montreal aerie, as the earlier studies have suggested, but open to the competing pressures of several languages and urban centres, whether Sherbrooke, Hull, Moncton, or Winnipeg. Missing as yet from this opening to comparative studies of the "national" boundary is any understanding of the role of the literatures of linguistic and ethnic minorities in the Quebec cultural institution.

That such explorations would prove fruitful in illuminating the ways in which the Quebec institution establishes hegemony, makes its exclusions that determine who is and is not a writer, what is and is not literature, has been demonstrated by the emergence in Quebec of feminist theory that has pointed out the patriarchal bias of these mechanisms and the marginal position of women writers and their literary productions. Closely connected to the social and institutional analysis, this other emergent discourse takes a new direction, foregrounding gender.

Feminist analysis is an instance of reading and construction of meaning in a troubling relationship with the literary institution. As Suzanne Lamy elaborates in "Les écritures au féminin," her contribution to the Brussels conference, the emergence of women's writing has accompanied the proliferation of alternative structures — in publishing, diffusing, and teaching this literature — that began in the mid-1970s with the founding of *Les Têtes de pioche* by the poets Nicole Brossard, France Théoret, and others. The need for such alternatives was felt after the

October crisis of 1970, when women became radicalized to the power that language wields and to the sexism of social institutions. While feminists aim to topple the dominant culture and replace it with a *culture au féminin*, a women's culture, according to Lamy, in the same collection Demers and McMurray identify the feminist manifesto as exhibiting an aim of perpetual marginality. Integration or separation? Develop a feminist critique of patriarchal institutions or create alternate structures for women?

This centre/periphery issue with respect to power and knowledge is at the heart of Quebec feminist theory, whether of deconstructionist or of radical persuasion, these being the two dominant feminist discourses in Quebec (Godard 1985a, 1987a). Participating in the poststructuralist enterprise, with its focus on the logos, writing, discourse, and meaning, feminist theoreticians and critics struggle to decentre the dominant discourse in a perpetual movement of *différance* and, paradoxically, simultaneously attempt to inscribe the feminine subject in discourse, to name women's experiences in their own language. The emergence of a feminine subject raises questions for literary theory and for the theory of discourse in general regarding the articulation of the subject in language and the reintegration of the referent in textual theories. It also raises questions about power and authority in language and institutions. As for Foucault, the major point of departure for all feminist reading and criticism is: Who speaks? To whom? In what circumstances? In the subsequent denunciation of the narratives of mastery/the master narratives of our civilization (Freud, Marx, etc.), whose loss is a symptom of our postmodern condition, the feminist project has developed an extensive critique of the totalizing ambitions of theoretical discourse that claims to account for all forms of social experience. Feminism has challenged theory over the distance it maintains between itself and its objects, a distance that objectifies and masters. It has especially challenged modernism's rigid opposition of artistic practice and theory. The resulting fiction/theory, to use Brossard's term, is at the forefront of postmodernism.

The importance of the emergence of a feminist discourse on/in the Quebec literary institution has been underlined by many observers. Jean Royer, among others summarizing the literary production of the 1970s, noted the innovative elements of feminist discourse as the most important in challenging and changing the course of literature in that decade: "women's writing ... questions writing itself." From its first appearance, this writing was preeminently theoretical. In October 1975, *Liberté* organized an international meeting of women writers on the theme women and writing. Nicole Brossard, as editor of *La Barre du jour*, extended the debate in launching "Women and Language," the first of many issues on women, with a question: "How can the woman who uses words daily make use of a phallocratic language which from the beginning is against her" (1975b, 8-9). The texts submitted for that issue were rich and varied, ranging from poetry through prose and drama, but united in their radical opposition to dominant ideology and in their pursuit of formal experimentation. The search for her own forms and symbols led the woman writer to a rupture with the forms of language. As Brossard describes this in her preliminary remarks: "Tenter la femme à son propre jeu de *maux*" ("Try woman at her own game of ills/words") (1975b, 9). In her other contribution to the issue, "E muet mutant," "Silent *e* Mutating," Brossard insists on the political importance of writing. In contrast to women's speech, which is inconsequential and evanescent, women's written words are public. "Writing is making oneself visible. To show all sorts of forms and experiences. To impose upon the gaze of the other before he gets a chance to" (1979, 49). The gesture of writing is concrete and takes the form of a book. "It enters into history. It participates in the collective memory." The woman who writes "becomes a subject" and "imposes her subject," "transgressing masculine discourse" (1975c, 13). Concisely framed here is the use by Quebec feminist writers of negativity to interrupt the organic unity and cultural hegemony of dominant or "master" discourses. The negative impulse is a transformative strategy, as Brossard's text illustrates, for the results are productive and generative, resulting in a diversity of stylistic and genre "corruptions" especially with respect to the emergence of the feminine in language. The silent *e* protests against the dominance of the masculine in grammar, as Louky Bersianik has, and in the process renews the resources of language as Brossard has done with *amantes* and *l'amèr*. Concurring in the Saussurean paradigm of the primacy of language as a symbolic mode for human communication, these Quebec feminists, with their French sisters Julia Kristeva, Monique Wittig, Hélène Cixous, and Luce Irigaray, with whom their theorizing is so closely connected, change language so as to transform relations of communicative and cultural exchange.

The emphasis on negativity evident in fiction/theories like Brossard's *L'Amèr* (written both against and with the mother) and Bersianik's *L'Euguélionne* (a utopian carnivalization of the Bible and Freud) reveals the deconstructionist bent of Quebec feminist theory imprinted with the differential analysis and focus on the margin of Jacques Derrida, Gilles Deleuze, and Michel Foucault. Difference, deferral, discourse analysis — in Quebec these terms were present from the first feminist theory in the 1970s, unlike in anglophone North America, where they have only recently come to challenge liberal feminist theory with its emphasis on images of women. Madeleine Gagnon raised the issue of women's difference in her speech at the 1975 International Writers' Conference. Positioned in alterity and the unspoken in a state of lack of being to the self, a state of "oppression" under the "narcissistic representation of the same" of the "phallocentric" logos whose power is inscribed in her, she is "double" and her speech is "subversive" (1976, 251). Gagnon expands on this in her contribution to the first feminist issue of *La Barre du jour*, in which she links structuralist, psychoanalytic, and Marxist discourses to analyze women's oppression in language. Language being a code, a social contract the dominant make for the dominated, it becomes yet another of the instruments of domination, another form of capitalist exploitation (1975, 46). Against the code, women intervene in anecdotes and pretexts, through ellipses, gaps, displacements, and metonymies that mark their attempt at subverting le "Nom du père" (the name, the no, the law of the father) through which the subject is positioned under patriarchal discourse (Gagnon 1975, 47-49). Biological difference is not the grounds for the oppression of women (Gagnon 1975, 51-52). The antagonism of men and women is constructed through the subject's interpellation by/in ideology, Gagnon contends, extending the analysis of Althusser to the question of sexual difference. Rather than seeking leadership positions in the social order by speaking out about their oppression, women should ally themselves with other oppressed elements in society to engage in a critique of institutions and the way they reproduce the relationships of domination. Gagnon briefly describes what such action of the "mistresses" against the "masters" would be like in the educational institution from which she speaks. Framed as norm and positive value, silence is not death but a temporary exile from which writing will begin again and re-create. In conclusion, Gagnon cautions that while it is important, in preparing a feminist revolution, to seize the opportunity to speak, to work upon language from her decentered position, the revolution must be carried out on the level of "real power, economic, political, ideological" (1975, 57).

Silence is at the heart of Nicole Brossard's concerns too, silence not on the near side of language in the unspoken but on the far side of language in the numinous. "Le centre blanc," the white centre, is the nodal point of Brossard's writing, the place where language turns back on itself to allow space for the reader/hearer to become aware of herself in the act of enunciation and self-reflexively to subvert mimesis and the representation of the female body. Brossard's theory has its grounding in the work of Wittgenstein on language and his foregrounding of the spectacle of language, its materiality and its paradoxes, especially Gödel's theorem regarding its self-referentiality. Brossard sets out to deconstruct patriarchal language, by voicing the silent e, which, though changing pronunciation, had itself remained silent, and by subverting singular meanings through polysemous word play — paradoxes, puns, elisions — that frustrate attempts to arrive at binary oppositions. Brossard's work on paradox is nourished by the deconstructionism of Gilles Deleuze. For Brossard, too, repetition is always difference and deferral in a process that challenges the rule of noncontradiction at the basis of Western logic and metaphysics. In her critique of origins, she draws on the work of Derrida, especially on the concepts of undecidability and oscillation to develop a theory of feminist writing as mobility and the spiral. These cohere in her critique of representation, the fixed identifiable product of the book that represents an originary moment being displaced in a mimesis of process, of a work always in becoming, "in the trajectory of the species" (1983, 101).

Here Brossard's project overlaps that of Irigaray and her theory of mimesis as an intentional miming of identity that overwhelms it. The feminine deploys the feminine self-reflexively, and in so doing reveals it to be a construct of patriarchal logic and explodes boundaries and categories in the refractory mirror of the speculum/simulacrum. Brossard's texts are characterized by boundary play that challenges the categories and classification, the rules of logic, on which the dominant Western — read patriarchal — discourses are founded. Like Gagnon, she plays with the paradoxical positioning of insider/outsider in undermining the fixed category of "woman" to allow for the emergence of women in all their plurality and diversity. Here, as in Gagnon, the female body is metonymy, not metaphor, in a text of contiguity or, as Cixous has framed it, an "endless" female text ("sans but ni bout") of the circulation of female desire (18). Brossard's theory has encouraged many feminist critics of Quebec writers to explore the rhetorical strategies and linguistic patterns of women's writing to create an alternative lineage, a "fillial" lineage, of "casse-textes," "puzzles" in a deconstructive practice of the play of the signifier.

Most wide-ranging in its laying bare of the aporias of the dominant discourse is *L'Échappée des discours de l'oeil*, by Madeleine Ouellette-Michalska. Taking on each of the intellectual disciplines in turn — philosophy, anthropology, history, psychoanalysis, and literature — Ouellette-Michalska reveals how all fields of Western knowledge have been characterized by a narcissistic game of mirrors and surfaces whereby the masculine eye establishes the dominance of its gaze. Woman is "interpellated to constitute the negative term of a binary system." In this process of differentiation, she becomes "the silent sign of a masculine principle which is omnipresent and vocal. Immutable and static, she incarnates the fixed place of origins. Unspeakable, she is the blank in discourse where the ashes of the sign accumulate," the token in exchanges facilitating the transfer of goods or knowledges (73). Fixed at the origin, she expresses nonbeing and nonplace. Projected to mythic poles outside of time, she represents time. "To possess her, is to possess time. To close the Eye and take one's pleasure in the origin" (147). Between what was and what will be, between her virginity and her death, is interposed narrative, the sublimation of male sexual pleasure, symbolic capture able to transcend time. Woman is the mirror in which identity is reflected. In preventing the Eye from "stumbling on the scandal of the void and the gap," she upholds the Law of the Father, the omnipresence of the phallus, transcendental signifier. As token of exchange, she effects the grafting of the social body onto the biological body: "The text cements the relationship of nature/culture in the communication system" (152). The textual body is substituted for the visceral body and enters into a game of (dis)simulation. The signs are fixed in their linearity and re-create the world by a game of substitution. Writing fills gaps in the network of mediation. But the unnamable must be named. "The literary institution is born from this desire and from the impotence of citing the unnameable" (233). Throughout the history of literature, as Ouellette-Michalska shows, woman has held the function of conveyer of "mystery, ecstasy, and duration" (257). Object of exchange, and not subject, woman is fixed as mother or whore, witch and hysteric.

To explore these spaces, silence and hysteria, the excesses of the unnamable and absent feminine, is, Ouellette-Michalska demonstrates in her concluding chapters on the work of women writers, "to destroy the Eye forever," to shatter the effects of the mirror, the reflection of the same, through "fetal contamination" with the mother's voice and through symbolic inversion (295). Woman no longer serves as absent token of exchange in the transmission of patriarchal discourse. The absence of intellectual rigour, the impressionistic collage, the absence of a logical problem, these are some of the characteristics of women's cultural productions that expose "the weak points and make a blot on the Eye" (309). Illustrating the politics of inversion that she describes as a feature of writing in the feminine, Ouellette-Michalska concludes her study of patriarchal discourse with a prologue in which she prepares to write her first sentence. *L'Échappeé des discours de l'oeil* was awarded the Governor General's Award for prose, signalling the valorization of feminist theory in the literary institution in the 1980s.

The critic who most eloquently advocated a new mode of feminist criticism as *fiction/theory* was Suzanne Lamy, who, in *d'elles* and *Quand je lis, je m'invente*, evolved a new mode of writing that is a blend of critical analysis and creative writing, narrative, poetry, personal essay, diary. As in Brossard's work, these multiple texts are in/formed by the practice of Irigaray in *This Sex Which Is Not One* and by Roland Barthes's theory and practice in *The Pleasure of the Text*. For Lamy too, criticism mediates in-between literary science and reading, a place of diverse encounters where desire circulates. A loving relationship or the search for pleasure is most frequently the initial impulse of her criticism. The texts in *d'elles* in which the affectionate bond is played out to its fullest erupt in Quebec critical discourse with a new vitality.

Lamy's analytical approach identifies instances linking speech and writing, the social and the literary, and explores the multiple determinants and meanings of the instance of enunciation. In each text, the sociohistorical element is foregrounded. According to Lamy there is no essential woman ("De corps parlant, il n'y a pas" [1984, 12]). Rather, the feminine is a social and linguistic conjunction, both the trace of a millennial culture and the effect of women's violent will to break with traditional forms, "whose adoption is never innocent" (32). Who is speaking? In whose interest? These are the questions that initiate Lamy's analysis. Since the desire to break with the dominant order is understood to be a collective venture of women within a certain historicopolitical configuration, Lamy focuses her analysis in each essay on a group of writers. Consequently, the key term among the critical concepts is complicity, like Brossard's synchronicity, a phrase to describe the position of the woman critic engaged in loving dialogue with the woman writer, producing a text both with and about the latter's text.

Lamy's analyses of women's literary productions focus on the specificity of their writing. She identifies a number of linguistic facts that are also social facts. Coming to writing has been difficult for women, but it is with the voice that all begins, Lamy agrees with Gagnon. Speech expresses the relationship to the real, to power, and outlines the social imbrication and immediacy of women's writing. Lamy identifies a number of oral modes specifically with women's speaking that account for its social origins in marginality and the forms their writing will take: gossip, dialogue, litany, polytonality, and intertextuality. Sub/version is how she describes the litany, an intermediate form, "ritualized, overexploited" (1979, 99), which women are using intentionally in a parodic manner to rupture old forms. This polymorphic quality makes feminist discourse an *écriture à deux*, "a dialogue in the full sense of the word" (39, 45). Dialogic, the one-within-the-other in the Bakhtinian sense of the polyphonic text, feminist discourse works to subvert the monologism of the dominant discourse. Suzanne Lamy's criticism embraces the same dialogic forms as the texts she writes about, subverting critical discourse.

The twinning of critical and creative text is evident in another sphere. Lamy writes only about contemporary texts. She distinguishes between "feminist writings, feminine literature, texts by women where there is 'writing'" (1984, 12). Lamy is interested only in the third category, though admitting that Christine de Pisan, Madame de Staël, and others were subversive in their time (1984, 6). Writing is an evaluative concept that determines her corpus. Nowhere does she engage in the feminist critique of the canon and re-visionary reading of women's texts of the past that have become the staples of United States and, to a large extent, Canadian feminist criticism.[4]

Quoting Pierre Nepveu, Lamy relates women's search to rediscover the body, daily life, and minorities to a "dis/placement, an unforeseen development of the theories of modernity" (1984, 32, 42). Franco-Belgian feminist Françoise Collin situates feminism more precisely in the "crisis of modernism," last avatar of the modernist world, symptom of a postmodernist one (qtd. in Lamy, *Quand je lis* 26). In describing how she would read otherwise, approaching from the other slope of life, Lamy offers a critique of the limitations of the theories that have in/formed her work: sociological criticism, structuralism, Marxism, and psychoanalysis, none of which adequately addresses women's specificity. Moreover, her reintroduction of the referent, the subject, and the reading process opens breaches in these dominant critical paradigms. "Interrogations" of modernity is how Lamy categorizes feminist writing and re-writing (criticism). Against Lacan's view of the real as impossible, feminist reading strategies oppose "the weight of the real, the reality of texts, the reality of their texts" (1984, 84).

This cohesive position adopted by Quebec feminists has had an impact on anglo-Canadian feminist theory as evidenced in *In the Feminine: Women and Words/Les femmes et les mots* and *Tessera* on *fiction/theory*. Bilingual, like all Canadian feminist critical periodicals, these publications testify to the liveliness of the dialogue between the two language groups. Indeed, the convergence of perspectives around postmodernist performance, deconstructive undoing, by feminist critics of both language groups is unique in the trajectory of critical discourses in Canada and Quebec. While criticism has evolved independently in the two cultures, the reaching out exemplified by feminist theory is characteristic of a general opening of Quebec criticism, an opening that is dis/placing the binary mode of framing difference long a feature of Quebec discourse. No longer exclusively bound up in its *différend* with Paris, Quebec literature and criticism is exploring its alterity in comparison with another minor francophone literature, that of Belgium, in *Trajectoires: Littérature et institutions au Québec et en Belgique francophone* (Gauvin and Klinkenberg). It is also exploring its Americanicity. The process is dialectical: American interest in Quebec is also increasing, as demonstrated in the issue of *Yale French Studies* entitled *The Language of Difference* (Godard 1985b). In an international colloquium, Quebec critics reclaimed a prodigal son, Jack Kerouac, whose fiction is being translated into the Quebec urban dialect, *joual*.

But America does not stop at the United States: it extends south over an entire hemisphere. The new focus of Quebec studies is revealed in *Voix et images*, with its list of foreign correspondents including representatives from Brazil and Mexico as well as the United States and various European countries. Moreover, the issue devoted to English-Canadian literature (Fall 1984) was followed by an issue two years later charting relations with Latin America. "La littérature québécoise, une littérature du tiers monde?" "Québec literature, a Third World literature?" asks Gilles Thérien, exploring "the position of third," the "included third" of colonialism, the "excluded third" of revolutionaries, a situation of detachment, a theme of dispossession. This north–south comparison foregrounds the issue of comparative literature and the heterogeneous element in Quebec literature(s): a similar voice, though different languages. In this confusion of languages, Quebec criticism may explore not its social impotence but its cultural and social ubiquity. This is an option for a society whose cosmopolitan inhabitants have colonized large areas of the Florida winterscape and who are familiarly known in Mexico as "los tabarnacos" for the uniqueness of their swearing, a society, moreover, that has initiated a change in its institutions, voting no to separatism and to the Parti Québécois. With a realignment of institutions inexorably comes a shift in discursive practices and a change in the discourse of literary criticism. Or vice versa. Genre yields to antigenre in a process of renewal.

THE POLITICS OF REPRESENTATION:

Some Native Canadian Women Writers

Native Canadian Culture had never before received such public attention as it did in Toronto in the spring of 1989. At the Theatre Pass Muraille, *Dry Lips Oughta Go to Kapuskasing*, the latest play by Manitoba Cree Tomson Highway, played to packed houses and critical acclaim. Like its complement, *The Rez Sisters* (1986 – 87), which also — though from a woman's perspective — explored Reserve life, the traditional culture of the trickster, and gender politics, *Dry Lips* won the annual Dora Award for the best production on the Toronto stage. Incidentally, this was Highway's *third* play to premiere in Toronto that year, *The Sage, the Fool, and the Dancer* having played to equally full houses at the Native Centre in February. A play for young people had more limited exposure at a branch of the Toronto Public Library during National Book Week. Over at the Cumberland, the audience mixed in the lobby to see Gary Farmer in another leading role, a fine comic performance by this Mohawk actor from the Six Nations Reserve near Brantford, in *Powwow Highway*, the latest version of the on-the-road-quest — Native style. There was a strong Native presence in the visual arts as well. Rebecca Belmore's (Ojibwa) "Ihkwewak ka-ayamiwhat: Means Women Who are Speaking" was featured in the issue of *Parallelogramme* that reproduced the texts from the 1987 exhibition, "Locations: Feminism, Art, Racism, Region — Writings and Artworks" (Belmore 10 – 11). This was a prelude to her summer appearance in the Harbourfront show of "Contemporary Art By Women of Native Ancestry," which followed an exhibit of art by the First Nations and "Indian Territory," the work of Ed Poitras, at Power Plant.[1]

Later in May, Native Earth Performing Arts invited everyone back to Theatre Passe Muraille for "Weesageechak Begins to Dance," a festival showcasing Native plays and playwrights including, among others, *Deep Shit City*, a new text by playwright Daniel David Moses (Delaware), and *Princess Pocahontas and the Blue Spots* by the gifted actress and performance artist Monique Mojica.[2] Soon after, poet Alanis Obomsawin's (Abenaki) new film, *No Address*, was among those featured on the opening weekend of the Euclid Cinema established by DEC (Development Education Centre) to screen politically engaged films. For many of the writers, these events climaxed a season of intensive workshops in Native cultural production organized by the Committee to Reestablish the Trickster. The publication of the first number of *The Trickster* has in itself been an augury, a testimony to the variety and vitality, the quantity and quality, of cultural productions by Native artists. All signs would seem to herald the emergence of Native culture as a forceful presence in the literary institution.[3]

Inscribing this cultural activity under the sign of *The Trickster* indexes the ambiguities of this interruption, however. Like the many manifestations of this cultural hero, Native culture is both destructive and creative, Coyote's "double hook" of darkness and light. Participants in the creative workshops run by The Trickster would focus on reviving traditional storytelling techniques in new forms.[4] Under David MacLean's guidance, storytelling for "television" explored the "creation of new conventions" as, indeed, would the workshops under Highway on "Storytelling for the Stage" while that on "Adapting Storytelling for the Written Page" promised to intensively explore the oral traditions and why they should be translated into written genres. Such intersemiotic "translation" will inevitably work upon them, dis/placing and hybridizing conventions. More explicitly enunciated in a workshop under the direction of poet Lenore Keeshig-Tobias (Ojibwa) entitled "Re-establishing the Voice: Oral and Written Literature into Performance," was the kind of challenge to the Canadian literary institution posed by this emergent literature: it posits the word as a process of knowing, provisional and partial, rather than as revealed knowledge itself, and aims to produce texts in performance that would create truth as interpretation rather than those in the Western mimetic tradition that reveal truth as pre-established knowledge.

Challenge to the Canadian literary tradition was overtly signalled in two of the sessions organized by Keeshig-Tobias and Daniel David Moses. The one entitled "The Missing Voice in Canadian Literature" proposed an "alternative orientation to the study of Canadian Literature" and looked at the role of Native metaphors and Tricksters. Framed in this way, however, it drew attention to the absence of Native texts in the Canadian canon and advanced an alternate canon from what has been an "invisible" visible minority. In this, it contests the claims to comprehension and universality of "Canadian Literature," in the spirit of an aesthetic of difference, where Native cultural producers join the denunciation of the politics of the canon by a number of others in favour of greater recognition of the differentiation of a variety of groups whose race, ethnicity, gender, or class has hitherto marginalized them in the literary field. In this challenge, however, the Native writer is situating herself or himself not just as the Other, an author of radically different texts from an entirely different mode of production. Those following *The Trickster* constitute a contestatory discourse that positions itself as a literature of resistance within the conventions, though marginally so, of the dominant discourse. The final workshop aimed to confront directly the question of cultural appropriation, the strategies whereby Native creative productions have been marginalized by the literary institution. As its particular focus it took the issue of intellectual property exploring the different concepts of property in Native and mainstream cultures — anonymous communal texts versus signed texts — in a seminar with the resonant title "Whose Story is it Anyway?"[5]

As this title announces, questions of property are imbricated in issues of the proper name and of propriety, of those tangled concepts of the authorial signature, of authority, and of decorum or convention, both social and literary. Who has the right to speak or write? What are the appropriate forms for their utterance to take? These, as Michel Foucault has taught us, are the important questions to ask in order to unravel the knotted interconnections of knowledge and power: who is speaking, to whom, on whose behalf, in what context? The ideological significance of conventions is part of that "political unconscious" of literature analyzed by Fredric Jameson. As he writes: "genres are essentially literary *institutions*, or social contracts between a writer and a specific public, whose function is to specify the proper use of a particular cultural artifact" (1981, 106). The relation between texts and institutions is emerging as the common project of the humanities and the social sciences, according to Dominick LaCapra. Genres and intellectual disciplines — discursive practices all — determine through their constraints the specific language uses of texts. "And discursive practices always have a significant relation to sociopolitical institutions — a relation that becomes obvious and subject to sanctions once intellectual pursuits are formally organized in institutionalized disciplines" (LaCapra 140). Whether a perfection of a genre or a disconcerting text that rewrites a genre, texts test and contest the limits of a genre or discursive practice.

"Appropriate form" or appropriation? This is an issue of great contention within the Canadian literary institution at the moment and the intervention of the Trickster workshop was confrontational, strategically oppositional, a deliberate interruption of the canonical norm. Moreover, it occurred in the midst of an intense debate in the Toronto papers which indicated that the emergence of Native culture has been neither assured nor easy. What has been played out in the press, at the same time as this cultural flowering has been moving audiences in the theatre, has been an enactment of the systemic racism through which this cultural production has been rendered "invisible" over the years. The "strategies of reproduction" — the economic strategies that agents use to maintain or improve their social position, the conditions of access through education, affiliative groups, etc. — whereby the literary institution reproduces itself in its existing norms and confers legitimacy on "authors" is exposed in this debate. Generally, such reproduction, which is the work of institutions conveying "know-how," is to ensure the mastery of its "practice" and consequently "a reproduction, of subjection to the ruling ideology" (Althusser 128), the repetition of the same.[6]

This "reproduction of the relations of production" (Althusser 128) is carried out through many representations, whereby individuals are constituted as subjects in their imaginary relationships to their real conditions of existence, that is, in and through ideology. As Althusser reiterates, ideology always has a material existence in that it is a practice (155). Moreover, "there is no ideology except by and for subjects" (159), that is, ideology "constitutes concrete individuals as subjects" (160) through representations which offer subject-positions wherein the individual as subject is made to identify with the Subject of that specific institutional representation or discursive practice. In this case, the literary institution interpellates individuals with representations of the Author-function which Subject-position individuals are invited to occupy.[7] As Althusser points out, within a class society, relations of production are "relations of exploitation" between antagonistic groups. In the present instance of the Canadian literary institution, the relationships between ethnically different groups constitute agonistic relations within an apparatus of struggle ensuring the oppression of certain groups and guaranteeing the conditions of exploitation and its reproduction. That the literary institution and the representations through which it is reproduced are sites of struggle is, however, camouflaged in the narrative of the hegemonic discourse which affirms its authority monologically by refusing to engage in dialogue with these alternate discourses, refuses in fact to acknowledge their existence as contestatory practices and hence to legitimate them as interlocutors.

What is at stake in the struggle is the production of value under competing modes of production. What is that "good" book that merits publication and constructs the author as subject? The representations of the author-position offered by the dominant literary institution were challenged for their systemic racism at the sixteenth annual general meeting of the Writers' Union of Canada (Waterloo, May 1989). Racism in writing was the subject of a panel discussion which involved McClelland & Stewart Publisher Douglas Gibson and Lenore Keeshig-Tobias. The narratives of this encounter differ according to the narrator and his or her representations of the debate. In one account, Sheelagh Conway, dissident feminist writer, quotes Keeshig-Tobias in support of her view that the Canadian literary institution determines value (i.e., literary "quality") according to the "values of Canada's male-dominant, middle-class white culture. Anything else is viewed as ancillary or, at worst, an aberration":[8]

> Publishers say they are interested in "quality" work, not an author's gender or race. ... Juxtapose sexism with racism and the problem is compounded. Makeda Silvera, co-founder of Sister Vision, Canada's only press for women of color, estimates that fewer than 1 per cent of such writers are published because Canadian publishers are unwilling to understand or acknowledge Canada's diverse cultures. Lenore Keeshig-Tobias, a native writer, says publishers have returned manuscripts submitted by natives with "too Indian" or "not Indian enough" scrawled across them. (Conway)

This editorial practice, wherein a "good" book is an ideologically correct book and the author-position is determined by racist norms, is corroborated by Marlene NourbeSe Philip, a Toronto black woman writer, who describes the publication history of her prize-winning novel, *Harriet's Daughter*, as it was rejected by Toronto publishers using similar phrases. "Not marketable" was a "euphemism for their concern about the race of the characters." Only after a British editor agreed to publish it did Women's Press bring out a Canadian co-edition (Philip 1989b, D7).

Once published, books must still find their way to reviewers and readers. Most of the publications of writers of "visible" racial minorities are the work of publishers themselves marginal to the literary institution. That this relationship is ideological, an oppressive relationship, is suggested by the relative fortunes of two women's presses in obtaining the University of Toronto Press as agent for distribution. Second Story Press, a new feminist press run by white women born of the split at Women's Press over this very issue of racism, though it has yet to produce any books, has been signed on by the prestigious university press on the strength of the editors' reputation (Kirchhoff 1989c) while Williams-Wallace, another small press which publishes literary manuscripts by women and writers of racial and ethnic minorities, despite a most respectable back list of writers like Dionne Brand, Claire Harris, and NourbeSe Philip, could not obtain this agency service.[9]

The other narrative in *The Globe and Mail* also characterizes the encounter as a dialogue of the deaf, representing it, though, not as a site of struggle but as theatre of the absurd. It is not my intention to abuse *The Globe and Mail*, but it advertises itself as Canada's only "national" newspaper. Given these claims to universality, its literary pronouncements function as canonical fiats. It is these claims to speak for "everyone" which constitute the monologic discourse of hegemonic formations and which must be interrogated for their politics of inclusion. In this second narrative, Gibson and Keeshig-Tobias "address[ed] the same issue without ever talking at the same things; they barely seemed to be addressing each other":[10]

> It was hard to say which was the more outrageous, Keeshig-Tobias's claim that non-native writers should not tell native

stories or Gibson's unequivocal statement that there is no
racism in Canadian publishing. (It should be added, by the
way, that Keeshig-Tobias's recollections of native-produced
manuscripts being rejected and heavily edited by mainstream publishers cut little ice with a roomful of writers,
few of whom are strangers to either rejection or editing.)
(Kirchhoff 1989a)

In his article, Kirchhoff frames this stychomythia with an account of
the defeat of Judith Merril's motion proposing a task force to examine the relationship of cultural minorities to the Canadian publishing
industry, defeated because it seemed "patronizing," according to one
East Indian-born writer, and to bear little relation to the bread and
butter issues proper to the activities of a trade union in the eyes of the
majority. As Kirchhoff suggests: "The matters of race did not detract
noticeably the other business of the AGM, such as reports from the
regional committees, plans to get more Canadian literature into Canadian schools, discussions of contracts and copyrights, and the status
of the Public Lending Right program" (1989a). That business-as-usual
attitude was itself a manifestation of systemic racism, an example of
the trivialization and blindness that renders invisible the demands
of the minority, for whom this question of access to the editor's approval,
this mark of value, is indeed a vital bread and butter issue — the one
without which contracts are phantasmagoric — is made clear in the rest
of the article. Under the guise of the seemingly neutral prose of the
reporter stating the facts, Kirchhoff re-marks in his parentheses and
asides the profound racism of Canadian society which is manifest in its
jokes that make fun of the very fact of racism and so conceal the work
of reproduction of this racist mode of production within the institution. This is the key tactic of ideology, as Barthes understands it, the
naturalization of belief as fact, the presentation as that which goes
without saying, as a system of facts, what is in reality a semiological
system, that is a system of *values* (1973, 131). The jokes of the Union members offer representations of "colour" which Kirchhoff reports — and
supports — that serve to efface the different hues of skin, colour which
marks permanent differences among people, in favour of differences

in the colours of clothes worn by individuals, a mere surface difference of choice and costume. These jokes turn the protestations of racism by writers of visible minorities into the games of the clown, laughable, and hence no threat to the majority. As Kirchhoff compounds the racism in his reportage: "None of this was malicious, but it was always there" (1989a). The failure to treat another's claims seriously as those of an equal is the strategy of the oppressor who hereby denies value and subjectivity to the other. In these jokes, the person of colour is cast as an object of amusement for the white person who alone is constituted as author-subject in these representations.[11]

In this article, there is also a report of a quarrel between a BC writer working on a novel set in the Queen Charlotte Islands and the Haida who refused him authorization to visit their land without him according them the reciprocal right to vet what he should write about them. This is the other facet of this question of the political struggle over representation, over who has the right to speak and what is the appropriate form for this utterance to take. This question of the right to represent individuals or topics belonging to a minority culture has been a contentious issue in Canadian literary circles at the end of the 1980s. It was over just this problem that Women's Press in Toronto split into two groups over an anthology which included narratives about minority groups (Indians of South America) written by white Canadian women. What emerged as the group in control defined racism as the use by a member of a dominant group of the experience of a disadvantaged culture or the use of culturally-laden devalued language as, for example, the term "black" in a negative context. This attempt to formulate an anti-racist policy, one which moved beyond a liberal non-racist policy based on rejecting overt discriminatory remarks to develop a more systemic analysis of racism, did not, however, entail an affirmative action policy for promoting the self-representations of women of visible minorities. Moreover, the nostalgia for purity, as we shall see, inverted the reigning discourse but did nothing to challenge its values nor the fact of hierarchization itself. It was a call by Keeshig-Tobias for an affirmative action policy with regards to Native writers that was dismissed by Kirchhoff as "outrageous" and subversive of the existing political arrangements.

This was not a startlingly new claim by Keeshig-Tobias. It has been reiterated on many occasions by women of colour, most pointedly in the introduction to an issue of *Fireweed* wherein the guest editors speak of the difficulty they experience in having their work published because they are not "saying it right" according to the norms of the dominant culture. "[S]o if you don't fit into that [one way of 'saying' that counts], then as far as they're concerned, you're not saying anything" (Bannerji 11). For Native women this poses a particular difficulty since "the princess" and "the squaw" constitute the semiotic valences within which Native women have long been represented in the dominant literature of North America. In the allegories of empire, the Indian Queen figured in the celebrated "Four Continents" illustrations of the early sixteenth century as the "familiar Mother-Goddess figure, full-bodied, powerful, nurturing but dangerous — embodying the wealth and danger of the New World" (Greene 19). Her daughter, the Princess, as Britannia's daughter, the Carib Queen, or the Statue of Liberty, leaner and more Caucasian, figures in the allegories of nationalism as the colonies move towards independence. In these configurations, the Native woman as sign was called on to represent both American liberty and European classical virtue. But in a semiotic field configured through relations of substitution, as well as those of contiguity,[12] the Native woman also figured all that was different from the Queen. As the savage Squaw, she configured the dark side of the Mother-Queen, the witch-healer medicine woman, the seductive whore, the drunken, stupid, thieving Natives living in shacks on the edge of town, not in a woodland paradise (Greene 21). No Roman sandals grace her feet; her complexion is dark and primitive. She is the despised object of conquest. That an "image of the squaw" produced by the dominant culture would become a literary norm that would determine the value of all subsequent cultural productions by Native women which would be measured against it is a fear expressed by Native writers Beth Cuthand, Jeannette Armstrong, and Maria Campbell, who see in the strong interest white women writers have expressed in their culture the mechanism whereby their self-representations will be excluded from the literary institution (Armstrong et. al. 1983). Within the semiotic field of the Native, these representations constitute one valence in relation to the white women's long expressed dream of "going squaw."

That this exclusion has already happened, however, has also been demonstrated. One of the high canonical forms of Canadian fiction is the vision quest, or shamanic initiation, wherein the Native woman (or man) initiates a white woman into various Native religious practices through which she attains her creative and personal "identity." Here the Native woman is configured as Queen, as Mother-Goddess, fount of all wisdom and ruler of a natural paradise. This has resulted in a vogue within feminist circles for narratives of women's spiritual transformation, fiction in the form of the vision quest of romance using all the fictional devices of reference to produce a strong effect of the real in the form of a fully psychologized heroine seeking freedom from patriarchy in the "green world."[13] In contrast, Native women's narratives have adopted entirely different formal strategies, discontinuous tales rather than coherently plotted quests, symbolic events rather than psychologized reactions. Moreover, they write miscellanies — hybrid genres — mixtures of sermons, narratives, poetry, ethnographical treatises.[14]

A number of recent essays have analyzed the "imaginary Indian," the Native as sign within Canadian discourse, an empty sign and consequently weighed down with what Gordon Johnston terms "an intolerable burden of meaning" (in King 65) in that the Native has come to bear the burden of the Other, all that the modern white person is lacking. Identity for this white person is acquired through this encounter with alterity, knowledge of the self attained through the wisdom of the not – I, an identity both personal and national. For it is through this encounter with the Other who is Native to this land that a "totem transfer" occurs and the stranger in North America "goes native" to possess the land, to be Native. Conveniently, as Margery Fee points out, this figure of mediation, the token or empty sign in the discourse between white men, that is, the Native, dies or disappears (Fee, in King 20 – 21). This leaves the white man in undisputed possession of the land: "The simultaneous marginality and ubiquity of the Native people in our literature can be explained to some extent, then, by our desire to naturalize our appropriation of their land" (Fee, in King 24).[15] This impossible necessity for incorporating the Other, for becoming indigenous in order to belong in the land they have conquered, has been termed the process of "indigenization" by Terry Goldie, who articulates the valences of the semiotic field for this transference of the desiring subject, those of fear and temptation, which encompass a gamut of codes: those of orality, mysticism, soul, nature, violence, sexuality, etc. (in King 67 – 79, especially 73).

Despite the critique of Native women writers and the recent attempts at demystification by scholars of Canadian literature, the Native woman has maintained her mythical status within the dominant culture. Indeed, she even seems to be consolidating it in collaboration with the Writers' Union and in explicit opposition to the denunciations of such a practice as "structurally racist." I refer here specifically to the new novel *Bone Bird* by Darlene Barry Quaife and the writer's description/defence of her project in an interview. Under the heading "Celebrating Native Spirituality: Writer feels society can learn from native ways," Quaife tells Isabel Vincent that writing about different cultures is the work of the imagination and that any attempt to limit this freedom is an act of censorship and the promotion of racism. The novel she is defending in these familiar terms of the esemplastic power of a disembodied imagination follows the highly conventional plot of the "coming of age" of a Métis woman on Vancouver Island through the influence of her grandmother, "a native medicine woman, who is the spiritual centre of the book" (Vincent). Quaife pictures herself as a missionary to her readers, desiring to share with them the "sense of spirituality" that white culture has lost but which she has found in her research into shamanism. In this, Quaife reiterates all the codes of indigenization: lack, desire, mystical purity, possession. All the while she maintains the benevolence of her appropriation which is "for the good of the Natives": "What's important is how a writer approaches their material. I didn't approach [*Bone Bird*] with the idea of exploitation. I wanted to celebrate what I have learned with my readership. I wanted to open up the audiences for native writers" (Vincent). She continues, ironically contradicting herself and thus demonstrating the constraints of discursive conventions in this ideological production of representations:

> I wanted to be accurate, but not record native spirituality.
> I wanted to *make it my own* because what's important is *the synthesis — the writer creating the myth.*

> If I had come to the material with the idea of exploita-
> tion, then I would deserve to be censored, she said. (Vincent;
> my emphasis)

Intention is ineffective in the face of discursive practice, however. Though Quaife is seemingly unaware of them, she faithfully manipulates the conventions of "indigenization," though camouflaging their normative and exclusive character behind Romantic appeals to the originality of the artist and the freedom of imagination which are decontextualized and universalized, "mythologized," hence ideological, according to Barthes. Quaife's desire to help Native culture find expression is meaningless in face of her blindness to the context of her utterance at the present point in history where the Native peoples in Canada are forcefully calling for an end to benevolent paternalism and colonialism and the settlement of their land claims, the acknowledgement of their ancient rights to the possession of the land. In this enunciative instance, Quaife's desire to "make [Native spirituality] my own" by "creating myth" is, in its denial of history, an exemplary instance of the perpetuation of colonial exploitation. The grounds on which Quaife claims authority to do so are the familiar liberal humanist grounds of our common humanity and consequent "empathy," not an acknowledgement of the justice of the Natives' struggle. For this would undermine the universality of "Truth." As Quaife asserts, an emphasis on differences stirs up dissidence. The function of the writer is to respond to the "shared view of the world" she has with the Natives. "After all, we all bleed the same colour." This indifference to the many socio-political differences with respect to their relative access to the literary institutions that separate her from the Native writers exemplifies the rhetorical violence with which the dominant discourse denies the legitimacy of the minority, conflating relations of ideological domination with those of economic exploitation.

The irony of Quaife's position is further compounded when she reveals that this spirituality she wishes to share is her imaginative re-creation: "In order to evoke a very vivid sense of spirituality and recreate native rituals, Quaife did a lot of research into shamanism. While she concedes that she *fabricated* most of the native rituals in the *Bone Bird*, she nevertheless believes that her interpretation of native spirituality is valid" (Vincent; my emphasis). Valid, it most certainly is, since it reworks the codes of the discourse of British (and French) imperialism and the Canadian development of this discourse as indigenization, and finds its validation in the literary institution as demonstrated in the action of the Writers' Union on the question of racism. Since it has numerous literary antecedents, it must also be true as revealed knowledge grounded in the authority of the text and the Word. But is it real?

This too is a moot point, since reality is determined by its representations and they are signifying systems, sites not for the production of beautiful things evoking beautiful feelings, but for the production of meanings and positions from which those meanings are consumed, meanings that are defined in a hierarchy systematically ordered within social formations between the dominant and dominated. These conflicts and contradictions are negotiated within social formations in which subjects are interpellated so that the cultural practices through which we make sense of the social process, and the means by which we are caught up and produced by it, are sites of struggle and confusion over partial and conditioned knowledges. The danger is when, like Quaife, we take our fabrications, our partial knowledges for the Truth, and generalize to make it a Truth-for-all. Such a speaking on behalf of, a magisterial discourse *on* another, effectively precludes the circulation of its different partial knowledges as interlocutors.[16]

This struggle over the politics of representation on the issue of race is part of a much larger theoretical debate on relations of power to knowledge: can men theorize feminism, can the bourgeois theorize revolution? Because of the power alignments in the current discursive configuration, any statement of a white on the question of racism will be positioned by that discourse as an utterance on racism rather than as a contestatory utterance, because it perpetuates the discourse of white on red, or white on black, reinforcing the dominant discourse by blocking the emergence of an emancipatory discourse *of/for* red and/or black and/or brown, yellow, etc. Such discursive practices become oppressive when the group in power monopolizes the theoretical scene and there is no counter-discourse, that is no debate among differing discourses. To claim that only a woman can write about women or a Native person about Native culture, is to make claims for essentialism that involve the confusion of ontology and epistemology, as Gayatri Chakravorty Spivak has pointed out. "Resisting 'elite' methodology for 'subaltern' material involves an epistemological/ontological confusion. The confusion is held in an unacknowledged analogy: just as the subaltern is not elite (ontology), so must the historian not *know* through elite method (epistemology)" (Spivak 1987, 253). To maintain these essentialist positions with regards to race and knowledge is to maintain the dominant discourse, albeit in simple inversion, rather than to challenge or change its norms and practices. "If the woman/black/subaltern, possessed through struggle some of the structures previously metonymic as men/white/elite, continues to exercise a self-marginalized purism, and if the benevolent members of the man/white/elite participate in the marginalization and thus legitimate the bad old days, we have a caricature of correct politics that leaves alone the field of continuing subalternization" (Spivak 1987, 253).

Underpinning this inversion is the recognition by the subaltern or dominated that his or her idiom within the dominant discursive formation has not allowed him or her to "know his struggle so that he [*sic*] could articulate himself as a subject" (Spivak 253). Within this hegemonic order, s/he was constituted as object of the knowledge of subjects. However, through struggle, acquiring some of the strategies and structures of the dominant, the subaltern rises "into hegemony," this process constituting a *dis/placement* of the dominant discourse and strategies of hybridization that undermine its monolithic position of power. Both speaking marginality and speaking against it, exploiting the ambiguity of their within/without position with respect to power, these emerging subjects destabilize institutional practices. That this is beginning to happen within the culture of Native Canadians is, as I shall argue, visible in I *Am Woman: A Native Perspective on Sociology and Feminism* by Lee Maracle and *Slash* by Jeannette Armstrong, written from within the political activity of the Okanagans, as they challenge dominant institutions and their representations of Native concerns.

While there are many continuities with the earlier cultural productions of Native women, notably in the strategic use of the miscellany, of traditional oral narrative forms, these texts contest their inscription

within the symbolic position of mystical orality and maternal spirituality of the dominant discourse by explicitly situating their texts discursively, as writing of resistance, and historically, within the project of the
contemporary Indian movement. Moreover, they are located within new
instances challenging the hegemony of the dominant literary institution, within publishing projects run by First Nations people to diffuse
their self-representations. No longer locked into "silence" as a singular
oral event or within the confines of a Native language, these texts in
English take as their interlocutor the dominant tradition in a polemic
which is overtly signalled within the texts. Moreover, although the
dominant discourse clearly reigns supreme, as witnessed by its deployment in systemic racism in *The Globe and Mail*, there is emerging in the
interruptions of *The Trickster* and Lenore Keeshig-Tobias the beginning
of a theorization of the marginalization of Native culture. The theory
finds a more sustained development within the texts of Maracle and
Armstrong which both extensively analyze the situation of the Native
within the context of a politics of decolonization and demonstrate how
marginality has been constructed by the hegemonic forces of imperialism and capitalism. But the emergence of this counter-discourse on
internal colonialism as a contestatory politics of representation is signalled in the change of form developed by these writers, the romance
vision quest of the dominant tradition into autobiographical and confessional modes respectively, as Maracle and Armstrong imitate — and
displace — the dominant genres in which the "imaginary Native" has
been represented. A critical aspect of their intervention is that these
are pre-eminently "historical" narratives.

Before analyzing these two texts in more detail, there is an important question that needs to be explored: the power/knowledge nexus
as articulated within different theoretical models of discursive formations. If the interpellative powers of representations and discourses are
so coercive that one is always subject under the discursive norm, how
can one elaborate alternate practices? How can the subject under the law
become a resisting subject? Subjectivity as the subject-position within
a discourse is synonymous with subjection, in Althusserian terms.[17] In
the clash of values which is played out as a clash of representations how
can the totalizing force of power be circumscribed? Where is there a

space for knowledges of oppressed minorities that make no claim to universality? The problematics of resisting subjects in subjection is a complex one involving considerations of the potentials for agency exercised within a situation of constraint and of the different models for conceptualizing the interaction of discourses. For this involves the pressing question of the relations between orthodoxy and heterodoxies in the interaction among the hegemonic culture(s) of dominant classes, popular culture(s), and high culture(s). Is the cultural field configured globally as successive levels in a hierarchy from dominant to subordinate classes, as a circulation of reciprocal influences between subordinate and ruling classes, or as cultural dichotomy with absolute autonomy between the cultures of dominant and subordinate cultures? Or, to phrase this problem in another way, how can what is positioned as object "inside" discourse take up a position as subject "outside" discourse? How can there be a position "outside" what is a hegemonic, and hence totalizing, field?

It is in such a double-bind, in such a self-contradictory and ambivalent instance of enunciation, that the subordinate "subject" is positioned. But it is by exploring the fissures and cracks which paradox opens in the claims of the dominant discourse that an alternate logic may be constructed, a logic grounded not on the binary codes of the law of the excluded middle, but in the logics of relativity or catastrophe theory with their serial or multiple interactions, their theorizing of chaos. This will open up a view of discourse as a field of contesting knowledges rather than as monolithic, totalitarian imposition of the Law. The time has come, as Chandra Mohanty writes, "to move beyond the Marx who found it possible to say: They cannot represent themselves; they must be represented" (354).

That one is never "outside" power, because it is "always already there," does not entail the acceptance of inescapable domination of absolute privilege, maintains Foucault, whose model for analyzing the institutional operations of power in the constitution of knowledges has been a non-Marxist theorization of ideology dominant in literary studies. "To say that one can never be 'outside' power does not mean that one is trapped and condemned to defeat no matter what" (Foucault 1980, 141–42). The response of oppressed groups to hegemonic culture is complex and frequently contradictory: accepted, forcibly perhaps, in some ways, it is resisted in others. The hegemonic discourse itself may be "marked by tensions and even contradictions" (LaCapra 78). As Foucault conceptualizes the discursive field, it is structured through a number of systems of control and distribution that function as "discursive police" to exclude such contradictions. It is a "system of subjection," characterized by its dissymmetry (1971, 37, 43, 47; my translation). Power functions within systems that produce polymorphous power-effects operative in micro-political climates. Each society, however, has a "general political economy" of truth, "that is the types of discourse which it accepts and makes function as true" (Foucault 1980, 130) that induce "effects of power." Although he argues against a "binary structure" of "dominators" against "the dominated" (1980, 142), Foucault's focus is on the strategies and techniques of exclusion through which discourses consolidate their power, rather than on the exploration of the conditions for the possible elaboration of new discursive formations. His theory of discourse has as its centre the workings of power, of the global economy — the "system of systems."[18]

Instead of locating resistance as merely a counter-effect of the networks of power, one may also begin to theorize from a situation of struggle, from the position of the subordinate engaged in lateral as well as vertical struggles. Michel Pêcheux develops the concept of discursive field and argues that no practice or discourse exists in itself; on whatever side, it is ultimately shaped and preceded by what it is opposing and so can never simply dictate its own terms. Meaning exists agonistically: it comes from positions in struggle so that "words ... change their meaning according to the 'positions' from which they are used within the 'discursive process'" (112). What is thought within one discourse is related to what is unthought there but thought elsewhere in another. In this way, "red" means something different in the dominant discourse from what it does in the Native's discourse of resistance. Institutional and social constraints act through the ordering of words and expressions within discourses. What is at stake in discursive struggles is this ordering and combining of words.

Pêcheux focuses on the processes of imbrication of discourses, their embedding effects and articulations, the structure of "interdiscourse"

(Pêcheux 113). Each discourse interpellates individuals as subjects of this discourse. But this subordination-subjection is realized in the subject "in the form of autonomy" (Pêcheux 114). The identification of the subject with him or herself, "the subject-effect," is coeval with the "inter-subjectivity-effect," an identification with the subject of another discourse (Pêcheux 118). There are no a priori dominant and revolutionary vectors. However, within a given ideological instance under given historical conditions these discursive formations are asymmetrically related to one another. They are, however, "sites of a work of reconfiguration" which may be, variously, a work of "recuperation-reproduction" or a politically "productive" work (Pêcheux 155): they may reinscribe the same and support the reigning discourse or work for change and displacement, redistributions in the discursive field, depending on whether the subject is positioned by the interdiscourse in identification or counter-identification with a discursive formation (158). Significantly, Pêcheux also theorizes a third position not caught up in binary relations of identity/negation. Displacement produces the "disidentification effect" (162) articulated in counter-discourses.

This formulation of a concept of counter-discourse or counter-hegemonic discourse,[19] is important in conceptualizing a vari-directional system. But other theorists have more specifically analyzed literary discourse as a field of centrifugal forces. Most significant among these is Bakhtin, whose conceptualization of the discursive field as one of competing languages of different social groups or "heteroglossia" ("polyglossia" being a competing field of foreign languages within a single national language) is developed through an analysis of fictional forms. Ideology, as Bakhtin/ Medvedev outline the grounds for a Marxist study of discourse, would study both the "forms of organized ideological material as meaningful material" and the "forms of the social intercourse by which this meaning is realized" (1985, 9). It is Bakhtin's initiative towards the classification of these forms of exchange among discourses which develops in greater detail the complexities of "interdiscourse," the characteristics and forms of imbrication, important for the theorization of counter-discourses. Bakhtin's work on the interface of signification and communication helps elaborate theoretical models of textual exchanges wherein discourses are displaced and destabilized. Interdiscursive (or intertextual) relations are played out in relations within and between texts, genres, and practices. These are contradictory movements between discursive sites within what is a "structural model of *uneven* development" (Stallybrass/White 196; my emphasis). Bakhtin asserts an open and future-oriented poetics, one that would rethink claims to the mastery of knowledge, and consequently "formulates the conflictual dimension, as the realm of the social determination of the weight and value of discursive elements" (Godzich 1978, xiii). In this, he sets out a materialist theory of discourse in which ideological creation, the production of meanings and values, is realized in historically specific things and actions. "Every ideological product (ideologeme) is a part of the material social reality surrounding man [*sic*], an aspect of the materialized ideological horizon" (Bakhtin/Medvedev 1985, 8).

This is central to Bakhtin's elaboration of the dialogue, a double-voiced discourse which is oriented towards someone else's discourse. Dialogic interrelationships among signifying discourses within a single context — "relationships of agreement/disagreement, affirmation/sup-plementation, question/answer, etc. — are purely dialogic relationships, although not of course between words, sentences, or other elements of a single utterance, but between whole utterances" (1984, 188). Inter-secting within the double-voicedness are two voices, two accents, two socially distinct practices. These voices may be subjected to re-evalua-tion when introduced into the first discourse, or even clash with hostil-ity. Sometimes, the other's word is not incorporated into the discourse, but remains outside though it is taken into account. This is a "hidden polemic" in which "a polemical blow is struck at the other's discourse on the same theme, at the other's statement about the same object." "[T]he other's words are treated antagonistically, and this antagonism, no less than the very topic being discussed, is what determines the author's dis-course" (195). This is an especially significant element of literary discourse which, as Bakhtin says, not only anticipates in advance the objections of its readers and critics, but reacts to a preceding literary style as an "anti-stylization" of it (196).

As well, there is "internally polemical discourse — the word with a sideward glance at someone else's hostile word" (196). The dialogic or double-voiced discourse — whether parody, irony, parallax, imitation (with a difference), stylization — re-marks convention by incorporating the word of another within it. The characteristic stance of the dialogic text is the one-within-the-other. Points of antagonism overlap, collide, and explode. They interrogate boundaries, challenge the hierarchy of sites of discourse, force the threshold, and move into the liminal, working the in-between, site of movement and change. In response to the desire for purity of the dominant discourse with its mechanisms of exclusion, they offer textual contamination, ambiguity. For the complexity of their double articulation arises from the fact that the discursive practices are both connected and disassociated: the logic of subject-identity that posits one subject for one discourse for one site or practice is confounded in this concept of discourse as a network of intersecting discourses or intertextuality wherein inside and outside are relational positions with respect to specific discourses not in subjection to a singular power. What such heterogeneity and hybridization effect through permutations and instabilities is the possibility of "shifting the very terms of the [semiotic] system itself" (White 1978, 58) by dispersing and displacing the very possibility of hierarchization. Here the importance of the dialogic for discourses of resistance becomes clear. It establishes a theory of a transformative practice grounded in critique and resistance. For the focus of the dialogic is on change, on bodies and social formulations as s(c)ites of instability and displacement. In these terms, the project of Native writers is not merely inscribed within the dominant discourse as opposition, but is a destabilizing movement in the field of power relationships.

"Heterogeneity," fractured genres, "polymorphous" subjects, "borderland" sites — these are the marks of "resistance writing" especially as practised by Native North Americans under "métissage" in their within/without elation to the dominant social formations (Harlow 98).[20] Indeed, embedded within the historical and material conditions of their production as a politicized challenge to conventional literary standards, resistance narratives are examples of "'heteroglossia,' in their composite forms as historical document, ideological analysis and visions of future possibilities" (Harlow 75, 99). This is indeed a "Manichean Aesthetics," as Abdul JanMohamed has termed it: "Even though an African may adopt the formal characteristics of English fiction, his rendition of colonial experience will vary drastically from that of a European, not only because of the actual differences in experience, but also because of his antagonistic attitude toward colonialist literature" (qtd. in Harlow 106). Like "minor literature," resistance writing draws attention to itself and to literature in general as a political and politicized activity. Immediate and direct involvement in a struggle against ascendant or dominant forms of ideological and cultural production is the task it stakes out for itself (Harlow 28). But, as JanMohamed's observation makes clear, this political engagement is co-terminous with "formal experimentation" (qtd. in Harlow 96). This is not, however, a formalist project. Rather, experimentation or the exploration of the formal limitations of the literary codes "imposes *historical* demands and responsibilities on a reader" (Harlow 95; my emphasis). Narrative is a way of exploring history and questioning the historical narratives of the colonizer which have violently interposed themselves in place of the history of the colonized. Experimentation, especially with structures of chronology, is part of this challenge, a radical questioning of historiographical versions of the past as developed in the "master narratives," in order to rewrite the historical ending (Harlow 85 – 86). Archaeology is undertaken for utopian aims. This results in a-grammatical texts whose palimpsestic mode produces mediations and/or contradictions. Given the ideological function of forms, when they are reappropriated and fashioned in different social and cultural contexts, the generic message of earlier social formations persists, producing sedimented structures, complicating the pressure on the genre for ideological change (Jameson 1981, 141). Exhibiting the identification of counter-discourse in their hybridity, these forms constitute "new objects of knowledge" (Said, qtd. in Harlow 116) that require new discursive practices in order to analyze them.

A third characteristic of resistance literature is that it be produced within a struggle for decolonization. Contemporary history, Jacques Berque has suggested, is the history of decolonization, the struggle to rewrite history by those without a history (qtd. in Harlow 4). History as it has unfolded has been the story of what the white man did, histories of colonialism written by imperialists. The struggle over the historical record is seen by all parties as no less crucial than armed struggle. As Frantz Fanon has described this struggle: "Colonialism is not satisfied merely with holding a people in its chains and emptying the native's head of all form and content. By a kind of perverted logic, it turns to the past of the oppressed people, and distorts, disfigures and destroys it. This work of devaluing pre-colonial history takes on a dialectical significance today" (Fanon 144; my translation). This awareness of the dialectical relations of the role of culture and cultural resistance as part of a larger struggle for liberation has involved theorizing differential subject positions for the author. S/he may write from opposing discursive formations and aesthetics: an "aesthetic of oppression and exploitation and of acquiescence with imperialism; and that of human struggle for total liberation" (Thiong'o qtd. in Harlow 8). This struggle for liberation may itself be conducted from different sites with respect to power, each with its own strategies and techniques, from positions of "exile" or "under occupation" (Kanafani qtd. in Harlow 2 – 3). This latter is the more complex, setting up a within/without posture for the writer in struggle under "cultural siege." In this, as Fanon suggests, the writer must resist both the temptation to universalize and de-historicize the struggle, that is, adopting the perspective of the imperialist, which functions as a strategy of containment for the contestatory culture, and the inverse posture of a "return to the source," a fetishizing of traditional Native culture as though the relation to the inherited past and cultural legacy had not been rendered problematic by the violent interruption of colonial and imperial history (Fanon 144; my translation). In this inversion, culture is transformed into artifacts, museum pieces.

Resistance literature, in contradistinction, takes up a position of dis-identification which explores the interference of a struggle for power on the transmission of a cultural tradition. It takes as its starting point the radical fact of its present situation as the culture of a colony. This insistence on the "'here-and-now' of historical reality and its conditions of possibility" is the *sine qua non* of resistance literature (Harlow 16). Indeed, distance, "scientific dispassion," and "academic objectivity" are rejected by writers and critics, as postures of isolation and universalization (Harlow 3 – 4). Central to the struggle is not just an attempt to reconstruct the history of the relations of power between those groups in struggle, by giving access to "history" for those who have been denied an active role in history and its making, but to transform historiography itself on the contested terrain of (re)writing "history" from the grounds of a "genealogy of 'filiation' based on ties of kinship, ethnicity, race or religion, to those of an 'affiliative' secular order" (Harlow 22). In the process, however, the objectivity and distance of imperial "affiliative" historiography is "contaminated" by "filiative" genealogies. What is foregrounded is history as narrative, history as telling, history as a process of unfolding of local stories, or provisional truths — narratives that make no claims to universal Truth.

Such an emphasis on the discursive constitution of truth effects a change in value that results from a critical parallax or shift in perspective, one which introduces into a singular discourse a rhetorical plurality or heteroglossia, the introduction of protocols of critique. Change in perspective inflects a disjunction in the relations of perception between the seer and the seen, the subjective "eye"/I and the represented world, as they are related to each other, but also as they relate to the source of perceiving consciousness "outside" (Terdiman 28). This shift in frames of perception and reference keys different discursive conventions and produces an instability, a confounding of several representations, in what the theory of perspective had taught us to be a hierarchical and fixed mode of relation. Such a functional change in a sign system is, as Gayatri Spivak writes, "a violent event" (1987, 197), a riposte to the rhetorical violence (de Lauretis 31) of the dominant sign systems with their positioning of the Native as Other, as token of exchange.

In turn, the disjunction in perception destabilizes the fixity of one's place in the structure, and consequently opens up "the entire problematic of *representing the other*" (Terdiman 28), the ideological inflection of all representation. Representations are practices, signifying systems, Griselda Pollock reminds us (6). Representation in its most common sense stresses that images and texts (of trees or persons, for instance) are ordered according to pictorial and/or literary conventions. But representation in a second sense signifies the articulation of the political processes, practices, and effects both determining and affected by representational practices. Understood here is Marx's distinction between *vertreten* where the Subject of Power "speaks for" in the political arena, through a proxy, an orator, the law, and representation or *darstellen*, representation as re-presentation, as in art or philosophy where in writing or on the stage, by portraits or actors, the oppressed subjects speak for themselves. This third inflection of representation signifies something represented to, addressed to, a reader/viewer/consumer and foregrounds the relations of seer and seen to the economic and political networks which constitute the "outside."[21] Here the rhetoric-as-persuasion of *vertreten* is displaced by the rhetoric-as-trope of *darstellen*: representation, it is made clear, is always re-presentation, something staged for a specific audience. Although the two modes of representation are unstable and constantly colliding — "the relationship between the imperialist subject and the subject of imperialism is at least ambiguous" (Spivak 1988, 297) — it is important, Spivak contends, to pay attention to "the double session" (1988, 279), to the enunciative instance with its power valences inflecting all presentations of the other. When history presents itself as narrative, as telling, it foregrounds this act of enunciation and thematizes those important questions: who is speaking, to whom, under what conditions. Representation as re-presentation, as narrative *staging*.

This interruption in the power of representation to dissimulate itself is analyzed in slightly different terms by Bakhtin in the contrast he develops between "monologic" speech, totalizing and authoritive which "cannot be represented — it is only transmitted" — and dialogism, characteristic of the novel as genre, which is represented speech. The words of others are put into quotation marks, "qualified" and "externalized," both represented and representing. In this clash of many speech genres, the word is shown as "incomplete" and "conditional" (Bakhtin 1981, 344 – 45). Such hybridization "appropriates" and "reworks" the other's discourse redistributively in a mode of "symbolic dissidence" (White 1978, 25) or resistance, a mode of "disidentification" (Pêcheux). In this double articulation, discursive practices are both connected and disassociated: the logic of subject-identity that posits one subject for one discourse for one site or practice is confounded in this heterogeneity and hybridization.

In different ways, *Slash* and *I Am Woman* thematize this representation as presentation or "re-accentuation," in Bakhtin's term, by re-writing the conventions of representing the Native. Through her autobiographical "I," Lee Maracle narrates herself as a political representative for women and for Métis. But this is a complex intertextual game, for interpellated in her title is *I Am an Indian*, an anthology of some of the first Native

writing to emerge from the Indian Movement in the 1960s, as well as bell
hooks' reprise of Sojourner Truth's celebrated declaration of 1851, *Ain't I
a Woman?*[22] Indirectly, then, she also represents Indianness. Métissage is
both theme and narrative mode in Maracle's text. The hybridization of
Armstrong's text develops through the strategies of fiction writing where,
deploying the techniques of the genre for represented speech, Armstrong
re-presents the autobiographical narrative of a Native man in quotation
marks, interrogated and provisional, staged within an ironic frame produced by the silences and repetitions of the represented speaker.

But the force of their political dis/placement of conventional representational practices is most immediately evident in the contestatory
politics thematized in their texts. Indeed the specific frame of their
discursive intervention, their critical parallax, is the elaboration of
Native Canadian rights within the context of anti-capitalist, anti-imperialist politics, both at the local micro-political level, in the discussion
of aboriginal land claims as it had become a matter for occupations of
cabinet ministers' offices by participants in a "Youth Conference"
(Armstrong 125 – 28), and as it had become the subject of debate over
the extent of these claims among the Okanagans whose reserves, not
covered by the Proclamation of 1763, are not legal (Armstrong 134), but
also on a continent-wide level in the emergent political force of AIM
(American Indian Movement) whose history and activities during the
1960s and 1970s are outlined through the eyes of Tommy Kelasket in
Slash and in "The Rebel," a chapter in *I Am Woman*. Both, indirectly in the
first, explicitly in the second, record important events, whether these
be the Okanagan tribe's hard-won moratorium on uranium mining
(Maracle 120, Armstrong 235) or the confrontation at Wounded Knee
(Armstrong 111 – 18, Maracle 126).

Both, moreover, explicitly ground this re-visionary historiography
in a struggle for decolonialization. One of Tommy's key insights which
he offers to his childhood friend Jimmy, a business administration
graduate who can't find a job, regards the subtle effects of colonization:
"Everything that the colonizers do, tells the Indians they are inferior,
that their lifestyle, their language, their religion, their values and even
what food they eat, is somehow not as good" (221). To avoid "feel[ing]
so shitty inside" (222), they admire and imitate the colonizer. What

Tommy doesn't state, though the novel reveals ironically through his silence and his gestures, is that the colonized also lashes out in inexplicable violence which is self-violence. In one of his many outbursts of rage, Tommy earns his nickname "Slash." Both his violence and his constant movement are the effects of self-hatred. His agitation to "DO SOMETHING" (120) leads him to chafe at directives to do things the "Indian Way": instead of "peaceful occupation[s], ... I wanted violence" (126). The framework of decolonization theory allows Tommy (and Armstrong) to view the Native's situation of powerlessness within a systemic analysis of power relations. Understanding that his problems are not just "personal," or rather that the "personal is political," is the political education Tommy painfully and slowly undergoes.

Maracle makes these points about the politics of personal and communal self-destruction more directly:

> The busting up of communities, families, and the loss of the sense of nationhood and the spirit of cooperation among the colonized, are the aims of the colonizer. A sense of powerlessness is the legacy handed down to the colonized people for achievement of the aim of the colonizer. LOSS OF POWER — the negation of choice, legal and cultural victimization, is the hoped for result. (120)

It is this powerlessness which produces violence, she argues. That she belongs to a conquered people who are "spiritually dead" is both the effect and the determinant of sexual violence. That an entire culture has been "raped" has made it impossible for them to love themselves, for Native men to cherish Native women. Admiring the dominant white culture, they adopt its values, seeing only "dark-skinned sensuality" in Native women as Other — the Squaw, not the Princess — raping them and beating them up (52–73, especially 71). Rage against the colonizer is deflected and turned inward on the colonized's own culture in a process of self-destruction.

Despite the extent of this oppression, this self-division from identifying against the self as Other, Natives have resisted and continue to resist. Indeed, as Maracle points out, there is a history of resistance parallel to

the history of colonization. It is a history which inspires the struggle
against destruction of homelands as on Meares Island in the Queen Charlotte Islands (Maracle 120) or in AIM's retracing of the "Trail of Tears" of
1838 when tribes in the southeastern United States were forced to move
to Oklahoma and leave their land for white settlers (Armstrong 96). But
resistance comes also through the knowledge of resistance. As Maracle
writes: "There is power in knowing" (123). Against the "destruction and
expropriation of knowledge," that is, against the practice of colonialism
(Maracle 120), Maracle proposes the strategies of de-colonization: "rewriting of history," which is not "betrayal" as it seems to the "elite," but
is the rebel altering her conditions, "re-writ[ing] her life onto the pages
of a *new history*" (Maracle 121; my emphasis). This is the "re-accentuation"
of the dominant discourse in the "hidden polemic," as Bakhtin characterizes the agonistic (dialogic) positioning of utterances and speaking
subjects within the discursive system. In Armstrong's novel, the focus
of Slash's travels across the continent with the Indian Movement is
to reclaim this expropriated knowledge of his history: "I hadn't even
heard of it," he says of the "Trail of Tears," "but then I guess that was
the point of this whole trip: to educate" (Armstrong 95). His narration
is re-presented as an alternate history, a history of struggle, the story
of the "many things" that he has seen which, even though he is young,
make him feel old in experience. "Few [of his people] have accepted
this teacher and taken her gifts." Consequently, he feels compelled to
offer his particular view, his "story" for his son "and those like him"
(Armstrong 253). Slash justifies his narrative in the framing "Epilogue,"
which thematizes the instance of enunciation of his personal (hi)story
that is representative of his tribal history.

The importance of these two books to re-visionary historiography is
that they document the struggle of Natives today within a history of
resistance. Writing from a position of "cultural siege," "under occupation," Armstrong and Maracle analyze their position within an active
struggle of decolonialization. This is an epistemic break, as we shall see,
with respect to the semiotic field engendering the "imaginary Indian"
in white writing on the Native — s/he is historicized not mythologized.
Nor is it history as timeless myth in traditional Native narratives of mystical orality which reify an "original source." Rather it is a new history

and historiography different from both, the history of struggle in the 1960s and 1970s in a hybrid narrative mode. This is history as narrating, as telling, in traditional Native fashion, but within recognizable dates and events and the conventions of "colonial" history. The narrative conventions of genealogical and affiliative orders of historiography are both operative. Nonetheless, these historical narratives make great demands on the reader for different historical knowledge, one not taught in schools. In this, they foreground their partial — fragmented and interested — knowledges. Examining their challenge to Knowledge and necessarily, as they forcefully claim, to power, I shall try to identify crucial locations in the texts where they stutter in the articulation of conventions, using these as levers to open out the ideology of colonialist and racist discourse in an act of explication. This will emerge as several fragments that will be read speculatively.

To read the spines of the covers of *Slash* and *I Am Woman* is to locate one such disruption of convention, one within the literary institution which mediates the meaning produced by these texts in the field of "Canadian" literature. Generally, along with the writer's signature and title of the book is labelled the publishing house which has produced the text. On Maracle's book there is a blank space. While the other textual apparatus of ISBN (International Standard Book Number) is to be found inside on the back of the title page, we are directed there only to "Write-on Press Publishers 1988," which further investigation reveals to be a publisher set up for the occasion. *I Am Woman* is a self-published book. In this gesture, Maracle takes charge of the mediation of her text so as to overcome the coercive powers of the dominant literary institution which would make her "speak it right," "speak white" either by refusing to publish her text or by shaping it through the editorial process to fit the conventions of Native life-writing, as happened to Maria Campbell's *Halfbreed*.[23] In this gap, and in the acknowledgements where she expresses her debt to "Native people, Palestinians, Chileans, Philipinos [*sic*], Eritreans, Ethiopians, El Salvadorans, Anti-apartheid activists and Black Canadian and American people" (Maracle iv) and dedicates her text "To my children," Maracle foregrounds the discursive formation in which her text is positioned as one of anti-imperialist resistance to the dominant white, Westernized literary institutions.

Armstrong's text is also positioned on the margins of the Canadian publishing institution, though its interlocutors are not those engaged in international decolonialization movements, but her people, the Okanagans, engaged in struggle over land claims, a fight against "internal colonialism."[24] On the spine of *Slash*, alongside the author's signature, is printed "Theytus Books." This, we learn from the publisher's catalogue, is "Canada's First Native Indian Owned and Operated Publishing House," a publishing project with which Armstrong has been closely associated as writer of books for children, *Enwhisteetka* and *Neekna and Chemai*. "Theytus," so the catalogue informs us, is a Coast Salish word that "translates as 'preserving for the purpose of handing down.'" With a variety of texts ranging from trivia games on Native lore to videos, archeological treatises, plays, traditional stories, and fiction, Theytus seeks to enlarge the concept of "education" and to produce new knowledge for/by Natives. This too is self-publishing, circumventing the dominant literary institution, in a way, however, with well-produced texts and catalogues, that mimics the dominant institutions. Armstrong's self-description is, in this sense, revealing:

> I've never really thought about being a Canadian writer; I've always thought of myself as a Native writer. ... In terms of Native writers, Leslie Silko and N. Scott Momaday, both Americans, have influenced me. Maria Campbell, who has shown so much endurance, has given me the courage to write. I recently was fortunate to meet Beatrice Culleton who wrote *In Search of April Raintree*. I really have a lot of respect for those two women, who have produced novels of real significance in terms of Native literature in Canada. (Freeman 37)

Like Maracle, Armstrong is less concerned with writing "authentically," "like a Native," within the semiotic field of the indigene or even within its negation, but in taking up a third position both within and without to create a new cultural community. She is not preoccupied with "Truth," but with good storytelling, with producing the tale to be told over and over.

The emergence of such Native publishing ventures in the 1980s, which has produced the category of "Native Literature in Canada," is the result of the political activism of Native peoples in the 1960s with the founding of such organizations as the National Indian Brotherhood (1968) and the subsequent advocacy of a policy of "Indian Control of Indian Education," as enunciated in a position paper of 1972. The need to establish course materials for such initiatives has resulted in a proliferation of curriculum-related materials, books, and tapes. Most of these cultural productions are specific to a Native language group, locality, or Indian Band, and do not trespass on the terrain of the dominant publishing industry. In this way, they figure as negation of the dominant paradigm. Theytus Books and Pemmican Press (in Winnipeg) have adopted a more ambiguous and con-testatory position, however, aiming to produce books for the larger Cana-dian market. Like other publishers operating on this scale, they receive block grants from the Canada Council. Unlike them, however, Theytus is not a capitalist enterprise operated for profit, but is run by the Nicola Valley Indian Administration and the Okanagan Tribal Council under the Okanagan Indian Educational Resources Society.[25] It is primarily, but not exclusively, interested in publishing the works of Native authors and has plans to help such writers through their apprenticeship at the En'owkin International School of Writing run in conjunction with Okanagan College and the University of Victoria (Kirchhoff 1989b). In this attempt to open up a space for Native literature within the dominant literary institution, aiming for a general Canadian market, the press has been only partially successful: its audience has been primarily Native people. Moreover, the efforts to reach that audience through educational material for schools has suffered in competition with larger publishing houses such as UBC Press which publish materials with Native content. In its ambiguous material conditions both within and without the dominant economic institutions of publishing, Theytus shares the hybridization of its texts directed at a dual audience.

Such heterogeneity marks the texts with respect to gender politics as well. It is here that Armstrong and Maracle have developed the most effec-tive interruption into the semiotic field of the Native, have most forcefully resisted being the Other through whom the anglophone Canadian can "go native," and find her cultural identity. Armstrong especially refuses the binary positions of Princess and Squaw available to her as a woman. Both reject the representation of Native women offered them in the dominant institution as women writers in that they refuse to develop portraits of the powerful Mother-Goddess, source of all wisdom, accessible through shamanic initiation. Indeed, Armstrong centres her narrative on the retrospective vision of a young man. That this constitutes an open challenge to the Canadian feminist movement which has invested so heavily in representations of Native women as it develops a "radical" feminism is made clear in the reviews of *Slash* in the feminist press. Typical is the one which, favourable in its recommendation of the book as both "powerful and easy," a book which offers a "glimpse" at the differing political perspectives of Indian and white politicians, concludes:

> One of the puzzling things about *Slash* is why Armstrong, a strong Indian woman, chose to write the story entirely from the viewpoint of a man. We don't get to know any of the women in the novel and the interesting things they are doing politically are glimpsed only through Tom's eyes. I found this somewhat frustrating, but not enough to distract me from the story. (MacKenzie 12)

Armstrong has engaged in a hidden polemic with the discourse of white feminists. To the demand of the women's movement in the white community for representations of strong women as the primordial focus of "good" women's writing, Armstrong has replied in a way that foregrounds the complexity of the Native women's political engagement on several fronts, where the struggle against racism is as important as that against gender oppression. That writing is a powerful tool for her as a woman, she is quick to admit:

> Men have easier access to other avenues for getting some of their understanding across — politics is one way that they express their resistance and are trying to make change. For Native women that hasn't been available, because of sexism; writing has been one of the only tools available to them. (Freeman 38)

As she points out, to adopt this masculine perspective was a hard choice, but was dictated by the fact that she was writing a historical novel. She is not writing the dominant "romance quest," though the confessional form fissures the generic purity of the historical novel, dis/placing it toward the mode of self-realization central to the quest genre. This is a quest not for a mythic Origin, but for historical (f)acts. Though there were some women, like Nova Scotia Míkmaw Anna Mae Aquash, who played leadership roles in the American Indian Movement, "it was the young Native male who was at the forefront of that movement" (Freeman 36). This is a text which took Armstrong more than a year to research, a chronicle designed to show the change over the past twenty years in Native politics from strong militancy of the early seventies to the "more positive approach" today (Freeman 36).

Nonetheless, though no longer the mystical, oracular wise woman, the Native woman remains a strong presence in Armstrong's fiction. Indeed, the constant quest of Tommy which seems directionless, without dénouement in its repetition and perpetual loss, is punctuated by his encounters with strong women who, for a time, give him an education in politics which reorients and centres his life. Crucial here is his meeting with Mardi when he comes out of prison following the fight in which he earned both his symbolic scars and his nickname. Like a will-o'-the-wisp, always somewhere ahead of him in the thick of conflict, her actions reported to him in the rumours and stories of other activists, Mardi introduces him to the Indian Movement and acts as a model of political activity. Later, Maeg, the mother of his son, fulfils the same role as teacher and source of inspiration within the Okanagan community. "A soft intensity" in her presence is what first attracts him to her (Armstrong 225), that and the power in her mother's words when she speaks to the meeting, words encouraging the group to a position of resistance in continuation of the ways of their forefathers on this question of land rights which they have continuously refused to abrogate in a treaty. Like Mardi, Maeg dies violently in an accident through her engagement in political activity. One way of reading Tommy's story would be as the narrative of his aimless wandering in the absence of a strong feminine presence: violence rules his life without the power of the grandmothers. This would be to read Armstrong's fiction as an idealization of the

feminine as inspiration and muse. Though there are traces of this narrative, it has been dis/placed, de-mythologized. These are not goddesses,
nor medicine women with oracular powers. Indeed, Armstrong forcefully counters such representations of the Native woman as Shaman in
her description of Maeg through Tommy's eyes:

> Her hair was thick, brown and wavy. It hung past her shoul-
> der and her skin was smooth and light brown. She hadn't
> worn any choker of beads or braids. In fact her clothes were
> just plain, not the usual "radical Indian" or "office Indian"
> garb. I hadn't been able to tell where she stood from her
> clothes. She was dressed too plain to have been one of those
> people who were "into" Indian medicine ways, in a cult kind
> of attitude. (Armstrong 225)

Armstrong here is re/writing the sign of the "imaginary Indian," in a
process of "*making* history" (Maracle 120).

Maracle's major interlocutor is the mainstream women's movement
which she hails in her title by foregrounding the question of gender
in her political analysis. In this, the intersection of struggles over race
and gender power alignments appears to be different in her work
than in Armstrong's. Nonetheless, Maracle explicitly thanks Jeannette
Armstrong and her family for introducing her to the "teachings of our
ancient ones, ... of my grandmothers" (Maracle 43), and to an understanding of spirituality and traditional Native ways. These are located
not on an a-temporal, mythological plane, in some pure moment of Origin, but in specific historical and material practices. What is "sacred" is
the will of the people, democracy. It is important not only for the Native
to practice democracy (Maracle 49) but also to share it with the rest of
Canadian society. This European "settler society" has laws which legal-
ize the oppression of the Native, whereas the laws of the Native forbid
oppression (Maracle 47). Like Armstrong, who also argues for the importance of Native theories of democracy (Freeman 38), Maracle proclaims
the importance of the political in Native spirituality against the "Traditionalism" which has "become the newest coat to cloak their hidden
agenda" (Maracle 47). She explicitly rejects an inversion of the semiotic

values of the indigene and a fetishizing of tradition that fails to take into account the interruption of imperialist history and the resulting conflict. Here, too, the inexplicable violence of the Native within this semiotic field is shown to be the effect of imperial desire, not something "natural" in the indigene. The importance of the grandmothers in giving love and discipline to help develop self-respect in Native children and interrupt the cycle of self-hatred and self-destruction that is the legacy of colonialism for the Natives is both human and political, devoid of the transcendentalism and magic of the Grandmother in the semiotic field of the indigene. There are none of the metamorphoses of Copper Woman and her daughters in the activities of Maracle's grandmothers!

Indeed, Maracle attacks head-on the values of mysticism, attributing them to the dominant culture rather than to the Native:

> I think that white people who indulgently refer to us as a spiritual people are unable to escape the chains of a parasitic culture. Parasites need a host to sustain them. They cannot sustain themselves. White people produce the stuff of life for white folks. Even in their own land, the majority of farm labor is non-whites or children. Since they rarely work at productive labor that is physical, they cannot conceive of laboriously unravelling their bodily person and discovering their spirit within. (Maracle 149)

As she points out, the way to discover a "spiritual being" is through hard physical exercise: "There is no easy route to spiritual re-birth" (Maracle 150).

Maracle interrupts the semiotic field by exposing the production of its values within specific social practices of exploitation. In this, she analyzes the operations of symmetrization and inversion operative in the Imaginary relations of White and Native, wherein the former, operating from lack and desire, mis-recognizes itself in an other, which becomes the Other, the absent full presence or plenitude of identity. In the Imaginary, this is represented as a relationship of I/you, of subject/object, which excludes the important social relationships. The contexts of relations of power are objectified and obscured, so that exploitation and oppression are masked when subjects are treated as floating atoms, as objects. These strategies of scapegoating through which a single discourse becomes the dominant discourse are exposed in Maracle's narrative through analysis of their processes. She also disrupts the dominant codes by hybridizing them.

This is especially evident in the case of spirituality which she frames within the transformative process of translation. Discussing the practices of Native spirituality, of healing through purification, she interrupts to define the word "Prayer," as begging, pleading. Contrasting Native practices in this regard as being closer to "putting our minds together to heal" (Maracle 148), she outlines the slippage in meaning between Native languages and English. "That is not the equivalent of prayer. However, there is no word for this process in the English language" (Maracle 148). Rather than advocating a return to source and to the "purity" of these languages, she argues for the invention of a hybrid spirituality. "We then must make one up or integrate our own word into the language. English does not express the process of ceremony. Yet, we are forced to communicate within its limits. We must differentiate and define our sense of spirituality in English" (Maracle 148). The result, however, will be to dis/place the concept of spirituality and prayer in English where instead of a unitary definition it will be polysemic. The translation effect is a "dis-identification effect," the politically productive work of polyglossia functioning here as heteroglossia which disrupts the hierarchization of discourses, English over Native.

While Maracle's text could be said to present the analytical framework for concepts that *Slash* re-presents, it adds an extra dimension, however, in its explicit analysis of the interlocking oppressions of sex and gender. Foregrounding the question of gender in the second chapter, "I Am Woman," Maracle charts the evolution in her thinking on this question as she moves from a belief that "it was irrelevant that I was a woman" (Maracle 16) to her present understanding of the centrality of this denial of womanhood to the imperialist project. Here Maracle also engages in a hidden polemic with Native politics and its effacement of gender. A feminist analysis is central to her theorizing of racial oppression. In refusing a place for women and for love, the Native has played out the colonialist reduction of a people to "a sub-human level" (Maracle 20). Through her analysis she hopes to infuse love into Native communities again and so increase self-respect. This is one of several strategies of "empowerment" (Maracle 113) she advocates which would re-align the binary axes of this semiotic field so that the Native no longer functions as negative, as Other, for White identity politics.

"Racism is recent, patriarchy is old" (Maracle 23). This is the position from which Maracle now views these as interlocking oppressions. She attacks Native men for standing up to recognize white women when they come into the room and accepting their word as final arbiter while they demand that Native women make written submissions to meetings. Native women are denied the opportunity granted men of defending their opinions in public debate and honing their reasoning skills (Maracle 25). To both white and Native men, women are considered mere "vessels of biological release for men" (Maracle 27). Interrupting the semiotic values of sexuality ascribed to the indigene as "Squaw," Maracle discusses the strategic importance of interrogating men in public meetings on their sexual activities (Maracle 29). Important in her feminist analysis here is making a distinction between sex and love.

But in raising this issue, Maracle contests the feminist movement too which, she says, has been embarrassed by the word "love" (Maracle 31). While Maracle's discussion of Native spirituality and her insistence on the primacy of patriarchy as oppression would seem to make her arguments appealing to North American feminists, as, indeed, its later publication by Women's Press implies, I Am Woman is no text for easy consumption. Maracle challenges the assumptions of dominant feminism, as of left-wing and Native movements, with regards to their attempts to limit and contain the truth claims of Native women. In this frame, the title of Maracle's book is an ironic staking out of claims to generalize about the oppression of women in face of the women's movement's refusal to recognize these truth claims:

> No one makes the mistake of referring to us as women either. White women invite us to speak if the issue is racism or Native people in general. We are there to "teach," to "sensitize them," or to serve them in some other way. We are expected to retain

our position well below them as their servants. We are not, as
a matter of course, invited as an integral part of "their movement" — the women's movement. (Maracle 20 – 21)

In this regard, Maracle's self-presentation also functions as a critical
intervention into the discursive formation: she positions herself as
the unspeakable, as paradox confounding discursive norms, as Native
woman *intellectual*, one, moreover, who is a school drop-out, but who
quotes T.S. Eliot (Maracle 88) and writes her text in poetry. "I here, now
confess, I am an intellectual ... I am lonely" (Maracle 130). The second
statement is a direct consequence of the first, since Maracle's position
violates all the discursive norms for the category "intellectual." She
has none of the semiotic values that would grant her word claims to
Truth. As she writes:

> There is nothing worse than being a woman who is dark,
> brilliant and déclassé. Darkness is the absence of natural
> (normal?) class polish. Admit this, all of you. I laugh too
> loud, can't hold my brownie properly in polite company
> and am apt to call shit, "shit." I can't be trusted to be loyal
> to my class. In fact, the very clever among the elite know
> that I am opposed to the very existence of an elite among
> us. (Maracle 131)

It is this heterogeneity of Maracle's discourse which disrupts decorum.
While her analysis of politics is conducted at times in lucid logic and
eloquent, balanced statements, at others it is conveyed in the vulgar-
ity of slang, when she addresses men about "getting your rocks off"
(Maracle 29) . Analysis alternates with anecdote in embedded stories
of many troubled Natives. These in turn are continually broken up by
poems which in condensed form probe the contradictory emotions,
varying from rage to love, which are expressed in this text.

These violations of decorum are more striking in that they disrupt the
unity of tone characteristic of written genres. That Maracle presents her
insights and theories in writing is in itself a major intervention in the
discursive norm of orality within which are positioned the utterances

of the Native. Introducing her text, Maracle self-reflexively focuses on its hybridity as "scraps," "scribbl[ing]" on what most people would consider "garbage" — "paper napkins, brown bags and other deadwood paraphernalia" (Maracle 1). Central though is the opposition between orality and writing, developed here not as the privileging of the former, as in the dominant discourse on Native cultural forms, but as a compulsion toward the latter: "writing when I should have been mothering," as she pointedly contrasts (Maracle 9). Although the text is presented as first-person narration, the textual marker of oral narration, this is not presentation, but re-presentation. For the text is a compilation of stories, a miscellany: although they give the illusion of truth, the anecdotes are fictional.

> It is the practice of writers to fictionalize reality and prostitute the product of their licentious fantasies. "Artistic license," they call it. (Whoever "they" are.) Being not different, I have taken both the stories of my life, the stories of others' lives and some pure fabrications of my imagination and re-written them as my own. ... Usually, when one writes of oneself it is called non-fiction — I dis-believe that. Hindsight is always slightly fictitious. (Maracle 3 – 4)

Self-reflexively framing her exposition and narrative in this reflection on the dis/placement of writing, on writing as trace and *différance,* on writing as the constitution of fictions of identity, Maracle foregrounds these representations of the Native as re-presentations where rhetoric is trope — the staging of Natives speaking for themselves.

This thematization of the instance of enunciation is central to Maracle's quarrel with the institutions of knowledge which she contests from her position as "intellectual." Writing, especially the writing of history, is a terrain which for her is mined with the racist texts of the settler society. The educational system valorizes and propagates writing. But it is the educational system where the dehumanizing gaze of the colonizer is most present, teaching the Native child that s/he is a "cannibal" (Maracle 103), effacing her history and replacing it with a mimicry of the colonizer's narrative. The educational scene as staged by Maracle is a scene of mindless repetition, the Native parroting the anthropologist's discourse without understanding the language (Maracle 47 – 48). Here the "trans-lation effect" of heteroglossia is engaged in its most productive work of dis-identification when translation is staged, is re-presented, as a crucial strategy in the colonialist struggle over discursive authority. This scene is also the child reading out of the history book, an "asinine practice" designed to "integrate" the child into European society. "The teacher called my turn. I glanced at the clean white page with black characters all over it. 'Louis Riel was a madman, that was hanged …' I could not buy that anymore than I could the 'cannibalism' fairy tale of fifth grade. I could not forsake my ancestors for all your students to see" (Maracle 111). Education is the primary thrust of racism, Maracle argues: "[s]chools have showed themselves to be ideological processing plants" (Maracle 113). Rather than abandoning the scene of writing to the settler education sys-tem, however, Maracle has taken up the pen to disrupt those represen-tations of the Native as cannibal, as madman, to expose the ideological foundations that are re-produced through such representations. In this, she stakes out a claim for alternate forms of truth: "your knowledge is not the only knowledge we seek" (Maracle 112). These knowledges make no claims to the universal since they are elaborated in polemical relation to the settler knowledge which does make claims to be singular Truth. Consequently, they acknowledge their provisionality and partiality.

Maracle's intervention in the disciplinary norms of historiography effects the dis/placement of bilingualism, the heteroglossia of the trans-lation effect. Running the danger of becoming a "crippled two-tongued slave" as her grandmother warned her (Maracle 85, 109), Maracle is still engaged in addressing the colonizer, trying to explain herself in his logic. But, as she makes clear, the implications of this will disrupt the fixed assumptions of the settler's language. More than "prayer" will have shifted its meaning: "knowledge," as we have seen, and "intellect" are opening up their semantic fields to include desire, as both passion and engagement. Knowledge, Maracle contends, is always interested, always a site of struggle for contending views. As she comments in conclusion in "last word," literature is such a field of contesting knowledges. Justi-fying the emotional range of her writing, Maracle takes issue with the common definitions of "anger" and "sadness" as used by a Native man to characterize Alice Walker's *The Color Purple*. In doing so, he was making a case for not displaying such negative emotions since they sell well to "white folks" and perpetuate negative stereotypes of Natives.

To Maracle, Walker's novel is not a "sad story full of hate" (Maracle 189): to hide the rage and madness created by the colonial process is to collaborate in maintaining an equally powerful mythology of the Native as untouched by imperialism whether in an "originary" tribal state or in peaceful assimilation to settler society. These are the "Truth" on the Native which Maracle seeks to disrupt by foregrounding the struggle for decolonization and the elaboration of a hybrid culture. Maracle will no longer collaborate in "whitewashing" history, in "writing r(w)ight." She will not keep silent about the oppression she has suffered. Nor, however, will she collude in the norms of the dominant discourse which values struggle negatively and privileges narratives which work toward unity and harmony in (Romantic) resolution. She will write neither a "long sweet book," nor a "short sad book." Nostalgia has been dis/placed in struggle. Exclusion has not yielded to utopia, but to the dialectics of history.

Armstrong, too, sets out to challenge disciplinary truths and to question the facts of history as they have been fixed in writing. Like Maracle, she refuses the binary opposition of a mystical orality as guarantor of Truth and stages her challenge to the dominant knowledge in the arenas of education and narrativity. The two are intertwined as they are in Maracle's text, for Armstrong also troubles the easy oppositions of orality/writing even as she denounces the latter as an instrument of oppression when wielded by the dominant educational system.

Significantly, the first narrative scene in *Slash* is situated in a school where Tommy is fooling around in the line-up for vitamins with his fellow grade sixer, Jimmy. This is a one-room school that goes only to grade six. But it is different from the residential school which offers the higher grades in that, as his cousin Joe says, kids there were "beat up for talking Indian" (Armstrong 17). The following year, the Native children are sent to school in town: at once they confront racism. The principal separates the Native children from the whites to talk to them about the rules: "You Indians are lucky to be here. We'll get along just fine as long as you don't steal from the other kids. I want you all to wait here while the nurse comes to check your heads and ask you some questions. Then I will assign you to classes" (Armstrong 23 – 24). Soon the white children in the school are calling them "frigging Injuns ... nothing but thieves, full of lice" (Armstrong 24). Armstrong outlines the way in which this stereotypical representation of the dirty, thieving savage is produced through institutional practices. The practice of scapegoating, of constructing the Native as imaginary Other, is analyzed step by step. She also exposes the destabilizing effects this has on the young people as perceived by Tommy's grandfather, Pra-cwa, who comments on the way they have become "ashamed of everything Indian" since they began going to school in town (Armstrong 25).

But the effects of this colonial alienation are extremely varied and complex. Armstrong deliberately eschews easy binary oppositions between the purity of traditional mores and the abasement of assimilation. Some of the Natives live in modern houses with TV's (Armstrong 25), others live more traditionally spending their evenings in storytelling, singing the Coyote Song or in the sweats (Armstrong 22, 37). Commodification and ritualization co-exist as social values. So, too, Natives both attend the Catholic church and are attentive to the teachings of the Creator of Indian spirituality (Armstrong 30).

This heterogeneity of response is especially true of the narrator, Tommy, who comes from a more traditional home where his family speaks Okanagan — indeed his grandfather speaks no English — and spend their evenings telling oral tales to which Tommy enjoys listening. But Tommy is also an excellent student at school, learns English easily, and is a good reader. The dichotomy between Okanagan/English, between oral/written modes of knowledge is dis/placed in Tommy's narrative as he moves easily back and forth between both modes of cultural production. He offers the dates, facts, and analytical mode of imperial history as he recounts the events of the 1960s and 1970s, including the confrontation at Wounded Knee and the march on Ottawa. But these are presented in a disjointed manner with many repetitions, empty moments, and embedded "oral anecdotes." Indeed, the circular form of the narrative with its opening and closing sections situated self-reflexively in the narrating instance, when Tommy explains his narrative goals and strategies, foregrounds this narrative as an oral performance that is paradoxically represented in writing. This framing device, however, introduces quotation marks to distance the reader from the tale unfolding in that its status as artifact is exposed. This is a staged representation, history as narrative, history as telling. Like Maracle's personal narrative, this too is a mixture of genres, not the ethnographical autobiography told to the white man, but the Native confessional mode developed in the Indian Movement crossed with the oral anecdote, and framed as self-reflexive written fiction foregrounding its narrative strategies. While, on the one hand, the text might be seen to develop generic links with postmodern historiographic metafiction, to adopt Linda Hutcheon's terminology, on the other, it shares generic features with a Native genre Armstrong much admires, "political oratory" (Freeman 37).

This hybridization is self-reflexively staged in the opening chapter in the oral tale (cautionary fable?) told by Tommy's cousin Joe, who is both a medicine man and a gifted tale-teller. The tale of "Hightuned Polly" and her dog that she "babied like some white woman do [sic]" (Armstrong 19) is a tragi-comic tale about the perils of imitating the ways of the colonizer. At a stampede, Polly's dog is in heat so that she is followed by a crowd of dogs wherever she walks carrying her dog. To stop this, Polly sews a buckskin pant for her dog. The following morning she finds her dog, a hole chewed in the pants, and a crowd of visitors surrounding her. But this narrative may also be read as a fable of the dis/placement produced by cultural heterogeneity, a *mise en abyme* of Armstrong's own narrative. For the blending of cultural conventions here, the pampering of the dog but the failure to limit its fertility through neutering produces in/appropriate effects. These frustrate appropriation, however. The unbridled fertility of Polly's dog, despite the attempts to limit and constrain sexuality, reinforces, even as it counters, the stereotype of the promiscuous savage. For there is both nothing and everything "natural" about this promiscuity. This is a translation-effect of laughter-producing heteroglossia: repetition with a difference works here to dis/place the identity politics of verisimilitude and mimesis by emphasizing contradiction and paradox, the heterogeneous truths of *mimesis tekhné*, of mimicry. While this is presented as an oral tale, one of the "good stories [which] came out towards morning" (Armstrong 19), and as performance disrupts the economy of the trace, of writing, this is no "traditional" oral tale related to religious beliefs like the myths collected in so many anthologies of Native stories, but a contemporary carnivalesque anecdote which deals with the dilemmas of colonialism. Still, it invites allegorical reading and, in this, offers truth as interpretation, fiction as the way to (f)act.

While this anecdote, strategically placed in the first chapter, "The Awakening," emphasizes the historical importance of narrative truth in Armstrong's novel, the fiction/fact opposition is undercut along with the oral/written binary by the positioning of this story in the middle of an all-night conversation where the main issue is the problem of assimilation and the principal narrative strategy is dialogue and political debate. Tommy's family is trying to decide what position to adopt at a meeting in Kamloops of all the Indians in BC where a decision is to be taken on voting for "who was going to be the white man's leader," Diefenbaker, in this case. Tommy's grandfather, Pra-cwa, a "headman," argues against suffrage on the grounds that they wouldn't want the white people voting for their Chief. "We live different than them and they live different than us." On the contrary, as Tommy's uncle reports, "some Indians think it's okay. Some of them in the North American Indian Brotherhood want to vote. They say it'll do some good. They say we would get a better deal on our lands." However, Pra-cwa fears they "could be getting ready to sell us out of our reserves and make us like white people" (Armstrong 18). Against this cultural interpellation which comes through "paper laws" — all the apparati of the state and its educational institutions — the opening chapter sets out a coded system of oppositional values from Native culture. But the narrative refuses to draw an imaginary boundary between the two antagonistic cultural codes, deploying them instead in such political debates and carnivalesque parody which serve to collapse differences.

Though they are made to seem similar, these cultural codes produce different subject positions for the Native. Through policies such as enfranchisement (18), taxation (19), regulation of alcohol distribution (20), and the "white paper" (28), the state enforces Native assimilation through dependency. Cultural stereotypes are another source of infantilization and consequent racism, as in Hollywood representations which come through the television and educational systems: "Like one teacher, who explained what she wanted in slow Hollywood talk. She said, 'You fix'um little story, Tommy, about how you live.' To the other kids she had asked, 'Please prepare a short biographical sketch of yourself'" (Armstrong 38–39). This rhetorical violence produces subjective violence for the Native interpellated into this discourse. But should he identify against himself with the white culture and opt for assimilation, he still faces alienation. Consequently, the narrative line of this apprenticeship story is feathered, divided. Tommy is offered a choice that is a non-choice as he advances in Chapter 2 to "Trying It On."

Whether "it" is embracing the materialism of white culture and becoming assimilated to its master narrative of development and progress or opting for the pastoral containment of the "old ways" of traditional Native culture is ambiguous. Instead, Tommy's growth is measured by his increased skill in reading, in interpretation. When he was a child, he could decode the English words of the "white paper" to read to his father and grandfather (Armstrong 18). As he grows older, his hermeneutical skills develop through learning to read cultural codes for their ideology of racism. Increasingly, this places him in a difficult position with respect to his people, seeing more than many, unable to steer a clear course of action between two alternatives which seem more and more similar, equally dubious. In the final pages of the novel, this brings him into conflict even with his wife Maeg over the issue of Native rights in the Constitution. Maeg argues: "This is a people's mission. We care for our rights and our land and we have a child. Maybe more than that, we have to clear the future for him. Nobody is looking out for our rights so we all have to do what we can. ... That's why I'll go on that express and carry a sign that says, 'CONSTITUTIONAL RIGHTS FOR OUR CHILDREN'" (Armstrong 236). With its focus on the future, Maeg's position entails a narrative of progress. While he acknowledges the importance of their rights to practice their ways and the need to alert public opinion to do something to protect them, Tommy is "uncomfortable about the whole thing" and reserves judgement till he can talk things over with the old people. By the time the trip is half over, he has managed to articulate his nagging doubt. He has perceived a split between the Indian politicians who are leading the caravan and the people who are singing to a different tune, one called the "Constitution Song": "We don't need your Constitution, BC

is all Indian land. We don't need your Constitution, hey yeah hey. ...
How much clearer can it be?" he asks. "We don't need anybody's constitution, what we have is our own already. We hold rights to the land
and to nationhood. We just need to have it recognized. We want to
keep it" (Armstrong 241).

What he has recognized are the racist strategies of the state bully-
ing the Natives into ceding all their land rights by threatening to leave
them out of the constitution unless they "negotiate." Power is in the
Natives' hands though, if they can just wait, for their bargaining power
is ownership of the land. They are a sovereign people, not colonized
Indians. But Slash's attempt to convince the leaders of the strength of
their position and the danger of negotiation is met with ridicule. They
laugh at him and treat him as though he were crazy (Armstrong 242).
His wife Maeg continues to argue with him that Canada will not go away
and that his way will only cause more hardship, "strife and bitterness"
for the people (243). She also continues to work with the "Constitution
Express." Her initial joy at their success in having aboriginal rights recognized later evaporates and she comes to share Tommy's view with
others. For him, the agreement promises a dark future, one with the
Natives as "second class citizens instead of first class Indians" because
without land they would be nothing:

> Many of our leaders would be lining up to get compensa-
> tion on their lands. That would be the worst devastation
> of all. Our rights would be empty words on paper that had
> no compassion for what is human on the land. I saw what
> money and power could do to our gentle people and I felt
> deep despair. Nothing much would remain after that to
> fight for. Nothing to heal our wounds in the fighting. We
> would no longer know freedom as a people. We would be
> in bondage to a society that neither loved us nor wanted us
> to be part of it. (Armstrong 248 – 49)

In this conclusion to the novel, in the chapter "We Are a People," it is
clear that no "resolution" has occurred between the antagonistic discursive formations of the opening chapters. No progress has been achieved

in advancing the Native cause. Natives still remain divided within themselves and, more strategically, as this political novel demonstrates, among themselves. The most devastating impact of racism has been to divide Native peoples in order to assimilate them more easily. For the seeming opposition between white cultural codes and Native ones turns out to offer no choice at all. The choice to assimilate into progress or to fetishize tradition is ultimately the same choice: to remain caught in a binary antagonism between a hegemonic discourse and its inverse, a counter-hegemonic discourse. What Armstrong's novel does, through the represented speech of Tommy, however, is to show the necessity for a third way, for a position of dis-identification where one may signify otherness yet refuse the trope of subordination:

> There are all kinds of us from the Native Alliance for Red Power working on this. The Beothucks are a symbol to us. They were a tribe of Indians on the east coast that were wiped out so the land could be open for settlement. You see, there was a bounty placed on them by the government and they were hunted down to the last one. That's how we fit into this society. They just want us out of the way, no matter how. It's called genocide. It's what's happening to our people right now. We are dying off because we can't fit in. Help is progressive. The ones that are just brown white men. The ones that fit in. Soon there will be no more true red men, with their own beliefs and ways. There is nothing wrong with our ways. Just because our people hate to be grabby, just because they don't knock themselves out like robots at nine-to-five jobs, and they don't get too excited about fancy stuff or what I call luxuries, they are looked down on and treated as outcasts and called lazy. Or else they get like us. They get angry inside and fight back some-how. Usually they end up dead, in prison or drunk. All of these lead to genocide of our people. You see they only give us two choices. Assimilate or get lost. A lot of us are lost. We need to make a third choice. That's what Red Patrol is about. (69–70)

Though Red Patrol is no longer an answer to the problem by the end of the novel, the necessity for a third position, one not established by the dominant discourse as its negation, is sited in a discourse of critique. Grounded in the interpretation of discourses, in the reading of codes, this hermeneutical activity is similar to the discourse of the analyst, attentive to desire in knowledge, the antithesis of the discourse of mastery.[26] As such, it foregrounds the passionately engaged nature of knowledge, implicitly criticizing the totalizing Truth claims of the discourse of mastery. Critique as the terrain of resistance.

There is no "solution" to the political problem, no moment of illumination in this novel, only continual struggle to find a third position, constant questioning of assumptions. Similarly, there is no fictional closure, no resolution, for the narrative circles around in its end to the beginning, that is, to the instance of enunciation where the narrator explains his need to tell his life story in order to provide a permanent record of the history of struggle. Whereas the Prologue opens with a focus on the act of narrating ("As I begin to write this story") and on the narrative as feigning ("The characters in this novel are fictitious. ... The events are based in actual events but are not meant to be portrayed as historically accurate" [13]), it ends with a poem, a lyric on the evanescence of nature, and so poses a problem in interpretation for the reader. Between historical fiction and the wind's displacement of all signs, there has been no progress, no development and almost no action: the narrative is composed mainly of reported speech. In short, this has been a "flat" book not likely to make the best-seller list in Canada. Repetition is an important rhetorical feature in Native oral narrative. Indeed, a-chronological ordering of material is a characteristic feature of Native "autobiography." But such repetition is routinely removed by white editors of such autobiographies to align them with the dominant codes of self-representation (Brumble 11). The formal experimentation of Armstrong and Maracle with structures of chronology challenges the limitations of the generic codes of the white colonizer's master historical narratives, not as formalist project, but to re-write the ending of the historical record. That the major challenge of the Native is to make the settler society understand that s/he has a history, that Native culture has undergone development and change over time and is not "'primitive' and therefore without a 'history,' is necessary before Native culture can be perceived to have 'art history,'" and therefore be part of the movements in art that have produced "high art" (Vastokas 8). Similarly, the Native must challenge the codes of settler society to show that there is time and, consequently, meaning in her/his narratives. The fact that there is a Native history must be established in order to decentre the values of origin, primitivism, and mysticism that have configured the Native in the discourse of indigenization. "It is crucial," we have read in the opening lines, that the narrating "I am an Indian person" (13), crucial, we come to realize, because the cultural discourse legitimates fictional form.

Form, as Bakhtin has shown us, is always a message in a specific sociohistoric configuration. Moreover, as he suggests, the inherited canons and modes of representation of the Western literary tradition do not permit an aesthetic based on performative values. Its high canonical genres are known "in their completed aspect" (1981, 3). The novel alone is developing in history. In this, it provides a critique of the fixity of genres by exposing the conventionality of the forms through parody. *Slash* re-accentuates the plot of growth and development characteristic of both the *bildungsroman* of the cultural hero and the histories of new nations ("Canada: The Building of a Nation"): both its lack of change and its palimpsestic mode are hidden polemics with the myth of progress, an implicit critique of this trope of imperialism.

But Armstrong's historical narrative challenges historiography on yet another ground, that of its truth claims. Knowledge is not Truth hidden in pre-existent facts to be discovered and reconstructed in language, but truth to be staged, constructed in the telling, "true simply as a consequence of being stated" (Spence 177). The two types of truth, historical truth and narrative truth, are established on different grounds, in contrasting criteria of accuracy and adequacy, and deployed in different narrative modes, "plain" as contrasted to "significant." In the former, observation language, description, is important, for it enables the verification of the logical connection between events. In the latter, these connections are outwardly invisible, present as "narrative fit," that is, the narrative account seems to provide a coherent explanation of the events in question. Nothing relevant is omitted; everything irrelevant is excluded. The pieces fit into an "understandable Gestalt" (Spence

182). Narrative may be thought of as a kind of theory that "represents an interpretation of a particular meaning," a meaning "dependent on the observer's system of interpretation" (Spence 292). The problem of establishing general rules is great when interpretations are narrative rather than veridical, the hermeneut functions more as pattern maker than pattern finder (Spence 293). Interpretation is "creative" (Spence 177). As Maracle wrote about Native historiography as narrative: it is "re-writ[ing] history ... re-writ[ing] her life onto the pages of a new history": this is the rebel "mak[ing] history" (Maracle 120 – 21).

Critical to this shift in frames of perspective in historiography is the narrative strategy of the fictionalized participant focalizer. For unlike the conventional historical narrative of knowledge as verifiable, pre-existent Truth, written from the distant, objectified position of a non-participant observer, both these narratives are the representations in quotation marks of political presentations by partisan narrators. The shift in frames of perception from outside to inside, from the eye to the I, inflects a disjunction in the relations of perception and representation, which establishes the grounds for this process of unfolding local stories, provisional truths. But such autobiographical narratives are a double challenge to discursive formations. As well as confronting and exposing the codes of settler historiography, these autobiographies break with the codes of Native "tradition." Autobiographies are "not a traditional form among Native peoples but the consequence of contact with the white invader-settlers, and the product of a limited collaboration with them" (Krupat xi). The first Native autobiographies were "told-to" narratives, the joint "collaboration" of an ethnographer or missionary and a Native. As such, their very textualization is a function of Euramerican pressure. They are, moreover, more properly "scientific" or "factual," than "literary," as is the case of autobiography in the canon of English literature. In this, they are the narrative of a "representative" of their culture, their story emphasizing the individual only in relation to her/his social roles, not as distinctive individual. The Native autobiography is consequently in its formation a double-voiced discourse, the collaboration of two persons of different cultures, modes of production, and languages. In this, the Native autobiography is a heterogeneous, hybridized form. Consequently, it stands in opposition to the settler society with its literary norms of "ego-centric individualism, historicism, and writing" (Krupat 29). When the written autobiography is utilized by a living person to present her/his Native voice not as vanished and silent, but as living and able to articulate her/his differences, it presents itself as contra-diction. Consequently, the autobiography holds potentials for challenging the discursive norms of the discourse on the indigene while dis/placing the fetishizing of Tradition.

For in the telling of an autobiographical narrative, a speaker posits herself/himself as the subject of a history, as the subject of a sentence, as "I." As Benveniste has shown, subjectivity is linguistically and discursively produced. "I," though, cannot be conceived without the conception of the "non–I," "you." Consciousness of self is possible only through contrast, through differentiation. Dialogue, the fundamental condition of language, implies a reversible polarity between "I" and "you" which are empty positions, shifters, marking the difference between now and then, here and there. "Language is possible only because each speaker sets himself [sic] as a *subject* by referring to himself as I in his discourse" (Benveniste 225). But since language is a system of differences with no positive terms, "I" designates only the subject of a specific utterance.

The basis of subjectivity is in the exercise of language. "If one really thinks about it, one will see that there is no other objective testimony to the identity of the subject except that which he himself thus gives about himself" (Benveniste 226). Since language itself differentiates between concepts, offering the possibility of meaning, it is by adopting the position of subject within language that the individual is able to produce meaning. When learning to speak, one learns to differentiate between "I" and "you," and to identify with the first-person subject-position. Subsequently, one learns to recognize oneself in a series of subject-positions (boy or girl, white or red, writer or reader, etc.), which are the positions from which discourse is intelligible to itself and others. Subjectivity is thus a matrix of subject-positions which may be inconsistent or even in contradiction with each other.

For this movement across the bar of language from signifier to signified occurs, as Lacan has shown, in the Imaginary, when the subject recognizes itself in a recognition of the self as other, in contra-diction. By cross-identifying in this way with the Subject, the subject is constituted as subject in ideology, according to Althusser, positioned within the social discourses available to the subject. Given that the coherence of the sign and of the predicate synthesis are the guarantors of the unity of the speaking subject, as Kristeva argues, any attack against the sign — or syntax — is the mark of a re-evaluation process vis-à-vis the speaking subject's unity. Writing history from the perspective of the subject in the process of making herself a subject through the constitution of an interlocutor, a community of readers, the "you" who bring her into being as subject, is to enact such a shift in sign systems that destabilizes the unity of the subject of the dominant discourse of history, constructing a different subject of (hi)story, a critical subject, the Native storyteller as "storian." Rather than offering a historical product, these fictions unfold an epistemological process, a way of knowing through telling and reading, and an existential process, a way of·forming an identity through discourse.

It is through such strategies of dis/placement and decentring of available subject-positions that these two Native writers have challenged established canons of address and representation. Through their representation of their political agenda as feminists and Natives, framed and staged as provisional narrative truths, Maracle and Armstrong have signified their otherness in the very act of refusing the trope of subordination. By locating interlocutors both within and without the Native community, by writing hybrid texts that address both audiences as "you," they have constructed a complex subject-position for themselves, frequently contradictory, as Slash and Maracle's narrator know well, but one that allows for the creation of a third position, a transformative practice, one of analysis and critique of the dominant binary discourses on the indigene. They are self-consciously entering the logical fray surrounding the "silenced" subject of racism. Quite literally, Maracle and Armstrong are storytelling for their lives. To write the story that will be told over and over, to create that community of "yous" to respond to their narratives, this "writing re(a)d" will discursively constitute both themselves as authors and their critiques of racism as provisional truths. In this, they will have begun to write the other, otherwise. Other, that is, from the perspective of the *dominant* discourse within which I write.

DETERRITORIALIZING STRATEGIES:

M. NourbeSe Philip as Caucasianist Ethnographer

This essay is about realigning geopolitical identities, about the transformation of languages and bodies, about inventing the "real," in this case "Canadian Literature(s)." At stake is the concept of a "national" literature in the case of a multilingual, multiracial state. This consideration of so-called national literatures as comparative literatures challenges the paradigms of the discipline of Comparative Literature, founded on literary nationalism where language is the mark of nationality and Literature, it is understood, must be territorialized. Deterritorialization, however, is the condition of literature in Canada.

The paradox of living between cultures, of writing between languages, is forced on M. NourbeSe Philip as that contemporary figure of alterity so ubiquitous in Canadian culture, the immigrant. The dis/placement of language she encounters in the competing fields of polyglossia produces a disjunction between the apprehension of, and communication about, the world around. In a new culture, signifiers have lost their habitual referent, are deterritorialized. She is caught in a border dialogue between mimicry, alterity, and silence. Not part of the continuing migration from Europe which established the settler colony of Canada as an extension of French, then British imperialism — with English and French as its official languages — she is a descendant of African slaves, over whom British imperialist rule was exercized as self-conscious disruption: she comes from another marginal place, Trinidad-Tobago, a colony of invasion and exploitation. An exile twice over through enslavement and emigration, NourbeSe Philip has made of language a place and taken up "the challenge that the anguish that is English" is for all African Caribbean people (1989a, 19). In this "obsession that ... is language" (Kirchhoff 1989a), NourbeSe Philip constructs a "demotic," drawing on Caribbean theorizing of the decentring of imperial English through a polydialectical jamming of its codes, or what has been called the "Caribbean continuum" (Ashcroft 45).

Writing within the tension of centre and margin — in Canada between margin and margin — she represents from the position of those already t/here, a boundary crosser, a transgressor, those marginal voices bordering on the known, themselves hybrids comprising both the known and the unknown. She shuttles back and forth displacing, yet simultaneously exposing, the irreducibility of the margin. The official explanation of her difference in Canada is cultural, yet she poses it as linguistic. She explores the creative potentialities of the interface of languages, strategies of code-switching and recontextualization, in the production of an interlanguage or counterdiscourse, that is a centrifugal system of sign manipulation. Pursuing a politics of the signifier, she invites us to read this *différance* in language as metonym of social and cultural forces traversing the text. In *She Tries Her Tongue, Her Silence Softly Breaks*, continuum is re-marked as vari-directional system not binary opposition. The multiple combinatorial potentials of the sign are the site of struggles to fix meaning in discursive signifying practices. This problem in discourse is a clash of cultures over claims to the "real," that is to "authentic" *Canadian* Literature.

For the African-Caribbean-Canadian who would be a writer, oppressed by the pernicious effects of sexism and racism, only too aware of the politics of the choice of language in the construction of representations of identity ("create new i-mages" 1989a, 78), this paradox of de/cons/ struction poses an additional challenge that makes her language self-reflexive. The continuum is a Caribbean reworking of English: in Canada, this "demotic" is a foreign tongue. The symbolic order instituting the categories of the sayable (or writable) exerts its authority in the conflict of languages: "We grow up speaking English, so it is comforting, but it is also something forced on us" (Kirchhoff 1989a). Writing to "decentre" language through the contra-diction of two heritages, NourbeSe Philip disrupts the discursive norms of Canadian English through hybridity, re-placing the imposed and imposing language in a new geopolitical terrain. Framing her difference in/as language. NourbeSe Philip's project oscillates between the valences of the syntax of ethnicity, between the dis-covery of this "nation language" — reclaiming "home" — and an in(ter)vention "decentring" all language — realigning the terrain — that is, between melancholy or memory and anticipation or project, between nostalgia and dissidence or, between a syntax of "retentive" and/or "restitutive" particularity and a syntax of invention or syncretic particularity (Sekyi-Otu 197). In this double gesture of recontextualization, NourbeSe Philip develops the creative potentials of the intersection of discursive formations to problematize the monoglossia of English-Canadian literature. Her relativizing moves from the Caribbean abrogation of English in a becoming English to destabilize the identity politics of "Canadian" literature which, through her foregrounding of the hyphen (Caribbean-Canadian), is re-configured as a polysystem of conflictual signifying practices.

Origin myths fixing the "distinctiveness" of nineteenth-century Canadian Literature affirmed the necessary unity of literature, language, soil to constitute Northrop Frye's topocentrism in which the question of identity is reframed as a question of position in space. "Who am I?" is translated as "Where is here?" This trope constructing Canadian identity erases the aboriginal peoples from the landscape and assimilates the French to the "mainstream," re-covering the resulting gap with a genealogical narrative of analogy, a myth of Renaissance. The promise that Greek culture will be renewed covers up the contradiction on which Canadian literature is grounded, the non-literariness of its literature. Canadian writers using English break the chain of literature, nation, language. While they find themselves in a double bind with respect to the writing of England, whose models they both must and must not use if they are to achieve recognition and authenticity, even greater is the disjunction of writing by someone whose language is other than English. This latter also inscribes a difference with respect to mainstream anglophone writing in Canada, Canadianness being co-terminous with the English (or French) language. When English is written as a second language and the cultural and textual codes of other literary traditions are grafted onto the modes of address and textualization of English, difference is inscribed within language as hyphen or translation effect — as estrangement or defamiliarization.

The economy of writing in Canada is organized around hierarchical divisions into mainstream and immigrant writers on the poles of language difference. These categories are set out in the *Report of the Royal Commission on Bilingualism and Biculturalism* which introduced and defined the term "ethnic" in official Canadian discourse. It assumes that Canada is the domain of "two founding nations" excluding the Native peoples who now call themselves "First Nations." Bilingual refers to French/English fluency only. "Other ethnic groups" make *cultural* contributions. Though the *Report* asserts that language "is the principal element" of a culture (I, xxxiv), it begs the question of what is to happen to the culture of "other ethnic groups" whose languages are not preserved. Paradoxically, the *Report* comments that "nobody will maintain that a group still has a living culture, in the full sense of the term, when it is forced to use another language in order to express to itself the realities which make up a large part of its daily life" (I, xxxv). Yet the *Report* points to the flourishing cultures of Acadians and Jews articulated in the languages of the "founding nations." This ambiguity of preserving culture while not necessarily preserving it is now entrenched in the state's bureaucratic apparatus of cultural valorization. Financial support of writing and publishing by English and French-Canadian writers is the province of the Canada Council, while immigrant writers and publications in other languages get grants in aid from Multiculturalism Canada which considers literature under the broader rubric of cultural productions. Native writing, if acknowledged at all, was for long the concern of the Department of Indian Affairs. However, in the last decade a separate programme for First Nations artists has been established by the Canada Council.

Bureaucratic practice structures a distinction between high and low cultures around the semiotic fields of founding nations/immigrants, English-French/other languages. This is, however, a formula for silencing literatures in other languages since it materializes as an opposition between literature/folklore, high/low culture. It maps out the opposition of "founding nations" with language rights and "ethnic others" with a culture divorced from language. Multiculturalism prefers to subsidize manifestations of traditional folklore, producing a hierarchical division of cultures around the oppositions literate, modern and oral, material, traditional. The immigrant is forced to choose between the two valences of the semiotic field of immigration, two non-choices which both ensure invisibility in the present political arena. On the other hand, s/he can produce literature in English and opt for assimilation, on the other, s/he can produce folklore in another language and opt for fetishizing the past in the production of museum pieces. These cultural productions — folkdancing, traditional foods, music, and material culture — are easily consumable by a mainstream anglophone audience since they mask linguistic difference and, consequently, reproduce the hegemonic values of this audience. Despite the etymology of the term (belonging to a nation), "ethnicity" is not the condition of everyone. WASPS are never ethnics. As NourbeSe Philip points out, however, the writer who comes from an ostensibly English-speaking country in the Caribbean is frequently not perceived as eligible for multicultural grants on the criteria of language, but the content of their work is not "Canadian" enough to be considered "good" and qualify for support by the Canada Council. Framing her critique on the grounds of a Caribbean "nation language," not the more common bureaucratic category of "Black Heritage," NourbeSe Philip challenges the categories effecting the official cuts and exclusions of Canadian cultural discourses establishing value in the Literary.

Most of the so-called multicultural groups are of white European descent as a result of Canada's long-standing "keep-Canada-white" immigration policy. "[M]ulti-culturalism is not anti-racism" (1990). As a policy of liberal cultural pluralism, it works to reproduce binary oppositions of white/colour and fails to expose the power relationships of systematic racism that work to erase difference. Multiculturalism might be dubbed a European charter myth of origins, an effective process of recuperation whereby diverse cultures are returned homogenized as folkloric spectacle, exotica, and nostalgia, oriented toward the past and, consequently, depoliticized in the present. In this formation, nationalism and culture are unified as media event. Cultural pluralism functions to obscure difference of class and race and pre-empts the possibilities for structural heterogeneity. The critique of Black peoples exposes a complex contradiction of Canadian culture where language creates one set of exclusionary practices of silencing and race another overlapping set of erasures, a contradiction signified in the positions of "silenced" other and invisible "visible minority."

The hierarchy relating these two fields, so that the African-Caribbean-Canadian is at the bottom of the social and intellectual pyramid, has been produced by mapping these inside/outside valences over the grid of civilization/barbarity, as NourbeSe Philip has suggested. However, these signifiers regulating exclusionary oppositions are mutually constitutive, "cultural treasures" acquired by "spoil" or by "toil." "There is no document of civilization which is not at the same time a document of barbarism" (Walter Benjamin 256). Art can be known only through the processes it erases, the triumphal procession of the conqueror or the labour which has gone into its making. Dehistoricized, decontextualized, the cultural object exists as monument because the connection between art and labour and art and history or politics has been e-rased. Aesthetic value rests in the very distance separating the work of art from its production, from its use value. In this way, its meaning is fixed and seemingly immutable. As NourbeSe Philip points out, the monuments of European modernism owe much to African art, but this debt has been occluded in their removal from a ritual activity and in the erasure of the circumstances of that removal. This has been accompanied by an appropriation of their aesthetic in the development of "primitivism" through which Eurocentric art practices arrogate for themselves reason and knowledge by rationalizing their exploitation in theories of racial and cultural superiority, that relegates the African Other to all that is inferior. "[P]rimitivism became a device to manage the primitive" (1987, 31): the work of art was fetishized, commodified, torn from its social fabric where its meaning was assigned within a social order. Obliterated or functionalized, the work of art is "civilized," the barbarism underpinning it has been erased, the imperialism and racism of this appropriation denied. While such works as Picasso's *Les demoiselles d'Avignon* or, in Canada, Rudy Wiebe's *The Temptations of Big Bear* are considered masterpieces and classics of their time and place, the works of art of the African or indigene are relegated to the vaults of the ethnographic museum and their "literature" received as anthropology or sociology. In *She Tries Her Tongue*, NourbeSe Philip exposes the "spoil" of civilization as rape and excision of the tongue. This allegory of empire at the origins of Euro-American literature in Ovid's *Metamorphoses* is also the barbarity at the heart of civilization contaminating the Canadian "Renaissance."

Ethnographic literature is invisible in literary histories because its history is not received. Nor can it be. Black literature especially is figured as a-temporal. In the decontextualization or erasure of textual production in the process of monumentalization is manifest what James Snead terms operations of "coverage against both external and internal threats — self-dissolution, loss of identity; or repression, assimilation …" Cross-cultural feuds involve discursive quarrels over "where one coverage ends and another begins" (Snead 214). One such struggle over identity constitutes European self-definitions as separate from African culture which, failing to recognize the General in the Hegelian *Aufhebung*, has "no history" only a "succession of accidents and surprises" (Snead 215). "Natural" Black culture plays "barbarity" to European civilization even in the Americas where both are settlers, albeit under different conditions. Such theories justify white supremacy in practices of Black slavery. In the form of oral history (first-hand accounts or testimonials from marginal groups) or as sociology (the ethnic as problem), the literary productions of ethnic groups are received in opposition to canonical "monuments." In contrast to literary texts which are considered as a textuality visibly more worked over than other forms of writing, this kind of ethnic writing signifies as the apparent "disorder" of speech (Barthes 1964, 25; my translation). Its value lies in the immigrant's speech whose authenticity is proportional to the marks of linguistic naïveté and (even) incompetence with which it is inscribed, broken language metonymically signifying not yet assimilated or "naturalized." Different. What writing is produced is read as confession of the emigrant's exile even if this should be the self-consciously wrought textuality of poetry which stakes claims to the Literary and participation in high culture in its very form. Poetry? The problem of legitimating it when it is written in a language other than English — or filtered through a previous and other culture and language in a translation-effect — is difficult in light of the discursive norms of culture territorialized so that "identity" and "nationality" coincide with a unique language.

Literary identity is thus a contradiction in terms when the poem in dialect belongs simultaneously to Canadian literature and Afro-Caribbean literature in exile. This break produced by emigration makes language deterritorialized, as a-signifying practice in what is a "littérature mineure" (Deleuze 1975). The absence of a territory occasions a break or rupture with power, forms, norms, hierarchies. This may manifest itself in the broken English of the translation effect, in a highly metaphoric language, or in the invention of an idiolect (a syncretic language), involving a shift from a referential use of language, no territory being possible, to an intensive use to compensate for the loss of making sense (Deleuze 1975, 42). In the absence of referentiality, "ethnic" discourse engages in the continuous fictionalizing of origins, constructing an identity in the imaginary.

Literary language is not a given but, as Barthes reminds us, a question of affiliation or transgression (Barthes 1964). The ethnic writer may buy into the language of power (English) or interrupt it by foregrounding the diglossia of her deterritorialization. Points of antagonism, overlap, and intersection between the dominant and the dominated, of the "Canadian" and its imaginary "Other," are powerful symbolic dissidences within this culture. Mapping where place, body, group identity, and subjectivity interconnect exposes the discursive sites where social classification and psychological processes are generated as conflictual textual complexes. Ideology and fantasy join, tracing lines of desire that are produced and reproduced through one another. The law of these displacements is the law of exclusion. Its Others — what it negates and excludes to create its identity as a classical-classificatory body — produce new objects of desire.

The construction of the "Imaginary Canadian" (Wilden) occurs in operations of symmetrization and inversion wherein the "Canadian," from lack and desire, mis-recognizes itself in an other, which becomes the Other, the absent full presence or plenitude of identity. In the Imaginary, where deixis is stripped of social specificity, the contexts of relations of power are objectified and obscured, so that subjects are treated as floating atoms and exploitation and oppression are obfuscated. Through such strategies of alibiing (Barthes 1973, 123) a single discourse becomes the dominant discourse. Discourse involves both the "forms of organized ideological material as meaningful material" (as sign) and the "forms of the social intercourse by which this meaning is realized" (Bakhtin /Medvedev 9). "[E]ach situation, fixed and sustained by social custom, commands a particular kind of organization of audience" (Volosinov 97). The literary text and language are sites of the constant making (and unmaking) of identities and meanings.

Within a specific discursive formation, this clash of competing discourses, in which "a polemic blow is struck at the other's discourse on the same theme, at the other's statement about the same object," is figured as "hidden polemic" (Bahktin 1981, 195). Meaning develops within discursive fields agonistically, shaped and preceded by what it is opposing and so never existing on its own terms. It comes from positions in struggle so that "words ... change their meaning according to the 'positions' from which they are used within the 'discursive process'" (Pêcheux 112). So "civilization" and "barbarity" are thought differently depending on whether they are thought by the anglophone Canadian or the African-Caribbean-Canadian. Classical literature, for instance, is promise of Renaissance for the one, but barbarity at the heart of civilization for the second. Power, though, privileges one discourse and speaking position, fixing it in a singular norm.

From their within-without position, the writing of minorities troubles the homogeneity of the ethnocentrism of the singular discourse of power, works at its limits, on the margins to interrogate its silences, absences, its politics of exclusion. It exposes boundaries, challenges the hierarchy of sites of discourse, forces the threshold and moves into the liminal, working the in-between, site of movement and change. The complexity of this double articulation arises from the fact that the discursive practices are both connected and disassociated: the logic of subject-identity that posits one subject for one discourse for one site or practice is confounded in this concept of discourse as a network of intersecting discourses where inside and outside are relational positions with respect to specific discourses not in subjection to a singular power. Through permutations and instabilities emerge the possibilities of shifting the terms of the semiotic system itself, of conceptualizing an open system as a site of struggle rather than a closed system of binary oppositions organized on hierarchical lines that conceal the operations of power by naturalizing these differences as fact.

Clashing discursive positions within the field could be configured by mapping other perspectives successively over these semiotic valences. In the case of NourbeSe Philip, viewed from the dominant discourse, from an initial opposition by a process of negation four terms are generated that lay out the horizontal and vertical axes of combination and between them four semantic fields or zones: 1) zone of Canadian masterpieces, 2) zone of authentic folklore of foreign provenance, both in "native language," 3) zone of inauthentic masterpieces (immigrant writing), and 4) zone of inauthentic folklore (ethnographer's report), texts "in translation."

THE CANADIAN LITERATURE SYSTEM

(AUTHENTIC)
"NATURAL" NATIVE LANGUAGE

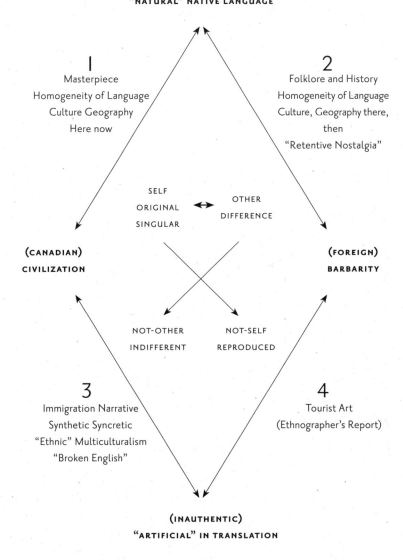

I
Masterpiece
Homogeneity of Language
Culture Geography
Here now

2
Folklore and History
Homogeneity of Language
Culture, Geography there,
then
"Retentive Nostalgia"

SELF
ORIGINAL   OTHER
SINGULAR   DIFFERENCE

(CANADIAN)   **(FOREIGN)**
CIVILIZATION   **BARBARITY**

NOT-OTHER   NOT-SELF
INDIFFERENT   REPRODUCED

3
Immigration Narrative
Synthetic Syncretic
"Ethnic" Multiculturalism
"Broken English"

4
Tourist Art
(Ethnographer's Report)

(INAUTHENTIC)
"ARTIFICIAL" IN TRANSLATION

Cultures in conflict are posed in the overlapping semiotic fields as a problem in discourse. What is at stake is a struggle over the "real," a struggle over the signifier "Canadian," in order to mobilize it for political ends by inflecting its meanings in different ways that cut and mark the boundaries of inside and outside. Who has the right to decide? Whose truth claims are legitimated? Whose interests are served? These are the stakes in the power/knowledge nexus. Identity of the "natural" Canadian is constructed through a narrative of conjunction or disjunction with the imaginary other by the subject in pursuit of an object of desire: Canada is defined in opposition to other states within a discourse of nationalism. These oppositions generate the respective contraries and oppositions on the terrain of displacement or artificiality, those not at home, of the not-other or immigrant and the not-subject or tourist/ethnographer. Movement is possible among these positions such that various residual and emergent contexts are included or marginalized.

The major narrative line constructs national difference in the possibly reciprocal relations between two oppositional geopolitical terrains, between 1 and 2. Movement from 2 to 3, between opposition and contrary, produces a narrative of immigration, of displacement in the improper language of "broken english." The intersection of 1 and 3, within the geopolitical terrain of Canada, produces a narrative of assimilation or multiculturalism that hierarchizes along the lines between native and imagined identities. The movement of the Canadian to another country produces, from the perspective of the Canadian subject, commodified tourist art or ethnographer's record. Both 3 and 4 are texts "in translation" rather than in the "native language." What is logically impossible, according to this model, is the inverse movement from 4 to 1: the Other's gaze as observer *in* Canada — what NourbeSe Philip terms her occupation as "Caucasianist," a Black woman's rewriting of Ovid's *Metamorphoses* — is excluded from the boundaries of "Canadian."

Yet it is just such a position rendered unsayable by the law of the excluded middle, ground of this logic of oppositions, that ethnic others — NourbeSe Philip explicitly — take up as position of *critical* parallax, foregrounding the contradiction of their within-without position, to expose the institutions of Canadian society that treat them as members only if they remain silent, invisible, assimilated to the dominant group whose power has fixed identity along the axis of its "real." "Inside" and "outside" are ever confounding sites, a matter of framing (Derrida 1987, 63), shifting, and realigning the borders as the viewing angle changes in a parallax, so that inside and outside function as relational positions, as a differential network of moveable signifiers, not as positive terms, as binary oppositions.

Those who can think in more than one language and who claim affiliations with more than one national culture find it impossible to consider language and culture as "natural" and unproblematic expressions of "experience." The translation effect means that no language can be considered transparent or referential. Meaning can never be fully recovered: the signifier is always excessive. Identity is destabilized and dispersed across a number of subject positions between the natural and the constructed. This produces the "disidentification effect" (Pêcheux 162) articulated in counter-discourses. Although there are no *a priori* dominant and resisting vectors, in a given instance under specific historical conditions these discursive formations are asymmetrically positioned to one another in relations of domination. As "sites of a work of reconfiguration," however, they may variously be a "recuperation-reproduction" work or a politically "productive" work: they may re-inscribe the same and support the reigning discourse or work for change and displacement, for redistributions in the discursive field. "Disidentification" is a third possible position, one not caught up in binary relations of identity/ negation, but in those of contradiction.

Disidentification is the third or neutral position envisioned by Claire Lejeune where "contraries cease being perceived as contradictions" (15) because they are framed not within the terms of logic which are "monologic" but in those of the dialogic. This "heterogeneity" or incommensurable difference is the terrain of paradox and oxymoron, confounding subject and object of desire in an "aesthetics of chaos" produced by an "infinity of possible tensions between appearance and reality" (Lejeune 37). The "foreignness of the third" will deploy itself in hybridized and infinitely cross-fertilizing languages.

This "trapeze of in-between" (Harman 116) in which the marginal is positioned outside the free-flowing regularity of "habitus" forces the condition of the exile, but may also be a learned ignorance, that of the observing ethnographer who has an eye on two worlds as s/he moves back and forth between them. As Caucasianist within Canada, NourbeSe Philip engages in the sense-making activity of mapping boundaries. In such reflection and self-observation, she is caught up in a "reflexive crisis" where unmediated, habitual action is challenged through the defamiliarization of the observing eye which subjects it to reflection, to mediated, interpretive action. The reflexive crisis is produced for both observer and observed. The dilemma of observation is to be both within and without, to make sense of difference on its own terms, then to have difference inform one's own terms. Every action is perceived embedded in historical necessity, as a text within a discourse. In-between, the observer looking ahead only looks behind while the boundaries which form habitus take shape before her eyes (Harman 120).

The act of mapping itself produces metamorphosis, rendering the world readable and, hence, explicable by transforming the strange to the familiar, hyphenating, that is shuttling back and forth between here and there, between now and then, transcoding, reconfiguring relations. Constant movement produces a disjunction that is loss, grounds of allegoresis or reading. In the resulting configuration of a provisional or invented identity is the emergence of a critical/creative discourse on the possibilities for constructing syncretic languages and literatures, of layering to form "new identities," Caribbean "demotic" as "Canadian."

CANADIAN? LITERARY? THEORY?

❖

Not the sardonic demand of A.J.M. Smith — "Wanted: Canadian Criticism" — this is not a narrative from lack as impetus for invention of a metadiscourse on Canadian literature and Canadian theory, repetition foregrounding the figures and narratives in which the demand has been continually articulated. Tropology, not topocentrism.

Interrogatives frame this as manipulation of texts on criticism and theory in anglophone Canada. Interrogatives insert gaps, interrupt the flow narrating the (im)possibility of Canadian theory. Question mark, inserted to problematize, to frame this textual in(ter)vention as diacritical pro-ject, functions as substitute for the hyphen, *trait d'union*, which works (the) in-between incommensurable terms, the space of the *différend*, shunting back and forth, separating, conflating Canadian/theory. Canadian-theory. Cantheory. Canadian? Theory? Disjunctive link? A space of *différance*. In this way, I remark the canonical question — how can a text be Literature when it's Canadian? — and its categories of plus/minus Canadian (Canadian/Theory), res(c)iting it within a discourse of contamination. This is, as Mary Douglas has suggested, to risk danger by exposing the permeability of margins and defiling purity, purity understood as the imposition of the logical categories of non-contradiction "tidily order[ing]" the values and ideas of a group into a standardized positive pattern that constitutes a culture and mediates the experience of individuals through a system of classification (38 – 39). It may be merely a ritual defilement pre-figured as opposition within that ideal cultural order. Non-sense, for instance. ("Ludic ruse.") Or scapegoat. ("N errative.") Possibly, hybridization as interrogative critique. ("Bricolage.") Displacement producing change? ("Polytics"?) In an economy of waste, or loss (*usure*), this is writing living on, bordering on. Not going beyond, though excessive. Paracritical. Symptomatic rereading some tropes of the Literary imaginary in anglophone Canada. Relativizing pro-ject. Interrogating truth-claims in writing effects.

N errative this text performs nomadically, a frame blurring borders, realigning categories, as it mediates between inside and outside in its role as "liminary" or introduction. The texts it frames overlap to a certain extent since they developed as reading in courses on Canadian literary theory mapping the institutionalization of Canadian Literature through the elaboration of critical fictions prescribing, describing, promoting, analyzing — constructing — the categories "Literary," "Canadian," and "Theory." Only parts of these conversations are overheard here. Some were developed only in oral form or seminar papers. Others have already appeared in print in different forums (Conway, Creelman). The resemblance is most marked in approach, in the strategy of symptomatic reading for the tropes, the contradictions, the moments when texts turn back on their presuppositions and write in excess of their meaning. This "interpretive re-reading" examines "the operation of the 'grammar' of each figure of discourse, its syntactic laws or requirements, its imaginary configurations, its metaphoric networks," and probes "its silences" (Irigaray 75). It is a reading not for meaning but to unfold the processes of meaning making. Repeating theoreticians' utterances, it is a reading *with* (and against) the text. Touching on. Re-inscription or transcoding "allows texts/language to live on. ..." Re-writing Andrew Benjamin, this may be articulated as "the possibility of rewriting is the possibility of theory (philosophy)." "Theory lives on in rewriting and re-writing survives even theory." Rewriting confronts the text as other, "as the site of differential plurality" and allows for the interpretive rereading of the word as a site of conflict, as the "recognition of non-correspondence as non-correspondence" (176). In interpretation, a process, what is presented is not the object of interpretation; rather, as it proceeds, an initial presentation points to something further that was not, at first, presented. What seemed to be original is not independent of the interpretive chain, but "always already a re-writing" (147). There is no inside/outside of re-writing, re-reading. The (im)possibility of re-writing is the condition of interpretation, of theory. The (im)possibility of theory. Living on ...

What these texts live on, border on, is what is othered, outtered by this framing, in the very uttering and inscribing as a discursive field — namely the discursive object the texts collectively construct, "Canadian Literary theory." The force of their interruption, however, at the site of differential plurality, is to displace the metaphors of the conflictual model that have dominated theoretical discourses in anglophone Canada through an emergent metaphor of dialogue or combinatory. This frames discourse on anglophone Canadian literature as a field of differential relations, not in the singular as "Theory." There are theories in circulation, working to different effect, producing differential subject positions that authorize some speaking subjects and some kinds of knowledges while excluding others. "Theory" is being thought beyond the relationship of inside/outside, not only beyond the opposition Canadian/foreign, but beyond the distinction world/language, landscape/langscape, that establishes asymmetric relations between original and reproduction, literal and figural. The distinctions maintained by such (im)possible purity are dissolved in a theory of contamination which, locating the figural in the heart of the literal, considers them equally textualized and contingent. Relational terms, distinguishing and binding to a common internally differentiated unit of value, they are not identities. Performances, rather, in that as figures, they deploy performatives, promising instead of giving (Derrida 1982, 209). Concern is shifted from a relationship between interpretation and object of interpretation to the implications and presuppositions of that particular interpretation or re-reading/re-writing.

This entails a shift from an economy of substitution (analogy, metaphor, condensation) to an economy of contamination (combination, metonymy, displacement). Not concerned with axiological issues in a regime of truth, the regime of interpretation focuses on ethical questions of effect: not on evaluating the Good and the True but on the contingencies of their exclusionary force. On the power of constructions, inventions. "North of intention." Beyond the author to the author-effect in the re-circulation of (critical) fictions. Ethics is no retreat from rigour of analysis but rather a shift in focus from questions of representation and adequation to those of language, action and their complex imbrication — a pragmatics of theories. This is staged as bringing to self-reflexivity the subjectification to institutions and knowledge. It is not a matter of an "abstract 'truth-value' but of how well it performs various desired/able functions for the various people who may at any time be concretely involved with it" (Barbara Herrstein Smith, 22), and entails an interrogation of the narratives through which such truth-claims are legitimated or "naturalized" as the "real" (Lyotard).

In the liminal, site of transformation, a frame is mobile, elastic, turning the subject under analysis in a different direction, a promise rather than a completed enunciation. The history of theories of the literary, like the histories of literary institutions in anglophone Canada, are still to be written. (This project is further advanced in Quebec. See my essay, 1990a). A question they have to contend with is the status of the Literary in colonial space. Literature, in the modern sense of the term, must be territorialized. Since the Renaissance, the mark of nationality in literature has been language. Canadians writing in English break the chain nation, language, literature. "Canadian Literature" is a contradiction in terms, for to be acknowledged as *good*, as "Literature," Canadians must follow the norms of writing in England. To be recognized as true, as authentically "Canadian," they must break these norms by writing "differently." Such purity is (im)possible in the Canadian situation where there is a non-coincidence of political and linguistic boundaries. Strategically rather than culturally formed, Canada has no authoritative culture with a collective sense of belonging. Literatures (in the plural) are produced in the languages of other nation states, deterritorialized, "minor literatures," as Deleuze has characterized them — nomadic — probing the "literary" (im)possibilities of idiolects, limit writing that may be innovative, marking a rupture, or non-sense, without meaning in the literary system (Godard 1987b).

The non-literariness of their literatures is the paradox that writers and theorists in Canada must confront, the ambiguity of their within/without position straddling literary institutions with opposing norms. Most frequently, this problematic has been framed not in terms of paradox or ambiguity, but in those of binary opposition, of "plus" or "minus" Canadian, in the phrase of Cameron and Dixon, who summarize thus the conditions of literary and critical response described by Northrop Frye, namely the requirement to broaden the conception of the literary to read the social and historical life of Canada as the Literary (the "Canadian context" or "plus"), in opposition to situating "orthodox genres of poetry and fiction" within "an autonomous world of literature" (literariness as criterion of the Literary or "minus" Canadian) (Frye 1965,

821–22, qtd. in Cameron and Dixon 138). In their Introduction, whose function is clearly signalled in the title, "Mandatory Subversive Manifesto: Canadian Criticism vs. Literary Criticism," Cameron and Dixon herald the succeeding "penultimate essays" (138) as attempts to detach Canadian texts from the sociological or historical meaning invested in "Canadian," away from a study of themes that constitute the repertoire of "Canadian consciousness" — a focus on context that collapses into an exclusive concern with content — to emphasize a discourse of the Literary "beyond nationality" (141) that will focus attention on the crafting of the literary object in an order of language — a focus on form in symbiosis with content, poetics not criticism (140).

What this manifesto overlooks, however, is that meanings are made through the theoretical frames brought to bear on texts; theories that discern the literary are produced as a function both of readers reading and institutions legitimating modes of reading. Moreover, the consequence of this manifesto has been to harden the polarized conceptualization of the Literary in anglophone Canada between Canadian/literary, Native/foreign, though it suggested the need for examining the Canadianness of this literature "within a consistent series of *comparative* contexts" (140; my emphasis) and for conceptualizing the Literary in relation to psychology, sociology, and philosophy (141). Significantly, the understanding of "context" has been extended beyond those of history and geography which have produced the dominant topocentrism or "geographical fallacy" of Canadian literary theorizing with its concern for discerning "where is here," of situating the subject in spatial terms, either taxonomically or phenomenologically, rather than with "who am I" (Frye 1965, 826) engaging in ontological speculation or the text as singular entity. Such polarization masks the fact that questions of cultural difference — of nation, class, race, gender, region — may well be the crucial frames that construct systems of meanings for readers reading texts. That they are Canadian, and not just part of World Literature in englishes, is surely one of the meanings that many readers make of anglophone Canadian texts whether or not these readers are Canadian. That this is no longer the only way to read these texts is equally clear, as the internationalization of studies of Canadian literature has demonstrated, especially in light of the world-wide academic interest in Margaret Atwood whose writing is analysed without any regard to her Canadianness.[1]

These different frames for reading Atwood situate her texts within different canons, arrived at through different concepts (norms) of the Literary. While the latter sees the Literary as a function of the author and the work either as an outstandingly crafted object or as an expression of an exceptional individual, the former makes explicit a political imperative and the work of Literature as mediation of the cultural values of specific interests. The terms "Canadian literature" or "theory" are not embodied in the texts or authors themselves but are invested by institutionalized reading practices and their narratives of legitimation. An interest in postmodernism or theory or Romantic poetry is not axiomatic in, nor productive of, an interest in Canadian literature. Without some form of nationalism (national difference, that is), the textual system of the Literary would not overlap with the textual system of the Canadian. Nationalism is the political imperative overdetermining this intersection. Such convergences are interested ones, made by readers produced to find such categorical distinctions meaningful by the institutions — academic, cultural, and governmental — that order the symbolic relations of a particular culture, establishing its categories of meaning and value. These are inevitably interested categories, relations of ruling ordering the desired/able forms and protocols of knowledge as discursive practices. Subjects are constructed by them in positions of dominance or subordination. The questions to raise are ethical ones regarding the exclusionary force of these contingent values. What interests are at stake in a particular critical narrative or allegory of reading? Allegory, as Paul de Man has argued, is a figure predicated on the discontinuity of a renunciation or break, a figure of the rhetoric of temporality, in which a doubling and simulation are effected. In this, a distant origin is constituted as a promise for re-collection that is un-realizable. Allegory thus speaks through the voice of the other, hence its disjunction and effect as re-venant. Memory which produces the recollection is the voice of the other speaking before in citations, signing in one's place. That is the place of the other. Split, othered, within the self. As double enunciation, allegoresis is the figure of reading. Tracing the figures of reading, the tropological moves of readers reading, exposes some of the narrative pragmatics and stakes at play in the politics of literary theory, theory which is, in de Man's words, "controlled reflection on the formation of method" (de Man 1982, 3).

"Canadian" is one of the elements — as presence or absence — to be theorized in any grappling with the Literary in respect to the literature produced in anglophone Canada whether explicitly or implicitly. What "Canadian" means in literary terms is a question that needs to be addressed if only to rephrase it as a problem in the meaning of the "national" as it operates in literary discourse. For the condition of belatedness as a literary field, a gap from Europe or supplementarity, has been a factor that successive generations of Canadian literary theorists, critics and, indeed, writers, have been obliged to negotiate. The contradiction at the heart of the literature. Its (im)possibility. This break is what makes the literature "Canadian," an absence that must be re-covered[2] through narrative which positions the Canadian literatures in some relationship — discontinuous or continuous — with the literatures in English or in French in Europe or in their far-flung post-colonial legacies as literatures of the "Commonwealth" or "francophonie." Canadian literatures thus need to be theorized as a problem in comparative literatures, as (a) field(s) of relational differences. The project of literary theory needs to be approached intertextually, interdiscursively. That is, one must locate Canadian literary theory through an examination of the history of its institutionalization and of the various narratives produced to negotiate the gap effected by the emigration of European settler communities to North America, whether these be the origin myths promising a brilliant new national literature either as re-naissant by analogy with, or as evolving in continuation from, the process that formed European literatures — continuity in the future — or origin myths of an unsung virginal wilderness emphasizing discontinuity, or myths of decline and fall that stress continuity in an elegiac mode. All e-rase the aboriginals with their different and oral mythologies.

Canadian literature is positioned thus in relational terms with respect to its European inheritance. Moreover, the very terms in which the argument for discontinuity — for the originality — of the Canadian literatures has been staged have themselves circulated widely beyond the boundaries of Canada — as Neoclassicism, Romanticism,

Modernism, respectively — though they have been articulated differently in light of the micropolitics of local cultures. Belatedness opens possibilities for graftings that produce hybrid formulations reworking the very presuppositions of the initial premises (Godard 1987d). To trace the specificity of Canadian literary discourse is a project doomed by an impossible dream of purity. A more productive strategy is to pay systematic attention to the highly selective processes of appropriation and realignment that have taken place throughout the history of the Canadian literatures. Theories have been borrowed, rewritten, and used for new ends — veritable patchworks — in order to theorize literary practices in Canada and *invent* Canadian literature. Sometimes and in some places, there may have been more interest in appropriating theoretical premises from England; in other places and times, the impact of American practices has had greater effect. While in other literatures an agonal relationship is said to have developed between so-called Anglo-American and French feminist theories, between gynocriticism and feminist critique (Showalter), feminist theorists in Canada have drawn on both strands in a productive cross-fertilization.

That there is a lack of homogeneity in the "Canadian tradition" of literary theory has been frequently argued in the case of Northrop Frye whose theories of "Literature" and of "Canadian Literature" are, in the view of Eli Mandel, "schizophrenic" (Mandel 1971, 3). Moreover, Frye's move in his "Conclusion" to the *Literary History of Canada* to enlarge the category of the Literary to include more than the traditional high genres of poetry and fiction and to reject an axiological approach in favour of poetics contradicted the approach of other contributors to the more narrowly "literary" chapters that are so heavily evaluative they raised Margaret Atwood's hackles (Atwood 1972, 23). Frye's approach was, as Sandra Djwa has suggested, a strategic manoeuvre in the effort to legitimate Canadian literature on the terms that Carl Klinck as editor of the volume had established, literature understood in a broad *belle lettristic* sense rather than in the narrower specialist terms, advocated by other editors. Occurring in the 1950s – 1960s, this may be read as a manifestory intervention in the process of professionalization on the side of English studies along the model of literary history as the history of ideas, institutionalized at the University of Toronto, against the attempted inroads of both "Leavisite" evaluative criticism and "New Criticism," with their narrower category of the Literary and focus on the close textual analysis of "practical criticism." That it had a certain force can be seen by the subsequent proliferation of "thematic" criticism, the dominant mode supporting expansion of the academic study of Canadian literatures in the 1970s. The concept of the Literary here is produced in certain allegories of reading at certain institutional conjunctures that work the gap producing the (im)possibility of Canadian literature.[3]

While the particularities of the terms in question may be unique to the situation of Canadian theory, this paradox is the aporia of any attempt to theorize the literary. The literary is what is inexplicit, what can only be read in theories of the literary. Literature and the rest, or remains. The literary and its theory are two events to be read as reciprocal figures. A paradox this is, for literature, a model in itself, can only be approached through another model external to it (Bessière 10). To specify the literary presupposes an exterior from which to demarcate it, noting a difference without giving it an identity. In its action, the literary attempts to establish itself as the plenitude of logos designating the order by which it is constituted. This order or set of presuppositions instituting categories is what can never be examined from within the system, the centre which is simultaneously, and paradoxically, the margin of the literary (Derrida 1967). However, it can only actualize itself by a continuous play of negation which situates it once again with respect to an elsewhere — figured as an adversarial or perhaps transgressive relation — by which the literary is authorized (Bessière 22). A third term is always invoked in any singular definition of the literary, even if the literary is discerned in terms of its literariness or poeticity, that is, in terms of its language. For the literary is inscribed in ordinary language and only through the use of this language may be recognized the marks of its literary usage. What began as a distinction between literary/non-literary becomes blurred, confounded. "The literary here is a strict relativization and a precise historical instance, indissociable from the cultural status of writing and of reading" (Bessière 24). Consequently, there is always a[n/other] in the literary: "the literary is a mode of heterogeneity, a complex of discursive activity" (Bessière 26). To specify the literary is to mark interpretation. This presupposes a figure of the writer, a figuration of identity such as the "persona" constituted in the linguistic interpretation of discourse, and a figuration of the reader who is constituted in the interpretation of that interpretation (Bessière 11). A second structure is produced in this doubling of language. This is not what is reflected by a model but what makes of its object the object of possible knowing, a mode of "prefiguration" (Bessière 12) or bringing to self-reflexivity. The state of this object and the movement of this object is determined by the literary from the limit of the act of writing, limit it never stops exposing as such. In that it reaches no literal and entails no totalizable object, the literary is "rhetoric." "Rhetoric" is not the negation of signification but its construction through a mediation that knows its limit" (Bessière 12). Rhetoric as mode(a)lization engages in exposing the imbrication of the literary in its network of languages, discourses, practices.

Before situating the following essays on the rhetoric of contemporary Canadian criticism/theory, I want briefly to track the narratives articulating current discursive practices, narratives of crisis and agon, for which I shall substitute excess and paradox. Writing on ... Living on ... The rhetoric of crisis is most forcefully mobilized in Robert Lecker's polemical inquiry into the canon-forming practices of the last twenty-five years which he characterizes as the "delegitimation crisis" (1990, 660). This in itself has produced conflictual responses which converge only in pointing to the persistence of the colonial cringe in Lecker's rhetoric that idealizes critical practice in the United States (Davey 1990, 674) and does nothing to unseat the hegemony of British classics in the Canadian academy (Ware 485). Underlining the paradoxes of Lecker's claimed neutrality that is at odds with the unarticulated values accounting for his judgements, his vaunted innovation of the advocacy of experimental texts struggling against a critical formalism, so that he "serves the conservative interests of his institution" (Ware 491), respondents turn the question of the canon into one of cannons, framing crisis as agon between opposing theories and values.

In the name of continuity, rather than discontinuity, Ware develops an evolutionary narrative producing a tradition of writing in Canada that has privileged a "feeling for place" over a "feeling for time" (Ware 489) in order to stake out a place in the canon for his own interest in eighteenth- and nineteenth-century Canadian poetry. He points out both the exclusion of poetry from Lecker's analysis and his conflation of post-modernism and post-structuralism. This collapsing of the "infinitized free-play" of post-modernism and the "radically disarticulating force of deconstruction" (Clark 84, qtd. in Ware 490) is a particularity of contemporary Canadian literary theory not found in the United States or in France where deconstructive reading has on the contrary developed through powerful disruptive readings of texts from earlier periods (Godard 1989). In fact, arguments have been made that post-structuralism is a poetics of Modernism, not of the Postmodern. In the United States, deconstruction has been almost synonymous with nineteenth-century studies through the institutional influence exerted by the Yale critics. Through this conflation of the "posts," Lecker writes in excess of his meaning, revealing himself to be defending a local alignment of theory and text which places him within the nationalist quagmire he professes to be beyond. Similarly, while Ware foregrounds his own political stakes in this institutional quarrel over the direction of studies of anglophone Canadian literature, whether or not it will have a place for anything other than reviews of current literary productions (and hence accord any symbolic meaning and value to his essays on earlier poets), the claims for history, for literary historiography as a pragmatics of literary knowledge on what seem to be conservative terms, have the effect of the new, adumbrating theoretical lines that will produce different textual and institutional configurations and narratives than those currently dominant, underlining the potentials for change in the residual historical mode (Cameron 1990, 124) when it abandons description for an analysis of symbolic mediation. (How many students have you seen recently choose a course on the Confederation Poets over one on the Canadian Postmodern? Regulation of scarce economic and symbolic resources producing the profession and the canon.)

I linger on this most recent phase in the on-going "crisis" of literary studies since it most forcefully exposes the political stakes in the debates, masked in most articulations under a claim for critical objectivity, or disinterested clarity, appeals to "common sense" and customary practice ("perfectly sensible," Darling 176; "neutral reader," Mathews 1989, 159; "me as an ordinary reader, a member of the great un(post)washed," Mathews 1990, 162), that are attempts to construct an "outside" from which to engage in theorizing the literary through the negativity of critique. This is a deictic process that constructs the speaker as subject "inside" and the theory under examination as object "outside" the enunciative contract with the reader. (I/you = we against s/he or them.) Positioning the speaker thus within "normal" relations is a strategy of alibiing, in Barthes' terms (1973, 123), an ideological manoeuvre of "naturalization," of masquerading a system of values as a system of facts.

This particular interchange also launches the customary salvos: History against Theory, plus against minus Canadian. At its most neutral, this tension is framed as the ampersand problem — "Literary Theory and Canadian Literature" (Moss 1987) or "Resistance and Reception ... [of] Theory" (Murray 1990) — two mutually exclusive categories whose interrelation is the object of inquiry. Will it still be Theory if it is Canadian theory? Theory as the "new" which, in demanding some form of accommodation, has resulted in "an uneasy fit," less "blindness of neglect" than "curricular superaddition" (Murray 1990, 52–53). In rejecting a model of the discipline as "conflictual and resistant" by definition or a model of domination by a single paradigm against which battle must be done, in favour of a metaphor of "sedimentation," Murray implicitly signals a position of acceptance. So too does Barry Cameron, in describing the contemporary theoretical "moment" as a complex of co-existing dominant, residual, and emergent paradigms (Cameron 1990, 124). A model of heterogeneity, it contrasts with the singularity productive of binary oppositions in a dominant model that would "wall out the chaos" (Cameron 1990, 138). Such insistence on homogeneity is a discursive strategy by which hegemony is exercized, fixing thus restrictively the thinkable, the sayable.

For the figuration of theory by those rejecting the readings that may be generated by various post-structuralist theories eschews such balanced phrases and heterogeneity for narratives constructed around the myth of the fall or around the alterity of theory — elitist, foreign, obscure. Both present current practices as consensual and normal, any change from which is regressive, not progressive. "A ... Twayne's Gonna Fall" (Darling; my emphasis). "Future Imperfect" not "Future Indicative" (Mathews 1990; my emphasis). "[T]he Critic's New Clothes" (MacLulich 1987), which like the Emperor's, prove to be so obfuscating, that it takes a child's detached clarity to discern the nakedness of theory's hyperbole. Child's play. The moves to trivialize (ridicule) or exoticize are exclusionary strategies regularly used to marginalize people or opinions by casting them as "outsiders" of low or abnormal status. The metaphor of the Fall frames the critical moment in a rhetoric of clash, as drama or theatre in the tragic mode. While this might lead to a consideration of the relation between "theory" as "controlled reflection" on method and "theatre" as site of transformation, acts of looking or "spectacle" connected through the Greek *theoreo* (to be a spectator), this is not a self-consciously staged theatrical re-presentation, but a rewriting of the biblical myth of the Fall in the prophetic mode.

Denouncing theory for its totalizing claims, these narratives are blind to their own apocalyptic rhetoric which has constructed this conjuncture within their interpretive chain as myth of the Fall. Where, asks Mathews, is the justification for the "guru" status of "postmodern critics" "regarded" as "Holy Writ"? (Mathews 1990, 163). Cameron *might as well be* calling Stich "an *unsaved loved one under conviction*" (Mathews 1990, 163; my emphasis). Rhetoric is mobilized here in support of a canonic or singular Truth in a discourse of power mined, however, by the force of its own rhetoric which, excessive, draws attention to its status as critical *fiction*, as contingent and provisional.

This is "resistance" as de Man has elaborated it, a consideration of contemporary literary theory as "pure verbalism," as "absolute fictions" in a tropological manoeuvre that denies its own fictiveness by asserting the primacy of a referential function for language and a mimetic status for art (de Man 1982, 11). Just as MacLulich with his fairy-tale fable produces a critical fiction as an elaborate fabulation, the myth-making critical fictions of Darling and Mathews resist the rhetorical or tropological dimensions of language and fail to bring their own fictions to self-reflexivity within the pragmatics and contingencies of the enunciative instance (whose interests are being served by their speaking?) and hence to scrutinize their self-figurations as writers and readers. Prophets, judges. Such self-reflexive allegories of reading, where critical fiction is framed as fiction, as contingent and provisional truth-claim, may be read elsewhere, in this collection and in some of the texts examined, as these tropological analyses bring them to a crisis. They may also be located in the future conditional narratives of Cassandra rewriting Homer and Giraudoux as the conflictual field of Canadian literary theories (Godard

1985c) or the fairy tale of metamorphosis framing a narrative of complicity or theoretical impurity, that of the insightful blindness of Canadian feminist critics to their theoretical presuppositions when Beauty, through the transforming eye of love, metamorphoses Beastly theory and makes it an agent for change (Kamboureli 1990).

It is interesting to note the differences between MacLulich's tale of the failure to achieve metamorphosis or change after the unmasking of the magic in the signifier "Theory," a narrative in which he is arguing for the status quo of thematic criticism as the repository of humanistic values, and Kamboureli's tale of the power of this magic to produce change in the form of heterogeneity opening up a hegemonic discourse through the trope of heterosexual cross-transference as figure of mixity.[4] The first deploys its fable by analogy to assert claims for the self-evidence or transparency of meaning, in an alethetic moment uncovering continuity; the second self-reflexively re-cites the fable as an allegory of reading and a model for generating other readings, that is as a model for mediating and constructing meanings which inevitably speak beyond themselves, their excess producing (powerful?) misreadings. Reading beyond the fable, here one finds a narrative of change, gendered difference of necessity at the present moment being positioned at a site of challenge to the discursive system of the literary, inscribed as it is in male-dominated discursive practices. "Allegories of reading."

These allegories "tidily order" values and ideas into a standardized pattern mediating a system of classification through the imposition of the categories of non-contradiction. The mutually exclusive terms, through which theory is totalized and scapegoated include the following (theory is on the left, the speaker on the right):

> totalizing/ open-minded
> ("these papers reveal oddly monolithic mindsets" Mathews 1990, 162)

> slavish imitation / original masterpiece
> (absence of "personal, original theories" Mathews 163)
> ("derivative or second-hand without meaning to be so" Serafin 21)

banal / interesting
("servant of banal trendiness" Mathews 171)

empty / full
("barren foolery," "simplemindedness," Mathews 170)

ecstatic / objective
("ecstatic-identification-with-the-god mode of discourse"
Mathews 172)

jargon / plain speaking
("obfuscation instead of clarity" Darling 172)
("jargon" "compelled to detract from perfectly sensible
explanations" Darling 176)
("jaw-breaking and mind-bending critical neologisms" Mac-
Lulich 1987, 32)

redundant / original
("He uses this word and its cognates approximately 75 times,"
Darling 173)

monstrous / ordinary
("Hybrid Curiosity" Garebian)
("The Martian of Estevan" Mathews 1989)

foreign / native
("Colonial Mentality" Serafin)

sick / healthy
("poststructuralist blight" Darling 175)

death / life
("strangling [his] critical enterprise" Darling 173)

error / truth
("terms ... frequently used wrongly" Darling 173)

The highest praise that can be bestowed on a critic is "that he regards [his subject] as the heartbeat of a culture, not as a semiotic exercize" (Kertzer 1990, 183). A crucial strategy of these polemics is to conflate institutional norms of knowledge, objectivity, originality, with emotionally prized values such as health, life, community, and to equate these to Truth. The speaker claims to be in possession of these values that are missing in the object of analysis.

The effect of these often contradictory valences is to deny that practioners of poststructuralist theories have developed new insightful readings of Canadian literary texts. The stress on originality and innovation with regards to literary truth, repeated in the denunciation of the importation of foreign theories resulting in "viral" contamination, underlines the Romantic grounds for this theoretical stance. To the neo-classicist, learning from the models of the ancients is a privileged access to universal literary truths. This is a strategic misreading, moreover, since the project of any theoretical position is, by definition, concerned rather with showing how meanings are made within a system of literary discourse that generates many potential texts and meanings. Their object is the elaboration of literary discourse and thematizes variously the act of enunciation, that is the production, reproduction, and reception of the literary (Godard 1987d, 27). Poetics as opposed to criticism, virtual rather than actualized meaning. Hypothesis generation or fictionalizing. "As if ..."

This entails, however, another dialectic, that of theories of language that are "representationalist," assuming a mimetic relation between a text and a pre-constituted "reality" that produces an expressive-realist theory of the text, as opposed to a post-Saussurean theory of language as a signifying system that mediates the construction of texts and meanings. Opposition to theory may well stem in part from the absence of "objectivity" guaranteeing the models of the literary and the indeterminacy of the taxonomies provided. To acknowledge the primacy of language as sign, both signifier and signified, is to accept the provisionality and the contingency of one's utterance. This elides the boundaries between the creative and the critical act. Such a slippage has a particular force in the Canadian academy where the role of poet-professor is a frequent one. Rejection of the rhetoricity of one's critical utterances may well be a strategy for retaining the figuration of critic as evaluator, as arbiter of taste, rather than as spinner of poetic fables. In Canadian society, the judge has more prestige and power, both political and economic, than has the poet. (Judges have yet to perceive their involvement in criticism evaluating the truth-claims of competing narratives.)

There are, however, other issues involved in the emergence of contemporary literary theories in the current Canadian scene entailing a shift in the alignments of the literary. Throughout the history of its theorizing, the literary has been defined negatively by what it is not by comparison to other forms of knowledge with respect to their truth-claims. Plato considered the literary in relation to both the theological and the political, and found it a less clear and singular form of knowing. Aristotle, however, thought that the literary was more powerful than the historical, since its insight was not limited to the singular event, but might be generalized and universalized. Twentieth-century theories of the literary carry the baggage of this theological and metaphysical tradition, reinforced by Romantic theories of the word as primal generating force. They also have inherited a neoclassical tradition viewing the literary as the repository of the best that has been thought, as the embodiment of a general and humane knowledge from the past, whose attainment is the highest human good. One of the intellectual developments of the nineteenth century, which saw the emergence of the disciplinary bodies of knowledge that shape modern universities, was the separation of the discipline of history from that of literature both, as Hayden White has demonstrated, concerned with the production and analysis of narrative.[5] The analytico-referential discourse of empiricism also turned its lenses on what it had hitherto ignored in its concern with mapping and exploring the globe and the properties of nature, namely on the subject engaged in observing these objects, with the resulting emergence of psychology and sociology as the "human sciences."

These empirical projects have all been brought to a crisis in the twentieth century by linguistics and the philosophy of language which have foregrounded the mediation of signification in the construction of these bodies of knowledge, pointing to their status as provisional or hypothetical modellings of the "real." As the growing number of narratives detailing the development of theory and criticism of the Canadian literatures has made clear, the literary in Canada has been approached through the lens of geography as a legacy of its status as a locus of "exploration" producing the "environmental determinism" (Cameron 1990) or geographical fallacy of dominant literary theories. Significantly, this has produced an identificatory fiction that evades the potential schisms of such fictions grounded in genealogical narratives which advance ethnic, racial, and linguistic differences. This has been modified by the imperatives of Romantic cultural nationalism with their demand for origin myths and privileging of history, so that the discourse of professional historians of Canada has become the most authoritative discourse discerning Canadianness. This reinforces the claims to legitimacy of literary historiography with its linear narratives in discerning the specificity of the "Canadian" literary over the synchronic hypotheses of poetics.

Into these models have been introduced since the 1970s the presuppositions of the philosophy of language drawing attention to the self-reflexiveness of all utterance, its (im)possible project of discovering the "real Canada," pointing out, like the child to the Emperor, that the new clothes are simulacra produced in a differential system of signifiers along axes of substitution and combination. When a country has yet to be "invented" (fixed in a single authoritative narrative), exposing the indeterminacy of any of the attempts at mapping it, is to condemn one, like Ferron's cartographer, to "an uncertain country." Its identity fictions are forever deferred, (im)possible projects. The possibility of fixing and defining becomes all the more desir/able a project. The insights of poststructuralist theory for those schooled in an empirical tradition valuing facts not as (f)acts (fictional acts) but as stable verities is unsettling for they upset the normal modes of ordering. Theories of signification do not construct the literary as the habitual discrete body of objects, as texts, that can be mastered and contained, but as an indeterminate flux that is invented and reinvented in allegories of reading caught up in a paracitical order of words. This order is (miraculously) taken for the "real": it certainly produces "effects of the real" (Barthes) through the classificatory relations it regulates and the institutional practices its narratives consolidate in naturalizing, by erasing the work of producing, the authority of specific interests/subjects.

Some provisional reports of reading are gathered here. These are inevitably interested reports, though the political effects of their interventions differ. All are concerned to position poetics, rhetoric, as part of the sayable in the institutional debate on a national Canadian literature. Some positional readings are also oppositional ones. Gender is such a point of diffraction implicitly and explicitly realigning interpretive chains. The readers frame their own allegories as tropological incursions, reading for the contradictions, the elisions, the figurations of some critical texts producing Canadian literary discourse. Concerned with what the text is saying, they also investigate how the text speaks beyond itself. Where are its silences? Its unexamined/able presuppositions? Like the allegories they read, these critical fictions are open to mis-reading, most immediately in the unspoken assumptions of the discursive context of their production, a communal conversation, overdetermination their joint publication exposes. Most central is the concern with the work of the signifier "Canadian" in the field of literary discourse. What happens to its tropological moves to unify when the complexities of gender, race, or ethnic and linguistic difference are introduced?

In "Canadian Literature Criticism: Between the Poles of the Universal-Particular Antimony," Lianne Moyes introduces questions of temporality to disrupt the totalization of "Theory" in current constructions of the debate which figure the "entry" of theory in the 1970s, by showing the problematic of the literary/the Canadian, and theorizations thereof, to be a long-standing topos of Canadian literary discourse. This disrupts the debates around the "importation" of theory that characterize the present critical scene in terms of the "rape of the virgin land," by demonstrating the continuity of the production and circulation of theories of the literary in Canada for a century before the current "moment," from E.H. Dewart's prefatory remarks of 1864, Northrop Frye's concluding summary of the *Literary History of Canada* in 1964, through Frank Davey's "Surviving the Paraphrase" in 1974. Beginning with A.J.M. Smith's articulation of the universal/particular binary, and situating the various critics/theoreticians within this paradigm, Moyes then takes up a

193

different line of analysis, postulating the "radical continuity" of these binaries with each other, mutually contaminating and constituting as "relational differences" in a signifying system of "Canadian."

This binary opposition, she contends, enables critics to "naturalize and authorize the hegemony of specific interests" within literary discursive practices of Canadian literature (29). These antimonies work in both diachronic analysis of the evolution of Canadian literary discourse and synchronically within any particular *moment* of these discourses. Adopting the synchronic approach of poetics, Moyes reads critical narratives as a system of cultural signification whereby a Canadian "national" culture is brought into being. Through her deconstructive reading against the grain to bring the contradictions of these manifestoes to a crisis, Moyes initiates an analysis of the ideological investments of literary theories as discursive practices.

Jennifer Henderson extends this line of ideological reading in the mode of politico-symbolic relations constituted by the territorial frontiers of critical and literary inscriptions through a problematization of the work of gender in the feminization of a Canadian literary in her essay "Gender in the Discourse of English-Canadian Literary Criticism." Noting an emergent feminist postcolonialist discourse that engages in textual strategies of metaphorical displacement and implicit assertion of homologies between the female body and territorialization that dominate this approach, Henderson explores the work of this trope in three "moments" that interrogate the borders set in place by each. Establishing first through a figural analysis the way in which "gender" is taken to be a category in the making of a national Canadian literature by examining the trope as deployed by some contemporary male theorists in Canada — how George Bowering, for example, sets up the "official Canlit" of the sixties and seventies as a "matriarchy" in which feminist discourse took the lead in establishing a "Canadian" discourse beyond the colonized discourse of an earlier period in experimental, language-centred writing — Henderson goes on in a second "moment" to show how this conflation of woman/body territory for occupation has functioned in a metaphor of the double or triple colonization of Canadian women writers as inscribed in the critical narratives of Irvine and Howells writing from the Empire on the occupied colony.

The sexual difference of the first inscription is reread within a second frame of othering, where the feminine territory is framed as the inscrutable, the oriental, whose codes must be uncovered if this "feminine hieroglyphics" (in Irvine's words) are to become readable, knowable to the imperial centre. Implicit in Henderson's analysis is a reading of these imperialist narratives that homogenize and unify the traits of this writing, allowing differences only in quantity so as to read gender as a metaphor for "a distinctly Canadian ethos," in contrast to collections by Canadian feminist critics that proliferate heterogeneous narratives and problematize the fiction of national identity by introducing questions of linguistic and racial difference.

Working still within a problematics of difference, the third "moment" in Henderson's essay introduces the question of exclusion of these differences as a disruption of the territorial imperative. The very different experience of colonialism and resistance of Quebec and aboriginal women, who are not produced as subjects of the emergent Canadian literary discourse able to exchange their symbolic value in the market of postmodernism and postcolonialism posited by the previous two analyses, is examined in the third "moment" which focuses on *Language in Her Eye*. A contradiction is discerned in this book. On the one hand, there is a move to essentialize "gynocracy" or "matriarchy," as Bowering phrased it, which Henderson notes (55) in Kulyk Keefer's separation of language and gender as constitutive of the subject, a manoeuvre that posits gender as a biological given outside the mediations of language and a symbolic system — a strategic tactic of the colonial subject to unify "woman" as site of oppression — and the displacement of this metaphor by the colonized subject who asserts the lack of a common denominator in the category of "woman" as in that of "nation."

Henderson cites Marlene NourbeSe Philip's challenge to the normal symbolic practices that constitute racial others as the illegitimate objects of cultural narratives in which white women are produced as legitimate subjects. The broadening of the work of feminism as the site of resistance to women's oppression into an analysis of anti-racism and anti-imperialism exposes the conflictual social relations underlying the articulation of the codes of nationalism, gender, race operative in the construction of a Canadian literary discourse. As Henderson concludes, such interventions produce "a point of diffraction" (56) in the discourse which, if repeated, could produce a realignment of that discourse to expose the racism that has been operative in the categories of Canadian giving legitimacy and consolidation to the socialization of Canadians.[6] How this might operate has been suggested in the strategies of Ovide Mercredi in the early 1990s as he has deconstructed the fictions of identity of Quebec as self-authorizing fictions of provincial difference by positing a strategic essentialism of the inherent aboriginal rights of "First Nations."

The other essays engage with a different moment in the construction of a National Canadian literature, specifically with contemporary nationalizations-naturalizations of deconstruction by several poets/theorists. Engaging in interpretative rereading of the metaphoric networks, these essays expose the contradictions and contaminations that reinscribe Canadian deconstruction in a metaphysics of presence it would claim to negate. This is particularly the case with Robert Kroetsch, as Darren Wershler-Henry demonstrates in "The (W)Hole in the Middle: The Metaphysics of Presence in the Criticism of Robert Kroetsch." In this essay, he tracks Kroetsch's deconstructive turn as it turns back on itself to reaffirm a metaphysics of presence through the privileging of the alethetic moment of uncovery of a pre-existent truth. The focus on metanarratives, the privileging of voice over writing, the figuration of writer and critic as questor or detective in a labyrinth seeking the answer to a puzzle, the strategy of synecdoche whereby the local functions as general unity — all these produce a negative hermeneutics. The search for absent origins paradoxically turns into the origins of absence. Absence, negativity, becomes reified as the essential Canadian. While Wershler-Henry posits this as a strategic affirmation of identity in the 1970s, when the texts were written, in the context of emergent Canadian nationalism, for Kroetsch to re-publish the essays with few changes and no prefatory discussion of the different historical contingency of the moment of publication is a further demonstration of the ways in which Kroetsch's archeology works to construct narratives of consolidation rather than like Foucault's to interrogate their hegemony.

"Tract Marks: Echoes and Traces in the 'Toronto Research Group,'" by Adeena Karasick takes up a similar question in the theory of bpNichol,

Steve McCaffery, and Barbara Caruso in the 1970s, exposing the tensions between the oral, sacred presence of their phonocentrism and the deferral of presence in the undecidability and *différance* of their grammatology. Quoting playfully from their texts, Karasick displaces this opposition between phone/graph in her strategic rereading. Tracing the implications of their meditations on frame, on the impossibility of translation, on narrative as relational combinatory, on the reader as producer of meaning, she rereads their theory through Steinian "insistence," Baudrillardian "simulacra" and Bataillian "excess" as a story of language writing itself. Like the TRG, Karasick's theory of writing privileges "game, risk, play" to produce a reading with their text in the mode of respectful parody, yet against the text as a forceful misreading or "realignment of (pre-existent) topographies" (85). Stealing this definition of reading from the TRG, Karasick meditates on the work of realigning. Is it replacing or displacing? Is this meaning found or meaning confounded, constructed? Playing with the possibilities, blurring the boundaries between them, folding them into one another in a superimposition, a palimpsest, Karasick stages their — and her — text as "contextactic n'arraticism." Patacritics. Or "tropological idiocies" (87).

The latter term is introduced by Christian Bök, writing in "Nor the Fun Tension: Steve McCaffery and his Critical 'Paradoxy,'" about McCaffery's later theory published in *North of Intention* and about the critical reception of that theory. Bök tracks McCaffery's parody of poststructuralist theory to the practice of *bricolage*, the Deleuzian rhizome of nomadic writing, and the Bataillian economy of usure. McCaffery's textuality with its structural infolding and staged logical contradictions is a challenge to the referential fetish, a celebration of feigning and ludic play that postpones the promise of insight and evaluation that its framing as criticism and reviews holds out. Bök carries out his investigation into McCaffery's poetics in two stages. After symptomatically rereading McCaffery's text to show how it "interrogates the formulae of the restricted economy" (95) and stages its own deconstruction, he then explores the way in which McCaffery's text has been positioned in Canadian literary discourse through a singular authoritative code that neutralizes the doubled structure and pragmatic ethos of his parody. This focuses on an interchange with Bruce Serafin who, in "Colonial

Mentalities," accuses McCaffery of stylistic monotony, superficiality, and a colonial mentality for being slavishly passive to the authority of European theorists. McCaffery, in reply, parodies the authoritative mode of Serafin to charge him with xenophobia and a reductive methodology, enumerating hyperbolically his citations from European theorists to deconstruct the binary Canadian/foreign invoked by Serafin.

Rereading Serafin through McCaffery within a general or unrestricted economy, Bök exposes the contradictions in this construction of "Canadian." Serafin disparages McCaffery both for his "eccentric" novelty and for his inability to properly "steal from the writers he uses and so make their ideas his own" (97). Exposing the paradoxes of this argument where what is at issue is the "appearance" not the "substance" of originality, Bök advances McCaffery's "laud[ing] the unoriginal" as a deconstructive turn of supplementarity, producing a semiotic dispersal through the demonstration of unoriginal difference, of a supplement always already at the source. McCaffery's disruption of the evaluative hierarchy original/copy by rendering it irrelevant in the context of literary analysis is a subversive gesture, suggests Bök, that "disrupts any valorized productivity," truth as "a writing effect." "Intention" displaced northward beyond nationalism to "invention."

Central to Bök's tracing the deconstructive gestures of McCaffery's text is his argument that parody, with its doubled structure and relativized codes, simultaneously authoritative and transgressive, is an example of the "double gesture, double science, double writing" that Derrida advanced in "Signature, Event, Context" as the deconstructive intervention which practices a "reversal of the classical opposition and a general displacement of the system" (96). This work of parody may be read horizontally onto the hyperreferential "echoes" in Karasick's text and onto the ludic play of A/o in my "Can/Con?" which mimics the fetishism of the graph in Stephen Scobie's *Signature Event Cantext: Essays*, reading therein a contradiction in his rewriting of deconstruction as an affirmation of the presence of the letter, framed within a restricted economy, against a Derridean poetics of postponement, displacement in an economy of loss or excess, marked by contradiction, aporia. Mimicry is a strategy of *différance*, of a relativized economy, as Irigaray has argued, not caught up in the logic of the selfsame, of mimesis. "Can/

Con?" re-presents the ludic letter of Scobie's text in order to read there another narrative which his focus on self-inscription had displaced, the construction of an alternate canon of Canadian literature that would put the margins at the centre, would make difference an identity, while erasing the continuum of violence that constructed such marginalization and exclusion. This strategic rereading exposes the ideological work of gender mediating and constructing differential interpretive chains and meanings.

"Theory/Text/Self: Scobietext," by Robert Rawdon Wilson, is another reading of *Signature Event Cantext* as "theory at play" which, through it, raises a more general question about reading theory. After establishing Scobie's authority as a reader of deconstruction and an explicator of Derrida in particular, Wilson reads Scobie against the grain, showing how the text is in excess of itself in its staging of the local/universal paradox. At the centre of this contradiction is Scobie's "dubious proposition" that the proper use of literary theory is to enable interpretive criticism. His deployment of deconstructive theory leads not to the elaboration of a model of deferral but to textual hermeneutics, to the detection of meaning in a group of Canadian texts. The truth-claims of Scobie's commentary stem from an *a priori* position for which the texts serve as demonstration setting in place a binary original/copy which the play on A/o seeks to interrupt. As well, Wilson exposes the contradictions in Scobie's elaboration of the free play of the signifier which he, as is also the case in my text, shows to lead not to the unbounded text and field of metonymic combinations, but to the bound text of the order of the same. Equally paradoxical is Scobie's slippery move on the question of the supplement inscribed in a general economy of writing which he reworks as an important feature (a mark of Canadianness) of the specific texts under analysis, positioning his argument thus on the horns of the universal/particular dilemma prevalent in criticism prior to 1974 (Moyes), and since, in the writing of Kroetsch (Wershler-Henry) and Scobie.

Despite this emergence of continuity in my narrative, a continuity staged through selection and framing within its interpretive chain privileging tropological readings, discontinuity is also figured in Wilson's text. Like the other reading of Scobie's essays, it began as a review commissioned by a "mainstream" Canadian critical periodical, but was rejected for publication because of its focus on theory. Constructed thus as the doxa of reading theory in Canada is a strong misreading that re-writes and re-positions texts by practitioners of theories through a refusal of the premisses of poetics over criticism, either by denouncing them as non-sense or by refusing to engage them at all — exclusionary silencing. A cautionary fable, this figures the field of literary discourse on the Canadian as contestatory, not to overcome this opposition in a narrative of the ultimate acceptance of metatheoretical readings, but to underline once more the impurity of all reading and the conflictual arena in which reading takes place. Though staged as readings for contradiction in a poststructuralist frame, these reviews suggest that Scobie's theory is not as eccentric as it appears. In this, they deconstruct the binary opposition of surface/depth, literal/figural which they track and position them as relational terms, textualized and contingent within a regime of interpretation. A hermeneutic circle with its double bind, meaning is predicated upon the interpretive chain whose presuppositions are always already in circulation, forever beyond interrogation from within its perimeter. It does matter nonetheless from what point one enters the circle, since meaning-effects produce truth-claims having different exclusionary practices mediating who has the right to speak, about what, whose cultural values will be considered normal, natural, properly "Canadian."

There is no inside/outside re-reading, re-writing. Beyond "intention," these (g)hosly essays live on ... in the (im)possibility of theory. Readers at work. Readers reading reading. ... Reviewers reviewing reviewing. ...

Writing Between Cultures

[L]earning all these words by heart, as well as memorizing all the verb-forms was like having stones rolling around in my head. The whole thing seemed to be humanly impossible.
⋄ Marie de l'Incarnation, "La Relation de 1654" (137)

White Girl: "School's a strange place. ...Your throat gets sore. ... You cough a lot too. I used even to cough blood. And they won't let you talk. They try to make you talk like they do. It's like stones in your mouth."
⋄ Daniel David Moses, *Almighty Voice and his Wife* (19 – 20)

A nation is not defeated until the hearts of its women are on the ground.
⋄ Cheyenne proverb, epigraph to *Almighty Voice and his Wife*

These epigraphs, from the texts to be analysed, highlight the toil and spoil of translation. Through them, I want to examine systematic interferences between languages in Canada at two different moments in the wake of imperialism. During the period of first contact between Europeans and Amerindians, as exemplified in the seventeenth-century writings of Mère Marie de l'Incarnation, Canadian concepts are translated vertically into European vernaculars and produced as Europe's other in a systematic erasure of horizontal translation among Amerindian languages that effects cultural and political hegemony. Turning in the second instance to the contemporary period, I shall examine the theatre of cultures of First Nations playwright Daniel David Moses who restages the trope of translation to expose therein the rhetorical violence of imperialism in a counter-hegemonic move. Whereas, in the first moment, the bilingual Amerindian translating is figured as potential traitor, as "lying thieving Indian," in the second, such duplicity is the power of Trickster, a culture hero who transforms the world.

I am more concerned here with non-translation than with translation "proper," that is with a refusal to translate cultural or linguistic difference which produces divergent political effects in the two texts. The selection of language in a multilinguistic milieu is always a politically charged process of constituting what Gramsci calls a "normative grammar." "An act of cultural-national policy," such choices enact relations of ruling as they contribute to "the formation and enlargement of the ruling class" and establish relations "between the ruling groups and the national-popular mass" and so organize the "cultural hegemony" (146–47). Language change as counter-hegemony develops through struggle with other models and historical phases working as forces of resistance to normative grammar. The "national language," as Gramsci notes, "cannot be anything but 'comparative,'" cannot be imagined "outside the framework of other languages" (146). It is this performativity of translation I wish to analyze through an examination of some of the tropes of translation which constitute the conditions of possibility, the field of the sayable, ordering the movement between languages and cultures wherein the Canadian literature institution is produced. A country in translation necessitates a consideration of literature not in terms of identity but of relationality with a consequent attention to asymmetries between languages as these order relations of ruling.

The absence of a single national language, and consequently of a homogeneous literary system, is a topos of writing in Canada as negativity.[1] It is, however, less an absence of words, a matter of lack, than of excess, the difficulty of choosing among many words, I would suggest, that is a dilemma for the Canadian in an instance of "national heteroglossia" (Bakhtin 1981, 295). If the boundary is the "hottest" site of semiotizing processes where meaning-making occurs, as Lotman argues (136), where the distinction a culture makes of an ordered "us" produces its particular type of disordered "them" and such disturbances lead to the creation of a new cultural "semiosphere" (142), this entails a concept of semiotic activity in a cultural milieu as more than binary alterity. A boundary both separates and unites in relation to an outside and is, consequently, polylingual (136–37). Moreover, the space it encloses is transected by boundaries at different levels forming variously continuous or discontinuous spaces, possibly even some combination of open and fragmentally closed spaces. The boundary then is a point of constant exchange of signs producing cultural value.

Within the Canadian context, under official bilingualism, there has been a tendency to conceptualize linguistic and cultural relations in binary terms. Canada's policy of official "multiculturalism" encourages First Nations peoples and immigrants to retain their cultures, though not their languages which remain unofficial.[2] Multiculturalism, as culture without language(s) and authority, or voices reconciliable in one voice, figures an end of translation in a fiction of unanimity. Against this, I want to argue, Canadian literature discourse has developed within contradiction, between cultures, between languages. Contradiction is embedded in linguistic signs in their centrifugal potential or differently oriented accents of diverse speech communities, multiaccentuality which the ruling social formation strives to make uniaccentual. Critics' calls for a hybridized "national" language, "Anglo-Ojibwa" and "Franco-huronne," in the mode of indigenization of Romantic nationalism in the nineteenth century, have given way to the creation of syncretic languages by polyglot writers mingling Chinese with English and Hindi.[3] Such contacts and interferences among languages, indeed the internal dynamism or dialectical aspect of the Canadian literature *poly*system within itself, may be traced through the boundary play of translation. During periods of cultural change, translation is significant in reorienting signs within multivalent accents, extending their vitality and development. In contemporary Canada, as in Renaissance Europe, translation is a mode of expansion or creation of knowledge through a proliferation of versions from different horizons of cultural perception.

A Cultural Turn

While currently there is a turn to more pragmatic policy analysis in Cultural Studies, discursive analysis continues to scrutinize rhetorical topoi and discern the ideological stakes of utterances. Such a metaphorics productively foregrounds the interpretive fictions or social logics of translation. A fluid activity, translation is conceptualized diversely in various "national" languages and in a variety of tropes at different historical moments. A historicized pragmatics is crucial for understanding the differences between the translation theories of Marie de l'Incarnation and Daniel David Moses, I would contend. If the connotations of metaphorical and hermeneutic activities from the Latin and Greek terms of *translatio* and *metapherein* persist in present-day understandings of "translation" as a transfer of concepts, they are enriched by other connotations.[4] Mère Marie de l'Incarnation gives the activity of transmission an expanded meaning of enrapture. Normative English language translation practice of textual equivalence is only one possible fiction, however.[5] The Anishinaabe term for translation, *aanikohtamowin*, combines a prefix for "link" with a stem for "story," to imply that translation makes a connection by telling a story about a word.[6] Explicitly postulating translation as creation not imitation, this emphasis on textuality contrasts significantly with English's focus on semantics or French's concern with rhetorical form. Such *storying*, I would suggest, informs Daniel David Moses's understanding of linguistic and cultural contact. So, translation develops a narrative that places a word within a social action. Each of these different articulations of translation activity frames specific understandings of the modalities of linguistic and cultural interference, establishing normative modes of contact, delimiting acceptable forms of relations and strategies of textual manipulation, and configuring speech genres. These relations produce certain hierarchies among signifiers, inscribing relations of power which may make the translator's turn a *conversion* or a *reversion*. Although the range of possible versions a translator may make is considerable, I shall concentrate on these stances to examine two different scenes of the passage between languages at different moments in the history of translation in the Canadas where the languages interacting are positioned within different axes of power; the one a scene of *instruction*, the other a scene of *insurrection*.

In the last decade, translation theory has taken a "cultural turn" (Bassnett and Lefevere). The insight of Bakhtin into the heteroglossia as well as the addressivity of language conceptualizes sign systems as neither unified nor transcendent but meaning-making within vectors of power. Languages are chains of potential relations among signifiers saturated with the play of social forces at a particular historical moment in a socially specific environment that orders the actualization of their connections. The translational utterance does not so much establish a match between languages as follow a particular trajectory toward the outsidedness of another language. Languages are always imbricated in relations of superiority or inferiority, asymmetrical relations which are agonistic and stratifying.[7] The word of certain speech communities is "authoritative," and taken for a general norm. There are languages and literatures of major and minor diffusion within global or even "national" marketplaces. Within such a model of the ideological inter-relation of languages, translation, or the rewriting of a text in a different conceptual horizon, is understood as one of a range of processes of "manipulation" within certain vectors. The concept of difference – of contradiction or syncretism – even of the *différend* (incommensurability) and *différance* (indeterminacy) – displace dogmas of fidelity as concepts of translation activity. In the complex multi-directional movement of living on, translation may enlarge or constrain a text's authority.

Translation traffics in power. In the double movement of interanimation that is translation, languages, subjectivities, are ex-changed, relativized. Such "dialogism" points to the incompleteness of all languages, to the absence of any homogenizing master language, not to posit the transcendence of the need to translate in some theological moment of signification or "pure language" but, on the contrary, to insist on the dynamic interaction and contamination of languages in the continuous *movement* of transformation in the making and unmaking of hierarchies. There is nonetheless a difference in the effect of such commerce in languages depending on where one is positioned within the axes of power, and on the direction of the transfer – downwards, upwards, or horizontally – along the hierarchy, whether one "translates" the self into the perspective of the other or translates the other into the language of the sovereign subject, or meditates on the difficulties of passage. The alienation of the self in power through recognition of oneself as a kind of foreigner in respect to a mastery one may yet attain differs from translation of the less powerful other who is transported into the self-same to be alienated from the self. The colonizing potentials of the latter constitute the "poetics of imperialism" (Cheyfitz 115) wherein the other is transposed into the master code of empire in an act of *con/version*, as I shall term this "turning," within a scene of instruction. An imperial politics of language in the Canadas in the work of Mère Marie de l'Incarnation[8] makes claims to *understand* "les Sauvages," refusing to acknowledge its own powerlessness in the necessity for, and the inadequacy of, its cultural translation: the "Savages" are understood as always-already European, superior Europeans, in fact, since they appear more zealous (submissive) in their devotion — easy converts.

The extent to which it is mistranslation and that the Amerindians can take up the language of Europeans without being confined to its limited meanings is what is at stake in the complex performance of "ghost" in Daniel David Moses's play. A focus on a "phono-semantic series" of signifiers (Haroldo de Campos 1982, 185), rather than on meaning that follows logic in its move from word to word by established connections, disturbs "transparency" and "transcendency" as strategies of colonial discursivity. Challenging the conventional hierarchies of "major" and "minor" literatures by granting precedence to the role of the translator or interpreter over the author and exploring the space in-between texts to write in what has been written out — the raced or gendered conditions of its transposition, the "middle passage" or transportation between points of contact, the tropes of turning, the activity of cutting — this is a translation practice which makes visible the *cultural work* of translation, its ethico-political effects. Such modalities of turning are concerned with horizontal relations between texts and languages as well as vertical relations of imposition, ones I shall characterize as *creative re/versions* staged in *Almighty Voice and His Wife* as scenes of negotiation ranging from armed insurrection to parodic resurrection. Translation studies converge here with cultural studies in an examination of the internexus of power, knowledge, and subjectivity, concerns that animate my analysis of strategies of non-translation in "Canadian" literatures at the height of and in the wake of the imperial moment.

Con/version

"At the heart of every imperial fiction ... there is a fiction of translation," asserts Eric Cheyfitz (15). In the Canadas, this is a story of a founding violence, a captivity narrative with many variants as French and Amerindians confined each other in forcible immersion. Jean Delisle begins his history of translation in Canada with the sentence: "Interpretation was the first profession practiced in Canada *after* the arrival of the Europeans" (1987, 33; my emphasis). That translation took place between different indigenous languages *before* their arrival is overlooked. He also neglects the violence of this professional debut in that the first translators were inducted into this profession by force — aboriginal peoples abducted and transported to Europe.[9] Contact with North America was produced in translation both literally (in the narratives of contact edited by Hakluyt which promoted settlement of the Americas) and figuratively: the "new world" came into being in a troping, overwritten by the "old" whose perceptions framed its inhabitants under the universalizing figure "Indian," as a resource for exploitation and an object for conversion. Metaphor or translation — a carrying across as transportation and/or transference — has been the "very motor" of the "perceptual apparatus" of colonization (Cheyfitz 109).

The dream of absolute power of the discoverer/conqueror is founded in an unacknowledged contradiction. The silence of the "Indians" of North America, proliferated in the literature of exploration in the figure of the "Indian" who speaks no language and the "Indian" who speaks "our" language (guides or "native informants") is, in fact, symptomatic of a different problem: the failure to recognize the figure "Indians speak a language and it is different from ours" (Cheyfitz 109). "We" do not understand this language and so its speakers appear silent or invisible to "us." This may also occur in its converse: "we" all speak the "same" language and "we" all revere the "same" object whereby "we" come to cohere as subject. In effect, this is a figure of non-translation for what it presents as a problem in *intercultural* communication turns out to be a problem in *intracultural* competence, a problem with metaphor. A contradiction within one language between the "natural" and the "figurative" is projected outward as two incommensurate languages (Cheyfitz 121 – 22). A failure at dialogue is figured as a genetic inability of the other: the inferiority of aboriginal languages, their "barbarity," becomes the imperial alibi for (rhetorical) domination. Two metaphorical machines encounter each other but only one is understood as rhetoric or art: the other is perceived as transparent or "natural." The translation of the "inferior" by the "superior" is simultaneously impossible, because of this qualitative discrepancy understood as intellectual deficiency, and inevitable, because of the same discrepancy understood as power differential (Cheyfitz 122). The Amerindian is thus perceived to speak both gibberish (speaking with stones in her throat) and with a "natural" eloquence in a language taught him/her by Europeans. Aboriginal oral utterances as varied as oratory and prayer are (re)ordered within European rhetorical forms. Clashes between Amerindians and European power necessitate the production of written texts within European formal conventions as, for example, in the many letters of petition from First Nations peoples to government officials filed in the colonial archives (Petrone). Translation moves here to obliterate difference, to eliminate the need for translation, to bring about its own end. The dilemma after Babel will be overcome when everyone understands "our" language.

A myth of a "common" language is central to the imperializing and civilizing project which equates speaking well with being human. Not to do so is to be a "savage." To speak well is to master a language, that is, to speak the language of the metropolis. Incoherency is translated into "coherent" speech which "makes sense" within what is so constituted as a "universal" language, a "colonizing" language. Translation of the "other" into the codes of the empire entails a mission of conversion, most explicitly one of translation as instruction in the language and culture of the master. The connection of learning a language and mastery in the movement of culture from one people to another transferred the Roman *imperium*, a model of an empire with Latin as a universal language, to other places and times maintaining the (imperial) idea of a universal rather than national character.[10] A version of the mediaeval theory of *translatio imperii et studii*, suggests Eric Cheyfitz, this offered a theory of history as the cyclical replacement of one empire by another that was simultaneously a theory of rhetoric and one of translation. The transmission of knowledge (*studii*) was co-terminous with a geographical transfer connected to a transferral of power. While in France this later involved adapting knowledge to the language of the addressee and justified writing in the vernacular (Lusignan 313), in the Canadian context, the Amerindian languages were refigured as Latin in a universalizing move that conceptualized the cultural transfer of empire as pan-European Renaissance or Catholic return to Apostolic fervour.

The *translatio* was both a theory of figurative language and a theory of the transmission of power in that it proposed a monologic theory of translation from and into (infraduction and supraduction) the hierarchically "superior" languages of Europe. At its centre is a "primal scene" in which an orator by his eloquence "civilizes" a "savage." This "imperial commonplace" is the narrative of the orator as first settler or colonizer, bringing humanity and civility to "wild savages" or "wild lands," found in Cicero's *De Inventione* and *De Oratore*, texts used for centuries in the teaching of rhetoric or eloquent speaking (Cheyfitz 113–14).[11] I shall turn to such a scene of instruction in the work of Mère Marie de l'Incarnation, a Canadian example in which Amerindian girls are taught to identify against themselves with the gospel's "poor in spirit" in order to gain greater power through transformation into French-speaking Catholics. This translation of the aboriginals *into* the terms of empire ironically writes them *out* of the empire as silent Other, eliminating the specificity of their cultures and languages and of the act of translation itself in the supraduction by conflation of Amerindian languages with Latin, a universal language.

First, though, I want to talk about another kind of non-translation that fails to recognize the Amerindians' cultural difference while paradoxically writing that difference out(side). This variant of the failure to acknowledge that aboriginals have cultures and languages which are complete and autonomous, so that horizontal translation between Amerindian languages might figure in the relations of exploration and settlement, or that a dialogic countertransference might occur in the passage between European and aboriginal languages whereby the European would be transformed in the activity of translating, propagates the myth of the "empty continent" which enables the transfer (translation) of "Indian" land into "Canadian" *property*. In this case, within the context of English attempts to settle Newfoundland,[12] the "Indians" are not overwhelmed by the eloquence of a European speaker, for there are no "Indians" visible.[13] They have been written out of the landscape entirely. The "new world" is figured as incomplete, in need of the completion or settlement of the "old." The land is first translated into British property in an imperial project framed in Latin, that universal language of Renaissance humanism, in which the Hungarian scholar,

Stephen Parmenius, bard of Sir Gilbert Humphrey's expedition, wrote to his Oxford friend, Richard Hakluyt.[14] Oscillating between documentary inventory, manipulating the figure of analogy to produce the "effect of the real" and naturalize the "new world" for civilizing prospects, and prayer for favours from British patrons, Parmenius's letter produces a subject of the enunciation wherein the spoken subject is figured as powerless in comparison to the addressee. The threat of subjection is reduced by mastery of Latin rhetoric, language of eloquence and (self-) control. In the "absence of any people," "Newfoundland" functions as a screen of vacancy, in a relation between Europeans through which the subject differentiates himself as universal and powerful, filling the void with representations as imitations.[15]

In the French relations of exploration and settlement greater attention is given to both Amerindian languages and to translation. Jacques Cartier acknowledged the need for interpretation, albeit with a violent capture. To the *Relations* of his voyages are appended glossaries of Iroquoian terms limited, though, to elementary phrases of numbers, food, basic questions. Moreover, Cartier's description of the coasts of the Maritime provinces and of the St. Lawrence River is mediated by not one but two modes of perception, a marking of distinctions as well as a search for equivalences. He notes that the peoples he encountered "appellent ung hachot en leur langue *cochy* et ung cousteau *bacan*. Nous nomames ladite baye la baye de Chaleur" (1986, 113). This is not an equal traffic in languages as the balanced rhetorical structure of the sentences would convey, but the prelude to a narrative of tricks and captures, where the reported calculation and feints of the Amerindians are met with ambushes and abductions by Cartier. Indeed, the pursuit of similarities dominates: this act of naming in a European language follows a passage of description under the sign of equivalences ("we" are all Europeans) of the quality of the wheat and rye growing at this site, description positioned between two sentences predicting the ease of converting these aboriginals.[16] This opinion is formed after initial contact with aboriginals who have readily accepted axes, paternosters, and other goods and given away everything they had in exchange until "they had nothing but their naked bodies" (1975, 18). Such a perception of Amerindian submission to European persuasiveness stands in unmarked opposition to the observation a week later that "Ilz sont lar-rons à merveilles de tout ce qu'ilz peuvent desrober" (1986, 116). Who is more credulous, it is difficult to discern. Reading between the lines, this contradiction manifests a cultural clash over concepts of property where a gift economy of hunter-gatherer culture confronts the private ownership of proto-capitalism and neither recognizes the other as a "system." Between these two sentences, Amerindians' dancing and speech-making ("harangue," Cartier 1986, 116) are noted uncomprehend-ingly by the European chronicler,[17] while the aboriginals' astonishment (*"estonnez"* 1986, 117) at the inside of Cartier's ships is emphasized as a sign of Donnaconna's goodwill.[18]

Relations between French and aboriginals are repeatedly constituted in this mode of misprision, the eye reading similarity, the ear distin-guishing difference. The failure to attend to the silent cultural signs ordering modes of address produces translation as metaphor, translation as violence. The authoritative certainty of the narrator in reporting these gestures as transparent in face of the incomprehensibility and hence untranslatability of the speech is nothing short of the marvellous. The European elides signs of resistance, that is, of difference: invisible, cul-tural incommensurability is thus transcended.[19] Cartier's "sauvages" are "gense" ("people"), potential Europeans, in need of moulding or devel-oping under a firm hand. We read aboriginal oratory as silence through Cartier's narrative rhetoric. What figures in his account is the venerable topos of *traduttore traditore,* the translator as traitor, here confounded with that topos of imperialism, the "lying thieving Indian," suffering the pollution of bilingualism, of being between cultures as "crippled two-tongues" (Maracle 109).[20]

It is the persuasive "technology of eloquence" (Cheyfitz 34) — rhetori-cal power enhanced by the representational machinery of writing, a "literall advantage" (Purchas 486) — in the service of religious conversion that figures prominently in the figure of *translatio* in the work of Mère Marie de l'Incarnation. Instruction is as effective a modality of figuring the Amerindians out of power as their elimination from topographi-cal description by Parmenius or their capture by Cartier. The figure of instruction involves a paradox of translation as non-translation, the learning of Amerindian languages in order to bring the aboriginals to a recognition of the universal power of Latin, of Catholicism as transcendent Truth, through the sacred writings of Christianity. Against the dangers of the forked tongue that would produce lies and errors in translation on the part of "native informants" is positioned the power of Christian ritual and rhetoric to guard against "delusion" (de l'Incarnation 1967, 76).

Containment is critical in Mère Marie de l'Incarnation's figuration of translation, but hers is a chosen captivity, the confinement of the cloister. This enclosure symbolizes "civilized" femininity which she seeks to impose on the Amerindian girls sent to be educated in the Ursuline convent at Quebec. Aboriginal women had the freedom of the forest and "canote comme des hommes" (de l'Incarnation 1971, 829). More disturbing to the Jesuits was their sexual freedom unregulated by the concept of "sin" (Karen Anderson 86). Realizing the impossibility of their goal should they not "civilize" the aboriginal women, the Jesuits brought nuns to New France. Attracted by the enlarged possibilities for her own spiritual and administrative activity in the forests of Quebec where the apostolic authority of cloistered nuns received full recognition — indeed, the pioneer nuns were called "Amazones du Grand Dieu" — Marie de l'Incarnation nonetheless sought to circumscribe her aboriginal pupils within the rules of discipline and surveillance of the cloister, instructing them through the Catholic rite of examination of consciousness in practices of psychological control to separate them from the negative (barbarous) influences of the forest. This is characteristic of the split subjectivity produced in feminist discourses with their contradictory values of enlightenment emancipation or autonomy and of feminine difference as passivity and dependence. Marie's scrupulous exactitude in following the rule of the cloister, despite its ultimate hampering of her avowed vocation to win souls, places her discourse more heavily on the scales of feminine submission.

Her *Correspondance* oscillates between these contradictory pulls of assertion and subjection punctuating her portraits of aboriginal women, some noted for their heroic exploits in freeing themselves from Iroquois captivity and making their way back to Montreal or Quebec on their own (1971, 329), others praised for their docility and submission to the nuns (1971, 72). So, too, Marie de l'Incarnation destabilizes her own authority as knowing subject, minimizing her skill in learning Algonkian, Montagnais, Huron, and Iroquois languages by attributing it all to divine inspiration.[21] Learning them, she wrote, was "humanly impossible." So, she continues: "I spoke lovingly to our Lord about it, and he came to my aid to such a degree that in a short time I had a very great facility in the language so that the activity of my interior life was neither hindered nor interrupted" (de l'Incarnation 1985, 127; my translation). By effacing herself to become God's instrument, she will make possible the perfect translation of the Word. Meaning transcends the material modalities of communication: apparent disparities are absorbed into a vaster unity. Her letters are mediated by these two modes of perception, a marking of differences, of error and delusion that transforms itself into a web of equivalences, of truth and illumination. The fall into the wilderness, into languages, serves as testimony to a providential mission to New France and as evidence of the particular grace bestowed on her as the devoted handmaiden of the Lord. This is, moreover, a particularly skilful rhetorical device for soliciting help for the project of New France.

The power of Providence manifests itself in rhetorical eloquence, as Mère Marie de l'Incarnation records it: "Le R. Père le Jeune qui est le principal ouvrier qui a cultivé cette vigne, continue à y faire des *merveilles*. Il prêche le peuple tous les jours et lui fait faire tout ce qu'il veut: Car il est connu de toutes ces nations, et il passe en leur esprit pour un homme *miraculeux*" (1971, 94; my emphasis). The transformative results of his preaching are evident in their effects, as Mère Marie observes upon her arrival in New France in September 1639: the Christian God is "praised in four different tongues [Montagnais, Algonkin, Huron, French]" by aboriginal preachers which she reads as prophesy of her future, teaching girls of this "barbarous country" the way to heaven (1967, 69).[22] Certainly, this promise of the easy conversion of the aboriginals makes Mère Marie forget the perils of the ocean crossing where they had almost capsized, catastrophe forestalled by divine intervention. Commencing her voluminous *Correspondance* with these providential signs, Mère Marie establishes the rhetorical form of her relation, a litany of examples of God's benevolence. An insuperable difficulty is introduced as prelude to a demonstration of divine power, the lesson of the *felix culpa* or happy fall. This scene represents the universality of Catholicism, for the diversity of languages masks a singularity of meaning: "Nous sommes tous ici pour un même dèssein" (1971, 88). Christian eloquence holds out the promise of a single, pure language, a miraculous speaking in tongues where there is mutual comprehension and unanimity of belief — a common desire — that transcends and redeems the fall into Babel. Translation undertaken in the ethnocentric aim of conversion produces a vision of salvation — for Mère Marie at least.

This goal of sense-for-sense equivalence is based on a theory of textual transfer grounded in the onto-theological discourse of the one True "Word" and its many distortions, formulated in classical metaphysics and biblical hermeneutics, and regulating the translation practice of the early church fathers working on the Vulgate (Robinson 55). The theory postulates a hierarchized dualism with everyone — except God and his Logos or "true meaning" at the top — an instrument of the level above and an instrumentalizer of the level below. Through divine inspiration, the biblical translator will become invisible, an instrument of God, and make possible the perfect translation of "Meaning," perfection being measured in the extent to which a translation supersedes the original. Such "originality" is achievable only through slavish imitation which valorizes divine authorship and erases all traces of textual mediation. Applied to non-biblical texts, this theory refuses to acknowledge conflictual relations between cultures and texts, assuming that translation occurs only between "identically-placed systems" (Bassnett 1990, 146).

Christian eloquence thus contains the threat of translation, the duplicity and lying of those who speak many languages and distort the one true Word with their accents. Skill in the French language, as well as knowledge of the Catholic catechism, limits the threat of bordercrossing with its attendant risks of impurity by imposing a rigid hierarchy. Not only does this make the aboriginal pupils tractable but it enables the nuns to carry out their surveillance more effectively, as in Mère Marie's account of Marie Amiskouevan, a model of docile devotion, whose bilingualism is testimony to the persuasiveness of the French missionaries. "Il ne se peut rien voir de plus souple ni de plus innocent; ni encore de plus candide, car *nous ne l'avons surprise une seule fois dans le mensonge*, qui est une grande vertu dans les Sauvages. ... Cette fille *nous a beaucoup aidé dans l'étude de la langue, parce qu'elle parle bien François.* Enfin cette fille gagne les cœurs de tout le monde par sa grande douceur et par ces belles qualitez" (1971, 95; my emphasis). Submissiveness is the significant quality for verifying the reliability of her translation for it is a sign of her perfect mastery of the cultural rhetoric of European translation practices. Taking up the role of subservient handmaid positions her within her "proper" role in the instrumental hierarchy, assuring the fidelity and transcendence of target language version in a movement of supraduction for the circulation of Meaning beyond all language. Marie's fidelity is corroborated in *Les Relations des Jésuites* where, following her marriage it is reported, "she gave proofs of a faith strong and animated by love," repelling the advances of several young pagans who were courting her, and reacting strongly to the ministrations of a traditional Shaman (*The Jesuit Relations* xx 128 – 29) to her sick brother. These proofs are gestures, tears and smiles — more secular than sacred signs — interpreted as rejection of aboriginal religious practices by the priest who presupposes cultural universals.[23]

This woman enters into the colonial archive with proper names (Marie-Magdeleine)[24] through her skill in languages, her aptness as a pupil. It is her knowledge of French which makes her so valued since she can act as go-between, both carrying the word of Christ to her kin and helping the nuns perfect their skills in the Algonkian language. In returning her to her people with new powers of reading, writing, and telling the gospel, the missionaries were making use of, and recuperating for their own ends, the aboriginal practice of according women authority to speak in public assemblies. Indeed, it was the resistance of aboriginal women to their teaching, and the consequent difficulty in converting the tribes, that had induced the Jesuits to bring the Ursulines to New France (de l'Incarnation 1971, 117 – 18). By educating the women, it was hoped, the entire tribe would be saved from such "diabolic" temptation, Christianized, and francisized. Particularly important in this regard were the dual constraints of silencing women as social actors while encouraging them to reveal their most private thoughts in confession and receive instruction in how to understand them, so learning obedience and humility. Returning the girls with official presents, charged as ambassadors to their people, reinforced the new hierarchy

being established of "Jesuits-Ursulines-aboriginal child-adult aboriginal" (Deslandres 106; my translation).

Marie-Magdeleine differs from the other Algonkians precisely in her
refusal to lie, lie avoided by speaking transparently, that is, (as) French.
Her lifestory, however, unfolds along the same lines as those of other
girls inserted into these relations — sudden and total transformation
upon baptism.[25] "Progress" is equated with a sedentary life, with confinement within the domestic space of "civilized" femininity. In her
early letters, Mère Marie expresses surprise at the way the aboriginal
girls accept the confines of the cloister. Though Marie Negabmat kept
running away into the woods at first, after her Christianized father
ordered her to return, she was transformed within two days into a
model of piety.[26] At this point, Mère Marie stresses the success of the
missionaries in establishing the power of the cloister. Nearly thirty years
later, she admits to her son that only one out of every hundred girls who
have come to them has been "civilized." When least expected, the girls
climb over the palisade "like squirrels" (1971, 802) and disappear into
the forest with their parents. Being cooped up in houses makes them
melancholy and ill.[27] Despite these failures in her vocation, Mère Marie
continues to uphold the importance of enclosure with the gendered
and class hierarchy it constitutes, rather than to abandon the cloister
to follow the aboriginals' itinerant life in the forest.

This gap between exemplum and actuality may also be a function
of Mère Marie's eagerness to detect cultural similarity in visual signs.[28]
Mimicry of gestures is how she measures the quality of Marie Negabmat's transformation: "elle tressallit de joye à la veue d[u] pourtraict"
of the Virgin Mary and prays twice, first in Algonkian with her friends,
then with the French girls (1971, 91). Agnes Chabwekwechich is considered exemplary for repeating the Christmas sermon to the children
in the convent complete with gestures (The Jesuit Relations xx 134–35).
What the aboriginal girls' readings of these gestural codes might be
is elided in this text which focuses exclusively on the correct repetition of ritual forms. Were they manipulating the codes to their own
profit, as the sons of Donnaconna had? (Cartier 1986, 143, 145). What is
the twentieth-century reader to make of Mère Marie's accounts of how
the girls showered the nuns with caresses as they never did their own

mothers[29] — indeed had come to think of the nuns as "truly our mothers, we lack nothing with them" (*The Jesuit Relations* x x 138 – 39)? Did they recognize their position as hostages and attempt to make the best of it? Was this duplicitous mimesis, playing up to the nuns in response to the latters' fantasmatic investment in transformation only to get new clothes and attention showered upon them? These, however, were not sufficient incentive for Nicole Assepanse to leave her mother (de l'Incarnation 1971, 96). Mère Marie records these contradictions without comment, demonstrating fantasmatic certainty in the cultural universality of gestural signs which she reads within her own narrative model of conversion as "true (Christian) belief."

So much has Marie Amiskouevan become the "civilized barbarian" that she has a French suitor and is on the point of assimilation. But the nuns appropriate her cultural fluency, her zeal in their service, for their ends and arrange her marriage to an aboriginal man, a student in the seminary. Moreover, they use her in the traffic in languages within their missionary aims of total conversion to translate French Catholicism downward. In the exchange of letters between New France and France, she figures in the textualization of this "civilizing" project: this anecdote of her conversion written in French serves as exemplum in the Ursulines' continual petitions for funds.[30] The plea for help for the future is underwritten by the description of the always-already francisized aboriginal. Marie and other aboriginal girls figure as objects of demonstration for the miraculous transformative powers of Christian rhetoric and the perfect submission of the Ursulines to the divine author's will as instruments in this conversion. Encounters between "native informants" and missionaries' master discourse involving questions of translation are reconstructed in a textual account that brings reader and native into a textual participation fusing external and indigenous cultural descriptions. Mère Marie's discourse oscillates between exemplum and prayer, constituting a subject of enunciation in the authoritative reportage of Amerindian life, abjecting herself in submission to the wealthy patron and the divine author.[31]

The potential betrayal of translation of Amerindian languages is contained in a troping that makes them "sacred" and affirms divine authorship. The French nuns and priests do not leave interpretation exclusively to the aboriginal peoples but learn their languages themselves in order to speak more eloquently, to persuade more effectively. They write glossaries and grammars to fix knowledge so they will not be dependent on treacherous aboriginals or nativized French *coureur de bois* as interpreters (Delisle 1975, 35). Mère Marie begins a letter to a fellow religious a year after her arrival in Quebec with a salutation in Algonkian which she immediately translates into French. These, she concludes the paragraph, are "à peu près ce que nous disons ordinairement à nos chères Néophites" (1971, 108). The figure of linguistic difference with which the letter begins slides into one of commonality. Translating upward and downward, into and from the French, is synonymous for Mère Marie, for the rhetoric of the utterances is the same, to transport or, more precisely, to transfer (French) Catholicism, to encounter the sublime as an instrument of divine providence. In this trope, she rewrites Canada into the Roman empire.

Travels outward to the "new" world are figured as travels back in time: New France is fused with biblical time and place. Indeed, contrary to others' perceptions that Canada is located in the regions of Hell, she finds it perfect Paradise (1971, 112). She has been transported to the time of Christ under the Romans, to the period of early Apostolic fervour conflated with the later inspired work of the Church Fathers translating the Vulgate, and represents skill in the Algonkian languages as knowledge of the sacred and universal language, Latin. As she writes: "Nous faisons nos études en cette langue barbare comme font ces jeunes enfans, qui vont au Collège pour apprendre le Latin. Nos Révérends Pères quoique grands docteurs en viennent là aussi-bien que nous, et ils le font avec une affection et docilité incroiable" (1971, 108). This trope of inversion as infantilization is repeated in the many allusions to the blessedness of spirit among those who are to all appearances poor and naked in the new world. Study is difficult and humbling, but is made easier by "God's Grace."[32] Learning to speak well (selflessly), putting on the drapery of rhetoric as in the figure of *translatio*, will lead ultimately to the authority of the spirit to persuade so that New France will become God's kingdom regained. It was also a potential site for martyrdom, a possibility Mère Marie, like the Jesuits, had constantly in mind (1971, 94). All her hardships and deprivations were read as signs of possible ravishment of a different order, framed by the excess of the counter-Reformation which translated extreme material suffering or sacrifice into the ineffable language of the mystical sublime. Barbarity is thus configured as sanctity. Translating downward into aboriginal languages is refigured as vertical translation into Latin, language of the ineffable. Even the forked-tongue translator may be converted when Latin becomes the universal Truth of the colonial encounter with spatial and temporal coordinates confounded in the process. This universal language is possible only by separating language and culture so that Eurocentric ideas are exchanged in any and all languages. In such a process of displacement, the aboriginal languages are surplus signs taken as waste, infinitely replaceable and expendable.

These texts subsequently entered the European literary system in the guise of non-fiction as the "truth" of "discovery," producing innovation within it, at a moment when Europe was inventing itself in spatial relation to the Americas, Africa, and Asia, as well as in temporal relation to the Greeks and Romans. To locate in the texts of exploration and settlement the specificity of aboriginal perspectives in the colonial encounter requires a shift in the object of investigation to the colonized in the production of de-colonized knowledge. Reconfiguring the subject-position of indigenous peoples as colonized, however, does not undo the ideological work of their exclusion as subjects to and of their own historical making. At the centre of this exclusion is the politics of translation implicit in such colonial texts as the letters of Mère Marie de l'Incarnation where the translator refuses to engage with the rhetoricity of the source text of Marie Amiskouevan, to consider where its social logic ordering the relations between words may work according to a different economy. Gestures are read with infallible certainty: the potentially disruptive logic of the Algonkian languages is e-rased in the trope that turns them into Latin, the language of imperial truth.

Re/version

Almighty Voice and His Wife reads as an inversion of such a theory of equivalence. Daniel David Moses reverses the object of investigation from the colonizer to the colonized in an attempt to undo the ideological

work of their exclusion as subjects to and of their own historical making. European rhetorical forms are re-ordered in Amerindian rituals
that constitute meaning as event rather than as representation. The
performative mode of his text brings readers and actors into a textual
participation by separating rather than fusing external and indigenous
cultural descriptions. Performance is written out, however, which writes
aboriginals into the discourse of empire to question its categories and
values. Viewing bilingualism not as a slippery slope leading to delusion,
where translation is figured as loss, Moses presents a theory of translation as creative difference, where ambiguity opens up a potentially
generative play of illusion. Cultural transmission for aboriginal peoples
may be assured through the creative enhancement of translation as
afterlife beyond colonization in a process of recycling as regeneration
through decay and dismemberment.

Language choice, translation, is a site of conflict. The language of the
master is masterfully wrenched to a different effect as Moses addresses
the problem of self-representation when one persists as a stereotype
"in translation." The obligation to "speak white" in the Interlocutor's
commands to Almighty Voice — "Come on, use the Queen's tongue"
(1992, 54) — is countered when he continues to perform a Cree ritual,
repeating its gestures, though not always its language. This failure in
representation points to an otherwise invisible rupture in the figuration of the "indigene." English has become the language of intertribal
communication but its hegemony is being challenged. For it has become
the instrument in which the First Nations collectively wage a political
struggle for land and self-government. In a strategy of decolonization,
words are opened to the play of cultural difference, resignified hetero-
geneously in the same "national" language, as in Moses's marvellous
word play on "ghost" which reanimates clichés to make English an
aboriginal tongue.

Straining not for the translative sublime, like Marie de l'Incarnation,
Moses offers a different kind of catharsis in the play of irony. Norms,
barriers, are made to be broken, transformed. Against a model of vertical translation producing subjugation, Moses develops a horizontal
model of translation between aboriginal cultures privileging creative
borrowing. For the topic of his play is an incident from the history of

the Cree people's conflict with hegemonic Euro-Canadian culture while Moses himself is a Delaware.[33] His play stages a double act of translation, both supraduction, in which the European language is reshaped by aboriginal cultural values, and trans-duction, in which someone from the Six Nations' community writes Cree history and ritual — with the acknowledged help of translators — the Cree language then retranslated in the published script into the dominant language, English. In performance, however, the Cree is untranslated, producing differentiated positions for spectators distinguished on the basis of language. This palimpsestic overwriting is a subversive move to work with and against the conqueror's language so as to render visible substantially different cultural assumptions and disrupt the hierarchy established through Mère Marie's linguistic theory of transparency. Moses analyzes performatively the material modalities of communication in all their contingency. Two metaphorical machines wrap around each other. The translator's duplicity is not a matter for a firm controlling hand but a feint making possible survival within a logic of contradiction that deflects such power to fix and define.

A number of Marie de l'Incarnation's tropes are taken up, their presuppositions exposed and transformed, most specifically, that of the faithful handmaiden with its accompanying figure of enclosure. An important addition to Moses's version of the story of Almighty Voice[34] is the attention given to his wife, White Girl, which is Moses's homolinguistic translation of the personnage known in historical documents as Pale Face. The play demonstrates the importance of what Jeannette Armstrong terms "soft power" (1991, 96), that is the feminine power of cultural creation and transmission, as the epigraph affirms. Significantly, the play is dedicated to Moses's grandmothers. It ends with a scene in which the character Almighty Voice, who has endured a long afterlife playing his ghost in the character of Mr. Bones in a Medicine Show, dances on stage. Literally dead, he lives on "in translation." Meanwhile his wife gathers her costume from the show where, dressed as a Mountie, she plays the Interlocutor (police and show barker simultaneously). She then holds it aloft, presenting a child-shaped bundle to the audience. Through the magic of performance, the cloth is transformed from the uniform, symbol of oppression, to swaddling clothes, promise of continuation. This marks a shift from death to new life which is the narrative movement of the play.

White Girl is no subservient figure: "pretty fierce for a little girl" (Moses 1992, 64). An assertive interrogator in this second act, she has been an active instigator in the first, an escapee from the convent school, breaking through all the walls that Mère Marie's successors have put up to prolong the cultural genocide. The hunger she feels in the school, the absence of game to hunt on the prairie, all point to the fatal effects of fencebuilding for the Amerindians from their perspective. With her mother-in-law Spotted Calf, moreover, White Girl is the keeper of ritual traditions and knowledge. Her power vision or "good medicine" protects Almighty Voice from the pursuing police, though her "bad medicine" as the once-baptized "Marrie" may have made him more vulnerable to their power. A frequent violator of the pass regulations designed to contain aboriginals on reservations, Almighty Voice has broken out of jail where he has been confined for killing a cow for their wedding feast, an insurrection that ultimately finds him encircled by more than one hundred Mounties with a cannon. A narrative of outlaws seeking an outside where they will not be surrounded, the captivity figure is now presented from the angle of those resisting it, breaking through the circle. The play stages the conflict of colonial conquest in this representation of the final incident of armed rebellion by aboriginals in western Canada a century ago while reasserting aboriginal cultural practices with the prohibited Ghost Dance and slippery Trickster. In this, Moses inserts the eclipsed aboriginal understanding of closure as death into the Eurocentric concept of "civilization" to expose the differential political effects of "capture." Insurrection is implicated in a move from *translatio* to *interpretio*, from the singular truth of the *Aufhebung* to the proliferation of contradictory versions necessitating interpretation within a historicized pragmatics.

The trope of invisibility is also examined through the contrasting logic of European and aboriginal cultures. The telescopic vision of the Mounties which allows them to see further into what is and so enlarge the circumference of their surveillance contrasts with the dream power of White Girl to foresee the future and make things happen. These two modes of vision — two different logics and temporalities — coexist, each ordering reality differently. From the prophetic perspective of medicine power, the problem of the "Vanishing Indian" — that the "only good indians are the dead ones" (Moses 1992, 68), or "the ones who are sainted" (1992, 89) — is only apparently so. As the Interlocutor proclaims, and the play enacts, "the most acclaimed magical act of the century [is] the Vanishing Indian" (1992, 58) who persistently reappears in a different form, not the disembodied Christian "Holy Ghost." Aboriginal culture only seems invisible to those who will not see. The complex play on appearance and reality, foregrounded in the white masking of the characters in Act 2 in a series of plays within the play, through which the matter of "passing" is explored, contrasts with its treatment by Marie de l'Incarnation. While she takes appearances for the real and reads aboriginal bodies as francisized, Moses creatively works with the problematic of representation as re-presentation in a specific socio-political instance of address to examine the manipulation of corporeal surfaces. As the Ghost says of the Interlocutor, "her touching masquerade seemed almost real" (1992, 82). She has become almost "white," though as the costume shows, the inverse of the "apple" — white outside but red within.[35] The performer's body is the primary signifier in which these competing narratives are played out. Against the transcendence of the disembodied word in the service of spiritual union in Mère Marie's theory of language, Moses foregrounds the embodied word in order to probe the relation of verbal and gestural signs. In this *mise-en-scène* which is a *mise-en-abyme* that foregrounds such "acting out of character" in the trope of cross-dressing in terms of both race and gender, the "tragedy of representation" as *lack* or absence is reversed in terms of its mimetic display in a subjunctive world of "as if" and, under the name of play, takes back everything, including the cultural genocide of aboriginals.

The logic of the masquerade is the logic of the supplement which overturns the hierarchy of firstness and secondness, of the One and the many, to posit the logic of the series, of variation. The gap in the interval between two enunciations is a sign of excess in the layering of discourses which constitutes them as partial, both incomplete and virtual, mutually interdependent within an historical instance of enunciation. Moses's investigation of representation extends to the slipperiness of language, the difficulty of holding anything fixed, even a proper noun. "Names, names, they're all the same," the Interlocutor parodies the Euro-Canadian perspective: "Dead man, red man, Indian. *Kisse-Manitou-Wayou*, Almighty Voice, *Jean Baptiste*! Geronimo, Tonto, Calijah! Or most simply, Mister Ghost" (1992, 55). This proliferating chain of signifiers fails to contain the character, however, despite the seeming fixity of the clichés. Under the name of Ghost alone he performs a number of roles in the Medicine Show, not only those of Almighty Voice and his friends, but those of the attacking Mounties and of the transvestite, Sweet Sioux, making use of a number of different performance styles from different racial and social milieux; minstrel show, vaudeville, folk singer, Western, pow wow fancy dancer. Contradictions proliferate: Jean Baptiste, as White Girl says, is the "name of one of their ghosts" (1992, 22), a Christianized "Holy Ghost." Conversely, Almighty Voice in jail is lost "like a ghost" (1992, 45). Ghost is a term aboriginals use for white people. The imposition of "civiliza-tion" on the two characters, their possible acculturation, is signified in their "saintly" names. Ghost stories, however, are an important narra-tive form on the Six Nations territory (Alma Green). Refusing the posi-tion of ineffable in the service of the nation's integrity, Moses attempts to make ghosts visible. This necessitates an examination of the other side of language, the cultural matrix that regulates the conditions of meaning-making. His challenge is to foreground eclipsed social values within the discursive modes of the dominant language. The encounter productively disorders the value distinction (distribution) between White and Amerindian cultures.

"To be seen is the ambition of ghosts," Moses writes as epigraph to another play, *Coyote City*. And he continues there with a story: "The ghost said to Coyote. Here we have conditions different from those you have in the land of the living. When it gets dark here, it has dawned in your land and when it dawns for us it is growing dark for you." The complex stereoscopic vision is available to Coyote, the Trickster who, as shape-shifter, embraces contradiction in his role as go-between. The plasticity of Trickster is such that s/he can transform into any shape — a fluctuating identity (Radin 165). Highlighting the connection between the tropes of inversion and of visibility, this epigraph also points to the cultural significance of one of the formal modes of representation in *Almighty Voice*, that of the shadow play, which focuses specifically on altered angles of vision and different states of being. Possibly, this constitutes a reworking of Plato's allegory of the cave so influential in Western thinking on representation as repetition, for it reverses his privileging of light as Truth to convey the enhanced power of seeing in the dark among the many copies and gives greater authority to the domain of illusion. In addition to the shadow play of the final scene, where the ghost dances for the baby's arrival, there is a shadow play at the end of the first act entitled "His Vision." In gesture only, it enacts the incident of Almighty Voice's crossing the police lines at night, invisible to them in the dark, moving behind the screen of representation to a spectral tipi where sit White Girl and her child. Almighty Voice breaks out of the circle of confinement aided by the cover of the dark which makes him invisible to the police. That the dark is valued positively is further conveyed by the final image where the religious allegory of Marrie/Salomé/White Girl and Jean Baptiste/Almighty Voice in which a woman kills a man (her "bad medicine"), has been translated into the terms of Cree rituals of cultural and spiritual power in which a woman gives life to a child. However shadowy it may be, this holds the promise of life to come, prophesying a future for the "Vanishing Indian." Certainly it proclaims that the heart of White Girl is not on the ground. For it counters her vision in the shadow play of the first scene of Act One when, confined in the school made of stone (19), she foresees Almighty Voice's death and the moon turning to blood.

Against the trajectory of the historical narrative of aboriginal decline in the first act, marked by the expansion of the prison walls so that the Eurocanadians "even turn the prairie into a jail" (26) and a place of death, is performed in the second act a ceremony of renewal, functioning like the great Midwinter Festival of the Iroquois as a new fire rite of renewal, a Dance of the Dead or Ohigwe, to cure paralysis or the spiritual death of melancholy (Kurath 48). Winter is also the sanctioned season for storytelling (Hitakonanu'laxk 41). If the epistolary genre constitutes Marie de l'Incarnation's translator as subjected to the higher authority of the divine addressee, the combination of storytelling and performance in Moses's play reconfigures the enunciation of the translating subject as polyvalent within the play of social forces. Even as the first act tells a story about some words to make visible the aboriginals' experience of colonization as spiritual and physical death, the second act meditates on the role of performance in opening meaning to an exchange between languages that is life-enhancing. Translation as performance goes beyond the creative expansion of *aanikohtamowin*, to introduce another modality of examining the silent and invisible force of cultural rhetoric with its politics of address. Performance enables Moses to set words against gesture, voice against body, in a complex layering that turns the rhetoric of imposition against itself to expose it as rhetoric and evaluate its technologies and effects. Translating the codes of empire downwards, in the barbed lines of the Interlocutor, foregrounds how anyone may learn them, mimic them, yet not be contained by them. The European doubling and projection in the representation of the aboriginal as displaced European is performed by the Amerindian in a depropriative mimesis or strategy of reversion. Reciting them back to a Eurocanadian audience gives them yet another spin by confronting spectators with the limitations of their cultural knowledge. Performance thus establishes a discontinuous space transected by a number of different boundaries, an opening of the field of meaning for the audience's interpretation, in what constitutes a breach of the fourth wall.

Performance, within the current discursive field in Canada, functions as a sign of aboriginal authenticity, for orality is a fiction of firstness constituting identity as *First* Nations in a social contract founded in the legible. As such it has power within a struggle over political rights. Traditional aboriginal performance occurs as both storytelling and ritual. Theatrical performance, however, constitutes a European high art form. A tension between cultural performance and aestheticized theatricality informs the complex structures of address of *Almighty Voice and His Wife*. As co-director of the Committee to Reestablish the Trickster (1990), Daniel David Moses organized a series of workshops[36] to encourage aboriginal playwrights to produce cross-over works, intersemiotically translating traditional storytelling techniques with their enigmatic teaching form[37] into the agonistic models of dramatic conflict of aesthetic texts. Performance is a space for gathering and dispersing energy that effects a transition or transformation. A turning in the here and now that introduces a breach in regular social relations, moving into the betwixt and between to furnish a critique of the crisis, performance recontextualizes and establishes fields in which to situate a gesture, a body, a word. As such, it is a repetition with a difference, a transformance emphasizing process and action, along the model of translation as rewriting (Godard 1990b). Initiation rites and political ceremonies, which are considered to be social dramas, effect a transformation in the status and bodies of the participants in the action, whereas aesthetic drama works its transformations on the audience of the performance (Schechner 171). Moses's theatrical production, like those of a number of First Nations playwrights, works between these two modes of enunciation, producing transformations on both levels for the aboriginal actors constituted as subjects of enunciation, and for audiences turned into participants and initiated into new cultural knowledges or a critique of institutionally received knowledges.

Indeed, the question of subjectivity is central to performance which is concerned with the manipulation of the fragmented body and of space so that they become fluid, transformed into event. Though limited somewhat by a fictional character, performance initiates a play of desire with the performer as catalyst. Through the play of doubling and repetition are constructed spaces for the projection of different postures of desire wherein subjects-in-process constitute themselves through investment in different objects of desire and emerge from the "event" transformed (Feral 135). Seeking not to say something, but to set in place a series of relations among subjects through play with a variety of transitional objects, performance poses a deterritorializing gesture, forcing an opening that reorients relations of centre and periphery (Feral 138). Setting aside representation, performance stages social roles as models for demonstration and critique of social technologies. Through the play of the "fictive body" manipulated by the actor rehearsing her own staging of the imaginary as a subject-in-the-making, the fixed subjectivity of scripted social behaviours or roles is unravelled. Enunciations are conceptualized as process rather than finished utterances within the making of meaning for social subjects. The criterion of performability in the theatre changes the function of the linguistic utterance so that it becomes only one sign in relation to others in a web of sign systems. The sense of the individual units of meaning depends on their connection within this network which foregrounds the imbrication of text and interpretation, performance enacting a movement beyond the text which reveals itself to be open to multiple interpretations, not tied to the prior letter of the law. Performance introduces into the consideration of translation a movement from a constative theory of discourse, which frames truth claims in terms of fidelity or resemblance, toward a consideration of meaning-making within the terms of appropriateness in response to the conditions of address or performative theory of discourse, that is, to a consideration of the ethical or political effects within a field of clashing languages (Bakhtin 1981, 418). Your word *against* mine.

This brings me to the important second act of *Almighty Voice and His Wife* where the narrative of an historical event from an oppositional perspective that exposes the deadly constraints of living a history under conditions not of one's own making shifts to a Brechtian defamiliarization of performance where that history is rehearsed in a number of stereotypical Euroamerican representational modes. The Interlocutor's pedagogic discourse punctuates with details of their finer points the different performance styles to underline their conventionality, their culturally specific pertinency as modes of exclusion. Superimposed on them in a theatre of cultures is the Ghost Dance, aboriginal ritual that disrupts the generic contract of Eurocanadian drama by substituting communal participation for individual psychologized crisis. In a syncretic move, Moses layers a variety of "national" rituals, from the Cheyenne preface to the attribution to the Cree of a ceremony of the Sioux brought north to Saskatchewan by Sitting Bull, after his defeat at Little Big Horn. Moses invokes him as "Chief Shitting Bull" in a final outburst of high invective (80).

The massacre of the Ghost Dancers at Wounded Knee is introduced in the gallows humour of Act Two, Scene One, titled "Ghost Dance," when the Ghost, relating the phases of Almighty Voice's last stand against the police, describes how he "crawled out of the pit" he had dug to protect himself from the gunfire. "Wasn't much good against a seven pound cannon, now was it?" The Interlocutor replies: "His leg was gone. Talk about wounded knee! The bones were shattered, pulp" (73). The effect of such historical references is to constitute this as a cultural performance, in that it invites spectators to merge the space of their lifeworld and the imaginary space of theatricality with the "real" space in which they are living during the performance, the space-time of 1897 in the Michinis Hills near the One Arrow Reserve. Such a conflation of representational, theatrical, and cultural spaces as event is reinforced by the physical presence of stage features. The mechanism of such referentiality, however, works only when the appropriate cultural context is supplied by the audience. The spectator is interpellated differentially depending on whether s/he connects the stage space to the conventions of performance and so aestheticizes the action or whether s/he links them also to the historical events of Wounded Knee as site of the Ghost Dance massacre as well as site of the 1970s political struggles of the American Indian Movement. The Interlocutor is more explicit in framing the conditions of aesthetic performance as spectacle within the technology of the gaze of empiricism and imperialism than in keying the audience for aboriginal ceremonial.[38] In making the latter connection, aboriginal members among the racially and culturally mixed Toronto theatre public of Native Earth Performing Arts would constitute themselves as subjects of the enunciation, a collective historicized subject who actively participates in the transmission/transformation of discourses.

Counterpointing the many versions of the spectacle, theatrical version of the panopticon, is the participatory ritual of the Ghost Dance. One among a number of messianic religions which emerged in the nineteenth century in response to what Dickason terms the "upward spiral of regulation" (315) after the defeat at the Battle of Batoche (1885) of Big Bear's campaign to unite the Amerindians and of the Metis' hope of a nation, the Ghost Dance was a "cultural reaffirmation in the face of strange new forces" (Dickason 237). Such movements worried officials for they strengthened the people's inner resources to withstand the intensifying onslaughts on their culture. "The traditional way, far from disappearing as officials hoped, was reincarnating in different guises" (Dickason 287). Rising on the American prairies in the 1880s, the Ghost Dance syncretically linked new practices with traditional beliefs and forms. The white robes worn by Ghost Dancers were adapted from the Mormons. The rituals themselves, exhausting dances which induced ecstatic trances in the dancers within the traditional sacred circle, stressed their individuality in a quest for eternal life. In the trance under the medicine man's hypnosis, individuals communed with the spirit world and had visions of their friends who had died. This vision made them personally invulnerable to the violence of white culture. Prohibited in Canada after 1906 (Dickason 287), with its focus on reproducing a state in which the dancer moves through death to a transformed existence, the Ghost Dance proves an apt metaphor for traditional aboriginal culture which was driven underground by such oppression.

Making the ghosts dance again is both to transmit aboriginal tradition and to symbolize the dynamic and creative elements of a living aboriginal culture. Literally and figuratively, to dance is to commune with the dead souls and communicate to the world of the living visions of those who have died, yet are alive in the spirit world. This is another temporality and subjectivity than the Eurocanadian, not a singular embodied existence, nor a disembodied existence founded in the dualism of body and soul, but a permeability of boundaries between spirit and matter, now and then, between languages and cultures. Significantly, the Cree language is concentrated in the opening and closing scenes of Act Two, in the opening scene, titled "Ghost Dance," where the Ghost replies to the Interlocutor's taunts by ordering her away so he can finish his dance,[39] a line which returns as refrain at the end of the play. That the Interlocutor shifts languages and symbolic codes and answers him in Cree in the final interchange of the play[40] signifies the transformative effect of the dance.

A dance of resistance, of shape shifting, of metamorphosis or transformation, the Ghost Dance falls within the purvue of Trickster's double-voiced logic (Radin 148), a logic of contradiction, in which life and death, inside and outside, divinity and buffoonery, folly and cunning are coterminous, different twists of a single "moebius strip" (Vizenor). Appearances are unstable in this logic, for something may well be the opposite of what it seems. Moses both aphoristically sums up the historical significance of the Ghost Dance religion and invokes the Trickster in the last line of Scene Eight, titled "Standup" when Almighty Voice says: "I'm a dead Indian. I eat crow instead of buffalo" (95). This sentence is a complex example of the translation effect, or intersemiotic translation working through the trope of inversion. In general English usage, "eating crow" is the equivalent of "eating shit." There are double cultural inflections at work here: "eating crow" in the lexicon of the prairies means biting into Trickster. The logic of inside out privileging contradiction rather than opposition specifically invokes Crow, the revered messenger from the spirit world (Mooney 232), who is a figure celebrated in Crow dances where he is linked with the messiah, dances which form part of the Ghost Dance ceremonies among some Cheyenne groups (Mooney 187). Crow it is who has breathed life into Almighty Voice's Ghost, the "skeleton crew," to attempt a performance of "number seven," a dance in Scene Three. Seven, incidentally, is the sacred number of leaders in the Ghost Dance. In this scene, "this Almighty Gas character" (or "big fart," as he calls himself to White Girl, invoking Trickster (Radin 140) in contrast with the ghostly white god) "joins in on the season's carnival of ruin" (Moses 1992, 68). The carnivalesque contradiction played out in these puns is that what appears dead, according to the binary logic of the Christian religion which separates body and soul, is from within an aboriginal perspective most vibrantly alive, both more embodied and alive in more than body. "Eating crow" is not just eating a bony skeleton rather than a fleshy animal, but a sharing in the metamorphic power of Trickster. Instead of a figure of death-in-life, the ghost playing tricks with death becomes a figure of life in excess of death. Playing on the ambiguities of the Ghost as both figure of the sacrificial victim in Euro-canadian narrative and figure of spiritual renewal in aboriginal culture, Moses takes up the mechanisms of racism, the jokes, slurs, and invectives, and spins them around, inside out, to play them back to a white theatre audience interpellated as the "you" of address. Affirming the magic power of the word to transform, this functions as a discourse of decolonization. Eating crow, the aboriginal has Trickster's power vision that shifts shapes, re-turns the spectatorial gaze by quoting the white man's words back to him (94), restaged so as to produce the Amerindian as subject actively ordering discourse. Far from disappearing, the ghostly Indian is dancing again in new disguises, transforming him/herself in the logic of variation.

Humour as defiance — this is the rhetoric of the "comic holotrope" that Chippewa writer Gerald Vizenor connects with Trickster. His explication of the trickster narrative, arising in "agonistic imagination" as "a wild venture in communal discourse, an uncertain humour that denies aestheticism, translation, and imposed representations" (x), echoes Paul Radin's earlier account of the parodic and satiric bent of the Winnebago Trickster "ridiculing traditionally accepted order" (152). Indeed, Trickster violates "fixed boundaries of custom and law" (Radin 185), resists all boundaries to remain "open in every direction" (188), a "promise of differentiation" (168). This principle of presenting "various points of view," discourses within discourse, is what enables a writer to "elude historicism, racial representations and remain historical," as Vizenor comments (xi). Moses has taken up Trickster's challenge to make visible this ramifying rhetoric of aboriginal culture and so refracts English making it a translated language. Aboriginal concepts are exchanged in any language, especially in English. As principle of differentiation, Trickster is interpreted anew by every generation (Radin 168). Indeed, under the sign of Hermes, or heterotopia, *traduction,* the mode of transformation specific to literary texts, works the combinatory logic of generation itself, "diluent les anciennes figures et composent formes ou formules inattendues et rétrospectivement nécessaires... d'une science *du vivant*" (Serres 16). *Interpretio* displaces *translatio.*

Asserting control over the discourse, over the representation of history, over the categories concerning identity formation, is a crucial tactic for a subaltern group to oppose hegemonic practices. Identity is no stable effect of a coherent entity but is constituted through the technology of language where the "I" or subject of enunciation remains contingent and provisional to institutional policies and practices articulated in historically differentiated discourses subject to contestation and to change. Variation is marked by a functional shift in a sign system constituting a discursive displacement with a transformation in the relation of object and subject of knowledge. Tracing localized economies of damage and neglect in writing as resistance challenges the monopoly of discursive practices and articulates different conditions of possibility which make visible the limits of dominant fictions of the real. Translation as resistance, then, would be a tactic of intervention in what constitutes the basis of "linguistic" as well as "national" identity in Canada.

Ghosts are dancing, Trickster reigns at Spadina and Bloor in downtown

Toronto. Moses, though, does not speak Delaware. In fact, there are too few speakers of the language now to constitute a linguistic community. Moreover, in his theory of language as in Marie de l'Incarnation's, aboriginal languages remain surplus signs, despite cultural difference in the conditions of language use. They are, however, within an economy where loss and gain are not the only terms for conceptualizing change or distinction. Rather within a regime of maximized exchange there is a theoretically infinite productivity not only of values, but of forms of exchange of values. Though Moses would locate cultural difference under the sign of Trickster, his/her principles of energy, of fluid boundaries and fluctuating identity, find analogues in the grammar of Algonkian languages with their emphasis on verbs that highlight action and on the addressee rather than the speaking subject. I've twisted the moebius strip inside out again with this paradox. In yet another twist, while I am studying *Aanishinaabemowin*, Daniel David Moses has just published a new play called, in echo of my argument, *Brebeuf's Ghost*.

Do linguistic boundaries necessarily coincide with cultural borders? Can a culture survive without a language? What constitutes cultural fluency? These are the thorny questions raised by the two examples I have analysed which are respectively the translation of language but not culture and the translation of culture but not language. "Language is not everything," as Gayatri Spivak reminds us, merely a clue to the point of dissolution of the boundaries of the self. Attending to rhetoric — the established modes of address — as it works in "the silence between and around words" is necessary to constitute a model for a different language that acknowledges its foreignness and avoids repetition of the ready-made (Spivak 1993,180 – 81). This ethical project of attentiveness to particularity also necessitates full consideration of the specificity of language whose syntax codifies a logic of relations, as in the case of the Algonkian languages where the marked category is that of the object of address rather than the subject. For differentiated knowledges, different positions for subjects are produced in the dynamic relations of language to culture with a more layered knowledge produced for the subject who comprehends both cultural and linguistic codes. Such discontinuous spaces of language and culture formulate a challenge to any "transcultural universal" (Bassnett 1993, 159) of meaning-making. The full implications of this argument for cultural difference have not been addressed here in that my argument has been presented through two texts rather than through a series of examples. That my analysis of the differentiated models of semiosis or translation has been so restricted constitutes a limitation in its tendency toward a binary model of opposition between a logic of identity or equivalency and a logic of non-identity or contradiction. To demonstrate my contention that translation theories are constituted in a particular historical instance of enunciation from within a dynamic field of variation will necessitate further analysis of other moments in the history of translation in Canada.

NOTES FROM THE CULTURAL FIELD:

Canadian Literature from Identity to Commodity

❖

Picking daisies? I wish I were. Anywhere else not here. It's a beautiful sunny day and the white daisies of high summer are giving way to the bright pinks and purples of Michaelmas daisies in the fields. "Here," though, is a computer and a pile of books and notes. These are not "Field Notes" in the Kroetschian mode, a poetic ethnography of life lived in a particular place, though I shall draw on their serialism with its shifting perspectival play. The field about which I write is the Bourdieusian "cultural field," the complex inter-relation of heterogeneous "habitus" — the lived social relations of ruling, taken-for-granted understandings and practices of the everyday — that interact dynamically to compose "the field of cultural production" in the context of the geopolitical entity known as Canada. And "here," I understand with Doreen Massey, as a spatial figure, that is, as "social relations 'stretched out'" (2).

Dionne Brand uses spatial figures or "chronotopes," as Bakhtin called them, to structure her fictions. "Here" in *In Another Place, Not Here* functions as site of conflict and decision to act, as in Adela's decision to stop her breath "Here" and Verlia's "red explosion" (22). "Here" contrasts with Verlia's dreams of escape and her Icarus-like flight into the sea where "she's in some other place already, less tortuous, less fleshy" (247), as well as with "Nowhere" (18), as Adela's ancestress in her loss and grief under slavery calls the place she is brought to, where she refuses to name her children. The opposition between these adverbs of presence and absence frames the tension in the novel as the legacy of slavery's dehumanization is compounded by racist discrimination and diasporic alienation. "There is little here here," to paraphrase Gertrude Stein's pronouncement about Oakland, California, neither in Toronto, nor in the Caribbean, nor even in Africa for the migrant in continuous displacement. There is only a struggle for empowerment and dreams of breaking free "in another place."

An oscillation between constraint and freedom is developed spatially in *At the Full and Change of the Moon*, Dionne Brand's second novel, where attempts to fix place and time under the regime of slavery are transformed a century after emancipation into the nomadism of diaspora. The map on Lieutenant-Governor George Hill's desk, which "can only describe the will of estate owners and governors" (52) for clearly authorized ownership, gives way to a "cartography ... of longings and muddled sight" (53). For, as Brand observes, "[m]aps are such subjective things, borders move all the time. ... Paper rarely contains — even its latitudinal and longitudinal lines gesture continuations. Paper does not halt land any more than it can halt thoughts" (52). Brand develops the trope of mapping as writing that constructs meaning, "the stroke of a pen designating a certain place on a map" (52). A map is a system of signs, not the territory: it is drawn from a particular angle of vision on the "real" which may conflict with other perspectives or mappings.

One such perspectival shift instigated the novel, as Brand recounted in a subsequent talk, "Is the Past a Fiction?" (York University, 4 Oct. 1999). In a museum she had discovered in elegant seventeenth-century prose the notation of a captain of a slave ship recording precise compass directions for landing a vessel safely on Trinidad. In the novel, these compass points form the intimate cartography of Kamena that he transmits to Bola, sign now of his longing for freedom and home, sign too of his failure to locate Terre Bouillante somewhere in the interior where the Maroons established a community beyond the regime of slavery. For "all his maps were discourses for settlers" (54), the "terrible poetry" of maps for the importation of slaves, for the commodification of women and men, maps of the coastline with its extreme conditions where "at the full and change of the moon" the tide would rise "four feet perpendicular" (53). There are no maps of the interior showing the way to freedom. But, as the novel unfolds, the compass does not remain steady to guide vessels to shore with their human cargo. It spins wildly on its axis as Bola's children and grandchildren, absorbing the cartography of longing through many stories, search not in the interior but outward over sea and land to every point on the compass, to South and North America and, reversing the middle passage across the Atlantic, to Europe. The Governor's map legislating property, as Brand writes, "cannot note the great fluidity of maps" (52). Informed by desire they are infinitely mobile, tracing the multiple shapes of longing for freedom yet entangled inevitably in the precarious human condition. With no fixed point, some lose their bearings.

I invoke Brand's fiction with its exploration of the discursive constitution of space under different formations of power to highlight both the persistence of a "geograficional" (van Herk 1990) imperative in Canadian literature discourses, despite the changing territories of the social imaginary which stretch now to encompass the Caribbean, and the central point of my argument, that even if the geophysical territory were the same, the conditions of possibility for mapping it with a pen have changed radically. In the transformation I am concerned with, occurring between the 1950s and the 1990s, literature works no longer in the service of the nation's identity within a Cold War competition between communism and capitalism, but to further its economic security in an era of global capitalism. "Culture," which was first disembedded from pre-capitalist traditional life-ways and positioned as a countervailing force to industry within a social whole, is now as an autonomous and self-regulating field of social reproduction and domain of value positioned asymmetrically as a counter force to democracy within an all-encompassing "economy" to whose ends it is subordinate.

"WHERE IS HERE?": TAKE ONE

In his "Conclusion" to the *Literary History of Canada* first published in 1965, Northrop Frye articulated in a celebrated koan what he saw as central to Canadian literature, the "theme of strangled articulateness," related to the perennial problematic of Canadian identity. As he wrote: "[the Canadian sensibility] is less perplexed by the question 'Who am I?' than by some such riddle as 'Where is here?'" This "paradox" arises from the "foreshortening of Canadian history" where many different social formations ("revolutions" in Frye's words) (1976, 338) occurring in rapid succession prevented the consolidation of any tradition of writing. The absence of a stable centre to culture has made it difficult for a writer to situate her/himself temporally in relation to a legitimate line of descent. And history, in the wake of Hegel, entails the establishment of causal chains forging such legitimating narrative linkages. However, there is "no Canadian writer of whom we can say what we can say of the world's major writers, that their readers can grow up inside their work without ever being aware of a circumference" (333). While great literature "pulls us away from the Canadian context towards the centre of literary experience itself" (334), drawing us towards a universal validity, Canadian literature lacking such "genuine classics" makes us continually aware of its social and historical setting, of the particularity of the "Canadian context." As Earle Birney phrases it, the writer is spooked only "by our lack of ghosts" (37). Instead, Canadian writers have tried, Frye notes, to "assimilate a Canadian environment" even as changes in communications technology are sweeping away the boundaries of that environment (1976, 338). Canadian critics, he proposes, should not engage in a canonical exercize of evaluative discrimination, but perform a kind of literary ethnography and focus on literature's relation to "Canadian life." Critics would record the reactions of "the Canadian imagination," rather than analyze the "orthodox genres of poetry and fiction" within an "autonomous world of literature" (334). "Where is here?" comes to signify a failure of the imagination to conceive of "Canada" as a community. Yet this should, I propose, be viewed less as a lack of an imaginary than as the consequence of specific colonial relations of power instantiating Canadian economic and cultural dependency. As Hayden White observes after Hegel, historical representation is "conceivable only in terms of its interest in law, legality, and legitimacy." Only the subject identifying with the social system and authorized by it can constitute a fully realized narrative representing the "real" as historical (1987, 13 – 14). Literary history and criticism contribute to a legislative project providing a vision of adequacy and redress for their politics of inclusion. Those on the margins of power, however, produce fragments, catalogues, rather than coherent narratives for a nation-in-formation.

Paradox is Frye's figure for this aporia when spatial relations that should bring cultural and aesthetic values into alignment and create "Canada" as a cultural presence with a self-legitimating tradition pull, instead, in different directions as the literary splits off from the social, myth from history. Labyrinth is another figure for such a structural absence in Margaret Atwood's reworking of space-time. In "A night in the Royal Ontario Museum," despite diagrams in all corners of the building, "YOU ARE HERE/ the labyrinth holds me, /turning me around ... a spiral" (96), spinning the speaker back in time. Like Lewis Carroll's Alice, she is caught in a recursive regression, an infinite series turning back on itself.[1] Or stutters like Stein with her Whiteheadian perspectivism — here is here is here — in which subtle variations and distinctions in perception emerge through repetition to inform different takes on a world in becoming. Through their lack of totality or coherency, these figures show by way of contrast the extent to which narrative strains for the effect of having filled in all the gaps.

What these various modes of incompleteness underscore is that "here" is a floating signifier or "shifter" (a "deictic" in Benveniste's terms). Not referential, it is correlative to the position of enunciation and designates co-extension with the speaking subject[2] who is constituted as such in the speech act, even as language is performatively constituted in the relation of address between "I" and "you." Just as these are reversible and reciprocal terms, so too "here" is interchangeable with "there" (which correlates with distance from the speaking subject), while "now" entertains relations of mutual complementarity or implication with "then." Indeed, it is only within such a reciprocal relation to "there" that "here" makes sense, not just in the constitution of subjectivity as "intersubjectivity," as Benveniste contends (266), but in its constitution as sociality within differing regimes of power, as Deleuze and Guattari argue, since juridical acts or their equivalents — "laws of social obligation" — are implicit presuppositions in speech acts (1987, 79). In a relation of "redundancy" or overdetermination (not identity), these presuppositions regulating pertinency have the force of "order-words" to carry out social transformation as they realign relations of "here" and "there," of "us" and "them." More than fashion an "imagined community" (Benedict Anderson), they establish hierarchies of power in the speech exchange with socio-political effects. And it is to such lines of force, I propose, that we should attend in considering the implications of Frye's utterance, "Where is here?" In what relation does "here" stand to "there"? And "now" to "then"? For it is only in such a relation that we can grasp "here" — and "now."

What conditions of possibility, what lines of force, shape the distinctions between inside and outside? As Bourdieu reminds us, while many relational theories restrict their "systematic analyses" of works of art to the "field of discourse," and consider the "field of position-takings" in and for itself "independently of the field of positions which it manifests," a "field of position-takings" is not constituted as a system just for analysis in a "coherence-seeking intention," but is the "product of a permanent *conflict*" wherein change results from a shifting balance of socio-economic forces (1993, 32 – 34; my emphasis). What is entailed in the move from "then" to "now," I propose, is a shift first from a concern with establishing sovereignty over a physical space through communications technology to securing the symbolic space of the nation-in-formation through a governmental apparatus of culture and, more recently, to securing global markets for the export of Canada's "knowledge industries." The shift in cultural values and national definition is not the consequence of some essential economic rationality but the effect of political strategies that aim to re-structure the social and political dimensions of capitalism so as to ensure the continual reproduction of the Canadian state. Such "structural readjustments" have profound implications for literature and for literary criticism in Canada in both material and formal terms. Not that these can be separated for, as Bakhtin and Bourdieu insist, genre is always a function of particular social relations of address.

Frye, though, separates text from history and context in what Eli Mandel has called "schizophrenia." While Frye develops a theory of genre as an "autonomous world" or "order of words" in his *Anatomy of Criticism*, it is based on achieved classics in a gesture that preserves the authority of a Eurocentric field of the Literary from the historical changes of writing in englishes. Yet in his analyses of Canadian literature, he advocates the historical over the aesthetic model of criticism to examine the "setting" of the writer (not the work) in a way that promises reconciliation of the divergence between examining "the literary" and examining "life." This opposition between the Literary and the Canadian informs his "Conclusion" to the *Literary History of Canada*. Congratulating its contributors on the "maturity of Canadian literary scholarship and criticism," he contends they have "outgrown" an understanding of criticism as "evaluation" and engaged instead in writing "cultural history" (1976, 333 – 34). Its "themes" are those of "exploration, settlement, and development" as these relate to a "social *imagination*" (334). While this has the relative advantage of facilitating the study "in all its dimensions" of a "relatively small and low-lying cultural development" (334), over a "huge debunking project" that would expose Canadian literature as a "poor naked *alouette*" (333) lacking dignity and hence authority, the *History* nonetheless becomes "something of a catalogue," rather than a fully realized narrative with a coherent structure (334). The narrative Frye discerns between the lines relates the establishment of a settler literature as *bildung* whether in the name of humanist values of self-development or of nationalist values of self-determination that would fashion citizens and foster identity.

I do not want to dwell on critiques of Frye's theories, but rather to attend to their implications for an emergent Canadian literature criticism as it was being institutionalized in the academy in the 1970s[3] and, more pressingly, to situate his theory within its historical moment in Canadian state formation and its "tactics" of "governmentality" (Foucault 1991) whereby, through cultural regulation and administration, the nation's boundaries were secured and its population constituted as citizens. This is, of course, to read Frye's theory as informed by a specific historical period, as contingent, hence ideological, despite his claims for the timelessness of the recurring, archetypal patterns in literary texts that are not mimetic reflections of a world of temporal flux but rather contain the world of nature since, "inside the mind of infinite man," they embody and show forth "the total dream of man." Literature manifests the "imaginative limit of desire" which, eternal, gives expression to an essentially unchanging human nature (1957, 119). In this, as Catherine Belsey points out, Frye's theory embraces contradiction for, unexplained, the relation between desire and language in an intuitive understanding of pattern and verbal structures, clashes with his notion of meaning's conventionality and systematicity whose principles can be taught democratically to any undergraduate. Turning aside from analysis of linguistic and social mediations in the production of meaning, Frye ultimately fails to break with the "empiricist-idealist position" that presumes literary knowledge to be the product of anterior experience conceived in a transcendent mind (Belsey 26).

The issue of inside versus outside posed by this residual idealism manifests itself not only in literary form in the tension between universal mythic pattern and the particularism of a Canadian "experiential catalogue," but in the very distinctiveness of the catalogue's content, uniqueness that implicitly differentiates, separates, creates borders. As "garrison mentality," this difference from an other takes the form of a retreat behind a border for self-protection from external threats which Frye posits as key to the "Canadian imagination" and literature (1976, 342). Moreover, this specialness of Canadian identity is premised on disembedding culture from the political economy and so neglecting the social dimensions of dependency. Aesthetic and social models of criticism increasingly diverge: not only does Frye's study of Canadian literature not help us learn something about the very nature of the literary, as he promised it would, but it fails to enlarge our conception of "what is literary." The effect of this theoretical "containment," as Heather Murray has suggested, is to protect his system of poetics from the challenge of (post)colonial writings (1987, 80). Paradoxically, however, Frye's commitment to promoting only "the best" that has been thought and written, though it was inspired by Matthew Arnold's ideas about English studies as a vehicle for secularized moral training and building Britishness, had long been adapted to Canadian nationalist aims of civilizing a disparate population to innoculate them against the related ills of anarchy and philistinism, of barbarism and materialism. Like many of his predecessors, especially Pelham Edgar and E.K. Brown, as Margery Fee has demonstrated, Frye promoted canonical British literature in the classroom, while facilitating the production of Canadian literature. His work for *Canadian Poetry* in the 1930s and his poetry reviews for "Letters in Canada" in the 1950s was the experimental terrain on which he claimed to have worked out his poetics. Marking boundaries, English studies encouraged resistance to American approaches, judged more populist and materialist. So Canadians did not necessarily need to construct a national literature for a distinctive identity, providing they could use "Britishness" to fend off Americans without falling too much under British sway. Canadian critics recognized this hierarchy of prestige, with Canadian literature placed third, which has led to the persistent marginalization of Canadian literature in the university English curriculum where it requires constant justification in the face of "absolute" standards.

Thematic criticism of the kind practiced in the 1970s by Margaret Atwood in *Survival: A Thematic Guide to Canadian Literature,* D.G. Jones in *Butterfly on Rock: A Study of Themes and Images in Canadian Literature,* John Moss in *Patterns of Isolation in English Canadian Fiction,* and a host of other critics, might be seen as an attempt to link the aesthetic more closely to the social were it not for its disregard for literary history and its total-izing gesture of incorporating every textual detail into one overriding "pattern" or "theme." Even more so when themes relate to geophysical space — the so-called "topocentrism" of Canadian criticism — texts are seen to represent the experience of a particular society which the artist has faithfully portrayed (a kind of pseudo non-fiction) rather than an ideological mapping by the critic (a critical fiction). Though apparently taking Frye's advice to do cultural ethnography, these thematic critics focus more on setting than on social structures or historical formations or language(s). This criticism operates a reduction from an anthropo-logical concept of culture as a "way of life," with a "characteristic style," incorporating a "structure of feeling" (Angus 39). Many relevant aspects of Canadian culture remain unexamined, especially the diachronic his-torical one subsumed in the timeless order of myth. A certain conflation occurs so that overlapping axes of cultural discourse become co-termi-nous. The high/low opposition of culture posited by Frye collapses into an English/Canadian binary, itself implicitly an opposition of Canadian versus American culture that equates with a conflict between public versus private ownership (Angus 38 – 39). Canadian literature plays the role of folklore or popular culture in other discursive formations, yet is distinguished thus from American mass culture.

The critical deployment of literature in this contradictory articulation for managing social tensions and producing subjects permeated cul-tural discourses in the period following wwii, symptom of an extreme anxiety over Canada's territorial boundaries. Literature was especially important in left-nationalist cultural discourses: for example, the Marx-ist writer Margaret Fairley taught courses in Canadian literature in addition to promoting Canadian writing in the periodicals she edited, in opposition to the general practices of the academy which focused on British literature (Kimmel). Such discourses of cultural identity marked the political culture from the period following passage of the Statute of Westminster in 1931, which accorded Canada full responsibility for foreign affairs, and so legally brought an end to Britain's colonial control over Canada's extra-territorial relations. While protecting Canada's external borders was indeed a critical project in this period of international strife, of equal concern was the consolidation of internal rifts within both the geographical and symbolic space of the nation. The "yellow peril" had been of particular concern since the 1920s when studies synthesizing data from the decanal census reports noted a greater propensity of Chinese migrants for criminal behaviour and mental illness that correlated with their failure to learn English and low educational achievements (Hurd). In the 1940s, Japanese-Canadians were stripped of their property in fear of their support for the Fascist cause. Immigration from Southern and Central Europe also created racial tensions with Canadians of British origin in view of their potential for internal subversion in the form of Nazi cadre among Italian and German migrants during the 1940s or of a Communist fifth column in the 1950s. Assimilation of these potential dissidents, when they were not forcibly interned, necessitated a vibrant Canadian culture with centripetal force to bind them to the nation-state. Moreover, there was also the persistent resistance of French-Canadians which had once again become a matter of national security during the Conscription Crisis of 1944. The problems this unrest caused for the project of a unified symbolic identity are intimated in Northrop Frye's brief mention of the two languages and cultures of Canada which oblige him constantly to resort to "synecdoche" when speaking of "Canadian literature [sic]." Any advantages such a complex "national culture" may hold are only "potential": "The difficulties, if more superficial, are also more actual and more obvious" (1976, 336).

The problem of managing such a diverse and volatile population through the "strategy of culture" (Innis 1952) had been a major concern of the Canadian state during the 1930s when a series of national institutions to regulate the exchange of signs, most prominently the CBC and NFB, had been established in order to bind space through coast-to-coast communication (Druick). In this development of a governmental policy for administering culture, the state followed a model initiated in the 1840s when, in the absence of adequate capital to finance the construction of canals to bind the physical space of the Canadas, government purchased them and financed their completion. Confederation in 1867 further extended this governmental tactic by centralizing the railway debt of the colonies. As Harold Innis contended (1956), such extensive government intervention was necessary to compensate for the inability or lack of interest of a capitalist class under colonialism to construct the transportation and communication infrastructure requisite for development of the economy of the new state and so established a "tradition" of government subsidy and ownership important in later developments in the field of culture along the model of transportation and communication. Culture, however, promised to provide a compensatory symbolic identity to counter absolute economic dependency, as well as to provide content for an "empty shell" of a nation "constructed through the rhetoric of technological nationalism" and hence available for foreign content —"American mass culture" (Dowling 333). Contradiction thus informed the discourse on culture in Canada where nationalist, welfare, and market models have long contended for preeminence (Godard 1999a, 29; Godard 1995).

A civilizing role for culture was widely advocated in the post wwii period precisely when the Canadian economy was increasingly being developed as a branch plant of American capital as the government facilitated us inroads into the natural resource industries. The Arnoldian idealism informing Frye's poetics was shared by many among Canada's intellectual and political elites. Individual artists, though, left out of the cultural policy arrangements of the 1930s that favoured the communications industries of broadcasting and film, began organizing to have state support for the high aesthetic forms in the absence of capital investment in the arts by the economic elite either through individual patronage or private foundation. Artists formulated their position at the Kingston Conference on the Arts in 1941 and marched on Ottawa in 1944 to present their demands to government via the Turgeon Commission on national reconstruction. Why, they argued, had Canada put such great effort into winning the war, if there was no country, no cultural identity, to come home to? It was not until the subsequent Massey-Lévesque *Royal Commission on National Development in the Arts, Letters, and Sciences* (1949 – 1951) that this concern found wider resonance in policy formulations. The Massey-Lévesque *Report* made an explicit connection between autonomous cultural identity and national defence: "If we as a nation are concerned with the problem of defence, what, we may ask ourselves, are we defending? We are defending civilisation, our share of it, our contribution to it. The things with which our inquiry deals are the elements which give civilisation its character and meaning" (Canada 1974). Nonetheless, the obsession with identity was fuelled by worry that, with the emergence of the US as a superpower following WWII, a slide into barbarism might well take the form of American mass culture overwhelming the Canadian state. The Massey-Lévesque *Report* is explicit on this need for a distinctive Canadian culture to secure the continued existence of the state. As it notes: "a vast and disproportionate amount of material coming from a single alien source [the US] may stifle rather than stimulate our own creative effort; and passively accepted without any standards of comparison, this may weaken critical faculties. ... Without a vigorous and distinctive cultural life" national independence "would be nothing but an empty shell" (18).

Evidence of the urgency of these concerns was to be found in the troubling outcome of negotiations between British and Canadian publishers between 1943 and 1945. The British were worried about the loss of overseas trade while Canadian publishers were chafing under their place in the publishing industry in the North Atlantic triangle when British publishers sold North American rights to New York publishers. Controlled by British and American publishers, the Canadian market was largely dominated by imported books with only a small output of original publications restricted to Canadian rights only. With a limited market, it was difficult for Canadian publishers to sustain their production let alone increase their capital. Canada could only be treated as a "country" under the Berne Convention and become a producer of cultural texts if the British publishers would recognize the Canadian market as separate from the American in the sale of rights. Despite British publishers' accord in principle on this question, they made an agreement with their American counterparts in 1946 to divide the world in two, with the United Kingdom having sole rights to book markets in the British dominions, colonies and dependencies and continental Europe, while the United States had exclusive rights in its colonies and dependencies (Parker 371). For reasons of geographical proximity, Canada was included in the us exclusive territories rather than the British. This had a significant impact on the translation of Quebec writing, for example. The works of Gabrielle Roy first appeared in New York and American practices established a norm for translation in English Canada. Reception of her work appropriated its emotional intensity for an anglo-Canadian identity and nourished a myth of Canada's feminized stance vis à vis us imperialist materialism (Godard 1999b, 507). Fearing that the publishing industry was in peril of disappearing and that Canadian culture would soon be caught in the orbit of American culture, the Massey-Lévesque *Report* recommended massive government subsidies to writers, artists, and publishers. This policy was not instituted, however, until the Canada Council was formed in 1957. Speeches at its opening ceremony manifested the perennial tensions in Canadian cultural discourse between nation and market as economies of value. Co-chair Père Georges-Henri Lévesque forecast the "expansion of humanism in Canada" in the search for "Truth" and "Beauty," while the chair, Brooke Claxton, both adhered to Thomas D'Arcy McGee's vision of art as civilizing to unify "the great new Northern nation" by "keep[ing] down dissension" and contemplated the great benefits of the council in economic metaphors of a "dividend" realized from "investment" (qtd. in Godard 1995).

Only one of the semi-autonomous cultural agencies forming the apparatus through which centralized pedagogical strategies tackled the problem of liberal democratic governance, that of simultaneously ordering individual citizen and national whole, the Canada Council nonetheless had a dramatic impact on the field of cultural production. Moreover, in the era of Sputnik, the council funded the massive expansion of the universities, supporting new libraries and facilities for art and music education, as well as providing scholarships for graduate education and fellowships for faculty research. Northrop Frye commented on the effects of the change in his "Conclusion" to the revised *Literary History of Canada* (1976) as a "colossal verbal explosion that has taken place in Canada since 1960" which made him feel as though he were "driving a last spike" and "waking up from the National Neurosis" (318 – 19). Here, then, was here.

"Where is here?": Take Two

"Where is here now?" What's the difference between "now" and "then"? Has there been a break or continuity? Writing a history of the present is always a fraught project when the only clock is variation. Have the shifts brought about irrevocable changes? Or have modifications been incremental in a continuous becoming? To a certain extent, nothing has changed: the nation remains the frame of reference for thinking the literary as it has been since the Renaissance linked language, literature, and bounded political territory. Criticism continues to turn around the problematic of identity, though literature serves to mobilize the claims of many groups for inclusion in a more broadly imagined community reconfiguring the nation. Diversity is proclaimed key to Canadian "post-modern" identity in an abandonment of a project of symbolic unity in favour of "disunity as unity" (Kroetsch 1989, 21) — a subversion of "total-izing systems" or "challenge to boundaries" (Hutcheon 1988, 183). Topo-centrism remains an ordering figure but now "Land [is] Sliding" (New 1997) when read as a trope operative in relations of power rather than as a static given available for naming and possessing. Criticism atten-tive to the mediations of language recognizes literature — and literary criticism — as ideological mapping not expression of pre-existent terri-tory. Within a different frame, from the perspective of global capital, everything has changed under the material conditions produced by the rise of a distinctively transnational capitalism. The 1950s post-war reorganization of the economy and decolonization movements laid the groundwork for a new economic world system. Transformations under way in the form of powerful new technologies, new forms of media interrelationship, a new global division of labour, and a market fully commodified announce continuation of the vertiginous pace of change to the Keynesian welfare state initiated in 1973 by the us unilateral repudiation of the Bretton-Woods agreement that made it both possible and profitable to speculate on international currency exchanges. Sub-sequently, the us emerged as sole superpower with global hegemony. Literature no longer "expresses" and so binds territory, nor retains its utopian dimensions as an ideal human realm of value. Instead, culture is caught up in struggles for economic domination through cultural exchange in a different economy of value that turns not on the mediating power of labour but on speculation on the market itself.

More than just uncertain, the nation has become a site of profound anxiety, a matter for "worrying" (Kertzer 1998) and conflictual articulations linked only by their inability to locate a "social community" or vibrant civil society to buffer the solitary modern subject (Davey 1993, 264). "Post-national" though Frank Davey may call the rhetoric of contemporary Canadian fiction, the nation remains the field of its material production where publishing is organized under the state apparatus of the Canada Council and Heritage Canada. Still, the competing models of the nation Davey identified, the "monolithic Ontario-centred 'caring' society" and the "open post-national arena of unrestrained economic opportunity," translate the ideologies of opposing political formations with different ways of relating inside and outside (262). The struggle between these divergent political positions is currently redirecting the tactics of governmentality away from population-making through culture. Two articulations of these positions emerged during the debate over free trade in 1988 in what has proven to be a pivotal moment in the restructuring of the Canadian state. One, taken by a number of prominent writers, argued on "political" grounds for continuity in government strategies on behalf of the country's "welfare" (*The Globe and Mail* A4). The other, that of the capitalist elite, adopted by a number of writers and right-wing journalists and paid for by the Canadian Alliance for Trade and Job Opportunities (a business group advocating Free Trade), argued for unfettered free speech and the "economic opportunities" of the individual (*The Globe and Mail* A6).[4]

This rhetoric has been deployed by the new right over the last decade to present as inevitable and necessary the dismantling of the welfare state and, consequently, the transference of the infrastructure of transportation, communication, and culture developed with tax-funds generated from all its citizens into the hands of the state's richest members, so increasing the gap between rich and poor. Such resurgent liberalism is eminently political, despite disavowals in the libertarian rhetoric, and constitutes a veritable transvaluation of value in that it gives precedence to economic rights above all others, those rights to maximize opportunities for individual profit. An ideal of thick social citizenship is abdicated in favour of lean economistic consumerism. It is not labour power that drives this new economy but speculation on surplus value. And in this era of economic fundamentalism it is difficult to make value claims for health, knowledge, or beauty. For the state no longer works to produce human capital through self-development or self-determination. Biopower has been replaced by the continual surveillance of a control society whose violence is increasingly directed at the economically disadvantaged in an age of downward mobility. Criminalizing the poor has become high sport in an economic system indifferent to human welfare. Any notion of a common good that might constrain individual self-interest has withered with, as Hegel warned, a resulting loss of civil society. In such a scheme of value, the patient labour of creating weighs less than the chance winning of a lottery ticket. Sound cultural production, good publishing, are evaluated on the extent to which they maximize profit for shareholders, not on the quality and force of ideas they put into circulation as these transform people.

Evidence of the impact of a shift in conditions of possibility is to be found in the changing discourses on culture at both federal and provincial levels with direct implications for policy. Since the passage of the Charter of Rights and Freedoms in 1982, procedural liberalism with its privileging of individual rights has been reshaping the Canadian state. Throughout the 1990s following on the heels of the Free Trade Agreement, there were continuous cutbacks to the cultural apparatuses for the exchange of signs founded in the 1930s, CBC and NFB, redirecting production to for-profit media companies. Even responsibility for financing the national debt was largely transferred from the Bank of Canada to the commercial banks whose profits increased geometrically. The Canada Council was not spared in this restructuring. After losses to inflation throughout the 1980s, and cutbacks through the early 1990s, a further five per cent cut in 1995 squeezed the arts communities financially. So, too, the arm's-length principal was compromised by reduced importance accorded jury decisions and more direct bureaucratic intervention by council administrators and government itself through programmes administered by Heritage Canada. These changes accompanied a shift in the council's mandate from working in the "public interest" on behalf of citizens to a corporate model of rationalization serving clients. Council funding was withdrawn from research and arts-service organizations, longstanding sites of policy articulation, which have translated artists' discourse from the symbolic to the political with power to affect the world. This implicitly consolidated an image of the artist as isolated genius, a heroic individual rather than an integral part of the body politic with claims on its resources. Heritage Canada's abrupt cancellation of funds in the third year of a five-year programme directed to publishers in compensation for new sales taxes and termination of special postal book rates pushed a number of them to the verge of bankruptcy when they were unable to carry out projects for which contracts had been signed. The situation was critical in Ontario, where the slash and burn tactics of its new Conservative government cancelled the loans guarantee programme to publishers in 1995, as well as reducing the Ontario Arts Council (OAC) budget by 40 per cent in less than two years. Always undercapitalized, the arts community lost a significant amount of working capital and, hence, the potential for generating more, initiating a downward spiral. Ironically, fewer performances or productions and a loss of revenue led to fewer applications for international travel or exhibitions and a reduction in taxes paid into government coffers.

The shift in cultural discourses was most noticeable in Ontario in the changing connotations of "balance" as this signifier rationalized and configured state intervention in cultural production (Godard 1999a). Since its founding in the early 1960s, the OAC moved from a participatory to a market model of the arts. In the report on its inaugural year, 1963–1964, the OAC's mandated sphere of action was configured in a medical or juridical metaphor of balance: the state would intervene to guard against the "deformity" of "one-sided development" in a heterogeneous field of values and so avoid "an increase in wealth" alone that would impede "real progress" which requires the development of "all the faculties belonging to our nature." Education in the arts would enable the full development of human potential. Now, the OAC is under the wing of the Ministry of Citizenship, Culture, and Recreation, not the Ministry of Education. In the pronouncements of its executive director in the report for 1996–1997, balance has been resignified as innovative "partnerships" linking individual arts organizations with specific

"private" enterprises or wealthy benefactors. For its chair, in 1998, creativity manifests itself not in the production of aesthetic objects but in
"creating partnerships, alliances, and other *imaginative* ways of earning
revenue" (OAC 1998b; my emphasis). Rather than ser-ving as "catalyst"
bringing divergent sectors of civil society together or as "peace corps"
bringing arts education to the hinterlands of Ontario (OAC 1964), in
1998 OAC developed a handbook to help arts groups generate "impact
numbers" to use in "credible arguments for the arts" when soliciting
sponsorships, including a computer model for calculating "the economic
value of volunteers" (1998b). In a neo-liberal regime ruled by numbers,
the function of arts groups has shifted from creative processes to the
collection of economic data quantifying outcomes so as to justify arts
activities in the corporate sector. Canadian culture becomes synonymous with the culture of capital.

This discursive change legitimated new articulations of culture that
hamper publication of Canadian literature texts and critical analyses
of them. Corporate sponsorship and donations have gone primarily to
large, mainstream organizations producing safe work by dead European
masters rather than to smaller groups featuring new aesthetic work by
living artists. This privileging of elite forms and the artist as isolated
genius fostering a rhetoric of celebrity also shaped the OAC's policies on
literary publication which, in 1998, introduced a distinction between the
high canonical genres of poetry, novel and drama — eligible for subsidy
in periodicals — and essays which were deemed non-literary and not eligible. Not only does this deepen the wedge between the aesthetic and
the social in that it runs counter to the broad definition of the literary
proposed by *Literary History of Canada* with its advocacy of "cultural history" (Frye 1976, 333 – 34), but it increases the symbolic capital of consecrated works over creative responses to struggles of local communities.
Culture is anywhere else, not here. These policies reinforced the more
restrictive definitions of the literary promulgated by the Canada Council which throughout the 1990s progressively glossed funding criteria
to exclude books addressed to "specialized" rather than "general" audiences. In 1996 these were specified as "primarily designed for a narrow,
specialized or scholarly audience" that used a technical language and
references to scholarly sources not deemed intelligible by the general

reader (Canada Council). While these policies worked in similar fashion to those of the OAC to disembed the literary from the social, they were cast in a more populist rhetoric. Yet they worked equally to promote the "easily digestible and familiar" (Lecker 1999, 453) and to posit the Canadian reader as in need of a remedial dose of civilizing culture in a neo-colonial model of citizenship. Still, it is significant that research addressed to such a scholarly audience is no longer the province of the Canada Council, as it was through the 1970s, but is now under SSHRC the responsibility of the Department of Industry.

Compounding the crisis engineered since 1995 by diminishing financial support from government has been the simultaneous deregulation of the market. Several recent incidents point to the implications of the new order of global capital for publishing in Canada and a more general shift from an era of culture as the glory of a civilized nation projecting an identity in international politics[5] to one in which culture is a pawn in an industrial strategy of economic security waged in the global arena of the "market wars" (Pennee). In pursuing a liberalization of trade, Canada has insisted that culture is a non-negotiable issue. Yet, when the federal government passed legislation to block the sale in Canada of split-run magazines that would siphon off advertising dollars supporting Canadian magazines, the World Trade Organization (an unabashed arm of American foreign policy like the World Bank, the International Monetary Fund, etc.) overturned the legislation in 1997, dealing a devastating blow to Canadian cultural policy. For these organizations culture is business. This legislation did not target the 81 per cent of magazines on Canadian newsstands which are American, only those that recycle editorial content from American home editions and sell advertising at a discount to Canadian advertisers.[6] Increasingly, international trade regimes place substantial limits on the ability of the Canadian state to influence the production and diffusion of culture within its borders. Mindful of this, perhaps, the Department of Industry focused only on business transactions and not the publishing programme in applying the foreign-investment policy in another instance.

Book publishing is an area in which the pressure of globalization has changed the playing field. According to StatsCan, Canadian-controlled publishers still originate over 80 per cent of indigenous titles, as well as

95 per cent of book exports. A number of publishers have closed down in the last few years, however, and others are increasingly orienting themselves to external markets, with children's book publishers adopting American spelling and banishing "Canadiana" (Hammond 26). Yet these publishers are cottage industries in comparison with the "global oligopoly" of multinational publishing operations currently engaged in an unprecedented flurry of mergers with other media, like that linking America On Line to Time-Warner. The latter closed Little, Brown Canada in 1998, reducing the ranks of foreign companies with substantial Canadian trade lists. A further reduction occurred in 1999 with the merger of Random House of Canada and Doubleday Canada into a mega-publisher controlled by the German multinational, Bertelsmann, a transaction not blocked under the foreign-investment policy. However, with the gift of McClelland & Stewart, one of the oldest and most active of the domestic publishers, to Random House in 2000, this multinational giant has a stranglehold on Canadian publishing. With its extraordinary financial resources, it can easily outbid Canadian companies for authors. The small publishers are consigned all the risk of discovering and developing new authors, while the multinationals reap the benefits of increased profits and capital gains. Canada thus enters into the system of trade imbalances between American publishing industries and their foreign counterparts in which, as Lawrence Venuti notes, profits earned in foreign markets support the American industry. As he quotes the head of Random House, "foreign rights are the necessary income to compensate for the high advances we often pay in the us" (1998, 161). Canadian literature is prized within this global economy since its multicultural diversity is readily exportable in translation. Though ethnicity has become a signifier of marketability, multiculturalism is accepted only in as much as it increases the cultural capital of the dominant culture. Dionne Brand's play with spatial figures charts the transformations in this geopolitical configuration. Her fiction, published now by American-controlled Knopf rather than by the Canadian-controlled little presses that supported her poetry, opens the dialectic of identificatory synthesis of (t)here out into a diasporic dispersal spreading across the globe. As Arif Dirlik reminds us, global capitalism has been the condition for the emergence of postcolonialism (73).

1995 was a watershed in yet another cultural arena, that of knowledge production about Canadian literature, not just in the production of Canadian literature. Back in 1973, Brian Stock challenged Canada's foreign policy on culture which, he argued, was light on information in contrast to such former imperial powers as England and France with the British Council and Alliance Française that placed education at the centre of their external cultural exchanges. Canada's organizational division of responsibilities among a number of levels of government and several independent agencies (CIDA, Canada Council for UNESCO, External Affairs, etc.) contributed to this policy vacuum. Canada had few bilateral agreements and so "Canadians go to Italy on Italian money but no Italians come to Canada under the auspices of the federal government" (22). A more concerted policy on cultural exchanges along these lines would have the advantage not only of fostering a growing sense of Canadian nationalism, Stock proposed, but the economic benefit of providing employment for the "overproduction of educated or technically qualified people" that Canada has historically exported (25). Today, following the internationalization of Canadian Studies, an inverse situation gives rise to a very different critique by Christl Verduyn who rails against the lack of "institutional and governmental commitment to Canadian Studies within Canada": "Such anemic attitudes are apparent in the amount of government funding for Canadian Studies within Canada as compared to Canadian Studies outside the country" (5). As Verduyn's protest registers, implementation of the measures Stock advocated have provided more work for underemployed foreign intellectuals than Canadians whose learned journals, publishing outlets, and learned societies have been constrained by forced cutbacks to government spending under the structural readjustment demanded by international money markets to reduce deficits and eliminate trade barriers.

At the same time, federal government policy has made a priority of selling Canadian knowledge industries abroad, both as industry and as ideological support to develop export markets. Participation of university presidents negotiating bilateral agreements for student exchange on the various Team Canada trade missions conducted by the Chrétien government into various parts of the "third world" testifies to the industrial component of this export initiative — a traffic in students. Responsibility for the cultural component was assigned to Canadian Studies associations throughout the world grouped under the International Council of Canadian Studies (ICCS) which is financed by the Department of Foreign Affairs and International Trade (DFAIT). The place of culture under global capitalism in the complex interrelation of government, economics, and security was cogently articulated in *Canada in the World/Le Canada dans le monde*, a 1995 policy document of the Chrétien government. "The promotion of prosperity and employ-ment" is of greatest importance, according to this document, followed by "[t]he protection of our security, within a stable global framework." "The projection of Canadian values and culture" is the third of these "key objectives" helping to advance the implicit economic and politi-cal formations of capitalism and liberal democracy (*Canada* i). The document recognizes "the role played by artists and creators in dis-seminating Canadian values and diversity throughout the world" and, despite budgetary constraints, pledges government support to work collaboratively with partners in Canada "to publicize our cultural assets abroad, and to promote our cultural industries and educational services" (38). In particular, support is assured for the most profitable aspects of culture, "our expertise in the communications field" that will strengthen democracy in Eastern Europe and participation in the "international television network TV5" that showcases francophone and visual culture (39). Linguistic diversity opens more potential markets. Canadian "cultural and educational industries" are to be celebrated so that they "can continue to compete at home and abroad" (39). But mar-keting Canadian cultural goods will also help promote Canadian trade opportunities: "We will seek to make better use of Canada's artists and scholars as part of a fundamental re-thinking of the way we promote ourselves and our products abroad" (22). More information on Canadian culture and learning will be made available to foreign service officers abroad so that they will provide "one-stop shopping for export-related intelligence and services" (23). The military metaphor here positions culture as secret agent in global economic struggles. What is unques-tioned though, and hence naturalized, as Donna Pennee observes, is that capitalism is culture rather than a particular political ideology (202). In the absence of recognition of capitalism as only one model of economic organization among many, a model backed moreover by a particular dominant world power, culture is positioned as countervailing force to democracy, no longer to industry. For in this imposition of the concept of exchange-value as absolute, as a single frame constituting the "real," the kind of exploration that makes demands beyond the instrumental, beyond the individual, and of any transformation other than exchange is constrained which, in turn, forecloses dissent.

BORDER CROSSINGS

What is striking in this policy document is the emphasis on diversity as export. But it is also the gateway through which exports pass, travelling on the multiple passports of the new global citizens cast in DFAIT's allegory as double agents. This new rhetoric manages the extremely diverse and mobile population of Canada through a strategy of dispersal rather than one of binding to territory: celebrating diversity becomes a way of containing it. This rhetoric finds an echo in Canadian literature criticism which increasingly focuses on the places of crossing or thresholds in a process of denaturalizing the relation between literature, language, and territory that Smaro Kamboureli has described as "releas[ing] [her] self from the hold nativism has on Canadian literature" (2000, 8). Border crossing with its mobility factor breaking open the encircled "garrison" functions as chronotope of the contemporary world system. I shall return to Kamboureli's particular focus on "diasporic literature" shortly, for her analysis of the "scandalous bodies" whose excess in comparison to the ethnic subject escapes the "centre/margin dialectic" and the control of the "desire-machine of the state" (26) differs in its strategy from other recent works of criticism. Increasingly, these are "outsider notes" (Hunter), analyses of Canadian literature by foreign scholars whose texts, impossible in their country of origin, are being published by Canadian publishers with the help of grants from ICCS. Yet those written by insiders also adopt the ethnographer's perspective in order to question the assumptions underwriting narratives of national self-identification so as to include its many fragments. Literature is still read synechdochically to take the pulse of the nation, though it is posited as imagined rather than as geophysical space. To a certain extent this strategy effects a deconstructive reversal of thematic criticism's cultural ethnography by exposing how what appeared supplemental to Canadian identity — ethnicized, gendered, or racialized difference — was constituted as margin in the very act of positing a centre. So we read about *Gendering the Nation* (Armatage et al.) that it performs a "crucial conceptual intervention into th[e] monolithic framework, with its assumptions of a unitary Canadian identity and its roots in seventies cultural nationalism." The centre is "always de-centred" in that "national identity is articulated against an imaginary centre and mediated through regional, ethnic, ... sexual and gendered identificatory priorities" (10). Yet the centrifugal impulse is paradoxically centripetal: supplementarity is *thematized* in narratives that seek to incorporate textual details into an overarching pattern. Moreover, these works draw on a methodology similar to that of thematic criticism and read literary texts symptomatically as history rather than reading literature alongside the texts of history and politics. This is a more general conundrum for contemporary cultural criticism, as David Scott notes, particularly for postcolonial criticism. A characteristic move of this criticism has been a "certain indefinite deferral of [the political]" (18). This move has enlarged the field of the political beyond the discourses and practices of the state by systematically interrogating the assumptions through which the political as such has been constructed (epistemic, national, humanistic assumptions, as well as those of gender and race) and arguing they are political in as much as they entail relations of power. Such a "politics of theory" has characterized postcoloniality, Scott contends, calling instead for a "theory of politics" that would fold the field of cultural critique into a critical strategy that addresses "macropolitical questions," questions of "rights and justice," of "political representation and community," of "the good" and "obligation" (19). The nation-state has not yet dissolved in the new world system but rather is orchestrating realignments in the transfer of power and resources that change the categories of the good and the responsibilities of citizenship to advantage certain groups over others. In this conjuncture, Masao Miyoshi warns, "preoccupation with 'postcoloniality' and multiculturalism looks suspiciously like another alibi to conceal the actuality of global politics" in the forms of "transnational corporatism" (728).

Territory and population rather than corporatism have been the main axes of investigating forms of the transnational in Canadian literature criticism. The focus on territory prolongs the geopolitical imperative to secure boundaries symbolically. But the topoi of the Canadian imaginary are now moving borders not enclosed spaces or static positions. And criticism works to denaturalize them in a further destabilization. Outside Canada, borders seem to be "floating" (Aziz) or dissolving, as the editors of *Borderblur: Essays on Poetry and Politics in Contemporary Canadian Literature* note, in view of the "widening critical approaches" generated in "cross-cultural exchanges" (Hunter and Chew vii). Inside Canada, borders persist, especially those mediating longstanding macropolitical international relations between Canada and the us. Borders are read now as metaphor in a system of signs, as "conceptual limits" (New 1998, 4) or "mythic patterns" (Angus 106), enabling fictions implicated in power relations. Ian Angus stresses the continuity of these formulations with Frye's "garrison mentality" (as a border invented to protect against being overwhelmed from outside) and W.H. New indicates how the oppositional positions conveyed in this metaphor need not inevitably lead to (en)closure but possibly to a productive encounter (1998, 15). Yet their articulations of the spatial imaginary mark a rupture with the "garrison" trope of the settler narrative in that both call for a radical recognition of otherness within. For Angus, this recognition constitutes a meaningful difference from both the European and the American social imaginaries. Drawing a line, a border in the wilderness, separates here from there in a "civilizing moment" that establishes a relation, a "limitation" (126), and prevents any closure of the metaphysical circle of interpretation. Taking the wilderness inside is a kind of "abjection," notes Angus (130), an ambivalence, an incompleteness, an opening to the Other, a becoming, unlike the American pursuit to contain the advancing frontier. "Questioning the border" maintains it, suspended in "relations of the in-between," those "between nations" as well as those "between the said and the unsaid" (127). For Angus, these are the conditions of possibility of an English-Canadian philosophy, for New of a Western literature and culture. "Borderwalking," New writes, is what occurs in "a territory" of "in-betweenness" — the "borderland" — characterized by transgression and revision, negotiation and transformation (1998, 27).

In this condition of indeterminacy, relations of difference may be simultaneously "consensual" and "conflictual" and so demand critical examination of the categories constructing difference. "Borderland" contrasts with the fixed conceptual edges of the "borderline" that "names and divides" as it stakes out territory (4). Canadian literature and culture are made to yield many anecdotes of restless encounters and boundary realignments in the contact zone, variously described as "giddy limits," "on the edge of everything," and the "centre of somewhere else." New's perennial concern with "articulating west" becomes his principal objective in later sections where historical shifts in the boundary between Canada and the US undermine any symbolic certainty in the 49th parallel — a highly mobile signifier. He also contributes a critical version to the many narratives about convoluted shuttlings back and forth across this metaphorical line as he straddles the border to analyze west coast fictions by Jack Hodgins and David Guterson and other American writers in a move to upset the "hierarchy of regions" (9) in which Ontario and Quebec claim centre. Celebration of a "living culture" and embracing local knowledge are two of the meanings New attaches to "borderlands" as he expands the trope to include the more abstract relations of connection to a wider world and limitless change (102). Despite this call to engage imaginatively with the future, neither New nor Angus fully addresses the implications of the in-between's provisionality to articulate more complex models of affiliation and enlarge the field of power to the gendered or racialized assumptions propping up historical geopolitical boundaries.

FILLING THE GAPS OF INTERIOR EXCLUSIONS

Questioning the border takes several forms in recent critical works concerned with population making. Most seek to fill in the gaps produced by exclusions within the national narrative but run the risk of consolidating the binary from the otherside in a centre/margin dialectic instead of rejecting the discursive categories in a process of disidentification. One form with considerable current political purchase explores the implications of "First Nations" literature within the competition over territory between two "Founding Nations" and those "nations" whose land they occupied. The concept of nations makes strong political claims within the struggle for aboriginal self-government by fracturing the symbolic unity of any Canadian nation. As developed by Dee Horne, the discourse of nationality is anything but a nativist project, though its political edge is blunted in her vision. "Unsettling literature," as she calls it, the writing of "American Indians" draws on trickster stories with their narratives of transforming traditions to "forge transcultural relationships" (155). "American Indian" writers have "talked back" to the dominant culture in asserting a position of enunciation in a way that "unsettles their colonial discourse" and articulates an alternative cultural politics that "eludes settler definitions" (153). Forged in the "vortex of colonial mimicry" through which the imperializing project of the settler culture has sought to civilize and assimilate it, "American Indian" culture has become "hybridized" (154). In its efforts to re-invent and imagine an alterNative culture, these communities have furthered the heterogeneity of the process, releasing contradiction and discontinuity in literary texts that subvert any singular identity. Hybridity does not necessarily entail a sublation of cultural differences, but may be a creative process for imagining new possibilities and "transcultural bridges" (155). Consequently, Horne calls on "settlers" to undergo a "process of decolonizing *métissage*" (155). For just as a palimpsestic writing over the epistemic violence of colonization would enable Marilyn Dumont to get out of the trap of "the circle" in which colonial stereotypes have enclosed her (xiv), embracing heterogeneity in a parallel gesture of cultural hybridization and inclusion of the other would release settler culture from its "garrison mentality." Horne's critical narrative performs such an unsettling gesture both in drawing extensively on the postcolonial theory generated in the diasporic return to the imperial centre by critics such as Homi Bhabha and Stuart Hall rather than working through the emerging cultural theory of Amerindians, and by using the terminology of "American Indian" throughout her book. Billed as "contemporary American Indian writing," Horne's analysis of six writers resident in Canada raises the issue of naming in relation to geopolitical territory only in a footnote that records the question of the troubling settler boundaries between Canada and the US without explicitly connecting the writers to Canada or invoking the alternate

261

political mapping of Turtle Island that posits a unity of the Americas (158). On the cover of a book published by the multinational publisher Peter Lang in a series devoted to American Indian Literature, this naming depoliticizes the struggles for cultural legitimation by First Nations as they relate to jurisdictional disputes over territory in the political arena of Canada. The turn to cultural critique in this transnational publishing economy bypasses questions of rights and justice and defers political issues of power. But this will facilitate the book's international dissemination. Moreover, in its recourse to a mimetic theory of identity derived from a postcolonial "politics of theory," Horne's study of Amerindian writing from Canada reinforces a Eurocentric metaphysics of being over a relational logic of transformation and becoming. So too, paradoxically, the rhetoric of subversion works in miming it to consolidate the authority of the narrative of settler *bildung* even as it attempts to introject the marginal in a poetics of abjection.

Similarly, the deconstructive move of Peter Dickinson through a metaphorical concept of nation consolidates as it parodically reverses the topocentric imperative of Frygean thematics. Such ambivalence is the effect of mimicry or "bad" mimesis that posits the margin as a distorted re-presentation of a centre. *Here is Queer: Nationalism, Sexualities and the Literature of Canada* presents itself as an "imperfect syllogism" derived from the staged encounter of Northrop Frye's "Where is here?" and of the lesbian and gay activists' slogan "We're here, we're queer, get used to it!" (3). The two models of identity are nonetheless rhetorically imbalanced with the geopolitical nation framed as interrogative and the sexual model of Queer Nation as exclamation. And though Dickinson sets out to denaturalize the normativity of the categories "nation" and "sexuality" by drawing on the fields of postcolonial and queer theory, it is their *hetero*normativity that is shown to be a socially inflected category when homosexuality is constructed as counter-identity. Dickinson aligns himself with the social constructivist analyses of Benedict Anderson and Michel Foucault who argue that "national" and "sexual" communities are discursively produced through the convergence of capitalism and print technology to create the homogeneous time of an imagined community. Dickinson joins Partha Chatterjee in critiquing the universalist assumptions of Anderson's theory of nationalism for failing to account adequately for its forms in Asia and Africa. Chatterjee questions specifically the conflation in Anderson's work of an imagined "inner" domain of community within a colonial order — a "national consciousness" — that does not inevitably coincide with the "material" or legal domain of a nation state (Dickinson 30 – 31). In this sense, Dickinson argues that a persistent homosociality in Canadian fiction both accedes to and resists the inscription of power relations on the body. Homosexuality exceeds the "national narrative of self-identification" (23). By analogy, the play of structural absence and embodied presence in the linking of "here" and "queer" extends to understanding the forms of affiliation of "Canadian, Québécois, and First Nations literatures," namely, that what has "*counted* as literature" is contingent upon extraliterary socio-political discourses (4).

A different (ac)counting of the literature from another positionality is what Dickinson proposes as corrective to "the identificatory *lack*" that has been the historical bias of Canadian literary nationalism which has been the result of a refusal to confront the "superabundance" of a destabilizing sexuality (4). Rather than repeat Frye's rhetorical question with all its "interior exclusions," Dickinson responds polemically with an answer, "Here is queer," that places queer, a transitive, "expansive signifier," across boundaries to "negotiat[e] the distance between 'here' and 'we're'" (38). For the tactics of Queer Nation are those of border crossing to occupy the spaces of and mime the privileges of "normality" in an interrogative and constructive engagement with an other. These tactics recognize the partiality and incompleteness of any process of identification that is inevitably contingent on a relation with an other in a syncretic rather than synthetic identity. Such "borderlands," Dickinson concurs with Angus, introject a cutting edge within identificatory projects intranationally as well as internationally (35). Through a series of "(re)doubled readings of national and sexual alterity" (28), Dickinson teases out the longstanding "tensions and triangles" of homosociality within Canadian literatures and shows how homoerotic desire complicates by moving across the intranational boundaries that have distinguished Quebec and English-Canada, and both "founding nations" from "First Nations" and Africadians. Yet, though his quotation of Frye out of context would seek to transgress Frye's critical project and that of Canadian literature criticism with its white, heterosexual national-ism—and publication of *Here is Queer* by the same press as *Literary History of Canada* adds a piquant irony to such transgression—Dickinson's method of symptomatic reading with its focus on the aesthetic over the socio-historical marks a continuity with Frye. As Dickinson observes, "'queer' is a literary-critical category of an almost inevitable defini-tional elasticity" (5). And literary category it remains in his book. How it has emerged in Canadian discourse, how it functions in relation to older categories of lesbian and gay collectivities, and how they have all become operational within the body politic as the state has legislated limits—these genealogical questions are not raised by Dickinson. In his analysis of the performative slippage of national and racial identities between Canadianness and whiteness, Dickinson quotes from critical studies on the politics of publishing and reviewing that have marginal-ized Dionne Brand's work. But "queer" is not subject to the same kind of scrutiny of the extra-literary supplement that makes it discursively performative. A counter-discourse to the national narratives, Dickinson's text nonetheless shares with them the gesture of straining toward a full and coherent narrative—albeit one of homosexuality—from colo-nial to postmodern periods. This centripetal project differs, however, from the fragmentary nature of previous studies on which Dickinson has drawn extensively that expose the heterosexual presumption in individual texts. Like Horne, Dickinson risks reessentializing the cat-egories—from the opposite side of the binary.

Multicultural Pedagogies

It is precisely such a move to fill in the gaps made by interior exclusions that Smaro Kamboureli rejects. Her aim in *Scandalous Bodies: Diasporic Literature in English Canada* is not to "construct a positivistic image of the ethnic imaginary" on behalf of either members of the diaspora or of the Canadian State (viii) but to interrogate the ways in which a politics of identity under the Multiculturalism Act in the act of legitimating ethnic difference commodifies ethnic subjectivity (x). Indeed, it is the very process of normalizing ethnicity that receives the full blast of her criticism. While both the Canadian State and cultural practices have

increasingly celebrated diversity, they have done little to redress historical practices of discrimination. Their discourses, moreover, inhibit any
critical examination of historical injustice and so function as a pedagogy of forgetting that makes possible a totalizing national discourse.
Although "ex-centric identities" have been embraced and so commodified, she notes, the "ex-centric" remains dependent on a centre (167).
Turning the discourse upside down merely reverses but does not displace
the Manichean categories. Kamboureli emphasizes the productivity
of the Multiculturalism Act which has created the space in civil society
for a dialogue on race and ethnicity. Yet, she observes, there is a constant risk of foreclosing dialogue in a fusion between the construction
of ethnicity and official attitudes. On the one hand, the Act interpellates the ethnic subject in her/his difference and invites (mis)recogni-
tion in a community homogenized in this difference whose authentic
performance keeps cultural diversity manageable by the state in a cen-
tre/margin dialectic. Multiculturalism as "mandated discrimination"
(92) consolidates binaries and reifies minorities in their unique identity with, as corollary, the extremes of "identity politics" and of diminished "literariness" under the imperative of an "essentialist thematics"
of cultural "preservation" (153). In tension with this "politics of difference" that would freeze past identities, a politics of "universalism" in
its blindness to difference stresses the equal dignity of all citizens (92).
Ethnicity in this instance becomes "a condition of commonality," a fundamental characteristic of Canadian identity shared by all Canadians,
not "a sign of contestation" against a troubled history of discrimination
(101). In a double gesture, this indifference to difference redefines the
Canadian nation as a multiethnic state and simultaneously disengages
ethnicity from marginality. Together these constitute two aspects of
the "sedative politics" of liberal pluralism that Kamboureli identifies
as the principal effect of Canada's multiculturalism policy which works
to harmonize differences and contain dissent in an image of a cohesive
national identity that makes a space for "negotiated difference" (174).
Kamboureli approaches this juridico-political agenda of state rationality and its discourse of consensus with a hermeneutics of suspicion and
focuses on the problematics of reading multiculturalism. "[A] continuous process of mediating and negotiating contingencies," she contends,

is necessary to understand diversity, a process that will seek to produce relational knowledge and a community of "hybridity" rather than of "consensus" (93).

For Kamboureli, as for Horne and Dickinson, the mimicry and hybridity of Homi Bhabha's postcolonial theory have displaced Frye's contradiction and paradox in the articulation of epistemologies of national identity. As she argues, it is necessary to recognize the material reality of difference, especially the contingent material reality of language, in knowledge production about Canada if one is to find a line of escape from the dialogue among communities that overlooks the history of their radical asymmetries in a too-easily affirmed consensus. "Cultural excess" (163) in the superabundance of destabilizing ethnicities that exceed the national narrative of *bildung* is how the diasporic "scandalous body" escapes inscription by state power in either the resistance characteristic of the 1970s and 1980s or the accommodation of the 1990s. While the former advanced a syntax of retention reifying immigrant identities in their immutable differences, the latter advances a syntax of utopian or virtual identity in which all are immigrants without distinctions. Kamboureli's approach differs from Horne's and Dickinson's in its turn away from a symptomatic reading of literary texts and a rhetoric of presentness to analyze the processes of legitimation of ethnicity in parallelled institutions of State and literature. Although Kamboureli does offer compelling detailed readings of the fiction of F.P. Grove and Joy Kogawa in a historicizing gesture, there is no attempt to constitute a coherent metanarrative of ethnicity as one of progress and establish patterns of sameness and repetition over time. Rather, Kamboureli reads for inconsistencies and discontinuities in the context of ethnicity between the 1920s, a decade of publication of a number of ethnic fictions from Manitoba, and the 1980s, a moment of consolidation of the State's multicultural policies within the charged climate of racialization. The greater part of her analysis, however, focuses on reading the Multiculturalism Act's pedagogical and performative force through the emergence of a media discourse on multiculturalism and on tracing the canonizing process of ethnicity in the literary institution through anthologizing practices from the 1970s to the 1990s. Interestingly, she does not analyze her own anthologizing, though *Scandalous Bodies* may be read as an implicit commentary on practice.

Through this genealogical project examining the conditions of possibility for a discourse on multiculturalism in all its disjunctions and incoherencies, Kamboureli attempts to move outside a logic of identity to trace the contingent forces of a becoming. At the heart of her concerns is the problematic relation of ethnicity to history, history understood as a system of power relations. In particular, she opposes a certain "postmodern multiculturalism" (171) promoted by the Multiculturalism Act and expounded by Linda Hutcheon that would appropriate ethnic differences to "enhance the dominant society's cultural capital" (170). The "postmodern mode of ironic pleasure" (170) makes space for marginalized voices but does nothing to alter their minority position. Nor does it help "look history straight in the face" so as to change relations of power (170). In contrast, Joy Kogawa's staging of the consolations of repression and nostalgia in *Obasan* offers an occasion to rework the history of racist oppression twice over. Against the amnesiac subject of Renan's national(ist) pedagogy of necessary forgetting, Kamboureli argues with Kogawa for the "double imperative not only to expose the contents of history, but also to change history's shape" (221). Though her analysis ends inconclusively with this encouragement to transform the past in the light of a different future, the greater part of Kamboureli's analysis has focused on the recent production of ethnic identities as they have been made marginal and, consequently, is implicated in the "centre/margin dialectic" (26) from whose repetitions she longs to escape. She attempts a break out in her opening manifesto in which she seeks to overcome a critical impasse and political paralysis. A manifesto would help her "rise above history" and announce a future safe from impending catastrophes, legacies of that history (7). Her paralysis is induced by the web of political debates around difference that deny complexity. The critical impasse is fostered by the critic's reflexivity when "self-location" fails to "immunize academic discourse" against the politics of the institutions she is complicit with (2). For her subjectivity is "historically formed" even if it is not totally "reduced to historical determinations" (22). "Janus-faced," she is simultaneously Canadian and ethnic. The particularities of her complex location are historically contingent and determined both by her own trajectory and by a Canadian national imaginary. This "shuttling self['s]" "prodigious doubling" resists making a choice between either condition but seeks to "produce a space where her hybridity is articulated in a manner that does not cancel out any of its particularities" (22). Hybridity, for Kamboureli, is the condition of diasporic subjects as distinguished from the binarity of ethnic subjects. Hybridity is also the haunt of the *angelus novus*, Benjamin's angel of history, suspended between past and future in the violent storm of progress. The diasporic subject caught in this contradictory in-between shares neither the ethnic subject's nostalgia nor her virtuality but, like the angel, transforms the past into a future that will be.

Hybridity may well emerge as a new idealism, Kamboureli warns, unless the critic questions the "metanarratives of development and progress that assent to hybridity" and the complex historical materiality of diaspora (23). Still, Kamboureli gets caught in this trap when she fails to analyze the politics of diaspora in the way she interrogates the politics of multiculturalism. And with the introduction of diaspora almost as an afterthought to her "book about ethnic literature" (vii) this constitutes a swerve into a politics of identity, albeit beyond the national arena. Adding "Diasporic Literature in English Canada" as subtitle to *Scandalous Bodies* makes it blend well on the list of a major transnational publisher that guarantees it wide distribution and critical attention beyond the borders of Canada in a way that contrasts with the "lack of commercial viability" (151) with which proposals for ethnic anthologies were received in Canada not two decades ago. The introductory chapter embraces disjunction when an analysis of the complex temporality of Benjamin's angel riffs into a commentary on another German angel in Wim Wender's *Wings of Desire*. Rather than advocating a community of hybridity as the form of sociality constituted in such a disjunctive temporality, Kamboureli might well have chosen Bill Readings' model of a "community of dissensus" (180) to convey a logic of complexity that exceeds the homogeneous time of the modern nation-state. Dissensus as a logic of relations attends to one's positioning and obligations in respect to history not by seeking consensus but by stretching toward the horizon of the *différend*, the heteronomous, the incommensurable. It posits the social bond as a question rather than as self-legitimating, as one of competing differences, a "whatever" community of "singularities" (186) brought together by the state of things (or "abstract machine") in what Deleuze and Guattari call an aggregate assemblage (1980, 116). The ethical obligation binds to this historical condition rather than to an Other, so this contingent community escapes structuring by the opposition of inclusion to exclusion. Such a historicized pragmatics foregrounds the relations of power, the violence, attending any coming together. For the different elements do not necessarily relate as symmetrically as the trope of hybridity implies. It is imperative for the critic to make visible the spoil and toil attending any civilizing gesture, as Benjamin enjoins, especially one seeking to theorize affiliation more explicitly in relation to power and advance the obligations of justice for the community in the making. The general effect of this recent criticism is that of open dialogue rather than defensive inwardness. Yet, as Malcolm Ross observed in 1976, much of the historical "scholarly labour remains to be done" in order to position Canadian literature not just in space, but in time (175).

BETWEEN THERE AND HERE: SURVEYING THE FIELD

There is no such thing as a "complete" diagram in the representation of a given field. Maps rarely halt and contain, but gesture toward continuations and/or disjunctions. The visibility of relations, the inclusion or exclusion of positions and details, depends on the scale of the map in question. A different scale of analysis, from greater distance or proximity, leads to a shift in focus and a new map. As surveyor, my perspective is not detached from the field under analysis but positioned within it and implicated in the shifts in critical stance I have outlined. Then, my essays in criticism adopted the general sociologizing tendencies of Canadian literature criticism in their attempt to diagnose the condition of a culture and society through a reading of its literary texts as sanctioned by the protocols of "expressive-realism." Yet it was less time than space that preoccupied me then, caught up as I was within the reigning topocentric imperative. In an early study of the phenomenology of urban space (1967), I analyzed the symbolic economy of the city with regard to the *différend* in political perspectives of francophones and anglophones as these constellated a "geography of separatism." For a longer study of the land in anglophone and francophone fiction (1971),

I examined differing phases of the emergence of a pastoral ideal as it was being elaborated within a predominantly urban culture. More than nostalgia for a disappearing way of life or a counterforce to modernity's materialism and industry, these rural idylls were bound up in an ideological conflict in which English Canada exerted its sovereignty over the territory of Quebec symbolically through this appropriation of its predominant genre, the *roman du terroir* (novel of the land), as well as of Quebec's historical past in fictions depicting quests to overcome the wilderness. Both the novels of settlement and those of exploration elaborate a gendered as well as a racialized narrative of the nation-information in which the masculine protagonist struggled to dominate a feminized landscape or was rewarded with a wife for his persistence in journeying through the challenging wilderness and fighting off the indigenous peoples.

I am, of course, summarizing these studies from the perspective of the discourses of today after analyzing the mediations operative in the production of cultural texts, most specifically language policy and cultural policy as tactics of governmentality (1995, 1999a, and 1998). In these essays, I have focused on the rhetorical figures through which power captures bodies as subjects in order to manage population. I have been elaborating a logic of complex relations — dialectic, dialogic, and rhizomatic — in order to analyze the dynamic interactions of disparate signifying systems and contingency's contextual mediations, rather than parse the allegories through which a nation's culture is expressed and its identity discerned. Patternings of content are now of less interest to me than (op)positions taken within a complex terrain.

Those positions currently structuring the field are the same as they were in the 1950s — the might of American capital — but its hegemony is now unchallenged on the world stage. The shadow cast by the power of the American empire across its northern border is much longer and penetrates more deeply as it reshapes Canadian culture to its market model. And the derilection of Canada's capitalist class in regard to the obligations of community is even greater in the 1990s. Dependency in the economic realm is no longer overcome through Canadian cultural policies that deliver programmes centrally through federal agencies in an assertion of a compensatory though feminized identity: government is disentangling itself from culture in response to pressures from the US for a level playing field for cultural *industries*. This leaves a few celebrities, feminized and ethnicized in respect to power — the Atwoods and the Ondaatjes — to float in the global firmament of culture under the logos of American multinational publishers. The conditions of possibility that enabled them to establish themselves as writers — that nationalist cultural policy — are rapidly changing and younger writers face uncertain publishing opportunities.

A Literature in the Making:

Rewriting and the Dynamism of the Cultural Field

❖

Quebec Women Writers in English Canada

Are Toronto and New York sites for the consecration of Quebec literature since the 1940s as Paris has long been? In reframing Antoine Sirois'
question regarding the horizon of expectation of Parisian professional
readers that influenced the awarding of French literary prizes to three
Quebec women writers (147), I am responding to Pierre Hébert's invitation to carry out a more sustained analysis of the "Carrier phenomenon"
with a study of the reception of Quebec literature in English Canada
and the US (1989, 109). However, I shall not undertake the systematic
analysis of the reception of the Quebec corpus by the English-Canadian
and American literary institutions that he called for, because I shall not
analyze the place of Quebec literature in the educational system. Also,
I shall consider only a few indices of its reception, namely the aesthetic
and social discourses of literary criticism. On the other hand, I shall
extend my analysis to include the field of textual production of Quebec
literature in English translation, since English-Canadian publishers' selection among the Quebec corpus — a selection that functions as a second
literary system with its own processes of admission, legitimation, and
consecration — makes visible the poetic discourse of the works and the
socio-cultural discourse from which is shaped a representation of Quebec
literature and an image of Quebec for English Canada. This representation is the effect of a narrative of decision-making by translators and
critics, for literary criticism, like translation, functions as a discourse of
legitimation creating hierarchies of value. A selective transmission
of the Quebec corpus contributes to the formation of a community of
readers, an English-Canadian public, and so works to consolidate an
identity for the nation.

Because I am mainly concerned with the position of women writers in these intercultural relations, the parameters of reception of Quebec literary works I have established may seem overly subjective. They are symptomatic, however, since I am building on similar findings in two independent studies of the reception of the Quebec literary corpus by the English-Canadian literary institution. As André Lamontagne, Annette Hayward, and Réjean Beaudoin observe, the works of Quebec authors most commented upon by English-Canadian critics were written by Gabrielle Roy, Anne Hébert, and Marie-Claire Blais. Jane Koustas has also noted that, according to the index *Canadian Translation*, the texts of Anne Hébert, Gabrielle Roy, and Marie-Claire Blais were those most translated into English.[1] The two phenomena are connected: the more one translates, the more critical reviews are published, the greater the symbolic capital, the more translations completed. Moreover, Mary Jane Green confirms the pertinence of Lise Gauvin's and Laurent Mailhot's observation that American researchers have paid particular attention to Quebec women's writing. Green notes that in *Quebec Studies*, the only American periodical devoted exclusively to Quebec culture, fully half the articles of literary criticism concern women writers. These analyze "the women writers already canonized in Quebec — Gabrielle Roy, Anne Hébert, and Marie-Claire Blais, as well as a more recent generation of feminist writers such as Nicole Brossard and Louky Bersianik" (115). Interacting with the hierarchical structure of the anglophone literary system, the reception of works by these two generations of writers exercizes a more conservative pressure in the former case and a more oppositional stance towards authority in the second instance. However, the significance of this feminization of Quebec literature is not the same in Canada as in the us. While the American canon is composed primarily of male authors, the Margarets — Atwood and Laurence — along with Alice Munro figure prominently in the English-Canadian canon. The dialectical relations between literary systems articulate a movement compensatory for a lack in the American system in the former case, whereas, in the second, the doubling of the systems works to legitimate a pan-Canadian culture through which the nation is feminized. Nonetheless, the situation in English-Canada is more complex, as we shall see.

Translation in the Structuring of the Field of Cultural Production

Over the last twenty years, the literary institution has been a privileged object of research in Quebec. In English Canada, however, academic criticism has more frequently embarked on deconstructive readings of texts. The author-function still holds sway in English-Canadian journalistic criticism which either celebrates the recognition of certain authors in a global cultural marketplace, or advances a liberal ideology of individual success by heralding the transcendence of the aesthetic imagination.[2] Such a concept of the autonomous subject is an ideological position that elides the relations of production and of transformation, that is, the social labour through which certain positions are produced as transcendent subject (*auctor*) while others are reduced to the position of marginalized other. This operation naturalizes and neutralizes historical and social relations by fixing in routinized institutional practices what are in fact arbitrary and differential values. Such autonomization in everyday habit derealizes the symbolic violence of a process of consecration that forces works to submit to a treatment of distinction. According to Bourdieu, the logic of relative autonomy in the functioning of the different instances of legitimation establishes a process of differentiation and exclusion upon a principle of cultural legitimacy. Modalities of cultural practice can be defined only as a system of differential positions taken in relation to other possible *prises de positions* within a political economy of the sign. Conflicts between different positions create the particular structure of a field through a dialectic of distinction between restricted and general fields of production. The differential deviation structuring the field functions objectively as antagonistic positions of genres and forms. Restricted positions are subject to limited circulation and long-term rewards, as is the case with consecrated texts, deemed classics and taught in the academy. Those positions receiving "large-scale production" compete in the marketplace in search of a profitable return on investment in the short run, as is the case with best-sellers. Without appearing to submit to the interference of economic, political, or religious power, the institutional practices of distinction reproduce isotopically the relations of power in a stratified society.

However, symbolic forms and systems of relation cannot be set apart from other practices in the everyday but must be considered within the entire range of lived social relations that Bourdieu calls "habitus," a social ecology of the sign. Symbolic capital is the social relation that consecrates the signifying practices of the dominant class within a heterogeneous field of cultural production, among a complex and constantly changing set of circumstances, involving multiple social and institutional actions. The signifying practices and cultural goods of that class wield the symbolic power with the authority to determine cultural and symbolic capital. While Bourdieu's theoretical model and analysis have focused exclusively on the dialectic between restricted and general fields of production as these pertain to class conflict, his attention to their positional properties as a social relation posits the emergence of other position-takings or habitus of groups with potentially differentiated conditions of social possibility. Women, for him, however, constitute only a "specific statistical category" or "target group" to whom works of "brand-name culture" (prize-winners) may be directed and so bring them into the socially dominant group (1993, 127 – 28).[3] This process of differentiating audiences occurs through struggles for specific stakes and rewards along a horizontal axis in which players in the sub-field of large-scale production seek to enhance their economic capital in contrast to those in the field of restricted production who exalt values of disinterestedness. A secondary opposition, intersecting vertically, entails struggles between a consecrated avant-garde and an emerging avant-garde or between different forms, such as the boulevard theatre and vaudeville, that are a function of the social quality of the works and their audiences. The dynamism of the system, the continuous changes within the field of production for the producers, arises from these struggles in the field within the structure of the distribution of a "capital of recognition" or "degree of artistic recognition" (187).

Crucial in Bourdieu's elaboration of the structure of the cultural field is the attention he gives to mediating forms of activity in the production and dissemination of authoritative ideas, texts, authors, etc. There always exists an array of intermediaries such as publishers, critics, journalists, librarians and, I would add, translators, among other diffusers, as well as the social networks and institutions in which they

276

are situated, such as publishing houses, periodicals, schools, scholarly societies, museums, and other such sites for dissemination. In this complex network of overlapping and competing institutional sites, these intermediaries all contribute to the production of the meaning and value of a work. An analysis of the differing positions and histories of translation and criticism in the field of cultural production opens up questions concerning cultural value which is, in Bourdieu's formulation, the constitution, preservation, and reproduction of authority and symbolic power in the field (270).

In analyses of the Quebec literary institution, Bourdieu is often quoted, but Jacques Dubois has had a greater influence, according to Denis Saint-Jacques, who notes a slippage that occurs in which "institution" displaces Bourdieu's concept of the "field" and so neutralizes "the position of the literary within the social configuration" (Dubois 1978, 43). Criticism is concerned less with the "habitus" — the social relations of power lived in everyday practices — than with the Apparatus and the Norm, the French normative standard producing a "conflict of codes" (Belleau 1986, 167) in the Quebec cultural apparatus. There is a greater focus on the modes of consecration and conservation than on the dynamism structuring a heterodox field with multiple position-takers in differentiated social milieux. This slippage occurs in a dialogue between Lise Gauvin and Jacques Dubois on a panel about the autonomy of the Quebec literary institution. Autonomy in this instance refers not to the internal self-regulation of the system of cultural production, as in Bourdieu's usage, but variously designates a technocratic vision of writing or the conditions of a veritable decolonization of culture. Literary criticism functions, then, as the ideologeme "autonomy" in a compensatory discourse of the Quebec field of production that affirms its specificity in a dialectical relation with an other, with both the colonizer ("l'Anglais conquérant") and the linguistic and cultural heritage of France (Brisset 32 – 33). Recognition of literary value in the field of restricted production constitutes a social relation in which the colonial power retains its prestige if not all its power. Concerned above all with the Paris-Montreal axis, Quebec literature criticism participates in the reproduction and circulation of symbolic goods by marking culturally pertinent distinctions with France for a self-regulating Quebec literary institution in the process of formation. This preoccupation also orients the discourse on the translation of Quebec literary works. "It seems to me dangerous at any rate," Lise Gauvin comments, "that only novels which have been recognized with French literary prizes are translated into foreign languages" (1982, 279). In this formulation, she indicates the complex position of the Quebec cultural field in constant interaction with other fields. Translation is indeed a dynamic mechanism through which cultural fields develop relations with each other. However, translation, as a discursive practice emerging from interlinguistic conflicts, does not transform meaning so much as it *invents* meanings as a function of the ideological conflicts *within* the translating culture.

Whereas Denis Saint-Jacques seeks to expose the underside ("l'envers") of the literary system and draw attention to the missing social relations of power, I want additionally to call for an *inversion* and insist on the importance of exteriorization, of differentiation through exchange, as an important mechanism structuring the field. A system is never completely closed even if autonomous or self-regulating: it can only be thought as system in relation to a becoming through struggles with different historical periods or competing schemas. The determination of value in a given system depends on the selection of a political orientation among divergent positions. Questions of language and culture are always problems of the relation between a dominant class and the people within the mediation of hegemony, according to Gramsci: likewise, translation negotiates the relations of prestige and power between languages within an international arena. Literary value is the value of distinction introduced when translation inserts an enunciation into a different system. However, the values produced on the market of exchange of these symbolic goods differ according to the position taken in relation to the dominant power and as a function of the direction of translation. I propose then to invert the vector of exchanges so as to examine the axes of New York – Paris and New York – Toronto – Montreal. Since wwii, because of American economic supremacy, New York has become the world's cultural capital. The French literary prizes awarded to Gabrielle Roy and Marie-Claire Blais in particular merely confirmed a previous American legitimation of their work in English translations published in New York and Toronto. France consecrated certain value:

Bonheur d'occasion, an American best-seller, and *Une saison dans la vie d'Emmanuel*, the work of "a genius," in the opinion of Edmund Wilson, the most renowned American critic.[4]

Moreover, the literary field(s) in Canada are not autonomous in the way Bourdieu formulated the concept. At every stage in cultural production, government financial support compensates for the lack of economic capital invested in publishing — grants to artists, block grants to publishers, fees to translators, funds to promote books and support readings of work by writers and translators. Publishers do not necessarily seek to please a bourgeois elite in the selection of titles and so produce cultural capital or to extend their audiences through titles chosen to augment economic capital. Government policy intervenes directly in the financing of cultural institutions by determining the categories of cultural production eligible for grants in aid. Translation in Canada is directly regulated by government since the translation of legislation and government documents constitutes the principal field of translation activity and, consequently, determines the norms of translatability. It was only in 1972 with the establishment by the Secretary of State of a programme of grants-in-aid of translation of Quebec and English-Canadian books into the other language, following on the heels of the Official Languages Act (1969), that literary translation developed in Canada, especially among the small, subsidized publishers.[5] There is inevitably a political dimension to the reception of Quebec books in English Canada, since the asymmetrical relations of power between Quebec and English Canada have traditionally been worked out on the terrain of the politics of language.

Quebec literary works selected by French or American publishers for prizes or translations respond to the criteria of these autonomous systems or may be rewritten and so modified as to conform adequately to their norms. A consecration in the restricted field of production of these systems may have important economic considerations for the Quebec writer in addition to symbolic capital, monetary rewards that the Prix David of Quebec or the Governor General's Award do not entail. The announcement of the Prix Fémina for Anne Hébert's *Les fous de Bassan* quintupled its sales (Sirois 158), while the impact of the Prix Fémina on the success of Gabrielle Roy's *Bonheur d'occasion* was not nearly as great as the novel's appearance in English translation as the May 1947 selection of the Literary Guild of New York in an edition of 750,000, a consecration in the field of large-scale production more directly tied to economic capital. Both these processes of selection differ from the rewriting in translation by the subsidized English-Canadian presses with their more transparent relations to political power. But a translation may also circulate in the field of marginal production, that of the avant-garde or another specialized audience such as children or women, and earn only a limited, critical success. It is the critical representation of this representation that confers "the public meaning of a work" by proposing "a social definition of its objective position in the field" that differentiates it from other positions (Bourdieu 1993, 118 – 19). Translations of Quebec literary texts have occupied the entire range of these positions, as we shall see, and issues of gender are operative in the distinctions among them that hierarchically structure the field.

Rewriting, or Changing Value and Knowledge

How does an "imported" literature function in a different system? What impact does this importation have on the fame and survival of writing? These are important questions for polysystem theory which concerns itself with the dynamic interaction of heterogeneous cultural fields. Translation, as "metaliterature," is a privileged mode of producing literary knowledge, according to André Lefevere (1977, 68). As "rewriting," translation constitutes a model of a dynamic system that relativizes knowledge, opening it continuously to an outside, to the *différend* of an agonistic postion or to the shock of the new. For change is produced through a movement of exteriorization or exotopy as much as through internal differentiations within a field and as such may be posited as a process of becoming, not a binary opposition. Borders are sites of intense semiosis where a new "semiosphere" is produced through the distinction a culture makes between an orderly "us" and a disorderly "them." Simultaneously within and without, the border both unites and separates and so brings about a realignment of the borderline and a redistribution of value (Lotman 142) that produces heterogeneous and mobile meaning. Criticism and translation are two important modalities of textual "manipulation" which, along with literary history, anthologizing, and many types of peritextual apparatus (prefaces, advertising, book jackets, etc.) engage in mediation between different fields or different positions in a field, and so realign borders. Such rewriting functions metatextually to determine its reception in the process of forming an audience by means of specific textual regularities and the performativity of discourse.[6] Forms of "rewriting" propose a certain ideology and a certain poetics in function of a given socioeconomic power by means of which one culture intervenes in another. The resulting refraction may accelerate literary innovation (by introducing new genres, new concepts, or new literary techniques) or, on the contrary, rewriting may play a conservative role and inhibit change (by selecting genres, concepts, or techniques that conform to established models) (Lefevere 1992, vii). Translation, in broadening the field of reception and the framework of a text's potential readings, plays an important role in increasing the text's longevity. As Lefevere concludes: "The fame of a writer and his or her position in literature are, to no small extent, at the mercy of his or her translator" (1977, 74).

Lefevere's theory of the textual and ideational manipulation of the literary to differentiated effects reworks a number of elements of polysystem theory. However, with his announcement of the "cultural turn" in translation studies, Lefevere insists more on the socio-cultural changes in the habitus, changes that may be analyzed through the operation of "patronage" (1992, 11). For Itamar Evan-Zohar, principal theoretician of polysystem theory, translated literature occupies either a primary or a secondary position, according to the state of the translating culture within the polysystem (22–24). The "normal" position, Evan-Zohar claims, may be found in established or stable literatures where translation occupies a secondary position with a conservative function of reproducing norms. Translated literature occupies a primary position with an innovative function when the translating culture is unstable. Such instability is a feature of the "new" English-Canadian and Quebec literary systems, according to Carolyn Perkes, which are, additionally, marginal in relation to the "strong" French, English, and American literary systems. In a process of accelerated constitution since the 1960s, English-Canadian literature is in search of new models to enrich its repertory of forms. Nonetheless, as Perkes observes, its forms have generally changed little despite the increased contact with Quebec literature, at least not those of the novel and short story, the genres most represented in the Quebec corpus in translation, which have reinforced the realistic tendency of English-Canadian fiction. An exception to this model of interaction, according to Perkes — an exception highly significant for my argument — is feminist writing in translation which, she contends, occupies a primary position aiming to transform the models of the target system and produce "adequate" translations. Such a project introduces changes in the English-Canadian peritextual discourse and cultural norms (1196). This approach to translation that evaluates its ideological adequacy or performative felicity challenges the discourse of "fidelity" with its corollary of equivalence and identity that predominates in the corpus of translators' prefaces analyzed by Perkes (1205–6). That there are several modalities for the insertion of Quebec literature in translation into the field of English-Canadian cultural production leads Perkes to conclude that the Canadian literary system does not conform to Evan-Zohar's hypothesis (1196). The problem, I propose, is on the contrary in polysystem theory's hypothesis itself that presumes a homogeneous reception of translations according to an abstract and idealist model. However, there is always differentiation and struggle among contending forces within a cultural field, in the present case between works apt for reworking to enter into the restricted field of English-Canadian cultural production, recognized with prizes and canonized in the education system — two instances of legitimation that consecrate through their symbolic acts — and experimental texts which, produced in a feminist habitus, circulate only in a marginalized field of production.

The concept of "patronage" is of help here in linking the position of reception within a field of production to socio-economic contingencies in the cultural field. Lefevere posits different modalities through which three aspects of power operate: ideological, or the formal and thematic constraints on genres of discourse; economic, or the conditions of possibility for living from the sales or salary of one's works; and the prestige of a particular style of life, or habitus. There is always a situation of "literary diglossia" stratifying the field, even in the case where a singular force — absolute king, totalitarian state, or monopoly of big-box stores — controls the three elements of power through subsidies or pensions or censure. But in such a non-differentiated system, the works not recognized would be called "dissident" or would be published only with great difficulty (Lefevere 1992, 17). This stratification of the field affects the conditions of possibility for publication in a differentiated field as well. Works that conform to the dominant ideology or poetics, and so are likely to be canonized, will easily find a prestigious publisher: works diverging from the doxa will have to make do with a *samizdat* or be published in a different system, unless they find a "rewriter" able to make them culturally pertinent (1992, 21). Such intervention on the part of influential rewriter-critics has positioned Quebec writers within the English-Canadian cultural field. Translation may also facilitate such movement into another cultural field, as it does with many texts written in minority languages in Canada whose English (or French) translations are eventually published while the original languishes in manuscript for lack of an audience. But publication in this second cultural field may shape the text to a different horizon of expectations, as we shall see with English versions of works by Quebec women writers. Those works suitable for canonization function in a long cycle of production oriented to the future, rather than in a short cycle of production oriented to the present and pre-established interests, as are best-sellers and other works in the large-scale field of production. In deciding what will be translated and for what audience, publishers also determine who translates, under what circumstances, and how they translate. This patronage function not only regulates the status of the translator, but intervenes obliquely in the other instances of reception, notably, in those of criticism and education where, on the basis of the works available in English translation, and within the literary schemas proposed by these translated works, readings, and interpretations are produced that make them intelligible to a unilingual audience. These operations constitute the textual and ideological effects of the market of symbolic goods that determine the translatable or the "threshold of knowledge" (Perkes) of textual difference.

If I insist on the importance of publishers in the reception of Quebec literature, it is not to contradict Pierre Hébert when he writes that one "can never insist enough on the role played by translators in making Quebec literature known in English Canada" (1989, 109), but rather to emphasize the relations of power that determine who will occupy the translator-function. Translators may well write in their prefaces and essays about the *bonententisme* in their recognition of the other (in what Sherry Simon has called the "ethnographic" impulse in English-Canadian translations of Quebec literature (1994, 53), that is their valorization of alterity), their translations nonetheless are forced to submit to the symbolic violence of the selective process of transmission by publishers within the competition of the market in symbolic goods that creates hierarchies of value.[7] Cultural nationalism always intervenes in these literary (inter)relations, but economic power structures the field. The difference in the reception of translated works, between their secondary or primary position as identified by Perkes, signifies a socio-economic stratification in the English-Canadian cultural field. The "realist" works of fiction by Gabrielle Roy, Anne Hébert, and Marie-Claire Blais, or rewritten to appear realist and express referential knowledge about some "unknown" corner of the nation, circulate in the restricted field of cultural production, produced by American publishers in co-editions with the large English-Canadian publishers — McClelland & Stewart, Stoddart-General (but not by the branch plant Oxford or Macmillan or Knopf). On the other hand, the works of a younger generation of feminists circulate in the marginal field of production, that of the avant-garde or feminism, published in periodicals such as *Open Letter, Exile, Canadian Fiction Magazine, Tessera*, or by "small" publishers, mostly writer-run, such as Talonbooks, Exile Editions, Coach House, and Women's Press, that transmit a different representation of Quebec literature.

"How Do You Say 'Gabrielle Roy'?"

Do you say [rwa] or [rəi]? Ted Blodgett's question, which I reformulate phonetically here, is asked every day in Toronto where the first French-language public school, opened more than twenty-five years ago, is called L'École Publique Gabrielle Roy. No other Quebec writer has managed to lodge herself so deeply in the imaginary and the habitus of English Canadians as Gabrielle Roy. With this question we address the ideological implication of her presence in the heart of the "Queen City." Is Gabrielle Roy a Quebec writer or a Franco-Manitoban writer or a Canadian writer of French expression? And does this school's name constitute an opening to embrace exogenous codes in an ethics of cultural difference that recognizes the alterity of the other? Or is it an identificatory translation that accommodates alterity in a play of surface differences to sustain a multiculturalist and pan-Canadianist vision of the nation? Through what dynamic in the dialectic of distinction does Gabrielle Roy compose an integral part of English-Canadian literary history? Under the sign of opposition? Or that of complementarity? As rupture? Or continuity? In the tension and disjunction of this operation of exchange and transference, inevitably incomplete because still in process, I reintroduce the protest of Lise Gauvin about the "distortion" produced in the displacement outside Quebec of the horizon of expectation in the transmission of knowledge through the circulation of symbolic goods. If a community and its knowledge can only exist in a "tragic situation," according to Gauvin, who experiences the rewriting of translation as a loss, then it must be in a Tchekovian drama in which the weight of cultural heritage weighs heavily on future possibilities. Yet it was under the sign of modernity that the work of Quebec women writers was first welcomed in English Canada, and that in a relation of inclusion or addition, not of the substraction identified by Gauvin.

"The Three Sisters" is how François Gallays frames this drama. In his essay, "Gabrielle Roy et ses deux 'soeurs': Marie-Claire Blais et Anne Hébert," he outlines a strong resemblance among novels published between 1945 and 1975 which are structured around the relation between two generations of women and set during the period of WWII. This was a period of great social change in Canada when massive industrialization accelerated modernization, but especially so in Quebec where the struggle for women's independence took the form of political emancipation. Feminism was militant during this struggle for suffrage, because Quebec women did not have the same civil rights as women in other provinces. It was not until 1964 that they were formally recognized as legal persons. Though they had a high symbolic status as mothers, their legal status was a subordinate one. This discrepancy infused passion into their emancipatory struggle at a time when feminism was less militant in anglophone

Canada. The transformation in social structures, in their habitus, may be read in the fictional heroines' quest for liberation. Annabelle Rea has also stressed the connections between these novelists in her essay, "*Le premier jardin* d'Anne Hébert comme hommage à Gabrielle Roy," where she notes resemblances between Florentine and Flora in the thematics of the body and maternity. In the motif of Demeter and Persephone, she traces the relations of mothers and daughters in the novels of women writers belonging to different generations in an alternative genealogy to write "une histoire à elle," in the phrasing of Patricia Smart (1988). In this herstory, women would be the subject and not the object of knowledge and resistance would take the form of political action to change the social order. The relations among women are viewed positively by these contemporary critics, in contrast to thirty years ago when such genealogies of women, especially that of Marie-Claire Blais' *Une saison dans la vie d'Emmanuel*, were attacked as a matriarchy embodying the colonized subordination of all the Americas, and not just Quebec (Major).

Over the last twenty years, feminist criticism has become an important discourse in the academy following an increase in participation of women in civil society which has conferred on them some cultural capital. Feminist criticism rewrites Quebec literature to make it culturally pertinent for this new order of discourse. It pursues, however, an orientation well established in journalistic criticism that celebrates the work of Quebec women writers for its pathos. This is highlighted in an interview with Carol Moore-Ede, the director of a CBC television production about Gabrielle Roy and Marie-Claire Blais whose novels, *Children of My Heart* and *Nights in the Underground*, had just appeared in English translation. She had tried in the programme to encourage the public to read these novels by evoking in their dramatization "toute la gamme des *émotions*" in the books. The powerful fascination that Quebec women writers have long had for Anglo-Canadians, she claimed, is because these women "have created the most despairing and the strongest images in all Canadian literature" (Anon. 52; my translation). These powerful emotions have a political function, as Walter Poronovich writes in *The Montreal Star*, for the promotion of Quebec literature is a federalist project to counter separatism: "If Quebec decides to separate CBC-TV can at least say in good conscience that it had tried earnestly to tell the rest of Canada who and what we Quebecers are." Neither of these critics noted another politics at stake here, that of gay liberation, for the scenario was written by Timothy Findley, a Toronto gay writer. The masked actors and nightmarish decor in the staging of Blais' fiction which contrasted with the realistic scenes, actual people, and landscapes depicting Roy's fiction, might well have represented the abject lesbian who could breathe only "Underground."

The Garden and the Cage, the title of Findley's dramatization, was borrowed from an essay about Gabrielle Roy's fiction by Hugo McPherson, published in the first issue of the influential critical periodical *Canadian Literature.* This essay elaborated what was to become the dominant representation of Quebec literature in its attention to the symbolic and affective aspects of the work — restrained despair contrasted with a sympathy for the characters, the poetry of their dreams, and the passion or lyricism of the novelist. In the work of both Roy and Blais, as we read in *The Montreal Star,* "[t]here is a persistent cloak of bleakness and frustration, fathered by years of aborted hope and fostered by inevitable despair. ... Lost souls. Dead souls ... All very depressing, yet somehow inherently beautiful in its reflection of life and living" (Poronovich). Anne Hébert's novels are marked by the same polarity, according to a *Montreal Gazette* reviewer: *"Les fous de Bassan* is a harsh book, as severe as the dour community it depicts. But it is also a splendidly lyrical book" with its "spellbinding, perfect language" (Simon 1982). While McPherson focused on the tension and oscillation between "the garden of childhood innocence and the past" and "the forces of the city, adulthood 'experience'" in the work of Roy, the TV dramatization linked Roy's work to the pastoral myth and Blais' fiction to the pain of urban living. Newspaper reviews and commentary focused principally on the emotional power of the fiction, on its conventional feminine aspect, in a depoliticization of the novels. Gabrielle Roy in particular is commended for her celebrations of "endurance" and "generosity."[8] There is no praise for her technical skill as a writer nor for the aesthetics of her fiction which are replaced by comments on the faithfulness of the representation and the significance of the themes, folklorized here in such a way as to make Gabrielle Roy's work pertinent for the large-scale field of production, that of popular literature.

The reference to "archetypes" in these reviews signals the frame of "thematic criticism" of Northrop Frye through which Roy's fictions are read. Frye's theories dominated English-Canadian criticism, orienting it toward an Arnoldian idealism that privileged an expressive realism deployed for pedagogical ends. McPherson was clearly drawing on Frye's theory of archetypes in reading a Blakean opposition between innocence and experience as the "controlling pattern" in Roy's fiction (49). He transformed her novels into existential dramas of "Everyman" in which there is no difference between rural Manitoba and "the Garden of Eden" (49), so powerful is the pastoral myth. Rose-Anna becomes for him a universal *mater dolorosa* who teaches us that we must engage in "a way of life in which the moment is all-important, and in which fortitude, compassion and love are the essential values" (McPherson 52). Roy's fiction has been made pertinent to the idealism dominant in English-Canadian academic criticism and she finds her place among canonized writers between the English poet William Blake and the American prairie novelist Willa Cather, and so becomes the bearer of universal value. Her work is thus dehistoricized and rewritten to conform to the humanist discourses which Canadian nationalists opposed to American materialism throughout the 1950s, as is evident in the Massey-Lévèsque *Report* on culture (1951) and in the founding documents of the Canada Council (1956). McPherson explicitly links this antimaterialist ideology with Canadian nationalism in his conclusion where he writes: "She has, however, given us a vision of ourselves which is immeasurably more powerful than 'the vision' of windy Prime Ministers and journalistic patriots. She convinces us, indeed, that the truth which Canada has revealed to her is a timeless truth. And she persuades us to bear witness to its importance" (McPherson 57). Roy's novels are read in English Canada as a kind of "pseudo non-fiction" (Elder 70) for their pedagogical force in the service of the nation. Fortitude in suffering is the "truth" of Canada they teach us.

McPherson's analysis exemplifies the "ethnographic" impulse of the dominant discourse on translation in English Canada — self-knowledge through an encounter with the other — and its central presuppositions: a literary work is taken to be an authentic representation of French-Canadian society and, by reading it, we will come to greater appreciation of this different society. However, while translators at least some of the time attempt to make the strangeness of this other culture palpable, McPherson's commentary exhibits an identificatory impulse that attempts to conceal the foreign provenance of the work in order to coopt it for an anti-American nationalist project of English-Canadian elites. Gabrielle Roy's country, as McPherson describes it, is a part of the "peaceable kingdom," as Frye calls Canada. But this is a feminized country. Gabrielle Roy's social status is effaced before her work, but especially before the myth of Canada as a stable country, maternally generous in its love and abject in its endurance of suffering, which becomes one of the forms of the signified: *Canadian persistence confronting America.* By conflating the nationalist demands of Quebec with those of Canada, English Canadians give more emotion and greater urgency to their own identity crisis. Quebec constitutes a sort of libidinal excess for anglophone culture. However, it is an image of Quebec and Canada that fits badly with the reality of technical and social changes created by the industrialization and Americanization of Canada during the 1950s. Yet, in the imagined community of Canada, as it has been conceived by an intellectual elite, the feminized spirit of Quebec urges perseverence and signifies resistance to American capitalism. Literary criticism manifests the ideologeme "fidelity" in a compensatory discourse of the English-Canadian field of cultural production, asserting its specificity in a dialectical relation with the dominant, materialist us and, simultaneously, with the dominated, with Quebec's cultural heritage. This latter relation of alterity is seen as supporting the new Canadian field which the critical discourse is in the process of creating.

In favouring an ethos of pathos in works of women writers where the depths of oppression are relieved only by the characters' emotional strength — rather than one of critique in the novels of Hubert Aquin, for example, that present revolt against a colonialist society with a more radical assessment of the situation and a more aggressive solution to end oppression — the English-Canadian field minimized the impact of that opposition by feminizing Quebec and so naturalizing the hierarchy of power. The "pervading presence of tragedy" identified by Poronovitch is presented as the inevitable suffering of the universal human condition, without political remedy. This critical rewriting is typical of the reception of Aquin's work, according to Chantal de Grandpré and Marilyn Randall, who note that his work is only appreciated (appropriated?) at the expense of a neutralization of its politics. While the response to his work is generally *"enthousiaste,"* criticism privileges knowledge of the human heart. Comments on Aquin's style as "effervescent, dazzling, convoluted" are accompanied by warnings that his "pyrotechnics" will not be to everyone's taste (Patricia Morley qtd. in Randall, 205). His fiction has not excited the same intensity of response from readers as the work of Roy, Québécoise in her very "passionate heritage" and "attraction towards the oppressed" (Gail Scott). Gail Scott's emphasis on the passion in the political forecasts the feminist rearticulation of politics in which "the personal is political," a development that undoubtedly has stimulated renewed feminist interest in Gabrielle Roy's work since the 1980s (Lewis 1984, Whitfield 1990). For activism and passivity are no longer binary oppositions in her work; and feminist criticism values positively the contradictory and the in-between that signify an excess rather than a lack in being or meaning.

This brief comparison of the reception of Aquin's work, or that of Jacques Godbout or Jacques Ferron — all three novelists associated with the project of Quebec independence and the "nouveau roman" — is instructive. They have received none of the objective signs of legitimation by the English-Canadian literary institution that the women writers who occupy the highest rank in the Canadian literary pantheon have. Nor any recognition from the French institution either, for it is the "three sisters" who received the major French literary prizes: Gabrielle Roy, the Prix Femina for *Bonheur d'occasion* in 1947; Marie-Claire Blais, the Prix Médicis for *Une saison dans la vie d'Emmanuel* in 1966; and Anne Hébert, the Prix Femina for *Les fous de Bassan* in 1982, following the Prix des Libraires for *Kamouraska* in 1971. These novels were also made into films, though only *Bonheur d'occasion* was screened in Toronto cinemas. Roy also received the Governor General's Award for fiction twice for the English-language versions of *The Tin Flute* (1947) and *Street of Riches* (1956).[9] And *The Tin Flute* was voted the best "Canadian" novel ever at the Calgary conference on the novel (Steele). This exceptional consecration of literary translations indicates how thoroughly Roy was integrated into the English-Canadian cultural field: she became a symbol of the bicultural national literature anglophone critics dreamed about. Although this may indeed seem to be an "assimilation tranquille" (O'Neill-Karch

96), it should not be overlooked that the French edition of *Bonheur d'occasion* sold well in Toronto in 1946, thanks to the high praise of the most renowned Toronto critic, William Arthur Deacon of *The Globe and Mail*. With his nudging, *La petite poule d'eau* was on the curriculum of the French Authors examination for the Ontario Senior Matriculation in 1956 – 1957 — the only book by a Canadian in either English or French to be studied in high school prior to 1968. But then, Gabrielle Roy's first publications had been stories written in English that appeared in the *Winnipeg Free Press* and the Toronto *Star Weekly*. Fulfilling the idealized image of a bilingual Canada, Gabrielle Roy's work responded to the dominant ideology as that of a Canadian of French expression.

If Roy enters without reservation into these ideological parameters, this is not the case with her younger "sisters" who are received conditionally. Not sociorealist novels like those of Roy, their poetic fictions are integrated into the field of restricted production, even of marginal production. Criticism in magazines and newspapers comments on their aesthetics and not just their themes. The novelist Aritha van Herk praises Hébert's *In the Shadow of the Wind* for its style "so pure and controlled that one stops and rereads paragraphs for the pleasure of the language" (1984, 10). Marie-Claire Blais' style attracts more negative criticism for its excesses. According to Keith Garebian, *Nights in the Underground* is "a mixture of *fin de siècle* decadent romanticism and contemporary existential seediness. It is part marmalade, part political claptrap — alternately sticky and brittle, concrete and abstract, sensual and intellectual ... and will disappoint all but her most loyal devotees." Although Mark Czarnecki signals the importance of the stylistic experimentation in *Le sourd dans la ville*, his ironically titled review, "Bloody Clouds of Words," concurs with Garebian's assessment: "without paragraph or dialogue breaks, page after page covered with neat rectangular blocks of text as daunting and compulsively readable as tombstones" (56).

Despite this reticence, at later intervals, Anne Hébert and Marie-Claire Blais received some forms of consecration. Alone among Quebec authors, the three women writers are included among the "Major Canadian Authors" for whom annotated bibliographies were published by the Toronto-based ECW Press.[10] A critical synthesis of the work of each of these authors appeared in US publisher Twayne's "World Author's" series.[11] Although American critics have written more about Blais — she was the most studied Quebec author in American periodicals during the 1970s (Mary Jane Green 115) — perhaps because of her residence in Massachussetts and the praise of the influential critic Edmond Wilson, Blais' work was the focus of a study in Toronto publisher Forum House's "Canadian Writers and their Works" series, as was the work of Gabrielle Roy.[12] That Anne Hébert was not included in this series, although she was the 1967 recipient of the Molson Prize for her work, demonstrates the preference for the novel, more apt to respond to the horizon of expectation of anglophone readers for faithful representations of French-Canadian society than is poetry which is more subjective and aesthetic. By 1971, only two of Hébert's books of poetry had appeared in translation with different small publishers. Her poetry had attracted the critical attention of only a couple of university professors reviewing it for little magazines such as *Alphabet* and *The Canadian Forum*, with one anonymous review in the *Canadian Author & Bookman* (1967). In contrast, seven of Marie-Claire Blais' works of fiction had appeared in English translation and her play "Puppet Caravan" was televised by the CBC in 1967. Her works were adapted for a number of different mediums — *Mad Shadows* was performed by the National Ballet of Canada a decade later — attaining through this multiplication of forms of rewriting a more complex position within the English-Canadian cultural field. Moreover, Blais had personal connections with the English-Canadian literary institution as a member ("ambassador," according to Sheila Fischman) of the Writers' Union of Canada, on the invitation of Timothy Findley. Anne Hébert, living in France and published there by Seuil, lacked such close relations to English-Canadian writers and publishers. The influence of the New York consecration of Roy and Blais undoubtedly had a significant impact on their insertion into the English-Canadian field, for the position of Anne Hébert changed dramatically with the New York translation of her novel *Kamouraska* in 1973.

NARRATING THE NATION: THE FEMINIZED SPIRIT OF QUEBEC

Works inserted into the field of large-scale production undergo a more radical manipulation than those received into a marginal position in the field, as the folklorization of Gabrielle Roy's novels demonstrates. The selective and limited transmission of knowledge which produces a decontextualized and partial representation of Quebec literature poses a more significant problem in the interaction between the two fields of cultural production. A few texts in translation function as synecdoche of Quebec literature. No explanations of the process or principles of selection are offered, however. The critical series of Twayne, Forum House, and ECW detach the three women writers from the context of the field of Quebec cultural production so as to better represent them as authors in the strong sense of the term, as exceptional, as authoritative. In the literary system, the author's name is a fiction that assures the quality of the writing by circumscribing its subversive potential. The author-function guarantees the cohesion of the work through its violent internal restructuring so as to make it respond to the expectations of unity in the receiving cultural field. Anglophone criticism privileges the author-function by celebrating the personal success of these women writers and by minimizing their relations to the Quebec field of cultural production with its readings of the "national" narrative. The unilingual English reader has no possibility of evaluating the respective position of these women writers within the field by comparing them to other Quebec writers, since it is only with English-Canadian writers or international writers in English translation that such comparisons can be made. Comparative analysis with English-Canadian writers may open up new perspectives on their works, as when Gabrielle Roy is read alongside Margaret Laurence as a Manitoba writer. Comparison may just as easily shift from a recognition of distinctive traditions into a camouflaging of their incommensurability, as in Coral Ann Howell's study of fictions by Blais and Hébert along with nine English-Canadian women writers. In *Private and Fictional Words*, she established a correspondence between the feminine and the Canadian as cultural difference without taking into account the cultural and linguistic hegemony that stratifies as it differentiates within Canada: "becoming feminized Canada gains real significance" (151). The women's "stories seem the natural expression of the insecurity and ambitions of their society and in many ways they provide models for stories of Canadian national identity" (26). Quebec women writers are included in this analogy between the feminine and

293

the nation, equally subordinate, which has been common in English Canada at least since 1928 when R.G. MacBeth praised poets Marjorie Pickthall, Pauline Johnson, and Isabel Mackay — "talented daughters of the Dominion" — who stayed in Canada rather than joining their masculine contemporaries to advance their careers in London.

English Canada has had a long tradition of including works written in French in studies about Canadian literature, at least since the publication of Henry Morgan's encyclopedic *Bibliotheca Canadensis* (1867). A significant socio-political role is accorded to knowledge of francophone literature in forming the nation, observes Pierre Hébert, contributing to the "entente cordiale ou de la bonne entente" between two founding peoples (1992, 18). While this equal treatment of the complete corpus of the two literatures continues in the encyclopedic tradition of such reference works as the *Oxford Companion to Canadian Literature* and the fully bilingual *Dictionary of Canadian Biography*, more common has been a model of supplementation and subordination. "AND Quebec," as Frank Davey observes, is the practice in most critical works or anthologies that relegate Quebec to a final chapter or appendix at the end of the book (1997, 13).

For a veritable ethics of cultural difference, however, as Gayatri Spivak argues, it is not enough to take note of the differences between the words and the rhetoric of "cultures-in-relation." What must be taken into account are the differences between two habituses, between those contexts of everyday life where power exerts itself by making distinctions between modalities of address or utterance regarding their felicity or adequacy in fulfilling the appropriate conventions, and hence their performativity. The partial inclusion of Quebec literary works within the field of English-Canadian cultural production decontextualizes and refracts them: a few works are admitted to innoculate the field against difference, against alterity, but not enough to effect real change in the field. A paradox ensues: what is most admired in Quebec literature — its unfamiliar or surprising knowledge,[13] its modernity, its powerful emotion — is rendered banal and ordinary. Rewriting the works participates in an operation of territorializing them, making them familiar, routine, whereby the self-regulation of the cultural field negotiates the insertion of symbolic goods from the outside. Symbolic violence operates as much by means of a process of inclusion as by exclusion when opposition is rewritten as complementarity. Symbolic capital affirms itself as continuity.

Yet it was under the sign of rupture, of modernity, that the works of these Quebec women writers were first hailed, modernism that had bypassed English Canada whose literature passed directly from Victorian idealism to post-modernism without pausing at the naturalism and symbolism of European high modernism (Kroetsch 1974, 1). Initially, English-Canadian criticism appreciated the objectivity and irony of their works that contrasted with the dominant idealization. This enthusiastic response constituted a compensatory movement for a lack in the English-Canadian cultural field and promised to enrich its literary corpus. Transforming the models, Quebec literature in translation occupied a primary position in the English-Canadian field, at least at the time of its initial reception. That this subsequently changed to become a conservative movement in which the translations took up the secondary position in the cultural field noted by Carolyn Perkes (1196) calls into question the binary model of polysystem theory. The operation of exchange and transfer of knowledge through the mediation of works in translation is necessarily incomplete because it is implicated in the dynamics of the "target" system in its evolution through conflicts between competing programmes of reading and changing historical phases. First contact occurred through a movement of exotopy in which writers of the target cultural field broke out of the constraints of the dominant aesthetic and ideological forms. Subsequently, realigning its borders and redistributing its values, the receiving system rewrote this peripheral knowledge so as to render it pertinent to the importing culture where it took up the diverse positions in which the habitus is subjected to hegemonic relations. The changing frameworks of academic criticism have been aptly identified by Neil Bishop in regard to the work of Anne Hébert: thematic criticism was supplanted by semiotic, narratological, and psychoanalytic criticism heavily influenced by continental French approaches (258). Since the 1980s, he notes, feminist criticism influenced by American critical practices has carved out a space for marginality in her work. Subsequent changes in habitus have occurred with the large-scale migrations across the continent and a transfer of population, and economic and political power towards the west. Gabrielle Roy's works have been more readily rewritten to correspond to the new critical frameworks of the intercultural and "la francophonie," where she is read as an analyst of multiculturalism (Dansereau, Waddington) or as a franco-Manitoban writer (Harvey).

This dynamic shift in habitus and critical doxa manifests itself in the successive refractions of Gabrielle Roy and her two "sisters." English-Canadian criticism participates in the production and transmission of symbolic goods by constituting the distinctions pertinent for the cultural field in the process of formation. In the first instance, a new objectivity incites the admiration of the English-Canadian writers. Comparisons abound with the great European masters of modernism. Hugh MacLennan, who aspired to be a Canadian Balzac, compared *Bonheur d'occasion* to the fiction of Charles Dickens, while his wife, the writer Dorothy Duncan, wrote that Gabrielle Roy reminded her of Scandinavian writers. She praised the novel for its sociopolitical timeliness (its honest dealing with the "unfortunate poor in Montreal") and the realism of its style (the most authentic French-Canadian dialogue). They recognized in Roy's work an aesthetic project with parallels to their own attempt to write the history of contemporary urban society. The success of Roy's novel established new models of writing that transformed the horizon of expectation for the urban fiction of MacLennan, Gwethelyn Graham, and other contemporaries, who became her fellow members of the Canadian Authors' Association. Alerted by MacLennan of the novel's considerable interest, William Arthur Deacon, the influential literary columnist at *The Globe and Mail*, noted resemblances to Flaubert. Without *Madame Bovary*, he claimed, there would have been no *The Tin Flute*: "The exquisite care of every homely detail, giving concrete reality to a stick of cheap furniture, to the drifting snow, to the taxi-driver's grandiose talk, is what this French master seems to have taught his apt pupil in Canada" (13).

Deacon's influence as rewriter of her work had an important impact on Gabrielle Roy's career. Their friendship was enriched by memories of their Manitoba childhoods which linked them against the cultural hegemony of Toronto and Montreal. Deacon thought Roy had earned such success because she was an outsider, first from Manitoba and then from France. He mounted an impressive publicity campaign for the novel in *The Globe and Mail*, an English-language newspaper with considerable cultural capital, making it known to a broad public. Because of his background as a lawyer, Deacon was able to help Roy in the material direction of her career, advising her on translation contracts for the novel. Simultaneous publication of the novel in the two languages was necessary, he believed, because the larger anglophone market would be important for the survival of francophone writers: "The need of money will ensure that the emphasis will be on Canadianism, rather than on racialism. ... Canadian literature will quietly assimilate the French" (qtd. in O'Neill-Karch 96). If, for him, it is primarily the constraints of economic power that orient the choice of publisher, and even of language, this argument advantages a specific political power. Constitution of an autonomous Canadian field of production, long overdue as British publishers refused to treat Canada as a separate market in their dealings with American publishers, became an impossibility after 1946 when the British and Americans concluded an agreement placing Canada within the American sphere of rights while Great Britain had sole right to market books in the other former colonies and in Europe (Parker 371). Recognition constitutes a social relation of subordination to American capital, American publishers having the greatest prestige in the English-Canadian cultural field: publication in the us confers symbolic as well as economic capital.

That Roy followed Deacon's advice and signed separate contracts with an American as well as a Canadian publisher increased her royalties. However, the translation made by Hannah Joseph for the American editor and reprinted by the Canadian, greatly facilitated that "assimilation tranquille" by transforming *Bonheur d'occasion* into a universal drama celebrated by American critics for its intense "pathos" (Lee). The textual effects of this manipulation established a model of ethnocentric translation for Quebec books translated in the us and then imported to Canada. Joseph's error in translating "poudrerie" (blowing snow) as "poudrière" (powder magazine) has been much discussed. But the title is also subject for debate since the literal version, "Borrowed Bliss," preferred by Roy, was not retained. *The Tin Flute*, selected from a higher socio-linguistic register and exemplifying the strategy of ennobling adopted by Joseph, accentuates the universal elements of the novel and conceals Roy's complex dramatization of Montreal's social stratifications. Unfamiliar with Quebec turns of phrase, Joseph chose to eliminate Quebecisms so raising the linguistic register of the dialogue and erasing subtle distinctions between characters' speech. This choice passively diminished the import of the novelist's analysis of class along with ethnic hierarchies. Joseph also transformed the characterization by changing the motivation and evaluation of actions. Azarius is presented as lazy when "se laisser vivre" is translated "while I'm waiting" rather than "let's go with the flow" and Florentine is no longer a member of the disadvantaged working class when the phrase "moitié peuple, moitié chanson" is translated "half slut, half song" (Montpetit 145). Joseph's translation deemed inadequate, *Bonheur d'occasion* was retranslated by Alan Brown in 1980. Not only did he choose to retain the title because it had become so celebrated in English Canada, but his translation did not clear up all the other problems, since he rendered this phrase, "half song, half squalor" (Montpetit 146). Nor did Brown signal the anglicisms in the dialogue of Roy's novel, although they had an important sociolinguistic value since the selected heteroglossia signified the characters' relations with economic power. The textual effects of these manipulations exhibit an ideology of naturalization based in concepts of transparency and "fluency" (Venuti 1998, 5) which, oriented primarily toward an addressee, mask the work of textual manipulation performed by a translator and the signs of cultural difference by effacing the traces of re-enunciation. The novel is presented as though written in English and not as a translation coming from a different culture.

The criterion of transparency exerted its force in the rewriting of Marie-Claire Blais' novels in the practice of her translators and in its reception by journalist-critics. Blais, like Roy, had the support of a special interlocutor in the most influential of American critics, Edmond Wilson, according to whom she wrote with great lyric force and biting satire "as shocking as Zola's" (148). He called her a "genius" and compared her fluid prose-poems to those of Rimbaud, Lautréamont, and even Virginia Woolf (153). Other critics subsequently compared her to the great European masters of modernism, to Claudel, Cocteau, Bernanos, and Mauriac for the power of her images of revolt (Callaghan 31), to Kafka,

Faulkner, and Dostoevsky for her exploration of the darkness of the human soul (Philip Stratford). In Wilson, Blais had found an exceptional rewriter with cultural capital who made her work pertinent not only in the American cultural field but also internationally. With his backing, she won a Guggenheim Fellowship in 1963 and moved to the us where she lived near Wilson and many other writers. Through him she met Toronto writer, Morley Callaghan, also much praised in *O Canada*, and his son, Barry, who published an early interview with her and subsequently translated some of her poems and plays for publication in his periodical, *Exile*. While Callaghan helped her negotiate with Canadian publishers, Wilson's high praise opened the doors to the most prestigious American publishing houses. They made contracts for translations of her work, engaging American translators. Such direct negotiations between publishers ensured rapid translation of Blais' work until *Nuits de l'Underground* (1978), with the exception of some texts dealing explicitly with homosexuality. These were translated later by small Canadian publishers, manifesting clearly the relationship between the prestige of the publisher who commissions the translation, the habitus of the translator, and the themes of the work to be translated.[14] American practice differs from English-Canadian in this regard, particularly since the establishment of the translation programme of the Canada Council where translators select a book to translate, then enter into contact with the author and a publisher. Through this intervention of the Council and political instances of power, the status of the Canadian translator is higher than the American who performs work-for-hire. In the us, the market of symbolic goods is structured by the economy: the field of publication has been in the process of intense capitalization since 1945 and today has become a veritable cultural industry dominated by Disney and Time-Warner. With Farrar, Strauss & Giroux as publisher, Blais' works were oriented towards the field of restricted production.

Marie-Claire Blais' earliest work fulfilled the expectations of an international market for it showed no regional particularities of setting or language. It was, however, her most "realist" novel, *Une saison dans la vie d'Emmanuel*, that won the Prix Médicis. Subsequently, her work became more subjective and rooted in Quebec realities with the three-volume, fictional autobiography of Pauline Archange. It was rewritten to conform

to the generic norms of the English *bildungsroman* in the translation of
Derek Coltman who cut the final eighteen pages of *Vivre! Vivre!* to form
a single volume under the title *Manuscripts of Pauline Archange* (1969).
Une joualonais sa joualonie (1973) raised difficulties of a different order for
the translator: a satiric parody of the Quebec national novel written in
joual and a *roman à clef*, a mordant satire of the Montreal literary milieu,
this novel crammed with Quebecisms was rewritten by the American
translator Ralph Manheim as *St. Lawrence Blues* (1977) in a way that elimi-
nated its foreignness. Although he kept the names of Blais' characters in
French, he oriented the text toward an American public with the title
which alluded to *St. Louis Blues*, well-known in the US outside the realm
of Jazz. For those familiar with Quebec literature, the title evoked the
"white niggers" of America, the ideologeme of oppression. From an aesthetic perspective, the translation succeeded well linguistically, since
Manheim retained the rhythm and the energy of the narrative.

From a Canadian perspective, however, as Ray Ellenwood pointed out
in a review, where a politics of language is always in play, the translation greatly distorted the pragmatic effect of Blais' novel. "Marie-Claire
Blais' book is about a particular kind of speech in a particular setting ...
This is not a nationalistic book — quite the opposite — but it *is* concerned
with the politics of language, with the way people speak, and how their
speech is bound up with class, education and opportunity" (1995, 105).
Like Joseph, Manheim fails to render the bilingualism of Blais' novel
and so obfuscates her dramatization of the socio-economic stratifications of Montreal. Removing the heteroglossia of certain phrases, not
signalling the English used in some contexts, Manheim elides the
political import of Blais' novel so as to make it more pertinent for an
international market. Imported into the field of restricted production in English Canada, however, this depoliticized and universalized
novel functions in a context where questions of linguistic identity are
at the heart of national politics. The textual and ideological effects of
Manheim's manipulation mask the difference of a text which takes a
controversial position on important linguistic issues. These strategies
have a significant impact on models of translation that favour readable,
ethnocentric translations. This American model predominates among
prestigious English-Canadian publishers and journalists whose criticism

is oriented towards the field of restricted production. When Ray Ellenwood translated *Nights in the Underground* (1978) for a Toronto publisher, he tried to render into English the historical and social specificity of the Montreal lesbian community characterized by a mixing of French and English languages. As he argued, highlighting Quebec's difference was an ethical issue: "I have a moral obligation to make my translation recall the original as much as possible" (1995, 109). And this strategy made the traces of textual manipulation visible in a translation that called "attention to itself" (1995, 107). As he commented, translation is a complex system of decoding and recoding on a number of levels, semantic, syntactic, and pragmatic. The translator, like the author, is positioned within a specific historical context subject to ideological-aesthetic constraints. Ellenwood's strategy of textual defamiliarization did not arouse the admiration of anglo-Canadian reviewers. Keith Garebian attacked his translation as symptomatic of a decline in Blais' writing: "The translation doesn't help matters. Ray Ellenwood has produced an atrocious bilingual hybrid: *'on demande a toi et moi* if we were Jewish ... *ils ont dit* they wouldn't punish us."

The purity of language is a fiction that reinforces anglo-Canadian hegemony. Anglophone critics consider non-pertinent to the dominant discourse any book that does not give the illusion that it was written directly in English, especially a book that exposes the bilingualism of Montreal, a francophone city which has long resisted the economic, political, and cultural domination of English. The concealment of language politics contributes to a depoliticization of the dispossession in the novels, which is perceived as an integral part of the human condition and not as the effect of a specific political oppression — the hegemony of English North America. In her translation of *Anna's World* (1985), Sheila Fischman adopted a strategy that respects the norm of naturalization. The English words in Blais' text help to establish the motivations and assessments of characters. The repetition of "drifter" and "drift away" relates specifically to Anna's father, an American "draft-dodger." Linked to the words "sexy," "gang," and "forbidden," they signify the increasing influence of an American culture of violence, a socio-political transformation that is invisible to the anglophone reader, as Kathy Mezei observes (1995, 144). That for many Sheila Fischman is the best-known

translator of Quebec literature indicates to what an extent the ideology of naturalization in the target language is esteemed as a translation
practice. Ellenwood's ethnographic impulse, that attempts to translate
into English an idiom open to the strangeness of its diverse appropria-
tions, is not legitimated in the field of restricted production where a
negative cultural value is attributed to translation. It should be noted
that Ellenwood has published his translations primarily with small
Canadian publishers like Coach House and Exile. Within the socio-economic hierarchy of the field of literary production in English Canada,
what has been most valued are rewritings of novels made to appear
realistic and to communicate an authentic referential knowledge of a
Quebec — feminized and unilingual in English.

The reception of Anne Hébert's work shows how Toronto is mostly
interested in "what New York wants," at least in the big daily newspapers which are the most important instances of rewriting works apt
to be consecrated. Hébert's work is admired at the price of a certain
decontextualization both generic and political. Read thematically for
its symbols and archetypes, her fiction is inscribed in a history of anglophone literature. The power of symbolic capital to stratify the field is
particularly noteworthy in the analogies elaborated by critics to establish the pertinence of *Kamouraska* in the field of anglo-Canadian cultural production. Although Hébert had published her first texts more
than thirty years earlier, had received the recognition of prestigious
prizes in Quebec, and her poems had been translated by celebrated
English-Canadian poets, her work was noticed by the anglophone public
only in 1973 with the translation of *Kamouraska*. William French, successor of Deacon as literary chronicler at *The Globe and Mail*, wondered
whether English-Canadian publishers were afraid of taking risks with
such works. The history of publication of *Kamouraska* reveals the presence of a "wall" preventing the cirtulation of symbolic goods between
"French Canada and English Canada": "It was published in Quebec and
France in 1970 to considerable acclaim, and won the Prix des Librairies
in France. Yet only now do we get an English translation of the novel,
just one jump ahead of the movie. And even this version comes to us
via New York, with translation by an American, Norman Shapiro" (15).
The "wall," according to French, was erected by the conservativism of

English-Canadian publishers, not (more accurately) by the prestige and economic clout of American publishers. In his review, French praises the power of the images — particularly the blood on the snow — and the combination of a story of passion with the narrative of a historical murder. Easily recognized here is the knowledge much valued by English-Canadian critics, intensity of emotion and a faithful representation of Quebec society. However, it is accessible to English Canadians only with the intervention of the Americans.

French's key points (minus the nationalist complaint) — the existing film version and the American translation — are reiterated by other journalist-critics. Paul McLaughlin emphasized the qualifications of the translator (an American professor) and the film, "directed by Claude Jutras and starr[ing] Génevève Bujold," which would soon open (37), but not the translation. Beverley Smith extended the analogy between novel ("a dazzling new height in artistic achievements" [1]) and film ("received with equal enthusiasm" [15]) by comparing them to the tense atmosphere and red imagery of Ingmar Bergman's *Cries and Whispers*. For Smith, the novel is legitimated by a British genealogy that establishes its symbolic capital: "Mlle Hébert's description of the passion that consumes her protagonists is powerful and stunning. The blood imagery is straight from *MacBeth*" (15). For McLaughlin, the pertinence of *Kamouraska* arises from its combination of a popular genre — a crime story — and a discourse highly regarded in English Canada, historiography. He asserted the authenticity of the novel's representation of French-Canadian society by emphasizing the historical truth of the plot — "this *actual* crime" — but he also praised Hébert's stylistic mastery — "maturity," and "imaginative control of language" — that produced "an eerie, black excitement that demands one's attention, without becoming contrived" (37). The art of Hébert is paradoxically an art of avoiding artifice in presenting a non-fictionalized world as reality, as the "truth" of Quebec.

Despite the geopolitical specificity of his title, "Quebec Gothic," French decontextualized *Kamouraska*. In contrast to the objectivity characterizing the celebrated naturalist novels evoked in his comparison of Hébert's novel to *Madame Bovary*, the gothic novel is notable for its subjectivity in the dramas of the unconscious that inform its symbolics. For the English-Canadian reader this is a significant genre, for the stories and novels of Alice Munro and Margaret Atwood have been called "Ontario gothic" and are praised for their magic realism, their atmosphere of the marvellous and mysterious infused in the everyday. This Ontario gothic has in turn been influenced by the "Southern Gothic" of Carson McCullers and Eudora Welty, writers of the American South. Recognizable here is the legacy of Faulkner, pioneer in the exploration of subterranean violence tearing apart insular communities. A comparison with this canonized American writer is intimated also in the much repeated phrases of the critics, "blood on the snow," "neige et fureur" — an allusion to Faulkner made explicit in van Herk's review of *In the Shadow of the Wind* entitled "The Sound and the Fury" — which established the Americanness of this mood of poetic terror much appreciated by Hébert's readers. An alert reader might also detect an allusion to "Wolf in the Snow: Four Windows on to Landscapes" by Warren Tallman, an influential English-Canadian critic. Published in *Canadian Literature*, this essay analyzed the theme of isolation and alienation in the English-Canadian novel of the 1940s and 1950s through the symbol of characters' relation to landscape seen through a window. The theme of a certain difficulty of being, like the imagery of windows and vast snowy spaces, was not unlike the psychological dramas of submission and revolt of the female protagonists in Hébert's novels. The instability of identity, a central problem for characters whose subjectivity disintegrates in proliferating fragments, has affinities with the "feminine gothic" which, according to Ellen Moers, represented women's troubling relation to creativity, the mixture of fear, guilt, and anxiety accompanying a heroine's efforts to transcend her condition by means of aesthetic creation or procreation of another being. *Kamouraska* and *In the Shadow of the Wind* respond well to the horizon of expectations of the market of cultural goods in English Canada where they belong to a genre of fiction highly valued in the us and Canada, and even in England, as comparisons of Hébert to the Brontës emphasize. That this is a feminine genre, a counter-discourse in which heroines pursue an interior quest that does not violate social conventions — in contrast to the masculine advenures of the picaresque, a canonized genre — fully satisfies the cultural expectations by feminizing

Hébert's work. This facilitates her insertion into the English-Canadian cultural field where she joins the pantheon of women writers — the "Margarets" — and bolsters the ideologeme signifying: *the feminine position of Canadian culture in relation to America.* This contradiction is central to the cultural discourse of English-Canadian nationalism. An oppositional discourse is represented in an ideologeme that displaces the symbolic violence of an economic subordination. Culture fulfills a compensatory function in securing a national identity.

Poetry in the Dialogue on Translation

What is striking in these reviews of *Kamouraska* is the absence of analyses of the translation and of comparisons with the aesthetics of Hébert's poetry which had been available in several English translations for a decade following the first publication in *Tamarack* (1962) of some poems translated by F.R. Scott. Two books of translated poems, F.R. Scott's *St-Denys Garneau & Anne Hébert: Translations* (1962) and Peter Miller's *The Tomb of the Kings* (1967), violated the normative fiction of the unity of language and the invisibility of the translator with their bilingual format. The difference in the reception of Hébert's fiction and poetry clearly exposes the distinction between the field of restricted production and the field of marginal or avant-garde production in English Canada. The "wall" of which French complained is not so much one between English and French Canada as it is that creating the internal stratification of the English-Canadian field of production. Among other differentiations, it separates a concern with form and language from a preoccupation with mimesis and theme. Narratives referencing a common humanity are valued over poetry or experimental texts that expose linguistic and cultural difference.

The work of distinction producing this internal hierarchy takes place in the criticism of Hébert's poetry. Through different critical frames of stylistic analysis, critics highlight the reticence and sobriety of her images rather than their sensuality or emotional excess. They emphasize the unusual aspect of her poetry, its place in the tradition of French modernism, and the difficulty it presents for translation into English. Reviews comment on the strategies of translation, influenced undoubtedly by the bilingual format of publication, Scott's three versions of his translations, and the exchange of letters with Hébert about translation. This *Dialogue sur la traduction* enabled a reader to apprehend the mechanisms of a dynamic reading of the poems that takes the form of a rewriting in translation. In publishing the three versions he had made of the poems following Hébert's comments on them, Scott presented translation as an inevitably incomplete process: "Une traduction ne peut jamais être considéré comme tout à fait terminée, même aux yeux du traducteur. Si telle expression ne le satisfait pas, il peut toujours en trouver une autre" (100). In this, he followed the poet's example in modifying the poem through the process of composition and in various subsequent editions. For the poet, too, is a translator, selecting the appropriate language to inscribe "an interior vibration." Reading is also translation, according to Scott, for the reader must extract meaning from a text. The words are not so much changed as charged with a personal meaning which is not necessarily that of the poet (101). The reading-translation that changes words into another language also charges them with different cultural values, for it confronts the limits of languages, their incommensurability, when the meaning of a word in the second language is not the same as in the first language. In their dialogue, Hébert points out some grammatical errors, some *faux-amis* (or illusory correspondences), while Scott replies in English, proposing alternatives.

Scott's general strategy of "literal translation" (81) proved limited in rendering "ses prunelles crevés," the final image of *Le tombeau des rois*, as "perforated eyes." The phrase has a "broader, more dramatic sense," Hébert commented, but Scott's version gave "more strength to the shocking image" (85). Upon rereading, he concurred with Hébert and changed his translation to "blinded eyes" which conveyed several possible meanings (102). Translating images is difficult, Scott concluded, because "each one must agree with others and complement them" (102). He learned to read images in a literary context which differs from the verbal context, a strategy of active reading/translating that engages with "true poetic signification," according to Northrop Frye in his introduction to the book, that is with the value of an image determined within an "order of words" or literary system (18). The mechanisms of the translating process are exposed in this dialogue: everything takes place under the sign of an irreconcilable difference between two languages and two modernist poetics. This process is an "adventure in experimental writing," observed Jeanne Lapointe in her preface to the book (23). Oriented toward the "source" language, literal translation makes explicit the foreign provenance of the work by producing textual effects that defamiliarize the "target" language in order to bring the reader to the poems. Scott's practice introduced a new model for translating poetry (the field of marginal production) which in the English-Canadian tradition has subsequently been "literalist" (Mezei 1984). Although a privileged interlocutor or rewriter for Hébert, Scott did not have the kind of widely recognized prestige of an Edmund Wilson to make her poetry pertinent in the field of restricted production, but only in the field of marginal production of left-wing and avant-garde periodicals. Exotopy constitutes a model limited to the field of marginal production, whereas that of fluency predominates in the field of restricted production in which the fiction of an anglophone Quebec is reproduced for a bourgeois public.

In translating, however, Scott paid more attention to the affective and sensory content of the images than to the sound and rhythm of words, which led some academic critics to produce thematic readings of Hébert's poetry. These readings inscribed the standpoint of the dominant idealism: they presented Hébert's work as an existential drama of innocence evolving into immanence through the experience or anguish of solitude. Laura Rièse underlined the symbolic dimensions of Hébert's and Saint-Denys Garneau's poetry in Scott's translation whose images conceal "a deeper meaning, something restraining and limiting their flighty aspirations, enlarged to comprise all humanity" (1962 210). The universal dimension of this quest distances their poetry from the "general patriotic urge" of their predecessors. Rièse's reading echoed that of Patricia Purcell [Smart] whose study of three volumes of Hébert's poetry, published in *Canadian Literature*, read them as three phases in an "intense interior drama of poetic and spiritual evolution" (Smart 1961, 51). The poet learns in the passage through a "dark night of the soul" (58) to conceive of poetic creation as a "Christlike mission" (61) leading to liberation. Where Smart developed a comparison with Camus' *L'Étranger* to highlight Hébert's modernity

(59), Rièse cited Sartre's *Huis clos*. Smart admired the "clearcut, unadorned style" of the poetry, while Rièse emphasized the striking originality of its metaphors, "not yet as startling as those of the French Surrealists but they come close to a certain abstruseness akin to Symbolism" (210). Hébert's work is thus simultaneously objective and subjective, resolutely modernist in its style though traditional in its subject matter.[15] Recognizable here is the dominant paradigm of Canadian Literature that rewrote Hébert's work to conform to an anti-materialist humanism. Rièse did not fully subscribe to its tenets, for she devoted a third of her essay to Scott's translation, to linguistic and textual manipulation, though she valued it for its "clarity and assurance," that is for its fluency and readability (210). Scott's translation is praised for retaining "the purity of the free verse" (210) which introduced a new poetics to the English-Canadian field of cultural production.

This positive evaluation of the translation was not shared by the poets who reviewed Hébert's poetry in translation. They rewrote her work to conform to the formalism sought after in transforming literary models considered too subjective and Romantic, but still within the framework of humanism's struggle against materialism. Robin Skelton and Louis Dudek regretted the loss of sonority in the English versification.[16] Their comparative analyses under the sign of cultural difference took into account the two different socio-political contexts of French and English Canada with their divergent ideologies and aesthetics. Skelton highlighted the balancing of objectivity with subjectivity in the tone, but regretted the loss of musicality. Scott translated the ritual meaning of *Le tombeau des rois* at the risk of losing the poetry. Nonetheless, Hébert's work exhibited an authentic "creative power" and, along with that of Phyllis Webb, Eldon Grier, and D.G. Jones, testified to the maturity of "Canadian literature" (82). Hébert is recognized in this case for her formal innovation, not for her powerful affects. Under the sign of a differential inclusion, Skelton outlined the difference in the modalities of identification of francophone poets for whom the symbolism and structure of versification conform to French models. Consequently, the problem of Canadianness is experienced differently for them. However, Skelton did not explicate this Quebec distinctiveness, and so minimized the political dimensions of Hébert's work.

This difference, according to Louis Dudek, stemmed from a transformation in addressivity and, consequently, different relations of power between the poet and her interlocutor which are more asymmetrical for French-Canadian than for English-Canadian poets because of the divergence in the evolution of modernism in the two cultures. Dudek emphasized this dual tradition, stressing the irreconcilability of the two literatures. Aesthetically more mature, French poetry revolted against Romanticism with Baudelaire in the nineteenth century. English poetry had to wait until the twentieth century and Ezra Pound for the same revolution. Consequently, this cultural transformation still underway informed the anti-Victorian satire of Scott, Klein, Layton, Purdy, and other English-Canadian poets, which interpellated an addressee directly, so inciting identification. Inheriting the French tradition, Anne Hébert's poetry is notable for its detachment and contemplative mood unknown in the English tradition. Peter Miller's translation of her poems (*The Tomb of the Kings* 1967) functions, then, as compensation for a lacuna in the English-Canadian cultural field and produces "aesthetic innovation" to advance modernism. Nonetheless, Dudek found the interiority of Hébert's poetry sterile. He much preferred the poetry of a younger generation, the poetry of the Révolution Tranquille of the 1960s, which raged against its own tradition. He conceptualized this development as an internal dialectic of Quebec society. It was positive, he suggested, because Quebec had too long avoided such dialectical evolution, remaining blocked in an anti-federalist, anti-English "obsession" (19).

Although he approached Hébert's work from an ethics of cultural and linguistic difference, Dudek ultimately performed a transvaluation of its politics. In emphasizing its interiority, he followed the example of F.R. Scott who, according to the franco-Ontarian critic Jean Éthier-Blais, had not rendered into English the triple symbolic orders of dispossession of *Le tombeau des rois*. Scott had understood the mediaeval context and the Egyptian concepts of hieratism, but he had not grasped their import in French Canada. By interiorizing, he had universalized the profound experience of Quebec's distinctive reality because he had not managed to convey in English "the contradiction of an entire being confronting an indefinable reality. [His rhythm] is too melancholy and lacks the negative tension that is the very source of inspiration of *Le tombeau des rois"* (Éthier-Blais 1970, 16). Anti-colonialist resistance, so pertinent in the Quebec field of cultural production, is concealed in the English translation which presents this specific dispossession as stemming from a universal human condition requiring no political intervention to counter it.

A Dialogue Among Feminists

None of these critics noted another political displacement in Scott's translation, sexual difference, with a consequent masking of the feminist implications of Hébert's poem whose subject is ritual rape. In her dialogue with Scott, Anne Hébert pointed out that he had failed to notice the child was a girl ("une esclave fascinée"), which he subsequently corrected with the introduction of the possessive pronoun in *"her* ankle." Kathy Mezei (1986) and I (1984b) noted this interchange as a key moment in the dialogue that raised a new problematic in translation studies, the question of sexual difference. What began as a dialogue about translation among poets became subsequently a dialogue between feminists about the asymmetries of power producing linguistic and sexual difference. The elaboration of a feminist theory of translation was pursued in *Tessera*, a bilingual feminist literary periodical that focused on analyzing the power relations sexualizing discourse in translation, narrative, and fictions of identity.[17] Feminist intervention in the theory and practice of translation has not been limited to the analysis of oversights in the translations of women's writing by male translators, as in the case of Scott's translation practice, but has taken as its field the whole issue of textual authority and the transmission of knowledge. How within a theory of (sexual) difference can the hypothesis of equivalence between languages be maintained? Who determines when equivalence is achieved? The ethics of sexual difference is doubled and compounded by an ethics of cultural difference that foregrounds the incommensurability of languages.

Feminist translation engages in interventionist practices of rewriting that draw attention to the process of translation and make visible the creative aspect of any re-enunciation. The feminist translator underscores the radical difference between an "original" context and the translating context, marks the parameters of the work of transfer, and explicates the modality of circulation of the translated text in its new environment. In this way, feminist translation practices highlight all the socio-cultural mediations effected by translation, especially the ideological, cognitive, and affective aspects. Translation, then, is less concerned with reaching a "target" culture than with exploring the space *in-between.* It focuses on those modalities of power that order the relations between languages and cultures determining the pertinency of contexts and that produce the feminist translator as subject of an enunciation. This utterance is a double discourse in that it is an interpretive transformation and transvaluation, not merely mimetic repetition. From this liminal space in-between there emerges meaning in excess of either original or target context which is accorded a positive value of criticism and creativity. For the reader of these feminist translations is forced to become an active reader in order to measure the distance between the conventional forms of linguistic prestige (cultural capital) and the emergent forms of feminist literary language, and so to *make* meaning. That translators of feminist texts have turned in their prefaces and other peritexts to language and writing as both theories and formal elements to bolster "their arguments of adequation" against theories of equivalency has transformed the discourse on translation in Canada, according to Carolyn Perkes: the knowledge represented in these theorizations of cultural transmission is no longer that of "landscape," as in the case of Gabrielle Roy, but of "langscape" (Perkes 1203). What is conveyed in the transfer between cultures is no longer representational knowledge of topography in an attempt to secure geopolitical boundaries but a probing of the socio-cultural gap between two unequal languages and cultures in an acknowledgement of differentiation. This interrogation of the ideological work of translation undermines any theory of translation as a "linguistic practice" (Perkes 1205). Translation understood as rewriting posits the alterity of languages and cultures as heterogeneities rather than as binaries. The cross-cultural project of *Tessera* posits a community of multiple voices engaged in many possible dialogues as a becoming through a process of critical transvaluation and social transformation. However, such a theorization of linguistic and cultural difference circulates in the field of marginal cultural production, in avant-garde periodicals, and feminist publishing houses without the cultural capital to produce authority across a wide range of social networks.[18]

In the contact with modern Quebec literature between 1945 and 1970, the repertory of literary forms in English Canada was modified through the introduction of more objective models. With the dialogue between feminists in the 1980s, there emerged a new literary genre, the "théorie-fiction/fiction-theory" featured in *Tessera*. Collaboration with Quebec feminists in this dialogue fostered the emergence of a new problematic in the Quebec novel, translation. Nicole Brossard, Louise Dupré, Monique LaRue, Hélène Rioux, and other writers concerned themselves with the fictive status of the translator drawing on their own experience of translation either as translated author or translator rewriting. As dialogue, translation has engaged English-Canadian with Quebec feminists in reciprocal conversations. And the dynamism of cultural fields interacting has produced change through the differentiation of exchange. Rewriting does not inevitably entail a loss, as is presupposed by the Oedipal model of lack, dominant in theories of meaning. Translation does not necessarily result in a tragic situation, as Lise Gauvin lamented. After all, Canadian feminists have rewritten Tchekov's *Three Sisters* as a comedy about relations between different generations of women (Cherniak). In the paradox lived by the bilingual translator — whose language is not one and who is unfaithful to two languages — translation is a figure of the excess of meaning or of multiplicity in an economy of abundance. Translation in this context bears a positive cultural value as a privileged means of access to a different form of creativity. The knowledge such alterity transmits is a knowledge that recognizes its difference, its limits, and consequently acknowledges the relativity of all knowledge. However, such theories of translation as swerve generating cultural innovation have as yet currency only in the field of marginal cultural production.

TRANSLATION AND NATIONS IN THE MAKING

The displacement of cultural categories provoked by language so made foreign to itself exposes the ambivalence of the narration of the nation which is subject to hegemonic and counter-hegemonic struggles dividing it from within. Is the feminine incorporated in the nation? Or, as site of contradiction, does the feminine question the nation as totality? The taxonomies of the forms of symbolic exchange are always mediated by the structure of the field. But the structuring of the Canadian "nation" as a form of "textual affiliation" created by reading the "national" novel is unstable (Bhabha 1990, 140). Far from having established authority supported by a pedagogical discourse in which the people is the object of a re-presentation of its past, as English-Canadian criticism claims with its preference for a literature of referential knowledge, the imaginary community of the nation is constituted through a process of signification in which the people is the subject of enunciation. In such a process of (re)writing, the distinctions established by criticism legitimate a hierarchy of sociocultural values, a hierarchy by means of which the "Canadian" nation attempts to consolidate itself through an encounter with its margins. A feminized, unilingual English-speaking Quebec? This is a necessary fiction for a multicultural Canadian community in the making. As for its remainders ...

Nonetheless, Quebec feminist writers refuse to recognize as stable any fiction of an anglophone culture relating to its margins. The centre does not hold but shifts to another location. The heteroglossia introduced into Quebec feminists' fictions about a woman translator does not participate in the defamiliarization of the fiction of an English Quebec, but in fictions in which French becomes one language among many others. The analysis of these feminist fictions from Quebec and of their critical reception is another story, a story of difference, one about the elaboration of Quebec discourses on English-Canadian literature. This (her)story testifies to the dynamism of cultural fields in interaction — of literatures in the making.

Relational Logics:

Of Linguistic and Other Transactions in the Americas

> We shall try to show that the *relation* between the same and
> the other — upon which we seem to impose such extraordi-
> nary conditions — is language.
> * Emmanuel Levinas (39)

> Canada is a land of multiple borderlines, psychic, social,
> and geographic.
> * Marshall McLuhan (1977, 244)

> C'est une Tour de Babel, pas une nation.
> * Paul Zumthor (18)

> Tupy or not tupy that is the question.
> * Oswald de Andrade (3)

Constructing the Americas

The re-invention of the Americas has taken many forms over the last
decade as the circulation of symbolic capital intersected with the traffic in commodities to produce a new global order. The invention of the
Americas was among the great projects of Modernity when, through the
traductio studii et imperii, a translation of knowledge and power, Europe
imagined itself temporally in relation to the Greeks and Romans whose
legacy it prolonged and spatially in relation to Africa, Asia, and the
Americas over which it consolidated and extended its hegemony in the
work of colonization. Whether framed as conquest, as the Black Legend
of Spanish contact with the Americas related, or as discovery, as the English and French narratives of a less violent engagement countered,[1] the
myth of America involved transformations and metamorphoses since

315

Americanness resulted from a differentiation between two states of culture. Establishing distinctions marking the transition between them was a critical aspect of making claims for a "New" order whatever its pertinent features might be. In its dual aspects, as Maurice Lemire has observed, the "American imaginary" established a dialectic between constraint and liberty (2003, 18), between the obstacles and challenges presented by the "land God gave to Cain" and the fascinations and promises of unknown pleasures in an earthly paradise or "land of Cockaigne." Ironically, this produced a situation in which any consideration of Americanness has been mediated by a third term, most frequently through the Europeanness in relation to which it was initially defined. As Jorge Luis Borges observed: "We are, we the men (sic) of the different Americas, so isolated among ourselves that we can barely even recognize each other, once described by Europe" (1966, 26). Or, as Quebec geographer Jean Morriset summarized the situation: "What all Americans have in common is their fundamental difference from Europe, without which they would have nothing in common" (211).

In the absence of direct influence of authors or movements linking Canadian or Quebec literatures to the literatures of Latin American countries, such reflections on the relation of the peripheral literatures of the Americas to the various European literatures reinforce the conventions of Comparative Literature, its grand project of a universal poetics founded in a certain Eurocentrism that privileges key periods of English, French, and German literatures such as the Humanism of the Renaissance and the *Weltliteratur* of the nineteenth century which postulate such unity.[2] Alternatively, an implicit critique of such a centripetal project and of the inherent disciplinary limits of comparative approaches to literature is formulated through greater attention to local manifestations and topographical particularities in the peripheral literatures as they intersect with the hegemonic practices of the Literary. However, this merely plays out the universal/particular binary from the opposite pole, the one long devalued, without changing the terms of the debate. In the Americas, this has often involved an inversion of relations of difference so that the work of mediation operating on the symbolic level involves the native other, who appears, as Maximilien Laroche has observed, as "the necessary third party, the point of intersection on this voyage which from the old continent to the new must lead the latest arrivals from their old identity to their new one" (1975, 124). "Making it new" in the spirit of an American poetics would break with Europe through the mediation offered by the image of the Amerindian that represents the metamorphosis of the European into the American in a process of indigenization.

The re-invention of the Americas, however, abandons such binary relations between centre and periphery, between European and aboriginal, in the search for different grounds for comparison which would avoid the passage through a hegemonic centre or its excluded other in movements of supra-or infraduction in favour of transversal or horizontal relations among the peripheral literatures of the Americas and analysis of the processes of mediation at work in such *trans*-actions. Work in the comparison of the francophone and anglophone literatures in the geopolitical terrain known as Canada suggests some of the ways in which such a project might proceed in the absence of direct contacts by focusing on culturally differentiated responses to shared contingencies of topography and history as these have been shaped by the forces of governmentality ordering institutional and textual relations. It is precisely the ways in which such relations converge so that the "zone of circulation of goods and people" — "the market" — is overlaid by a homologous "circulation of symbolic goods" "legitimat[ing]" the power of the marketplace to expand its capacities of integration that Wlad Godzich finds productive of new possibilities for comparative literature. For analyses comparing peripheral literatures introduce a centrifugal force that accentuates the "heteronomous function of literature" in a "counter-hegemonic" move which modifies the circulation of symbolic value and so contributes to a "New World Order" (Godzich 1992, 46). The function of "resistance" Godzich ascribes to inter-American comparisons in their reinscription of the local over the universal in a renewed cosmopolitanism seems problematic in view of the "globalization" to which he connects it (52). Literature's centrifugal power of distanciation and differentiation appears limited by the convergence of centripetal forces he invokes, of multinational corporations, transnational organizations such as the EU or communication networks such as CNN and rapid financial exchanges on a planetary scale (52).

317

Nonetheless, much of the impetus for what Jean Morency describes as a "disconnection" from Europe and an "americanizing wave at the core of cultural expression" (18) arises with a new transnational order that proposes greater integration among the nations of the Americas. And, as Godzich rightly observes, literature and other representational forms work to naturalize and so legitimize the networks of economic exchange, contributing thus to the production of symbolic goods.

It is with such symbolic goods and the materiality of expressive forms that I am concerned in this essay where I shall analyze some of the representations of contact and exchange that circulate in the Americas, proposing differential logics and politics of exogamic relations. In the process, certain discursive regularities emerge in the enunciative strategies of what are minor literatures in the Deleuzian sense; those produced in major languages which make these languages swerve and stutter in their re-enunciation from the periphery as Quebec French, Black Canadian English, or Brazilian Portuguese proliferate rhizomatically. For what is urgent in this "discovery of America by the Americans" (Laroche 1989) is the necessity for negotiating complex relations. Beyond the uncertainty of the colonial period and the recentring in the institutionalization of a national literature, the repossession of America by Americans results not in the constitution of a singular American identity but in a critique of the appropriation of that identification by a single community claiming the unification of states (the us), a critique formulated in the name of a pluralization and diversification of the Americas. When the trajectory from centre to periphery or from periphery to centre is abandoned, and the compass needle turns back on itself, the poet's words retrace a nomadic wandering from periphery to periphery in a gesture that deterritorializes the notions of centre and periphery, observes Edouard Glissant (1990): "Le Même c'est la différance sublimée; Le Divers c'est la différance consentie" (Glissant qtd. in Bernabé et. al, 127). Such a preoccupation with diversity and complexity informs the logics of relations which are my concern in this essay as, in different figurations encompassing diverse intersecting networks, they represent the "multiple processes of transculturation" (Bernd 109) informing a new hemispheric imaginary.

The possibility of closer relations among the nations of the Americas under the North American Free Trade Agreement [NAFTA] and with projected new governance structures for the Organization of American States has raised questions about what forms such integration might take beyond those of commodity exchange. "Possible or impossible integration?" ask Michèle Rioux and Christophe Peyron, organizers of the conference "Construire les Amériques" in Montreal in November 2003 which addressed the "limits of market logic." Noting the resonance of the expression "the Americas" in the social imaginary and the great number of transformations underway in the arena of trade agreements with short and long-term consequences, Rioux and Peyron ask, "What integration will be promoted?" What kinds of institutions will be created? Will the "social dimension" be taken into consideration in these agreements? Addressing these two issues is crucial, they contend, since the situation in which such new forms of hemispheric governance are being contemplated is marked by great economic asymmetries. The us, with 80 per cent of the GNP, controls a disproportionate share of the hemispheric wealth and the other countries are united principally in their objective of negotiating a preferential bilateral deal with the us. Evidence of the dislocation in international relations produced by such economic disequilibrium comes from the trade relations under NAFTA where between 1989 and 2002 Canada's exports to the United States increased from 73 per cent to 87 per cent while, despite efforts to diversify, Canada's exports to Mexico have remained fixed at less than 1 per cent of total trade (Rioux and Peyron).

While political scientists and economists continue to deliberate the implications of policies being implemented by national governments in the context of such transnational organizations as the Summit of the Americas,[3] exchanges are also taking place in cultural fields where the work of symbolic mediation gives shape to verbal and visual representations of these new economic and social relations. Less concerned with unequal relations of power, such cultural manifestations often celebrate diversity while formulating keywords for conceptualizing unity across North and South America. In the summer of 2003, Power Plant, a contemporary art gallery in Toronto, organized an exhibition of works by artists from Canada, us, Mexico, Cuba, Guatemala, Colombia, and Brazil. No particular meaning was attached to the provenance of the artists: what was highlighted was the legacy of Minimal art and its linguistic underpinnings from Conceptual art as these had been taken up variously in the works presented. Indeed, the exhibition catalogue stressed difference: the exhibition "reveals the diverse ways that artists make incongruous the literal and self-referential precepts of Minimal/Conceptual art forms by introducing the often messy, often poetic, complexities of daily life" (Wallace and Figueroa). Through the incorporation of narrative and metaphor into their work, these artists "combine the pure with the impure," creating a "dynamic" in which they reciprocally accentuate each other. Emphasis is placed on the volatile relations of form and content which play out the dialectic of global and local in the selection of an international art movement as the axis of comparison for diverse artists of the Americas. As the local or "the specificity of place" arises in the work, it links not to the symbolic content of national identity but to everyday experience, the curators note. Whether working and exhibiting in their own locality or participating "seamlessly" in the international arena, the artists in the exhibition are positioned in a "field of interpretation" in which perception of forms is post-national. As the curators claim, "[b]ringing together artwork from different nations within the Americas serves to provide a perspective on the works' similarities and differences. In spite of the virtual demise of national borders through mass communication systems and corporate globalization, the internal dynamics of the local context persist. Toronto is not Sao Paulo, Sao Paulo is not New York, and New York is not Havana" (Wallace and Figueroa). Despite this disclaimer, "Stretch," the title of the exhibition, provides a powerful metaphor for connecting such disparate linguistic and cultural sites across the North/South divide, a figure with enough elasticity to twist and bend even the economic incommensurabilities that fracture the hemisphere into some new disorderly order. Through the production and circulation of such symbolic goods as "Stretch," representational practices, both visual and verbal, converge with the operation of the marketplace under the free trade agreements to naturalize hemispheric integration under the sign of increased flexibility.

Commemorations in 1992 of the 500th anniversary of Columbus's arrival in the Americas incited much comparative and critical reflection throughout the hemisphere on the impact of the resulting clash of cultures. Nowhere were the north-south networks so effectively established as among Amerindians who in a counter-hegemonic move from below joined throughout the hemisphere in protest against the violent legacy of European imperialism and so gave substance to George Manuel's vision of a Fourth World with self-government for the indigenous peoples of greater Turtle Island. The enlarged economic community created by NAFTA, in part a tightening of continental ties in response to the economic power of the European Union, led to greater reflection on the political and cultural implications of this integration for North America. In South America, the development of such economic groupings as Mercosur, stimulated the emergence of a continental consciousness. However, the forms which such awareness has taken have differed greatly from country to country. If for some the economic dominance of the us has resulted in a flow of migrants northward, for others this has led to internal collapse under the pressures of structural readjustment programmes. The traffic in people as well as goods is unequal. Canadians head south to Argentina to film the workers' movement reclaiming factories and to study other forms of participatory democracy at work in the social forums of Brazil. In Canadian universities, Caribbean and Latin American Studies attract more student interest than Canadian Studies programmes.

This interest in new social movements resisting the dominance of us corporate capital has not translated into a similar increase in comparative cultural studies. Comparative studies of literature in the Canadian context have remained predominantly those of intra-national comparisons of the Canadian literatures, pluralized beyond the conventional English/French language binary by the studies of literatures in other languages, especially Italian and German, since publication of *Configuration: Essays on the Canadian Literatures*, the pathbreaking work of E.D. Blodgett (1982).[4] In Quebec, however, there has been a much greater interest in literary comparisons among different language groups, the analyses of Maximilien Laroche (1975) on Black American writing in comparison with Quebec literature leading the way in this regard. The affirmation of the autonomy of the Quebec literary institution from that of France has frequently taken the form of an insistence on the Americanness of Quebec literature through a comparison with the literature of the United States, as in Pierre Nepveu's Governor General's Award-winning *Intérieurs du nouveau monde: Essais sur les littératures du Québec et des Amériques* in which he analyzes the internalization of the image of America by its inhabitants so that they find replies to the burning question, "comment 'habiter' le paysage, comment établir un rapport à l'ici qui ne soit ni de l'ordre de la couleur locale, ni de la pure nostalgie des racines, ni de la fusion païenne?" (Nepveu 1998, 175). This dialectic of interior/exterior, of how a subject comes to dwell in a place and is constituted as subject through a relation with the outside, with alterity, informs all the writing in the Americas, although the forms in which these endogamous/exogamous relations are represented and negotiated differ. A reorientation in the relations of address produces a significant change in rhetoric. For instance, the impetus to compare Canadian anglophone and francophone literatures participates in a move to stress Canada's multilingual difference as a bulwark against the homogenizing invasion of us culture. Yet the great interest in comparative studies of Quebec and Brazilian literatures, an exception to the usual forms of comparison within the same language which hinge inevitably on the mutual relation to a European colonizer whose language they have inherited, speaks to the very difference in which the colonial legacy has been lived in French. In his monograph analyzing the grounds for comparing these two literatures on the basis of their long histories of colonization, Bernard Andrès contends that there are equally important reasons for pursuing such a project in the present, namely the shared linguistic isolation of the two groups in their respective continents, "francofonia *versus* anglofonia e lusofonia *versus* hispanofonia" (Andrès 216). With their lesser demographic presence, and the consequent incomprehension of their speech, Québécois and Brazilians are further minoritized in their Americanness. The rhetorical stances of comparatists manifest as much diversity as the social and political vectors at play in the dialectic of alterity. Difference, consequently, is key to the discursive formation of the Americas.

Managing diversity and difference has been the function of governmental operations in the territory now claimed by the Canadian state and other states in the Americas in the textual production of official discourses on identity. The construction of an American imaginary involves even greater divergences, though the means remain similar, the development of metaphors and emblems with the ability to lend an appearance of reality to an abstract conceptual system whether the nation state or the vaster hemisphere. Such representational practices would "structure the field of action of others" which, for Foucault, is the work of governing (Foucault 1982, 221). The post-colonial moment in the Americas is characterized by a number of shared socio-historical contingencies, among them the impact of European contact on indigenous peoples, the forced transportation of peoples from Africa, European imperial governance, massive migration from Europe and also from Asia, as well as migration within the Americas. Presently, all the states are in various degrees of economic dependence on the US. Nonetheless, these conditions have not become problems for ongoing debate and attempts at public solution everywhere. Moreover, they have been imagined and represented differently from diverse historically and socially concrete geopolitical sites. Everywhere there are multiple encounters, many potential "contact zones" (Pratt). Edouard Glissant writes of this context: "Diversity needs the presence of peoples, not as an object to sublimate, but as a project to relate." In this essay I shall explore such projects through the diverse logics at work in metaphors for managing diversity produced in some of the cultures of the Americas within that "*transversal relation* without any universalist transcendence" which comprises the opening to the heterogeneous, principal feature of an emergent hemispheric discourse (Glissant qtd. Bernabé 127; my emphasis).

Imag(in)ing Transversal Relations

Such transversal relations may be conceptualized as a mode of Gramscian cultural elaboration constituting, through the friction of contradictory "spontaneous or immanent" discourses, a "progressive" hegemony emerging in response to the pressures of a "popular collective will" (Gramsci 145 – 46). Building solidarities across heterogeneous social formations, these centrifugal processes differ from the centripetal communicative rationality of states which, with their centralized administrative, educational, and cultural apparatuses, elaborate a vehicle of "common potential communicability" distinct from the variety of dialects of "cultural identification" (Hobsbawm 62 – 63). It is in regard to such discursive constitution of sociality that references to the nation as "invented" (Gellner 169) or "imagined" (Benedict Anderson 4) or even as "narrated" (Bhabha 1990) have become increasingly common. Within the denaturalized "nation," an individual subject's allegiance is transferred from a ruler to one's fellows in the "imagined community" or civil society. Such concrete historical and social relations are cemented to abstract rights through micropolitical representations or "signifying relations" within "schemata of value" that posit and organize the social into symbolic networks (Castoriadis 255). Representations of language and territory, I propose, have worked powerfully in the Canadian context to solicit subjects' adhesion differentially to such symbolic networks that are shaped by even as they shape political institutions. In the Brazilian context, corporeality linked to language has been a site for the elaboration of signifying relations constitutive of cultural identification.

The discourses of language and space — of langscape and landscape — as well as those of anthropophagy circulate in accounts of the specificities of culture, as well as in fictional narratives. For the "creation of images and figures" supports processes of signification that constitute the "social imaginary" instituting "identitary operations" to make a public and common world exist for the individual who is produced as subject through these operations (Castoriadis 238). A "deep horizontal comradeship of community" is formed by and informs the representational practices in which people "imagine themselves to form a nation, or behave as if they formed one" (Benedict Anderson 6 – 7). These practices — which range from bank currency, through censuses, maps, museums, and various forms of record-keeping and writing — create attachments that bind subjects into "simultaneity through time" enabling the imaginative grasp of a "territorial stretch" so as to "think the nation" (Benedict Anderson 63). Once imagined in the particular relations of kinship or clientship, subjects now recognize themselves and their interests in the abstraction of the sovereign state through affiliations as, among other things, sports fans, music lovers, fiction readers, or speakers of a language. For language indeed is one of the most important representational modes of the social as cultural artifact. But language is not the only such representation, nor even an image for thinking the nation as simultaneity in the Canadian and Brazilian contexts, where linguistic and territorial boundaries do not coincide and many jostle for position on the same territory. Languages may separate and exclude, as readily as they link and include. Language is never neutral or complete but open to historical forces and "dialogic" reworking from agonistic perspectives (Bakhtin 1981, 294) in an unending struggle between differentiated socio-political positions asymmetrical in respect to power. In the Canadian context, languages are differentially legitimated so that while English and French are "official," other languages such as Spanish are not, though all bear the marks of cultural difference. What appears to be a similar case of binary difference in the Brazilian obligation to choose between the Tupi-Guarani languages of the Amerindians and the Portuguese of the invading Europeans becomes a complex paradox in Oswald de Andrade's celebrated pronouncement. Inserted in English into the Portuguese of his famous "Manifesto antropófago" (De Andrade 3, 7), "Tupy or not tupy" rephrases as existential dilemma the relativity of Montaigne's question, "Qui sont les vrais barbares?" The plurilingualism of de Andrade's pronouncement and its parodic reworking of Shakespeare transform this ironic inversion into an emblem of Brazil's cultural syncretism and the métissage of its peoples. The appetite for the Other which characterized European expansion in the Americas is countered by the cannibalism of the Tupinamba in a reciprocal process of devouring and appropriating.

Just as languages are positioned unequally within this heteroglossia — this Tower of Babel, as Zumthor's newspaper quote calls it (Zumthor 18) — so too discourses clash over how to represent the social imaginary. Another important figure for the predicament of a nation whose linguistic and territorial boundaries do not coincide is the spatial trope so provocatively proclaimed by Marshall McLuhan — "Canada, the borderline case" (McLuhan 1977). Both figures foreground troubled relations to community, the uncertainty of social cohesiveness, in terms of ethical or psychical disturbances. With the trope of cannibalism, instability is registered in the body in both its physical and figurative aspects, as mixed race subject of a conflicted body politic. Unsettling in its ambivalence, such abjection induces a state of continual crisis that poses a limit to the concept of nation. Whereas Babel figures the social imaginary in terms of a communicative exchange between a "we" talking about a "them" with implications for the conceptual limits of collective identity, the discourse of borders represents the image of community in terms of sovereignty and geographical limits. The blurring of boundaries between inside and outside in the discourse of anthropophagy complicates any relation of self/other or, indeed, any limit to the reversals in their relations. While the community invoked is differentiated linguistically and racially, it is imaged in economic as well as physical terms of consumption which extends the discursive field to matters of commodity exchange and capitalist exploitation.

These discourses of shared intelligibility, territorial security, and reciprocal appropriation propose different forms of identification for subjects and favour different axes of relation. Instability arises from within the community in the metaphor of Babel but threatens from without in the trope of border. The porous borders between languages and bodies in the trope of cannibalism signal a general cultural instability of multivalent relations, a "chaos-monde" (Glissant 1995, 33), but also the dissolution of limits on violence in the contact zone. Divergent versions of sociality manifest themselves in this mythologizing of origins, ends and points of transformation, with border referring primarily to international relations with the us, as the Borderlands Project succinctly articulates (Lecker 1991), Babel configuring complex intra-national relations among francophones, anglophones, and allophones and with anthropophagy confounding intra-national with inter-national relations in regard to power figured as consumption. Nonetheless, the north-south axis and Europe/America relations are vectors in all three discourses, implicated palimpsestically in intra-national relations. While discourses on language circulate most widely in francophone articulations of the social imaginary, anglophones have more frequently represented the symbolic network of society spatially through "bordertalk" (New 1998). These contrasting discourses have informed different conceptualizations of the symbolic order through which the socio-cultural relations of the community bring themselves into being in the political institutions of the state, differences distinguishing so-called "ethnic" from "civic" nationalism.

Babel and border, moreover, resonate widely in fictions of francophone and anglophone Canada preoccupied with social as well as personal identification. Distinctive in the Brazilian discourse of anthropophagy are its historical dimensions, the way in which it draws on practices of the early contact period between European and American cultures in order to represent exploitative relations in the twentieth century where disparities of class and neo-colonialist hierarchies of capital give a new meaning to cannibalism.

Representations of the social imaginary occur in visual forms, as well as in the cultural discourses and fictional narratives that are my principal concern, and make visible the symbolic nuances of the differentiated figuration of conflicted identifications. An important aspect of nation-state formation in the Canadas has been a history of stormy parliamentary debates over language and of turbulent sign wars in public space which has constituted a veritable language landscape informing cultural positions as well as politics. A significant instance may be found in the depiction of the debate on language in the first parliament of Lower Canada in 1792 in a painting by Charles Huot that hangs today in the Quebec National Assembly. What seems at first glance to be a problem of form in this tableau, its lack of central focus, or of any controlling mythic theme, gathers significance in its historical context as an account of the first public debate about choice of language in a situation of heteroglossia, the vote for the first Speaker of the Legislative Assembly that found the Panet brothers, like Cain and Abel, on opposite sides of the question: Louis-Philippe Panet supported an anglophone for the office, while his brother Jean-Antoine was eventually elected to the position on the grounds that it was imperative to speak the French language of the majority of members. The melée on the floor of the House conveys horizontally the confusion of Babel at an important moment in the constitution of civil society under British rule.

Langscape and landscape remain in dialectical tension in the social imaginary, however, as these figures take shape in cultural discourses and creative practices. *Babel* is the title of an installation by Montrealer Tom Bendtsen, exhibited at Toronto's Koffler Gallery in 2001. His monumental stepped tower built with 7,000 books spirals upward in a symbolic striving for perfect knowledge and command through language.

Through the interrelationships of titles and languages, including works on economics in Chinese and social theory in French, encyclopedias, and popular series like the Hardy Boys, hardbound and paperbacks, a complex system of thought is articulated. Yet, given the fissures destabilizing the tower of books, its toppling into a transversal sprawl is imminent. In this self-dissipating structure, Bendtsen represents knowledge and language as precarious and contradictorily self-defeating.

Equally paradoxical in its significance is the elusive image of the border, as in the slight mounding of friable earth on the prairie created in 1873 by employees of the North American Boundary Commission to mark the 49th parallel separating Canada from the US, perceptible now only in a photograph of that moment (Fagan F1). Linked to territory rather than language, this imaginary differentiates along a north/south axis. The Border has loomed large in political debate in English-Canada, especially since September 2001 when the flow of traffic across it ground to a halt. The Border, as Drew Fagan noted, had been turned "into Canada's lifeline" and the thirty-six-KM line of trucks blocking the border-crossing was ominous (March 16 2002, F1, 8). Greg Curnoe, a London, Ontario artist, who had a commitment to the regional, to what he called Souwesto, envisions borders differently in his 1989 lithograph, *America.* The border becomes less a line dividing than a playful experiment in semiosis as he redraws the continent to place Mexico at Canada's southern boundary, eliminating the US completely. Curnoe's embrace of the local led him to excavate traces of a First Nations presence in London, but this map, based on work by André Breton, had in earlier versions served first in a nationalist gesture as a cover for the *Journal of Canadian Fiction* (1972), then internationally as poster for an exhibition of London regional artists at Havana's La Casa de Las Americas, before becoming a challenge to the limits of political commitment marked by Canada's political leaders following the 1988 election on Free Trade. Highlighting the shifting nature of boundaries, and the fragility of the structures on which identifications depend, Curnoe adopts a rhetoric designating the boundary as a site of negotiation that distributes resources and power. In this he proposes a complex answer to Northrop Frye's celebrated question "Where is here?" that has long haunted anglo-Canadian culture, one that engages regional particularity in spatial terms beyond national boundaries in transnational issues of colonization and culture. This paradoxical map addresses some of the issues I examine through a comparative frame where the dynamics of local cultural rhetorics become readable across time and place, though their differences are never erased in a fluid transmigration. Babel and border, labyrinth and map, function, then, as conceptual limits establishing epistemological as well as aesthetic and political frameworks.

All three frames are in play in the figure of cannibalism with its introjection of alterity in a transfusion that produces renewed vitality and creative powers compensating for an initial loss. Indeed, sixteenth-century accounts of cannibal practices in Brazil emphasize the bravery of the enemy who has been captured, given as partner to the widow of a man killed in the struggle, and later eaten festively by the Amerindians who honour his courage through the ingestion of his blood while simultaneously destroying him (Forsyth 1983, 152 – 53). The Other is in this sense fully incorporated into the social body in what proves a productive cross-fertilization. The last shot of Nelson Pereira dos Santos's film *Como Era Gostoso O Meu Frances* (1970; *How Tasty Was My Little Frenchman*, 1971) zooms in on the face of Sebiopepe, a Tupinamba woman, as she devours her Frenchman, Jean, with no apparent regret. Romantic love seems of lesser importance than fidelity to tribal ritual in this film which subverts the conventional captivity narrative and its identification with the European protagonist's escape efforts to focus on the radical heterogeneity of exogamic relations. The disturbing image is followed immediately by a quotation from a 1560 report on a massacre of the Tupiniquin committed by Europeans, framing Sebiopepe's act as ritual vengeance as well as the sexual consummation of the bawdy pun on *comer* (to eat). On multiple levels the film stages such complex interplay of version, inversion, and reversal as these strained fidelities of eros and language.

Visualized in Sebiopepe's gesture is the central project of Oswald de Andrade's *"movimento antropófago"* to "digest" foreign models and techniques critically in order to rework them in a new synthesis that can then be turned against the foreigner. Jean is ritually consumed after the Tupinamba have figuratively devoured the technological knowledge he brings them about how to use cannons. Produced during the second phase of Brazilian Cinema Novo, dos Santos' allegorical narrative extends *antropofagia* aesthetically to its limits, going so far in its study of indigenous cultures as to stage much of the dialogue in Tupi. Cultural conflict pervades the film on multiple levels, prominent among them language which is used dialectically, as in the retelling of the myth of Mair, the Tupinamba white god-ancestor. This fable performs a metacritical function challenging the authority of representational practices in the ironic counterpoint of word and gesture while symbolically narrating the phases of imperialist conquest. Alternating between Tupi and French, as Sebiopepe and Jean exchange the role of narrator, the story twists and turns as Jean is increasingly absorbed into the tale and begins to act out the role of Mair, recalling improvements he has made in the Tupis' way of life. Sebiopepe resumes the narration in Tupi, recounting the Tupi revolt against the god, and their ultimate destruction through his posthumous powers. The bilingualism and shared narration represent on the level of discourse the ritual absorption of the foreign body in the cannibalistic devouring and so constitute a new origin myth of literal and figurative métissage. In a similar paradoxical episode, the plasticity of languages and their uniqueness are challenged critically in the "language test" used by the Tupinamba to differentiate between the Portuguese, their enemies, and the French, their allies, among whom Jean claims to be counted. Dos Santos ironizes cultural stereotypes in this test. While the Portuguese confirm their reputed gluttony by repeating culinary recipes, Jean puns in French on the ambiguity of identity: "Ces Barbares marchent tous nuds: / Et nous, nous marchons incogneus" (Etienne Jodelle qtd. in Madureira 122). Who then indeed is the barbarian? In a reversal of the conventional perspective, the Tupi now are unable to distinguish between European languages. They elect to keep Jean alive because of his willingness to teach them to fire the Portuguese cannons. His trade in destruction is the currency he negotiates with the Tupi, while his access to Tupi gold is what he negotiates with a French trader in an effort to escape.

The black humour of this scene ironizes the anthropophagic politics of the film as well as its historical allegory from which the film distances itself by "cannibalizing its archive" (Madureira 122). Quotations from historical accounts of Jean de Léry, Villegaignon, and André

Thevet about the rivalry of French and Portuguese in Guanabara Bay and especially Hans Staden's captivity narrative are fragmented and interspersed throughout the film as intertitles along the model of the contemporary newsreel. What appeared to be a return to a colonial origin, evoked through effects of documentary authenticity produced by a hand-held camera, turns into self-conscious performance within a cycle of reproductions. The questions raised by this juxtaposition of archival document and news item, as also by the contradiction between voice-over and images, undermine the film's historicity and its project of epistemological critique by revealing it to be complicitous with the very violence it seeks to subvert. Nonetheless, the camouflage of historicity and the cyclicity in the allegory are tactics to evade censorship under the dictatorship then in power and so subversively critique the nature of contemporary social relations with their alliance of militarism and "savage" capitalism — Jean's legacy — that would maintain Brazil in a state of underdevelopment, in the abjection of the "aesthetics of hunger" central to Cinema Novo as formulated by Glauber Rocha. Violence is generalized in the vertiginous play of reversals which directs critique cannibalistically at both exogamous and endogamous relations in the exchange of bodies and languages in the wake of imperialism. The stakes of blurring inside and outside are more extreme in the case of anthropophagy than with border play or Babel, lodged as they are within the body as well as in language and territory. So too is its critical bite sharper.

CULTURAL DISCOURSES AND COMPETING VERSIONS OF THE SOCIAL IMAGINARY

Babel, a figure stressing the chaos of relations in light of the incommensurability of languages and the incompleteness of understanding, is more frequently used within francophone cultures to describe contact with alterity that is often agonistic. Border, though, is anglophone, especially in English Canada where difference is conceptualized spatially in metaphors of mapping regional or cultural as well as international boundaries. Mapping focuses on territory rather than population-making in the constitution of the social and so prolongs the geopolitical imperative to secure boundaries symbolically. Such topocentrism has tended to generate images of affiliation expressing a homogeneous and harmonious collectivity — Northrop Frye's "peaceable kingdom" — having a secular and universal membership without tribal loyalties. Indeed, the thematic criticism informed by Frye's influential "Conclusion" to the *Literary History of Canada* fostered such unity. The distinctiveness of Canadian "cultural history" and "social *imagination*" (Frye 1976, 333 – 34) was to be found in its "garrison mentality" (1976, 342). Retreat behind a border for self-protection from external threats enabled the realization of a narrative of "exploration, settlement, and development" (1976, 334) that posits the establishment of a settler literature as *bildung,* whether in the name of humanist values of self-development or of nationalist values of self-determination. Implicitly, this image of the fortress in the wilderness constructs an overriding pattern incorporating a structure of feeling that distinguishes Canadian culture and literature from that of the us where the liminality of the frontier had been embraced in the name of radical liberation from the state's constraint.

The north-south axis of such border-talk is explicit in Marshall McLuhan's celebrated pronouncement, "Canada: The Borderline Case," title of a talk he gave at Harvard University in a lecture series on the "Canadian imagination." The boundary between Canada and the us is McLuhan's primary focus, "a typically human creation," as he cites in his epigraph, which is "physically invisible, geographically illogical, militarily indefensible, and emotionally inescapable" (1977, 226). Such a decentralized and flexible image of identity means that Canada readily "mediates between the First and Third worlds" (1977, 227). This position of "betweenness, the world of the interval, the borderline, the interface of worlds" is where major economic and cultural change takes place, he concurs with Harold Innis (1977, 233). McLuhan connects this figure of liminality to the American frontier thesis, emphasizing the "feeling for space" shared by the two most northern American countries that distinguishes them from Europeans or Asians (1977, 231). Speaking within the us, McLuhan stresses the similarities rather than differences between the two countries and so does not linger on the divisive aspects of the border, its marking of margins, abysses, or limits. Borderland rather than borderline is his focus: a relational concept, borderland as interface between cultures in a contact zone releases a creative "vortex of energy"

(1977, 239). What Canadians and Americans share in their preoccupation with the "environmental mystery" is a reversal of figure and ground with significant implications for culture (1977, 235). Spatial liminality substitutes for face and voice, so its creative energy fails to infuse the solidarities of "a public aesthetic vision" or the cultural work of linguistic transformation (1977, 243). English is only ironically engaged in such borderplay, for the "Canadian language" is inadequate to the toponymic task of mapping space (1977, 229). Moreover, it lacks conceptual distinctiveness, its abjection played out in the pseudo-diversity of englishes, humorously described by Stephen Leacock, as "English for literature, Scotch for sermons and American for conversation" (McLuhan 1977, 230). The condition of the "Canadian nobody" situated in more than one world is defined *as* border (1977, 228). Border figures ambiguously as both defence against an exterior force and transformative opening to an outside. Linguistic transformation does occur with considerable violence in the "ancient quarrel" of French settlers against the English (1977, 239). Elsewhere, however, McLuhan dismissed the importance of language as creative interface and claimed that it was the electric instantaneity of the present age that explained the revitalization of Quebec culture, not nationalism with its linguistic conflicts in calls for a territorialized "langue québécoise." De Gaulle's gesture of linguistic solidarity was outdated, McLuhan claimed, clinging to notions of country and language as forms of identification rendered obsolete by the "coolness" of Trudeau's federalist strategies with his deterritorializing of language (1968, 38). Quebec separatists advocating a distinctive society responded derisively to these remarks with a proposal that McLuhan be sent to the electric chair (P.S. 77).

McLuhan's concern with "[t]he Canadian borderline [with the US], as well as the numerous frontiers *within* Canada's borders ..." (1977, 245) has found more recent articulation in W.H. New's *Borderlands: How We Talk About Canada* and Ian Angus's *A Border Within: National Identity, Cultural Plurality, and Wilderness*, each of which takes up a different facet of McLuhan's account of the "Canadian imaginary" in the practice of literary criticism and cultural studies respectively. Borders are read as metaphors in a system of signs, as "rhetoric" of relationship and organization (New 1998, 5) or as "mythic patterns" (Angus 106), fictions implicated in power relations that exclude and include. Both Angus and New caution against the danger of accepting the boundary rhetoric as language of historical truth and so mythologizing points of origin and transformation that they come to seem natural or axiomatic. The hierarchizing of regions, the territorializing of ethnicity, the distribution of power in boundary rhetoric may seem inevitable unless challenged so as to expose the selectivity of its determinations. Angus stresses the continuity of his formulation of the rhetoric with Frye's "garrison mentality." New, however, indicates how the oppositional positioning conveyed in the metaphor need not inevitably lead to enclosure, but may possibly bring about a productive reinterpretation if understood as overlapping discourses where edges become thresholds (1998, 29). These articulations of the spatial imaginary mark a rupture with the "garrison" trope of the settler narrative in that both call for a recognition of radical alterity or heterogeneity within. Drawing a line, a border in the wilderness, separates "here" from "there" in what Angus considers a "civilizing moment" that establishes a relation, a "limitation" (126), and prevents any closure of the metaphysical circle of interpretation. Taking the wilderness inside is a kind of "abjection," Angus contends (13), an ambivalence, an incompleteness, an opening to the other, unlike the us pursuit to contain the advancing frontier. "Questioning the border" maintains it, suspended in "relations of the in-between," those "between nations" as well as those "between the said and the unsaid" (127). For Angus, these are the conditions of possibility for an English-Canadian philosophy; for New, they are the conditions for the emergence of a West Coast literature and culture straddling the 49th parallel that will upset the "hierarchy of regions" (1998, 9) in which Ontario and Quebec claim centrality. "Borderwalking," New writes, is what occurs in a territory of "in-betweenness" — the "borderland" — characterized by transgression and revision, negotiation and transformation (1998, 27). In this indeterminacy, relations of difference may be simultaneously "consensual" and "conflictual" and so demand critical examination of the categories constructing difference. Canadian literature and culture are made to yield many anecdotes of restless encounters and boundary realignments in the "contact zone," such historical shifts undermining any symbolic certainty of the 49th parallel. Celebrating a "living

334

culture" and embracing local knowledge are two of the meanings New attaches to "borderlands," as he expands the trope to include the more abstract relations of connection to a wider world and limitless change (102). Nonetheless, the call to engage imaginatively in creating the future is contradictorily linked to an argument in defence of cultural specificity and territorial integrity, albeit along an east-west axis crucial for a "western" regional imaginary, rather than the more common north-south international divide.

This focus on boundaries contrasts with the articulation of internal division within the same territory from the perspective of Quebec where Jocelyn Létourneau, pursuing a well-established formulation of thinking identification processes in terms of language and culture, has written: "Le trilingualisme, manifeste chez un grand nombre de jeunes gens issus des 'communautés culturelles,' témoigne précisément de la nécessité, pour tout locuteur d'identification ou d'héritage non canadien-français ou non canadien-anglais, de se positionner par rapport aux deux 'mondes dominants'" (110). While a focus on mapping borders may substitute for the thick ties of a shared idiom in anglophone Canada, language may inversely be theorized as ecology in a complex creative network. Language and territory are associated figures for thinking relations, though one may take precedence over the other, depending on the lines of force operative in these modes of affiliation. These are not identical logics of relations: the mapping of territory into bounded spaces, albeit with shifting and expanding frontiers in the one instance, differs from the knotted layering of languages in the other which produces "ancrages croisés" and "ambivalence" (Gauvin 2000, 115). The images of borderline and knot or spiral are linked to conflicting accounts of the nation-state as contractual or cultural which have pitted anglophone proponents of a federalist "civic" nation divorced from cultural particularity against francophone advocates of a so-called "ethnic" nation whose thick relations of culture, most pre-eminently of language, constitute a "distinct society."

A hyperconsciousness of language has been notable in francophone cultures in the Americas, according to Lise Gauvin, a veritable "tourment" unknown to those who confidently inhabit a linguistic mass not the margin. "Langagement" is her neologism for the omnipresence of an explicit discourse on language and narrativization of the necessary choice among languages in Quebec literature (Gauvin 2000). Posing the language question as relation has been fundamental in the very constitution of a field of literary production in Quebec, as Marie-Andrée Beaudet observes, the dialectic of alterity both positing unbounded heteroglossia and establishing a limit through a logics of relation. Quebec writers have always had difficulty making language their own in all its multiplicity and range: "Ce n'est pas une question de connaissance de la langue comme d'aucuns l'affirment. Mais c'en est beaucoup une de *rapport* au langage" (Beaudet 1991, 34). Desire for "une langue à soi" has long haunted critical thinking in Quebec: although it has changed over time, this "linguistic imaginary" has repeatedly asserted itself at strategic moments to become ultimately an end in itself, "substituting for collective as well as literary identity" (Gauvin 2000, 27, 32). Concerned both with affirming a French presence in North America and developing a specific Canadian idiom different from France, this imaginary has manifested itself in projects ranging from Henri Bourassa's promotion of "le parler français du Canada" at the beginning of the twentieth century to *Parti Pris'* experiments with the orality of *joual* as a literary language supporting separatist demands for Quebec independence in the 1960s.

In theorizing languages as ecology, I take my lead from Pierre Nepveu whose study of contemporary Quebec literature, *L'Écologie du réel*, introduces as epigraph a quotation from Borges' "la Bibliothèque de Babel" that spatializes linguistic relations: "Les mêmes volumes se répètent toujours dans le même désordre — qui, répété, deviendrait un ordre: l'Ordre." For the problem of heteroglossia, Borges poses a paradoxical solution in the expanding series. The library's ubiquitous and lasting system of hexagonal galleries gives the illusion of infinity to the wanderer. The philosopher or mathematician who constructed it knows the labyrinth to be finite and circular, but the voyager experiences it as an endless doubling in an infinite regress. Connected to a multilingual and multidisciplinary library noted for productive chaos and cyclicity, Babel becomes a synonym for critique and creation. The myth of Babel prefigures the event necessary to set history creatively in motion, rather than the unattainable perfect command of language in a reach toward heaven. In this chaosmos, reordered through the traveller's perspectival shift which transforms apparent disorder into new relations, Nepveu locates a figure for the contemporary literary imaginary of Quebec. Pursuing an inner adventure within a condition of exile, Quebec writers have forged a modern rhetoric of alienation and hallucination. This new culture, "indéterminée, voyageuse, en dérive," is intensely creative: no longer confined to repetition of the familiar, it does not limit itself to noting differences, but, attentive to pluralism, develops an ethic able to create forms to sustain "a constant dialogism" (Nepveu 1988, 217). Translation functions as one of the figures for this cultural imaginary which, while constituting a sociality in all its concreteness, seeks no foundational stability but remains open to the outside in a state of perpetual emergence.

Nepveu embraces Borges' aesthetic of transversality. For the vertical mediaeval world exemplified in the tower of Babel has toppled over into the horizontal world of modernity with its linguistic sprawl. The "extratemporal vertical axis" of Dante's hierarchical world has been displaced by Rabelais's new chronotope that relates "time to ... earthly space ... a time measured by creative acts," by growth and becoming (Bakhtin 1981, 206). In the early modern period's multilingualism, borderplay between literary language and social heteroglossia coincided and contributed to the renewal of "antiquated literary" forms by moving them closer to the "interests of those strata of the national language that have remained ... outside the centralizing and unifying influence of the artistic and ideological norm established in the dominant literary language" (Bakhtin 1981, 67). Social heteroglossia makes a *"dialogical contact"* with the image of another language, "both represented *and* representing" (Bakhtin 1981, 45) and so opens up a critical perspective on language challenging the myths of a singular and of a unified language.

Adopting a different historical approach to the diversity of languages, Paul Zumthor, Quebec theorist and novelist, also explores the figure of Babel, a contemporary hieroglyph for translation, as a limit posed through an ethic of relation. Like Nepveu, he insists on the creative energy released by this figure of incompletion ("l'inachèvement") rather than on the loss of some primal unity. Indeed, in its allusions

337

to architecture and building relations, the metaphor emphasizes the constructed over the natural. Examining many versions of the story of Babel, especially biblical and archeological accounts, Zumthor notes the radical ambiguity of the trope which connotes both incoherent mélange and excessive ambition, confusion and intellectual hubris. A mythic perfect harmony has purportedly been lost through an ethical or conceptual failing, an original unity dispersed through migration. While spatial oppositions are important in the story of Babel — wandering versus fixity in the horizontal relations among humans: the tower rising to the firmament, the god descending to see in a double verticality — it is the paradox of language which is central to the myth, Zumthor concludes. The impossibility of universal communication despite the fantastic prodigality of languages lies at the heart of the oldest version of the story. Geographical dispersion of the people is not introduced until later versions. Moreover, as Zumthor proposes, the multilogue had already commenced in paradise with the expansion from God's transcendent utterance, through the monologues of God and Adam, to the dialogue of Eve and the serpent. What the Babelic narrative introduces is the possibility of collective communication, in which each in his own tongue speaks to his fellow human being (Zumthor 195). In this possibility for mutual recognition and social interchange resides the most complete realization of the human potential. Language consequently can only be thought as a plural *relation* between languages. Yet this heteroglossia ultimately frustrates the desire for understanding, leaving incomplete humanity's search for a perfect language and total comprehension. Translation is inevitable then, since even in a return to the historical tradition to interpret the myth, there occurs a drift, a displacement of narrative sense over time as well as space. Creative wandering this is, however. Zumthor, like Edouard Glissant immersed in the "chaos-monde" (1995, 33), would rebuild the tower of Babel in every language, for the advent of a non-totalizing ethical relation, along the lines of the benefits of collective labour that Hegel saw as Babel's gift to humanity.

Language in Quebec has long figured as the "ethical relation between the same and the other" (Levinas 39). However, during the nineteenth century with the first intimations of Romantic nationalism, this relation took the form of a search for an exotic alternative to the imperial languages of Europe fuelled by pessimism about the inadequacy of Quebec French for authentic literary texts. As Octave Crémazie wrote: "[T]he more I reflect upon the destinies of Canadian literature, the less I think its chances of leaving a mark on history. What Canada lacks, is a language of its own ... Unfortunately we speak and write in a pitiful fashion, it is true, the language of Bossuet and Racine." What was necessary to escape the predicament of "literary colonials," he argued, was a language different from French which would excite in France readers' interest in a text from its periphery. "If we spoke Huron or Iroquois," he insisted, the "works of our writers would attract the attention of the old world. This masculine and nervous language, born in the forests of America, would have the poetry of the wild that is the delight of the foreigner. They'll enthuse about a novel or poem translated from the Iroquois where they wouldn't take the trouble to read a volume written in French by a colonial from Quebec or Montreal" (90–91). Crémazie's sentiments were shared by many in the Americas, although the hybrid languages advocated, Iroquois and English in Boston, Anglo-Ojibway in Ontario, Tupi-Guarani and Portuguese in Brazil, differ from the franco-huronne of Quebec (Godard 1981). By the twentieth century, however, only in Brazil was there still interest in such a linguistic experiment, in large part because of the impact of the *movimento antropófago* which positioned itself with the cannibals, not the "noble savages," in a movement of negativity.

Inciting interest in Tupi-Guarani was a project of the *Revista de Antropofagia* which published studies of its principal linguistic features highlighting its capacities for complex conceptual and psychological operations (Salgado 6). The anthropophagical movement sought to revive a longstanding practice for, well into the nineteenth century, Tupi-Guarani remained the vehicular language of Brazil. This was no nostalgic return to the past, however, but a critical salvo directed at all orthodoxies, oppressions, and repressions of contemporary society in the name of a total revolution. Oswald de Andrade urged his readers to become cannibals—"Socialmente. Economicamente. Philosophicamente" (3). A dialectical reworking of the valences of civilization and barbarity would produce a transvaluation of all values, sexual as well as political. In such a Nietzschean reversal, he called for a transformation of "Taboo into totem" (3). Praising Freud for his interest in the "enigma of woman," de Andrade's parricide would make way for a kind of matriarchal communalism where, in the absence of repression, pleasure and wealth would be more equitably distributed. In the wake of the French Revolution, the Bolshevik Revolution, and the Surrealist revolution, the "instincto Carahiba" of the cannibals who met Villegaignon would install this new order of "Carnaval" with its endless dethronings of American films or Catholic hierarchies or servile colonial imitators. Sociopolitical and cultural revolutions are intertwined in de Andrade's utopia which he identifies with both communism and surrealism. Anthropophagy infuses creation with critique as in de Andrade's witty pseudonym "Marxilar" — a fusion of Marx and *maxilar* (maxillary) — a neologism announcing the radical reach of his bite. The negativity of the cannibalist metaphor as critical instrument extends to every aspect of *Revista de Antropofagia*, even to the neologism *"dentiçoes"* (dentitions) given to each issue, underlining the subversive project of "devouring" established cultural forms with their derivativeness or any homogenizing nationalist culture. Brazilianness for the anthropophagical movement resided in its voracious absorption of the disparate, the heterogeneous, its portmanteau words, and baroque perspectival shifts through which it critically reworked endogamous and exogamous relations simultaneously.

Mario de Andrade in particular denounced the Brazilian penchant for slavish imitation of aesthetic movements and displaced it with the violence of cannibal devoration on both thematic and formal levels in his fiction *Macunaíma*, which first appeared excerpted in the *Revista de Antropofagia* (1928). *O herói sem nenhum caráter* (a hero with no character), as the subtitle informs, Macunaíma, a colonial cypher like the "Canadian nobody" (McLuhan 1977, 228), embodies the cultural trope. At the interface of bodies, not territory, Macunaíma is a trickster or shape-shifter whose metamorphoses between races and genders literalize métissage so that he is not one but many characters at once, Black, Amerindian, and European. Although he is introduced as a hero in the opening paragraph and noted for his ability to do extraordinary things, Macunaíma functions more like a picaro moving through a series of episodic encounters as he travels about the country which enables de Andrade to comment critically on the pervasive violence of Brazilian society as well as on this anti-hero complicit in the voracious culture. The cannibalist theme is treated in all its variations: an ogre offers Macunaíma a piece of his leg; Ci, an urban guerilla (in the film version), devours him sexually; and pirhanas eat him alive. The rich devour the poor, and the poor consume each other in desperation. In a preface to his cinematic adaptation of the novel for the Venice Film Festival in 1969, Joaquim Pedro de Andrade wrote that "*Macunaíma* is the story of a Brazilian devoured by Brazil." The film develops more forcefully the novel's critique of Brazilian society, turning the giant Veneceslau Pietro Pietra into a grotesque figure of the predatory capitalist with his anthropophagous soup and so savaging allegorically the repressive military rule and its economic policies. As Joaquim de Andrade explained his "cannibalistic hermeneutic": "Cannibalism is an exemplary mode of consumerism adopted by underdeveloped peoples. ... The traditionally dominant, conservative social classes continue their control of the power structure — and we rediscover cannibalism... The present work relationships, as well as the relationships between people — social, political and economic — are still, basically, cannibalistic." Those who can, "eat" others through their consumption of products, or even more directly in sexual relationships. "Cannibalism has merely institutionalized and cleverly disguised itself" (Joaquim de Andrade qtd. in Stam 239). Scatological humour, unbridled sexuality, and magic transformations are the camouflage in which *Macunaíma* veils its critique of the power relations preying upon the body.

"Somos concretistas," urged Oswald de Andrade (7). To which, in conclusion to his Introduction to the re-edition of the *Revista de Antropofago,* Augusto de Campos replied: "Somos Antropófagos" (1976 n.p.). In the interval between the launching of the anthropophagical movement as socio-cultural critique in the 1920s and the contestatory aesthetics of abjection of the Cinema Novo in the 1960s, the *Noigandres* group, comprised of poets Augusto and Haroldo de Campos with visual artist Décio Pignatari, mobilized the creative force of the cannibalist hermeneutic for an "intersemiotic praxis" that exploited the materiality of language itself, its graphic and sonorous properties, to break with the sentimentalism of Brazilian romanticism and renew cultural discourse (Haroldo de Campos 1992, 233). Through re-edition of the works by and writing critical commentaries on such authors as Machado de Assis, Oswald de Andrade, and Mario de Andrade, the de Campos brothers engaged in a "dysphoric" practice of "unreading" which critically reconfigured the field of Brazilian writing, escaping its historical positivism by focusing on "disruptions, infractions, margins and monstrosities." Through this cannibalization of the archive, they produced an anti-tradition which included their own "transvalorization" among the new constellation of fragments (Haroldo de Campos 1992, 233 – 38). For the "historical impertinence" in their synchronic approach emphasized the "concept opératoire" of the "fold" with its opening to the heterogeneous in neo-Baroque aesthetics and so linked their poetics to the Baroque, "the art of the counter-conquest" (Haroldo de Campos 1998, 551 – 53). "Rewriting, remasticating" its predecessors critically, the *"concreto barroco"* configured a new synthesis which was then turned against both Brazilian and foreign cultural traditions redirecting the flow of history (Haroldo de Campos 1992, 255). Criticism and creation are implicated in this double dialectic. Anthropophagy transmutates into concretism which functions, then, as anti-colonial discourse.

The *Noigandres* group's "desacralizing" and "carnivalizing" of the archive extends beyond the field of Brazilian literature and history. The "new barbarians" with their "devouring jaws" seek nothing less than "planetary redevoration" (*"redevoração planetário"*) with their "ludic combinatories," their "parodic transmutation of values," and their "multilingualism" (Haroldo de Campos 1992, 251). "Europe is under the sign of devoration" (Haroldo de Campos 1992, 231) when the periphery swallows up the centre. A national imaginary is no "Platonic unity" but a "dialogical movement of difference" marked by rupture, fragmentation, and continuous reworking (Haroldo de Campos 1992, 237). The dialectic of universal and particular, of totality and fragment is played out in a "vectorial field" whose "radial axes" include Marx and Engels, Mallarmé, and Joyce (Haroldo de Campos 1981, 5). Mallarmé's development of a visual notion of "graphic space" and of the controlled play of chance combined to form the "multidivisioned or capillary structure" of the "constellation-poem" (Haroldo de Campos 1981, 5). Joyce's "polydimensional limitless flow" materialized in an "atomization of language" where the whole "cosmos" was infused in each word conceived three dimensionally as "verbivocovisual" (Haroldo de Campos 1981, 6). In revitalizing the European canon by rewriting it as neo-Baroque, de Campos stressed the manifold and multifacetted in its legacy. A focus on the "phonemic level" of the word orients toward an open form, open both to the poet in a "catalytic procedure" of composition in which elements disintegrate and cluster in new transformations, open to the reader in that the work is "porous," "accessible from any place one chooses to approach it" (Haroldo de Campos 1981, 6 – 7). A poem is thus a "tension of things-words in space-time" (Augusto de Campos 1968, 72) rather than a "word-sign" (Haroldo de Campos 1992, 33).

This understanding of the poem as an "object in itself," rather than an interpreter of objects or feelings, constitutes its "concreteness" in a dialectical relation with abstraction (Augusto de Campos 1968, 72). Engels' conceptualization of a complex dialectic of intellectual work in which the material mediation of the economy is "indirect" rather than "mechanistic" forms the basis of concretism's "sociological semiotics." For just as the absence of direct correspondence between the economy and thought means that the radically new might emerge within an underdeveloped economy such as Brazil, so too the dialectic of universal and national proposed by Marx stresses their mutual "interdependence" and the consequent importance of a "multiplicity of national literatures" for any understanding of Literature (Haroldo de Campos 1992, 232 – 33). Marxist dialectics consequently inform the radical dialogism of the *Noigandres* group's "open work" which from the periphery "appropriates" and reworks hegemonic codes producing a poetics that is simultaneously national and universal (Haroldo de Campos 1992, 246 – 47). The cannibalist introjection of the other in the technique of "interpolating" foreign cultures and Brazilianizing them produces "unexpected dialectical syntheses" opening up multiple possibilities (Haroldo de Campos 1992, 39, 241). Speaking in the "interstices of a universal code," the reciprocal appropriation and continuous recycling participates in a general movement of "transculturation," a critical "transvalorization" capable of "expropriation, de-hierarchization, deconstruction" (Haroldo de Campos 1992, 242, 234). Concretism, in its encoding of multivalent movements of difference, holds out the promise that the apparently permanent may yet be transformed and so doubles its symbolic mediation with a political in(ter)vention that covertly resists the censorship of the dictatorship as well as neo-colonialism. Central to such textual transfusion is translation, a practice for which Haroldo de Campos has generated a profusion of neologisms — "recreation," "transcreation," "transtextualization," "transparaization," "translumination," "poetic reorchestration" and, most provocatively, "mephistofaustian transluciferation" (1982). The cannibalist aesthetics of transversality is marked by excess in a fusion of contraries that contrasts with the logics of borders and Babel which, like the Canadian mosaic, attempt to manage diversity by keeping fragments discrete within a larger structure.

Narrativizing Discourses of Space and Language

Although more radical in its resistance to cartographic enclosure with its implication of imposed cultural boundaries, Dionne Brand's turn to the paradigm of mapmaking shares with much recent anglophone Canadian fiction a tendency to theorize cultural contact across boundaries by superimposing maps over linguistic difference. Fiction participates along with cultural discourses in the articulation of a spatial imaginary expanding in narrative form the implications of this rhetoric of relation as a mode of identification. While it symbolically secures territory, contemporary fiction's deployment of the metaphor of the map also questions the border discourse by exposing the selectivity of its hermeneutic determinations and the logics of their relations. A number of fictions invoke the mimesis of cartographic representation explicitly so as to show through narrative plotting the impasses to which this understanding of an isotopic relation of map to territory can lead. Only provisionally signifying cross-cultural encounters, maps induce a series of perceptual revisions that realign the social imaginary.

Aritha van Herk's *Places Far From Ellesmere*, subtitled "Explorations on Site," and generically innovative — "a geografictione" or "a fiction of geography/a geography of fiction" (1990, 40) — displays the contradictory possibilities of the map topos on its cover. As ground, a vertically oriented black and white official map of Alberta signifies the map visually

as representation of structures of order and containment, whether imperial, national, or in this case, patriarchal. The compass mark for due
north placed in the centre below the title suggests that readers will not
lose their bearings. Not, that is, unless they are already "lost to women,"
terrified of women and so of the north (van Herk 1990, 123). Overlaid
horizontally as palimpsest, a brightly coloured, hand-drawn map offers
an imaginative revisioning of arctic space in which a city map of Calgary
is positioned near the Arctic Sea and the Mackenzie River delta, above
which floats on bright blue sea — or maybe sky — Ellesmere Island, in
the shape of a curvaceous female body. The maps convey graphically
the perceptual transformation narrated verbally as the phases of van
Herk's intellectual and creative development are marked by successive
topographical displacements in this fictional memoir. These shifts are
only implicitly encounters with other languages. Rather than relating
the traditional immigrant lifestory in terms of the loss or acquisition
of languages that mark the centrifugal move from family farm and
Dutch at Edsberg to the cities of Edmonton and Calgary and English for
school and work, the movement from one geographical site to another
registers ongoing perceptual transformations related to changes in
modes of reading and writing. The final move northward to Ellesmere,
"a Woman's Island," does rely on a bilingual pun to bring out the feminine subtext in the toponymic marker. But the ability to read this into
the landscape is the consequence of the heightened feminist awareness
the narrator brings to this site, consciousness raised to a higher degree
by her reading *Anna Karenina* while on the island.

Idiosyncrasies of reading maps are mirrored in reading novels. The
north incites "exploratory reading": in this place of border inversions,
the narrator reads the "eternal book" while Anna steps out of the pages
to read "this book of the north" (van Herk 1990, 130). The narrator proves
thus both a resisting and an overactive reader of Tolstoy's celebrated
novel. Dismayed by the narrative closure Tolstoy has written for his
heroine, whose sin has been an overly mimetic reading of English novels
which leads her to imitate their plots and commit adultery, van Herk's
narrator attempts to "un/read" the novel so as to keep Anna alive. This
active reading rewrites the novel to produce a new narrative in excess
of Tolstoy's closure, writing beyond the pages into Ellesmere's "pristine"

white space of potential imaginings — "the text a new body of self, the self a new reading of space" (1990, 113). In its utopian revisioning of space and plot, *Places Far From Ellesmere* rings changes on the habitual north/south axis of border discourse. A liminal space, the north is the point closest to Anna's Russia while still remaining at home and, conversely, the point closest to home from which it is still possible to read Russia. The estrangement of translation is unnecessary when Anna reads and may be read in English. Yet although the late 1950s of van Herk's youth was the height of an era promoting Canada's northern destiny, the southern border is always implicit in the northern frontier. For these were also the Cold War years when security issues were paramount and the Canadian arctic a liminal zone between us and Russian missiles. Reconfiguring space and by implication the national imaginary, van Herk attempts to turn it toward more feminine and life-affirming ends.

Alternative kinds of map that function as both a defence and opening of borders structure contacts between cultures in two other novels which address the problems of inter- and intra-national boundaries differently. Both Helen Weinzweig's *Basic Black with Pearls* and Margaret Atwood's *Surfacing* play with the metacritical double bind of maps used mimetically that undermine any objective referentiality or order they might impose. Both also briefly invoke a clash of languages as they territorialize ethnicity, concentrating diversely, however, on issues of immigration and colonialism respectively. In Weinzweig's novel, Zbigniew is multilingual and works as a translator in the courts. However, he is the estranged husband of Shirley Kaszenbowski from whose perspective the fiction is narrated. Shirley has left the marriage to follow a (fictive?) lover Coenraad in the course of his spying around the world. Tension in the marriage relates to conflicts back in Poland, tensions arising from Polish pogroms against Jews that are played out between the partners in the marriage and in relation to class conflict within the Canadian context, divisions which are represented geographically rather than linguistically. Shirley is above all a reader of secret codes on postcards and, especially, of maps. Like van Herk's overactive reader, Shirley makes meaning with any and every sign, exhibiting a preference for numerological decipherings based on word counts, line counts, sequencing systems. Shirley reads Coenraad's authorial intent into the most mechanical of

346

links through her practice of making arbitrary connections, reading for "zig-zag patterns" (Weinzweig 8) or between the lines for the unsaid, often "confusing hope with facts" (Weinzweig 35). With such tactics she approaches an essay on Dutch elm disease in a Canadian botany journal found in her mail box at the King Edward Hotel to which she has been directed by a clue interpreted in a pamphlet by the Canada First Committee located in *En Route*, Air Canada's inflight magazine. There she reads about "Canada being treated like a kept woman" in tandem with the repetition of "abdicate" (Weinzweig 10), a phrase which introduces a political allegory into the narrative of marriage breakdown.

National imaginary is soon replaced by municipal, however, for this clue has taken Shirley to the King Edward Hotel in Toronto, her home, to which she returns as a tourist. Among what elm trees is she to locate Coenraad? Spreading out a map of the city on a restaurant table, she scans its network of lines for Elm, a search that will take her not into the white page ahead, like van Herk's reader, but reading beneath the palimpsest of cartographical features and back through the meandering labyrinths of memory to confront the confinement and pain of her immigrant childhood. The map keeps her in line, its verticals guarding against her habit of "walking in circles" through cities (Weinzweig 27). Moreover, it demarcates the boundaries between her present bourgeois neighbourhood and the inner city ghetto where she grew up. Class divisions are spatialized along with ethnicity, distinctions read in the north/south orientation of the city. Ironically, Shirley needs the map to find her way back downtown, for she has lost contact with the Ward, the Spadina-Dundas area, to whose Elm Street she is eventually led by the map. Nonetheless, the map proves no ordinance model of certainty but as hermetic and ambiguous as Coenraad's codes: "there were not only two Elm Streets, but Elm everything else. ... twenty-six in all" (Weinzweig 27). Finding one's way becomes more a matter of following hunches to choose among apparently identical signifiers. The ordered differences the map imposes begin to break down as Shirley is pushed and pulled between present-day streets and the undertow of memory. Even this subjective order dissolves when Shirley learns that the hotel clerk has put the botany article in every mailbox so "elm" was not a private message.

What ensues is a dizzying series of borderblurs and shifts in frame that reverse and then inverse again the relations between outside and inside, container and contained, between reader and character, speaker and listener, between Shirley and her alter ego, Francesca, the dutiful wife. Shirley experiences a parallax in the art gallery. So absorbed is she in looking at a painting that she merges with it, "advancing into the canvas" until she is able to see through the underpainting a wraith-like figure of a girl, who calls out for help to save her from the captivity of a tyrannical father (Weinzweig 55). "Everything is a matter of perspective" (Weinzweig 56), Shirley avows after this surprising interchange. In breaking out of the frame and leaving her marriage, Shirley has abandoned all conventions including those of perception. In this story of immigration, the map metaphor manages the contradictory transformations in perception of a double estrangement effect. A city, at first foreign, becomes home and then *unheimlich* again. Open to such continual modification, the territorial borders of this body politic remain mobile. From an immigrant's perspective, however, the social imaginary appears conflictual and disorienting in its demands for creative reinvention.

For Atwood's protagonist, the parallax which radically transforms her perception and induces borderblur seems possibly to have taken her beyond the realm of the living in a merging with the spirit of place. Travelling by canoe into northern Quebec, she retraces the voyageurs' route to the mythic *pays d'en haut* in the heart of the continent as she journeys back to childhood scenes, to the place her family summered, in search of her father who has gone missing. Both intra- and international borders are at stake in *Surfacing*, as in the other two novels. The border between Ontario and Quebec is marked linguistically by "a sign that says BIENVENUE on one side and WELCOME on the other." "[H]ome ground [is] foreign territory" (*Surfacing* 11). Problems in communication are depicted as the protagonist struggles with her school French to understand the French and broken English of the neighbours who have told her about her father's disappearance. "This is border country," she observes, and the "mélange of demands and languages [on the signs is] an ex-ray of the district's entire history" (*Surfacing,* 26, 15). With "Coca Cola Glacé" concluding the list, the most recent phase of imperialism is announced. Along with the American flag on every powerboat, Coke symbolizes the invasion of commerce, technology, and environmental blight from the south, corporate take-over which is the dramatic focus of the narrative since Americans want to buy her cottage and turn it into a commercial fishing lodge. Most disconcerting for the protagonist is the creeping nature of this imperialism, so that Canadians mistake each other for Americans because of the indistinguishability of the accents.

Technology's power to extend the reach of empire over space is focused in the map paradigm which is deployed in a number of different ways. The ordinance map of the district hanging on the wall of the cottage, to which the protagonist turns to help trace her father's movements, reveals a history of colonization in the changing place names. Current government policy is translating English names into French ones though, significantly, "the Indian names remain the same" (*Surfacing* 105). On the father's drawings, the place names remain in English. Numbers on the drawings correspond to those he has marked on the district map beside the red x's he has placed there, a private code mapping the aboriginal sacred sites he has found and whose petroglyphs he has drawn. Reading the map and travelling to the site marked on the drawing of an antlered figure, the protagonist cannot bring public and private signs into alignment so as to find the rock paintings. Only when she dives below the surface of the lake to examine the cliff face is her vision transformed so she can understand the signs of Amerindian culture and escape from the divisive logic of territorial boundaries and language into a holistic universe in which subject and object merge. Immersed in this "other language" (138), she undergoes a metamorphosis and becomes part of the landscape — a tree leaning, a rock — shape shifting like the spirits of her parents who haunt the site. Though they are "against borders" (*Surfacing*, 180), theirs is a different kind of elimination of boundaries than that effected by American technological transformation, one which enables her to bring the rock drawings to life rather than to kill wildlife. But invisible as she has become with the trickster powers of the spirit world, this altered perception may not be enough to halt the pressure for continental integration. Moreover, the protagonist's metamorphosis, like her father's,

349

has been mediated by the Amerindian other whose culture has been consumed in this imperialist transaction of indigenization. Only their enigmatic signs now mark the trace of the Amerindian interaction with the land. In these novels, the dialectic of continuity and innovation is played out through landscape as identificatory fiction where mapmaking makes readable new possible relations along a number of different geopolitical axes within and between nations.

In contrast, a number of recent Quebec fictions which also develop the issue of cultural clash along a north/south axis frame this violence of subordination in linguistic terms through the necessity of choosing a language. The Quebec/us connection flows with different registers of intensity between English/French in Nicole Brossard's *Le désert mauve* and Louise Dupré's *La memoria* in which the figure of a translator mediates between overlapping languages and cultures. A change in perspective incited by the northern light enables Maude Laures to rewrite the story of a violent murder in Arizona in a more hopeful light while Emma, the translator in *La memoria*, is able through the repetition of translation to carry out the work of mourning for a husband who has abandoned her and for a sister long vanished in the us. In both these fictions the translator works through a traumatic loss to create a community of witnessing. Plurilingualism is experienced less as violation than as a form of verbal and textual polysemy: fiction becomes then a site of invention, a veritable laboratory of possible worlds. The trope of translation manages the contradiction of cultural transmission under conditions of linguistic uncertainty in which every language is the language of the Other.

Nonetheless, within the dialectic of universal communicability and self-alienation which this trope of linguistic choice narrativizes, a number of fictions conclude not with an opening to new forms of community but with a reaffirmation of tradition. In this they highlight the function of the Babelic story in negotiating internal exclusions by binding a population through a common language. The protagonist of Monique LaRue's *Copies conformes* lives in translation in San Francisco where she has difficulty making herself understood to a bank machine, ironically, since her husband is researching computer software for a universal translation programme. Accents disrupt technology's capacities for the "exact reproduction" necessary for machine comprehension and networked solidarity. Reinforcing the limits of universal connectivity in the wired world and the American myth of linguistic homogeneity is the carnivalesque joke on the tape given to Claire recording Diran Zarian's heavily accented voice repeating Plato's allegory of the cave which privileges conceptual mimesis over material modes of representation. This dialectic of abstract and concrete reproduction is played out on many levels in this narrative. The family have spent a sabbatical year in California during which their son has become at home in English and Claire herself has become so immersed in local culture that she has stepped into the pages of Dashiell Hammett's *Maltese Falcon* and is living out the role of Brigid O'Shaughnessy, alias Brigid O'Doorsey, from whom she is renting a house. Claire must ultimately choose among modes of repetition. Should she stay in California living a simulacrum? Or should she heed the call of memory and follow her husband back to Montreal? Jack Kerouac's *On the Road* in the window of the City Light Bookstore is a cautionary example of the fate of losing one's language. Claire's choice to return to Montreal reaffirms the venerable Quebec myth of a language of one's own and the provincial motto, *Je me souviens*. So she participates obliquely in the project of Jacques Poulin's protagonist who, in *Volkswagen Blues*, sets off across the continent to bring Kerouac back home to Montreal. At the us border he proclaims, after Heidegger, "*Die Sprache ist das Haus des Seins*" (Language is the dwelling of being) and so affirms the ties of language over territory even in minoritized Franco-American English where mimesis stutters.

Francine Noël's dramatization of the complexity of communication in multilingual Montreal through the topos of language choice in *Babel, prise deux* also affirms the importance of French as vehicular language of general communicability for the many migrant groups. Allegorically, the tension between triumph and tragedy, between the cover image of *Femmes de Caughnawaga* (a sculpture by Marc-Aurèle Suzor-Côté, linking to the origin myths of Quebec in the colonizing encounter with the Amerindians in which the Mohawk women are dressed European-style) and the frontispiece (which displays the origin myth of a different culture and another aspect of the interface of peoples with the confounding of languages from the Genesis 11 account of Babel in Hebrew script), is played out through the plot which gathers in members of different communities. Fatima, member of an old Quebec family, is a speech therapist working to help a girl regain her French through a palimpsest of other languages spoken in the city streets. Her close friend Amelia, a translator who has migrated from Spain, has finally decided to settle in Montreal. A trip back to Europe on her mother's death has made Amelia aware how much she has changed and, despite the pain of the mutation, she is now less uncomfortable in Montreal than in Europe, even though she is at home nowhere. However, having proclaimed her belonging as a Québécoise, Amelia is killed in an airplane accident on her return journey. In this failure to include the immigrant shuttling between languages, Babel proves once more to be a contradictorily self-limiting model of communication.

In *Babel-Opéra*, Monique Bosco also emphasizes the tragic aspects of this myth in what is less a heteroglossic text than a heterogeneous mixture of genres where the dispersion of the people in the biblical story of Babel prefigures the Holocaust. Written from the perspective of a survivor of this genocide, Bosco's narrative concludes with an image of Canada as a cold land of exile, a provisional refuge, rather than a promised land. It is a place, however, in which she, Sisyphus-like, must build Babel again. By opening wide the doors for the exiles arriving from every continent, Canada, she hopes, is where Babel will be built anew so that the universal and the singular may be reconciled, where "chacun a le droit de vivre selon les lois de son coeur, toutes origines confondues" (Bosco 93).

A dialectic of continuity and innovation, of the enduring and the catalyst, informs both landscape and langscape as identificatory fictions. But origins are even more confused and contested when the dialectic is intensified as it is in Brazilian literature with its endless cycle of reproductions and coincidence of opposites. Confounding origins and teleology alike, cannibalism as trope and theory of culture rejects Aristotelian notions of form which centre plots on a moment of crisis, whether of decision-making between alternatives or of a sudden perspectival shift, bringing about transformation and resolution. Instead, the anthropophagical aesthetic engages in a play of endless repetition whether this be in a proliferating cycle of stories, as in the narrative *Macunaíma*, or in the cumulative repetitions with a difference of the de Campos' transcreations. Mario de Andrade's hero has "no character" — not only because he is the paradigmatic Brazilian with no "original" culture of his own but because he has no psychic identity within the conventions of the novel, a permanent psychologized entity manifesting itself in exteriorized emotions and actions. Macunaíma is a great transformer with no stable identity — a shape-shifting trickster. Born black into an Amerindian family, he later transforms himself into a handsome white prince. He also transforms his brother Jigue into a "telephone machine," to call a local cabaret or to curse the villain Pietra, and an Englishman into the "London Bank Machine." Before returning to his homeland, he transforms the city of Sao Paulo into a giant stone sloth. At the end of the narrative he turns himself into the constellation, Ursa Major. Fusing fantasies, symbols, and satire, de Andrade's combination of heterogeneous elements attempts to synthesize Brazil in all its complexity. Macunaíma's various instantaneous journeys from one part of the country to another dissolve spatial boundaries and suspend temporal limitations, allowing him to roam through Brazil's history and sustain multiple points of view.

In creating his eponymous hero, de Andrade has orchestrated popular and folkloric motifs to create what was initially received as a compendium of Brazilian folklore. However, as de Andrade later avowed to his critics, the magical transformations of his hero owed more than a coincidental resemblance to the adventures of Kone'wo, a courageous and astute hero; Kalawunseg, a liar; and Makunaíma, the tribal hero, in oral narratives of the peoples along the Orinoco River in Venezuela and Brazil collected by Theodor Koch-Grünberg, a German ethnologist, and published in 1917. Mario de Andrade announced his surprise that these critics limited his copying to Koch-Grünberg when, as he writes, "I copied everyone ... I confess that I copied, sometimes verbatim," ethnographers, Amerindian texts, Portuguese colonial chroniclers, and Brazil itself. Even the idea of satire is not his own. The "only original thing," he claims ironically, is that of being discovered by chance by Pedro Alvares Cabrals (de Andrade qtd. in Madureira 112 – 13). Undercutting any claims to founding an original national culture, de Andrade's open admission of plagiarism foregrounds the novel's intertextuality, its artifice or status as writing rather than orality, its absorption of everything that can be expressed. This literariness ushers in the death of speech as the epilogue confirms. Narrated by a parrot who alone has kept from oblivion the language and happenings of the vanished Tapanhuma,[5] and told in the depths of the forest in an intoxicating new tongue to a man who will be intrigued enough to write them down, the cycle of stories is recycled, mimicked, endlessly translated. Dissipating any claims to indigenous authority, this last parrot of the aboriginal languages flies off to Lisbon, leaving the stories in transit between languages, between cultures, open to yet other reconfigurations and transvaluations.

With their "mephistofaustian transluciferations," Augusto and Haroldo de Campos follow a similar parabola back to the site of the masters' authoritative voices undermining any claims to pure speech in their dionysiac rewritings. Like de Andrade, they engage in a practice of self-reflexive plagiarism as de-propriation or "transtextualization" but the relations are inversed so that the forms of European texts are reworked isotopically from a peripheral language rather than the world view of Amerindian culture being recreated in a European language. In his many writings on translation, Haroldo de Campos emphasizes its double aspects as critique and creation: writing ruptures and fragments even as it configures and constellates in surprising syntheses. The translation of creative texts, always a recreation or parallel creation, is consequently a parody in the sense of a parallel ode or a plagiarism in the sense of a transverse rendering of tradition. Indeed, translations of Joyce can only be "travesties," especially if they are the "afro-anglo-homeríade" of Derek Walcott's *Omeros*, the "trans-*helenização*" of his own *Iliad*, or the "*jubilante e joycintilante*" of Augusto de Campos' versions of *Finnegans Wake* (Haroldo de Campos 2002, 19 – 20). Thoth presides over this book of the dead in his dual responsibilities for the deceased and for language which is generated at the site of loss or absence. Writing from the exile of multilingual Trieste, Joyce's carnival of languages, his "*irlandes babelizante*," is rendered into the de Campos' "*brasilírico idiomaterno*" through a "radical *phono-etimológica*" practice that releases a proliferation of neologisms (Haroldo de Campos 2002, 35, 19). As "labyrinth" and "palimpsest," Joyce's "monsterpiece" functions as an encyclopedia of transtextualization with its exhuberant inventiveness in the mixture of languages where a word contains an entire cosmos (Haroldo de Campos 2002, 32). "Transcreation" entails then a reciprocal appropriation and revitalization as the transmission of the signifying form rather than of any referential content transforms both Joyce's text and the possibilities for the Brazilian language.

The double dialectical dimension of translation which transfigures both originating and target languages and, indeed, undercuts any monologic privileging of either origin or telos in what is always a reciprocal interanimation of languages, informs the "radical transfusion operation" of Haroldo de Campos' "transluciferation" of Goethe's *Faust* (1982, 185). The problem for the translator, as he outlines it, is to recreate a "phonic ambiance" in which Griffin will be motivated through a chain of signifiers within the text so that the convergence appears necessary rather than accidental (1982, 184). Dionysiac rather than playful, de Campos's translation manifests a "subversive" "hyperfidelity" that rebelliously refuses to "serve a content submissively," electing instead to be faithful "to the reproduction of form" (1982, 182). What this entails is using the "poetic function" as a "device for textual engendering" to recreate in the translator's language a poem as "an isomorphic re-project of the original's design" (1982, 183). Attending to the "elective affinities" of sound and meaning inevitably modifies the shape and content of the words as he demonstrates in his reworking of the wordplay on griffin (Greif) and "*greifen*," seizing or taking possession, a word associated with Goethe's view of the active life (1982, 183). Working with this "phonosemantic series" to sustain the "iconic effect" of the whole with its phonic repetition and alliteration, de Campos retains some of the puns on grey and old man while sacrificing the sense when "*grimmig*" (angry) is displaced by "*grasso*" (heavy) or "*grés*" (sandstone) (1982, 186). The blood flows in this transfusion which while killing off the father nonetheless honours him by creating a revitalized existence for him in a different body.

The choice of texts to rewrite is highly significant. Most of de Campos' transcreations engage hierarchical relations of infraduction or supraduction as in his "transparadisation" where the double dialectics of his translation of the Hebrew Bible in a proverbial and aphoristic style, mingling colloquial with the solemn or poetic, Portugueses the Hebrew language and Hebraizes the Portuguese. Irreverent and reverent simultaneously, this process parallels his "transluciferation" of Goethe, a writer who himself "carnivalizes Hell and carnalizes Heaven" (1982, 182). Like the translations of sacred texts into the vernacular during the Renaissance, this process of cannibalizing the Babelian library both enriches the lexicon of Brazilian language and enhances its prestige. But the transversal aesthetics of "transculturation" became more significant in de Campos' later translations when persuing "elective affinities" with Mexican poet Octavio Paz in the recreation of *Transblanco (em torno a Blanco de Octavio Paz)*. Paz, himself a translator and theoretician of translation, shared de Campos' understanding of the translative aspect of all textuality: every text is at once unique and the translation of another text in an endless chain of translations. Translation entails invention and as such constitutes a unique creation. Paz's *Blanco* (1966) plays with typography on the page, shifting the margin 180 degrees to the bottom of the page with a line running vertically to the top with a reorientation of perception akin to the Copernican revolution, and not without resonances to de Campos' *Galáxias* (1963). *Branco*, de Campos' transcreation of the poem, follows this typographical innovation with its differently coloured fonts to emphasize similarity within difference. For as Paz comments in a letter to de Campos remarking the subtle shifts in emphasis, the Portuguese version is more "concise" and hence "better" than the Spanish (de Campos 1994, 121). Attentive to the "alliterations, puns, and other verbal echoes," de Campos has focused as usual on the phono-semantic aspects in translation in what he calls a practice of *"diamantizaçao"* (1994, 120).

Where *Transblanco* differs is in the radical expansion of the concept of translation to include all forms of rewriting: not only does the book contain both the Spanish and the Portuguese versions of the text, but also literary criticism, historiography, a prefatory introduction, and even an extensive exchange of correspondence between the two poet-translators from 1968 to 1981 about the process of translation. Additionally, de Campos wrote poems in response to the translation process and commentary on Paz's work, so giving textual materiality to the concepts in their titles "signs in rotation," "constellations," "galaxies." An anthology of poems "liberating the word" presents face to face Spanish and Portuguese versions of other poems by Paz. More than the phonetic transposition of *Blanco* into *Branco*, *Transblanco* enfolds them both in a "choreography of the internal dance of languages." Intersemiotic translation is at its most expansive here in the polyphonic dialogue of the poem as collective project, as open, unfinished work. Transculturation manifests itself as a dialogical movement of difference between Brazilian and Mexican cultures. What is re-established in this transcreation is a dialogue among writers begun in seventeenth-century Latin America. Explicit dialogue in the feminine wit of Mexican Sor Juana in her polemical confrontation with the theology of Padre Vieira of Brazil, implicit dialogue in the tropological discourse of Gregorio de Matos, the Bahian, Caviedes, the Peruvian, and Sor Juana whose anticipation of tropicalism, biting satire, and surrealism contributed in different ways to formulating Baroque poetics (Haroldo de Campos 1992, 242 – 43). *Transblanco* reveals the diverse ways that de Campos and Paz have ingested the Baroque with its disjunctive syntheses, insistent interrogations, and dynamic paradoxes. Their attention to these differences and to the mediations operative in this transtextualization establish translation as an important figure for the ethical relation of same and other in a dialectic of return and reversal.

Each of the tropes — borderline, Babel, or anthropophagy — manifests a project to relate. While the intersemiotic translation of *Transblanco* most powerfully facilitates the interanimation of peripheries, all three are metaphors for transversal relations open to the outside. Taken together they propose different logics of cultural contact through which to give symbolic force to the "territorial stretch" of a hemispheric imaginary.

Notes

The Critic, Institutional Culture, and Canadian Literature: Barbara Godard in Conversation with Smaro Kamboureli

1   Paper presented at "New World Coming: The Sixties and the Shaping of Global Consciousness," Queen's University, 16 June 2007.

2   "Feminist Challenges to the Production of Knowledge and Creative Practice," forthcoming *Atlantis*.

3   See Susan Jackel, "Canadian Women's Autobiography: A Problem of Criticism," in *Gynocritics/Gynocritiques: Feminist Approaches to Writing by Canadian and Quebec Women*, ed. Barbara Godard (Toronto: ECW P, 1987): 97 – 110.

4   Most recently, "The Risk of Critique: Voices Across the Generations," in *Academic Callings: The University We Have Had, Now Have, and Could Have*, eds. Janice Newson and Claire Polster, forthcoming.

5   "Theory at York," ACUTE *Theory Group Newsletter*, no. 11 (May 1992): 2 – 3.

6   "The Oral Tradition and Contemporary Fiction" (1974), *Essays on Canadian Writing* 7/8 (Summer 1977): 46 – 62.

7   "Crawford's Fairy Tales," *Studies in Canadian Literature* 4, 1 (Winter 1979): 109 – 38. Rpt. in *Nineteenth Century Literary Criticism*, vol. 127 (Detroit: Gale, 2003): 181 – 92.

8   "Between One Cliché and Another: Language in *The Double Hook*," *Studies in Canadian Literature* 4, 2 (Summer 1978): 114 – 65.

9   "The Avant-garde in Canada: *Open Letter* and *La Barre du jour*," *Ellipse* (1979): 23 – 24, 98 – 113.

10 See Robin Mathews, "Research, Curriculum, Scholarship and Endowment in the Study of Canadian Literature," paper presented at ACUTE, McGill University, May 1972.

11 See Smaro Kamboureli, "Theory: Beauty or Beast? Resistance to Theory in the Feminine," *Open Letter* 7, 8 (Summer 1990): 5 – 26.

12 "My (M)Other, My Self: Strategies for Subversion in Atwood and Hébert," *Essays on Canadian Writing* 26 (1983): 13 – 44. Rpt in *Anne Hébert*,

ed. Janis Pallister (Cranbury, NJ: Fairleigh Dickinson P, 2000): 316‒34.

13 Now ACCUTE, Association of Canadian College and University Teachers.

14 A shortened form of this conference paper appeared as "Theorizing Feminist Discourse/Translation," *Tessera* 6 (Spring 1989): 42–53.

15 Rusty Shteir et al. "A Big Divide?: Humanities and Social Sciences Together," RFR/DRF 32: 3/4 (2007) : 13–61.

16 Alessandra Renzi and Stephen Turpin, "Nothing Fails Like Prayer: Notes on the Cult of Saint Precario," *Fuse* 30.1 (January 2007): 25–35.

17 See Gilles Deleuze, *Negotiations: 1972–1990,* trans. Martin Joughin (New York: Columbia UP, 1995): 175.

18 See Fuyuki Kurosawa, "The State of Intellectual Play: A Generational Manifesto for Neoliberal Times," *Topia* 18 (2007): 11–42.

STRUCTURALISM / POST-STRUCTURALISM: LANGUAGE, REALITY, AND CANADIAN LITERATURE

1 On the same occasion, I read the paper "From Deconstructionist Project to Postmodern Aesthetic: The Criticism of Robert Kroetsch," published as "Other Fictions: Robert Kroetsch's Criticism" (1984b).

2 Stan Fogel presented a similar paper, "Lost in the Canadian Funhouse," at a session on the 1970s in Canadian Literature, MLA, December 1981. At the same time, I reached the opposite conclusion in: "New Critical Fictions: Phenomenology, Structuralism, Post-Structuralism, Feminism" (1981a).

3 This descriptive term is that of Timothy Reiss (1982): "In what follows, the name *discourse* will refer to a rather large and somewhat ill-delimited definitional field taken over, at least partially, from the studies of Michel Foucault. Firstly, *discourse* — here — is a coherent set of linguistic facts organized by some enunciating entity. Such a statement elicits at least two comments. In the first place it is clear that the term *discourse* means *any* semiotic system as

practiced, not necessarily a simply linguistic one in any narrow sense ... In all discourse not only are the linguistic (semiotic) facts, the signifying elements, organized by some entity, but we may assume they are not aimless. They *show* some goal" (27 – 28).

4   To paraphrase Terry Eagleton (1983).

5   The programme for these meetings was organized by Sandra Djwa, with my help on Quebec criticism.

6   These were by Gérard Bessette, Jean-Charles Falardeau, and David Hayne, among others. Some of these texts, in translation, may be read in Larry Shouldice's anthology (1979). Northrop Frye was honoured at a special luncheon of the association.

7   Bruce Whiteman (1981) speaks of Davey's conventionally referential and author-centred work on Souster and Dudek as an exemplary piece of "phenomenological criticism."

8   In this essay, Mundwiler explores the key to phenomenology, the epoché, or bracketing of the world, which he finds paradoxically reveals mimesis.

9   See also "make it new" in "The Poet as Critic" (1977, 12).

10   These are chapter headings in David Cook (1985).

11   To paraphrase Tzvetan Todorov (1977).

12   Germaine Warkentin (1979) used Jakobson's model to draw a distinction between different modes of writing in tension in David Thompson's journals. See also Sherrill Grace (1985).

13   See also B. Godard (1979) and T.D. MacLulich (1978, 419).

14   See for example the work of Georges-André Vachon and André Vanasse, or Barbara [Godard] Thompson (1967).

15   "Understanding that human time does not precede man, but is the manner in which man himself chooses to live, Grove and Purdy, Avison, Aquin and Richler, each in his (or her) own way, urges his (or her) readers to stop indulging in thoughtless living and conformity which erase the difference between man and beast and, through a spiritual and imaginative resurrection, achieve the essential step of disengaging themselves from the restrictive pattern of horizontal duration" (301).

16 For more discussion of feminist theories of reading see *Tessera* (1986) and my essay, "Mapmaking: A Survey of Feminist Criticism" (1987a).

17 For a more detailed examination of Kroetsch's criticism, see my essay "Other Fictions: Robert Kroetsch's Criticism" (1984a).

18 The parallel between deconstructionist and new critical readings was made at the MLA, New York, 1983, in response to a description by Barbara Johnson of the classroom application of deconstruction, characterized by its close reading of the text, unravelling ambiguities — deconstructive retracing. The difference, according to Johnston, is in the *différance*, the deferral. New Criticism reconciles ambiguities into a synthesis while deconstruction remains with the fragments.

19 See also my "Other Fictions" (1984a).

20 *Borderlines* was a cultural studies periodical published by a Toronto collective of academics and artists.

21 See also "Fred Wah: A Poetry of Dialogue" (1984).

22 To paraphrase Tzvetan Todorov (1977, 31).

CRITICAL DISCOURSE IN/ON QUEBEC

1 Lyotard's *La condition post-moderne* was written in Quebec, commissioned by the Ministry of Education.

2 All translations in this text are my own unless otherwise indicated in the list of works cited.

3 I use the term modernity here as a literal translation of the French. As used in Quebec, the word describes the period termed *postmodern* in English Canada, but it also refers to the preceding period of high modernism. The designation of periods in Quebec corresponds to that in France, where dada and surrealism were a central part of modernism.

4 Interestingly, most of the feminist criticism, the readings of texts by Quebec women writers, has been the work of feminist scholars living in English Canada and the United States. Quebec feminists have concentrated on fiction/theory.

THE POLITICS OF REPRESENTATION:
SOME NATIVE CANADIAN WOMEN WRITERS

1 "Contemporary Art By Women of Native Ancestry," York Quay Gallery, 1–30 September 1989; "Edward Poitras: Indian Territory," Power Plant, 1 June–10 September 1989.

2 This play received full-scale production by Nightwood Theatre and Passe Muraille in the 1989–1990 season.

3 There is promise of continuity too in anthologies of Native women's writing: *Writing the Circle: Native Women of Western Canada*, eds. Sylvia Vance and Jeanne Perreault (Edmonton: NeWest, 1990). Also in preparation in 1989 was Ts'eku collective of Vancouver, "Native Women: Celebrating Our Survival," for publication by Press Gang.

4 I quote here from the posters and application forms for a series of workshops held 14 January to 19 June 1989, Committee to Reestablish the Trickster, 9 St. Joseph Street, Toronto.

5 For a more detailed analysis of the Native copyright system where the right to tell a story is exchanged within a context of the acquisition of ritual knowledges, see my *Talking About Ourselves: The Literary Productions of the Native Women of Canada*. The CRIAW Papers/Les document de l'ICREF No. 11 (Ottawa: CRIAW, 1985).

6 Representations, it should be remembered, are signs, a relationship of a signifier to a signifier within a system of differences, as Saussure formulated the process of signification. Meaning is produced in a network of differences not through reference to a "real Indian." As Peirce affirms, a sign can only be received by another sign, an interpretant, in a chain of semiosis.

7 The literary institution also offers many more subject-positions as reader, as teacher, as historian, etc. As well as the individual genres, texts offer different subject-positions for authors and readers.

8 Conway's statistics come largely from Anne Innis Dagg's book, *The 50% Solution: Why Should Women Pay for Men's Culture?* (Waterloo, 1986).

9 Ann Wallace states that they were told the University of Toronto Press had too many accounts and would be adding no new presses. Subsequently, Second Story joined them.

10 Kirchhoff's title in itself signals the slant of the article towards the dominant group.

11 To reproduce these jokes would be to reinscribe this racist discourse. The interested reader may find them in the newspaper.

12 As Saussure has shown, meaning and value are produced in a differential network of binary oppositions through the logical operations of selection and combination.

13 For further discussion of these archetypal patterns using Native Canadian material see the texts by Annis Pratt, "Affairs with Bears," and by Gloria Orenstein, "Jovevette Marchessault: The Ecstatic Vision-Quest of the New Feminist Shaman" in my edited volume, *Gynocritics/Gynocritiques: Feminist Approaches to the Writing of Canadian and Québec Women* (Toronto: ECW, 1987).

14 For a fuller discussion of the clash between white and Native "images of the squaw," see my "Listening for the Silence: Native Women's Traditional Narratives," in *The Native in Literature: Canadian and Comparative Perspectives*, eds. Thomas King, Helen Hoy, and Cheryl Calver (Toronto: ECW, 1987), 133–73.

15 For further analysis of the Native as sign of Canadian nationalism in the making, see my analysis of the search for a Canadian language as Anglo-Ojibwa (1981).

16 As Lacan outlines this discourse of mastery, it is the "tyranny of the all-knowing and exclusion of fantasy," a discourse which "gives primacy to the signifier (S_1), retreat of subjectivity beneath its bar (S), producing knowledge as object (S_2), which stands over and against the lost object of desire (a)" (*Feminine Sexuality* 161.)

17 For a detailed examination of the predominance of models of the subjected subject see Paul Smith, *Discerning the Subject* (Minneapolis: U of Minnesota P, 1987).

18 Ironically, he describes these operations of exclusion within the dominant discourse of eurocentric racism: the place of disciplinary Truth is contrasted with the place of non-Truth, "une exteriorité

sauvage" (Foucault, *Ordre* 37; my emphasis).

19   The first term is that of Pêcheux (157). The second is the formulation of Abdul R. JanMohamed, 281–99. The term originated with Gramsci, "counter-hegemonic ideological production," quoted in Barbara Harlow, 14.

20   See also Paula Gunn Allen, *Sacred Hoop: Recovering the Feminine in American Indian Traditions* (Boston: Beacon P, 1986), 78, and Gloria Anzaldua, 4.

21   Pollock (6) elaborates here on K. Marx, *The Eighteenth Brumaire of Louis Napoleon* (1852). An analysis of Marx on two modes of representation is also to be found in Gayatri Spivak, "Can the Subaltern Speak?"

22   See Gooderham and bell hooks.

23   Campbell describes the reshaping activities of an editor in a debate at Women and Words, July 1983 ("Writing from a Native Woman's Perspective," audio tape). Maracle's book was subsequently republished by Women's Press.

24   This concept has been used in Canadian political analysis to explore the inferior economic situation of Québécois and, more recently, as a model for the position of Native peoples in Canada in a state of "cultural siege." See Kenneth McRoberts.

25   Information on the history and practices of Theytus Books in Iris Loewen, "Native Publishing in Canada" (unpublished paper, 1987). For this and other relevant material, I thank Viola Thomas of Theytus Books.

26   As Lacan formulates it, the discourse of the analyst focuses on the question of desire, gives primacy to the object of desire (a), over and against knowledge as such (S2), which produces the subject in its division as the structure of fantasy (S), over the signifier through which it is constituted and from which it is divided (S1) (Lacan 161).

DETERRITORIALIZING STRATEGIES:
M. NOURBESE PHILIP AS CAUCASIANIST ETHNOGRAPHER

No notes.

Canadian? Literary? Theory?

1 I refer here specifically to the Margaret Atwood Society, which mounts two sessions at the MLA every year, involving international scholars who study Atwood as a single author, not Canadian literature and Atwood as one of its a major authors.

2 I emphasize here the constructivism of "re-covery" (cover up) rather than the alethetic unveiling of a pre-existent truth in the "un-covery" of Kroetsch's "Unhiding the Hidden" with its Adamic myth of radical innocence.

3 Heather Murray has analysed the emergence of English studies as a discipline in Canada in *Working in English: History, Institution, Resources* (Toronto: U Toronto P, 1996).

4 The fable "Beauty and the Beast" has been used by psychoanalysts as the paradigm for female sexual development in the fixing of a male object of desire (Barchilon), hence as a model of sexual difference and heterosexual desire.

5 English studies emerging late in the nineteenth century, in Canada before England, has thus struggled with both the Arnoldian neoclassical burden of assuring access to universal truth in a secular age, and the Romantic nationalist imperative to utter the originating truth.

6 Further incidences of the disruptions in the territorial imperatives of the Canadian literary discourse produced by attention to ethnopolitics are analysed in Alison Conway's essay "Ethnic Writing and Canadian Literary Criticism."

Writing Between Cultures

1 The lack of "haunting ghosts" lamented by Earle Birney in "Can-Lit" functions, paradoxically, as an identificatory fiction for Robert Kroetsch: Canadian writing manifests "resistance to a speakable name" (1989, 41).

2 The terms of reference of the *Report of the Royal Commission on Bilingualism and Biculturalism* (1967 – 1972) which first framed the issues

of cultural and linguistic diversity established a clear hierarchy between "the two founding *races*" (English and French) and "other ethnic groups" (*Report* I xxi).

3 Jam Ismail is such a trilingual writer. For more detailed analysis see my essays, "The Oral Tradition and National Literatures" and "The Discourse of the Other: Canadian Literature and the Question of Ethnicity."

4 *Translatare* refers to the displacement of people as well as to the physical transportation of objects and to the transfer of legal jurisdiction as well as of ideas: it might also connote being carried away in transport — enraptured — as well as taking possession of something. "Translation," which emerged in English in mediaeval and neo-classical texts, connoted the circulation of translinguistic meaning conceived as separate from the medium of language in which it was expressed. *Traduction* emerged in sixteenth-century France from the Italian with a different semantic field meaning to lead across, to transform, or to bring before justice. Developing at a moment when translation becomes an object of discourse in rhetorical modes, not in the mode of conceptual learning, the French translator is understood to be transferring texts from one well-demarcated language to another. Translation here implies the adaptation and acclimatization of the foreign in what is a secondary and inferior activity. This contrasts with the English "translation," which means the circulation of signifieds beyond all reference to either the near or the foreign in some ineffable transcendence.

5 Consider also the German *übersetzung*, "to set above," which emphasizes the intertranslatability of languages as an interactive and reciprocal game between self and other, or the Hindi *anuvad*, connoting "the word sitting beside you" and "the word in dispute," establishing translation as contradictorily linking similarities and confronting differences.

6 There are some eleven dialects in Anishinaabemowin (Ojibwe), which is spoken primarily in Ontario and to the south of the Great Lakes. One of seven Central Algonkian languages, contemporary

Anishinaabemowin forms a distinctive subgroup evolved from Proto-Algonkian, spoken about 3,000 years ago. Linguistic variation falls into two primary groups, northern (including Algonkin and Severn Ojibwe) and southern (including Chippewa, Eastern Ojibwe, Odawa, and Saulteaux). Between the two are a number of definable subdialects. The Nipissing dialect to the east combines northern and southern features (Valentine 20–23). This term for translation was given by a speaker of the Severn dialect. A nineteenth-century dictionary gives *"ahnekuhnóotuhbeega"* for "translate" and *"ahnekuhnóotahga"* for "interpret." The suffix *"beega"* means writing. "Story" is transcribed as *"enáhjemowin"* (Edward Wilson). A lexicon drawing heavily on the Odawa dialect of Wikwemikong renders "interpret" as *"aanikkanoottamaake"* which combines the suffix *"aanikko"* (to join or tie together) with the suffix *"akke"* (to work with or make). Story or narrative is *"tipaacimowin"* (Piggott and Grafstein). Within this range of variants, the emphasis is on the active manipulation or work of bringing two languages into contact.

7 "Language is not a neutral medium" easily made "private property," for it is "overpopulated" with the languages of others, languages to which it responds or which it anticipates. "Expropriating it, forcing it to submit to one's own intentions and accents, is a difficult and complicated process" (Bakhtin 1981, 294).

8 Marie Guyart, born in 1599 in Tours, grew up in a baker's family and married a silk maker, Claude Martin. Widowed at nineteen and with a year-old son, Claude, Marie helped run the transportation business of her sister and brother-in-law before entering the Ursuline order at Tours in January 1631, where she was bound by the rule of strict enclosure under the directives of the Council of Trent. With Madeleine de la Peltrie and two Ursuline nuns, she set sail for Quebec on May 4, 1639. At the request of her son, a Benedictine monk, she wrote a spiritual autobiography detailing her mystic visions, "La Relation de 1654," which, despite her instructions not to do so, he published along with her voluminous correspondence five years after her death in 1672.

9   Taignoagny and Domagaga, sons of Donnaconna, the chief of Quebec, were kidnapped by Cartier on his first voyage in 1534 and returned to Quebec in 1535 when he kidnapped their father. On his third voyage, Cartier planned to send young men to live with aboriginals, but the immersion project ended after only two days when the aboriginals conspired against the French. Captivity figures importantly in the apprenticeship of translators in the exploration phases of the colony when, in the seventeenth century, Champlain sent young men to live with the Hurons, Algonkins, and even the enemy Iroquois. They were subject to torture and other trials. After proving their courage, they were adopted into the tribes, as was the case with such celebrated *truchements* as Etienne Brulé, Guillaume Couture, Jean-Paul, and Thomas Godefroy. For more analysis of these early interpreters see Jean Delisle, "Les interprêts sous le régime français." For an Amerindian perspective on multilingualism see Métis historian Olive Dickason (79).

10   This was explicit in the development of the Carolingian Empire when Alcuin followed the details of the opening scene of *De Inventione* in a letter to Charlemagne in response to requests for the rules of rhetoric so that the emperor might rule properly (Cheyfitz 112–13).

11   This topos still informs such nineteenth-century Quebec texts as the celebrated *roman du terroir, Jean Rivard*, where oratory and improvement of soil and *habitans* are the making of a hero as political ruler.

12   On June 24, 1997, Newfoundland celebrated the 500th anniversary of the landing of John Cabot (Giovanni Caboto) to claim the land for England.

13   This policy is different from that of the French who took Beothuks back to France to train them as interpreters before 1508 (Delisle 6). In the late sixteenth century a French sailor observed that the Amerindians in the Straits of Belle-Isle traded in French, English, Gascony, and Basque (Delisle 23–24).

14   Parmenius was among those who died on that fatal expedition

of 1583, but an epic poem he wrote of the settlement project and his letter to Hakluyt, both in Latin, survive as the first texts written in (British) North America. The letter, translated by Hakluyt, was published in his compilation of "explorer's" relations (*Principall Navigations* 1589) of which it is, despite its brevity, rhetorically exemplary.

15 Parmenius's text exemplifies translation in the Renaissance with the desacralization of languages and the emergence of vernaculars as state languages and, consequently, of national(ist) discourses. Becoming national is, paradoxically, for a language to become colonial and colonizing: colonial in differentiating itself from the universal language Latin, colonizing in representing itself mimetically as universal. Parmenius's letter, written in Latin, was published in the English translation of Hakluyt, an ardent promoter of England's colonizing projects, who removed from his dead friend's text lines where Parmenius commented negatively on the coldness of the climate because of icebergs in May. Such textual manipulation in translation is in keeping with Hakluyt's literal use of *translation* in the strong sense of transport from one place to another, in a passage that is potentially enrapturing, "captivating" its reader.

16 "Nous congneumes que se sont *gens* qui seroint fassilles à convertir ... Je estime mielx que aultrement que les gense seroint faciles à convertir à notre saincte foy" (1545, 1986, 113; my emphasis), quoted approvingly by Hakluyt in *Discourse of Western Planting* (4).

17 A frequent comment in Cartier's *Relations* is "Par default de langue ne pensames avoyr congnoissance."

18 This rapture is read by the French as a sign that Donnaconna — wearing his bearskin, "haranging," and *seeming* ("comme s'il eust voullu dire que toute la terre estoit à luy" 1545, 1986, 116) to protest the planting of a cross in the name of the King of France — "qu'ilz ne habbatroyent ladite crois en nous faisant *plusieurs harengues que n'entendions*" (1545, 1986, 117; my emphasis). Florio's translation — "woulde not remove the Cross we had set up" (1580, 1975, 23) — leaves out the last phrase which records French inability to

understand indigenous spoken languages, seemingly a matter less important to the English.

19   The Amerindians excel in the double-play of illusion, staging a performance of sorcery in which they imitate Christian rhetoric and ritual in the name of "Cudouagny" to warn Cartier against travelling to Hochelaga. Cartier considers the refusal of Taignoagny and his brother to accompany him up river, as they had promised in France, to be "treason" and "trickery" (1986, 143), but the miming of Christian ritual is related neutrally, without comment on its evident parody (1986, 145). How could Hakluyt, reading this passage, have interpreted the aboriginals as "easily converted"?

20   Significantly, French interpreters or *"coureur de bois"* received similar nicknames: Jean Nicolet was known as *Achurra* (*"homme deux fois"*) for his linguistic skills while François Marguerie went by the name *"homme double"* (Delisle 52, 61). This ready acceptance of Nicolet and Marguerie by the aboriginals earned them suspicion from the priests. When Etienne Brulé and Nicolas Marsolet helped the English occupiers of Quebec in 1629, they were considered traitors by the civil authorities as well (Delisle 39).

21   She compiled an Iroquois dictionary, a French-Algonkian dictionary, Algonkian-French dictionary, and a catechism in Huron, all of which have been lost, making analysis of her translation practice impossible.

22   "Car entendre louer la Majesté en quatre langues différentes: voir baptiser quantité de Sauvages: entendre les Sauvages mêmes prêcher la loy de Jésus-Christ à leurs compatriotes, et leur apprendre à bénir et à aimer notre Dieu: les voir rendre grâces au ciel de nous avoir envoyées dans leur païs barbare pour instruire leurs filles, et leur apprendre le chemin du ciel; tout cela, dis-je, n'est-il pas capable de nous faire oublier nos croix et nos fatigues, fussent-elles mille fois plus grandes quelles n'ont été?" (1971, 88)

23   She is known as "Magdeleine de Saint Joseph Amiskweian" (xx 126 – 27). "When she saw certain Jugglers breathe upon her sick brother, and sing to him, she only wept; as soon as these Charlatans had been driven away, the poor child began to laugh, indicating

by her tears the horror that she had for their ancient superstitions, and showing by her joy the pleasure she took in seeing her brother inclined to have recourse to God" (xx 128 – 29).

24 That this is her full name is suggested in the notes of Dom Guy Oury to his edition of the *Correspondance* (124). The hyphenated name ironically invokes both that of the Virgin Mary, immaculate, and of Magdelene, the sinner, and so combines the double tropes of conversion in Mère Marie's discourse, that of ease of conversion, because she is always-already European and "naturally good," and that of potential infidelity in need of a strong shaping hand.

25 "Elles perdent tout ce qu'elles ont de sauvage si tôt qu'elles sont lavées des eaux du saint baptême en sorte que ceux qui les ont veues auparavant courir dans les bois comme des bietes sont ravis et pleurent de joye de les voir douces comme des brebis s'approcher de la sainte table pour y recevoir le véritable agneau" (1971, 112).

26 "Elle n'y fut pas deux jours qu'il y eu un changement admirable. Elle ne sembloit plus être elle-même, tant elle étoit portée à la prière et aux pratiques de la piété Chrétienne, en sorte qu'aujourd'huy elle est l'exemple des filles de Québec" (de l'Incarnation 1971, 95). *Les Relations des Jésuites* records the same transformation, but portrays baptism as an act of violence when Père Le Jeune throws Marie into the river for not obeying her parents (xx 132 – 33). Aboriginal peoples did not punish their children, to Père Lejeune's great disapproval: he favoured a family structure of paternal authority (Karen Anderson).

27 "C'est pourtant une chose très difficile, pour ne pas dire impossible de les franciser ou civiliser. Nous en avons l'expérience plus que tout autre, et nous avons remarqué de cent de celles qui ont passé par nos mains à peine en avons nous civilisé une. Nous y trouvons de la docilité et de l'esprit, mais lors qu'on y pense le moins elles montent par dessus notre clôture et s'en vont courir dans les bois avec leurs parens, où elles trouvent plus de plaisir que dans tous les agrémmens de nos maisons Françoises. L'humeur Sauvage est faite de la sorte: elles ne peuvent être contraintes, si elles le sont,

elles deviennent mélancholiques, et la mélancholie les fait mal-
ades" (de L'Incarnation 1971, 809).

28 Significantly, the Ursulines did much of their teaching of Catholic
doctrine to aboriginal students with the help of images illustrating biblical narratives and the catechism.

29 "On ne peut exprimer les caresses qu'elles nous firent, ce qu'elles
ne font jamais à leurs mères naturelles" (1971, 97).

30 First narrated in the letter of 3 September 1640 to "A Lady of Rank"
as testimony to the Ursulines' accomplishments at the end of their
first year in Quebec, Marie Amiskouevan's story is related a year
later (24 August 1641) in thanks for the charity bestowed and to
"beseech" the convent in Tour yet again "[v]ous m'obligez infini-
ment de [la charité] que vous nous voulez faire" (1971, 123). Repeated
in *Les Relations des Jésuites*, this appeal for money is glossed with a
narrative of its transformative effect. The little house and plot of
land that will be provided for the seminarians will aid in their
assimilation to an agricultural mode of life. "If such piety touch
the hearts of many, the Savages will quit the forests to come to
us: and the parents will give their children to the seminary" (*The
Jesuits Relations* xx, 126 – 27).

31 The ultimate phase in this narrative of the providential work of
civilizing aboriginal girls involves Mère Marie de l'Incarnation's
translation by the Catholic church into the realm of the Beatified
for her miracles and visions, for her powers of eloquence in teaching and writing. An important document in the case for her Beati-
fication was a letter from descendants of the Hurons to whom she
had ministered.

32 "Nous étudions la langue Algonquine par préceptes et par méth-
ode, ce qui m'est très difficile. Notre Seigneur néanmoins me fait
la grâce d'y trouver de la facilité" (1971, 112).

33 Originally from the New Jersey/Pennsylvania area, the Lenni-
Lenapé or Delaware, an Algonkian-speaking people, came north
to Canada as United Empire Loyalists. The largest group settled
at Moraviantown in southwestern Ontario, with a smaller group,
to which Moses belongs, settling on the Six Nations reserve of

the Iroquois confederacy for whom they had previously served as "Peacemaker" to the Iroquois "Warrior." A minority among the Iroquoian-speaking Six Nations, the Delaware language now has few speakers. For this history see Hitakonanu'taxk and O'Meara.

34   Perhaps the most famous of those focusing on the male hero is the story "Where is the Voice Coming From?" in Rudy Wiebe's book of the same title (Toronto: McClelland and Stewart, 1974).

35   "Apple" is a pejorative term for the acculturated aboriginal.

36   These workshops had titles such as "Storytelling for the Stage" and "Re-establishing the Voice: Oral and Written Literature in Performance." In discussing features of aboriginal writing, Moses confirms the importance of Trickster in his plays as extending both verbal and visual possibilities: "The trickster is the embodiment of our sense of humour about the way we live our lives. It's a very central part of our attitude that things are funny even though horrible things happen." Performance and "the example of traditional Native story-telling ... has been for me a freeing thing. The pieces I write look like plays or poems or short stories, but I'm interested in how they sound and how they work when they're spoken" (Moses and Goldie xiv – xv).

37   "As you read the stories, as you listen to them it is expected that you make your own interpretations and draw your own conclusions as to the meanings within them. ... There is a strong Native belief in not interfering with others, but instead in giving them the chance to have their own thoughts, to make up their own minds and express themselves freely. Storytelling to us is a community experience, a coming together of people, to share in our past, our way of life, and in and of ourselves as a people" (Hitakonanu'laxk 41).

38   The Interlocutor sums up the seige where Almighty Voice is surrounded by the RCMP: "Imagine Red coats and wild Indians. What a spectacle! Where are my glasses?" (Moses 74). S/he is silent about the Ghost dance ritual, however.

39   "Ghost: *Awas kititin ni-nimihiton oma ota. (Go away. I'm dancing here.)* ... *Nahkee. Kawiya-(ekosi). Ponikawin poko ta kisisimoyan. (Stop. Let me alone. I have to finish my dance)*" (54 – 55).

40　"Ghost: *Piko ta-ta-wi kisisomoyan ekwo. (I have to go finish dancing now.)*"
　　"Interlocutor: *Patima, Kisse-Manitou-Wayou. (Goodbye, Almighty Voice)*"
　　(96).

Notes from the Cultural Field:
Canadian Literature from Identity to Commodity

1　Alice: "Would you please tell me which way I ought to go from
　　here?" The Cheshire Cat: "That depends on where you want to get
　　to" (Carroll 170). Carroll's paradoxes exemplify Gödel's incomplete-
　　ness theorem (Hofstadter).

2　This is distinct from the subject of the statement or *énoncé*. Ben-
　　veniste's theory posits the process of speaking or discourse with
　　all its contingency as a mediation.

3　The Association for Canadian and Quebec Literatures was founded
　　in 1972, the Association of Canadian Studies the following year.

4　Signatories of these advertisements are identified by profession
　　but not political affiliation, although some (Tom Flanagan, David
　　Frum, etc.) became identified with the Reform Party. The Cana-
　　dian Alliance for Trade and Job Opportunities was listed in small
　　letters as financial supporter of the ad, and published one of its
　　own on the facing page. Advocacy of free trade is presented not
　　as a politicized act but as a defence of the freedom of "economic
　　opportunities for our fellow citizens," claiming that nothing in
　　the agreement constitutes a "threat to any form of Canadian cul-
　　tural expression" (*The Globe and Mail* A6).

5　Addressing the issue of "The Projection of Canada Abroad," the
　　Massey-Lévesque *Report* notes the blurring of "information and
　　cultural exchanges between states." "Information about Canada as
　　a nation serves to stimulate our international trade, and to attract
　　tourists and desirable immigrants. ... Exchanges with other nations
　　in the fields of the arts and letters will help us to make our reason-
　　able contribution to civilized life ..." (253–54).

6　American domination of other sites of cultural consumption is
　　massive, as the following statistics reveal: 95 per cent of annual

screen time in cinemas, 90 per cent of drama on English-language television, and 79 per cent of the revenue for recorded music (Magder). Publishers have long earned most of their revenue as agents importing books.

A Literature in the Making:
Rewriting and the Dynamism of the Cultural Field

1   Koustas analyzed the percentage of their work translated, not the absolute number of translations for each author, finding that 90 per cent of Anne Hébert's work has been translated, 75 per cent of Gabrielle Roy's, and 60 per cent of Marie-Claire Blais'. Michel Tremblay, Hubert Aquin, André Major, and Jacques Poulin are the next most frequently translated authors, followed by Nicole Brossard, who with 40 per cent of her work translated, is the only writer of the younger feminist generation to appear in these statistics. Novels are the genre most translated (Tremblay's success on stage is an exception), which explains the ranking of Brossard, all of whose novels have been translated.

2   Academic criticism is not exempt from this privileging of the author-function since the deconstructive readings are frequently of single texts by authors who are acknowledged celebrities, as in the multiple rereadings of Atwood or the rush to publish essays on such rising international "stars" as Anne Michaels.

3   Elsewhere, in regard to feminist publishing as a "labour of love," I have developed a more extensive critique of the gendered difference of Bourdieu's concept of "disinterestedness": "Representation and Exchange: Feminist Periodicals and the production of Cultural Capital," *Tessera* 22 (1997): 104-21.

4   Significantly, criticism in the French media repeated Wilson's phrase and words of praise for Blais' novel without always citing him.

5   Between 1760 and 1960, only sixty books were translated between the two languages while, under the auspices of the Canada Council's translation programme, sixty-six books were translated between

376

English and French in 1974 alone. For the decade 1972–1981, the costs of some 452 translations were subsidized (Ellenwood 1983).

6   I refer here to J.L. Austin's understanding of the performative as an effect of any speech act which, taken up by an audience, for whom it felicitously (adequately) meets the conventions in a particular situation of address, has force as event. The audience is created in relation to this enunciative situation.

7   Even though literary translators in Canada are paid with funds from the Canada Council — an amount much below the market rate for political and commercial translation — they must first find a publisher who will accept their project and who will then make an application to the council for funding.

8   "Straight from the Heart" is the title of a review of the translation of *Children of My Heart* where Zonia Keywan notes: "The drama in Roy's book lies less in overt action than in emotions" (73). David Cobb expands in another review: "Her characters tend to be simple folk used as archetypes of all our endeavours to find happiness and wrest some sense out of chaos ... Her narratives are straightforward, uncomplex and celebrate the virtues of courage, loyalty, endurance and spiritual generosity" (10).

9   At this time the prize was awarded only to books published in English by the Canadian Authors' Association of which Roy, along with Ringuet and Germaine Guèvremont, became a member.

10 Paul Socken's bibliography of Roy was included in the first series in 1979; Delbert Russell's of Anne Hébert appeared in 1987; Irène Oore's of Marie-Claire Blais appeared in 1998.

11 Delbert Russell's *Anne Hébert* appeared in 1983, followed by M.G. Hesse's *Gabrielle Roy* in 1984, and us-based Mary Jane Green's *Marie-Claire Blais* in 1995.

12 Philip Stratford's *Marie-Claire Blais* was published in 1971; Phyllis Grosskurth's *Gabrielle Roy* in 1972. The three novelists were the subject of two critical essays in the pioneering anthology *Traditionalism, Nationalism and Feminism: Women Writers of Quebec*, edited in the us by Paula G. Lewis in 1985.

13 Gabrielle Roy wrote to William Arthur Deacon in 1954 that Quebec critics did not want to listen to her theme of "human love regardless of nationality, of religion, of tongue" (O'Neill-Karch 92).

14 David Lobdell, a translator who is gay, later translated *David Sterne* and *The Execution* for Oberon Press and Talonbooks.

15 Anthony Purdy makes a similar observation about *Kamouraska*, writing that it is not "postmodern" but "modernist in its composition and Victorian gothic in its subject matter and setting," combined "in a seamless work of art." "Clearly the formula is a winning one" (133). Hébert was the object of study for sixteen international academics listed in the 1996 *Répertoire International des Etudes canadiennes*, with ten working on Roy, thirteen on women writers of Quebec, but only four on Blais and three on Antoinine Maillet.

16 Subsequently, I arrived at the same conclusion in analysing Scott's and Miller's translations in comparison with those of Alan Brown (1976b).

17 See *Tessera* 6 (1989), "La traduction au féminin/Translating Women" and *Tessera* 3/*Canadian Fiction Magazine* 57 (1986), "Feminist Fiction Theory."

18 I have developed this analysis of feminist translation and the dialogue between a contemporary generation of English-Canadian and Quebec feminist writers more extensively in "La traduction comme réception" (2002).

RELATIONAL LOGICS:
OF LINGUISTICS AND OTHER TRANSACTIONS IN THE AMERICAS

1 Jonathan Hart (2001) analyses the ways French Jesuits and English protestants, through their accounts of contact with the Americas, waged a rhetorical campaign to emulate and supersede Spain's accomplishments in the New World, exploiting what became known as *La Leyenda Negra* of Spanish conquest to advance their claims to better governance.

2　More recent attention to disjunctive literary aesthetics and movements originating in the Americas, studies such as Omar Calebrese's
(1991) of the neo-baroque and Stephen Slemon's (1995) of the counter
hegemonic, postcolonialist force of magic realism have not yet had
an impact on the periodization of comparative literature.

3　In March 2005, a conference, Quelles institutions pour les
Amériques/What Institutions for the Americas?, was held at Laval
University. Organized by the Centre d'études interaméricaines, the
event was one among many such initiatives in recent years.

4　Interest in relations with other literatures of the Americas has been
confined primarily to studies of writing in a single language, as
in Sherrill Grace's (1989) examination of expressionism in English-
Canadian and American literatures, and Maximilien Laroche's
(1970) and Max Dorsinville's (1974) analyses of the impact of colonialism on Haitian and Quebec literatures.

5　de Andrade changed the name from Tupinamba to Tapanhuma to
introduce the notion of a Black indigenous group and thus write
himself into the founding myths as a Black Brazilian.

WORKS CITED

Allen, Paula Gunn. *Sacred Hoop: Recovering the Feminine in American Indian Traditions.* Boston: Beacon, 1986.

Althusser, L. "Ideology and Ideological State Apparatuses." *Lenin and Philosophy.* Trans. Ben Brewster. London: New Left Books, 1971. 127–88.

Anderson, Benedict. *Imagined Communities: Reflections on the Origin and Spread of Nationalism.* London: Verso, 1991.

Anderson, Karen. *Chain Her By One Foot: The Subjugation of Native Women in Seventeenth-Century New France.* New York: Routledge, 1991.

Andrès, Bernard. *Coerçao e Subversao, O Quebec e a América Latina: Ensaio sobre a constituiçao das letras.* Trans. Pascal Lelarge. Ed. Porto Alegre. Universidade/UFRGS, 1999.

Angus, Ian. *A Border Within: National Identity, Cultural Plurality, and Wilderness.* Montreal: McGill-Queen's UP, 1997.

Anon. "Les femmes écrivains du Québec fascinent les anglo-canadiens." Rev. of *The Garden and the Cage. La Tribune,* 14 February 1979, 52.

Anzaldua, Gloria. *Borderlands/ La Frontera: The New Mestiza.* San Francisco: Spinsters/ Sister Lute, 1987.

Armatage, Kay, Kass Banning, Brenda Longfellow, and Janine Marchessault, eds. *Gendering the Nation: Canadian Women's Cinema.* Toronto: U of Toronto P, 1999.

Armstrong, Jeannette. *Slash.* Penticton: Theytus, 1985.

——, Maria Campbell, and Beth Cuthand. "Writing from a Native Woman's Perspective." Audiotape from *Women and Words.* Vancouver: July 1983.

——, and Douglas Cardinal. *The Native Creative Process.* Penticton: Theytus, 1991.

Ashcroft, Bill, Gareth Griffiths, and Helen Tiffin. *The Empire Writes Back: Theory and Practice in Post-Colonial Literatures.* London: Routledge, 1989.

Atwood, Margaret. *Surfacing.* Toronto: McClelland & Stewart, 1972.

——. "A Night in the Royal Ontario Museum." *Poets of Contemporary Canada.* Ed. Eli Mandel. Toronto: McClelland & Stewart, 1972. 96–97.

——. *Survival: A Thematic Guide to Canadian Literature.* Toronto: Anansi, 1972.

Austin, J.L. *How To Do Things With Words.* Cambridge: Harvard UP, 1962.

Aziz, Nurjehan, ed. *Floating the Borders: New Contexts in Canadian Criticism.* Toronto: TSAR, 1999.

Bachelard, Gaston. *The Poetics of Space.* Trans. Maria Jolas. Boston: Beacon, 1969.

Baktin, M.M. and P.M. Medvedev. *The Formal Method of Literary Scholarship.* Cambridge, Mass.: Harvard UP, 1985.

Bakhtin, Mikhail. *Esthétique et théorie du roman.* Paris: Gallimard, 1978.

——. *The Dialogic Imagination.* Ed. Michael Holquist. Trans. Caryl Emerson and Michael Holquist. Austin: U of Texas P, 1981.

——. *Problems of Dostoevsky's Poetics.* Ed. and trans. Caryl Emerson. Minneapolis: U of Minnesota P, 1984.

———— / Pavel Medvedev. *The Formal Method in Literary Scholarship: A Critical Introduction to Sociological Poetics.* Trans. Albert S. Wehrle. Cambridge, Mass.:Harvard UP, 1985.

Bannerji, Himani, Prahba Khosla, et al. "We Appear Silent to People Who Are Deaf to What We Say." *Fireweed* 16 (1983): 8 – 17.

Barchilon, Jacques. *Le conte merveilleux français de 1619 à 1719: Cent ans de féerie de poésies ignorées de l'histoire littéraire.* Paris: Champion, 1975.

Barthes, Roland. *Le degré zéro de l'écriture.* Paris: Gonthier, 1964.

————. *Mythologies.* Trans. Annette Lavers. London: Paladin, 1973.

————. *The Pleasure of the Text.* Trans. Richard Miller. New York: Wang & Hill, 1975.

Bassnett, Susan. *Comparative Literature: A Critical Introduction.* Oxford: Blackwell, 1993.

Bassnett, Susan, and André Lefevere. *Translation, History and Culture.* London: Pinter, 1990.

Beaudet, Marie-Andrée. *L'ironie de la forme: Essai sur "L'élan d'Amérique" d'André Langevin.* Montréal: Pierre Tisseyre, 1985.

————. *Langue et littérature au Québec 1895 – 1914.* Montreal : L'Hexagone, 1991.

Belleau, André. "Action et enracinement." *Liberté* 3 (Nov. 1961): 691 – 97.

————. *Le romancier fictif. Essai sur la représentation de l'écrivain dans le roman québécois.* Sillery: P de l'Université du Québec, 1980.

————. "La démarche sociocritique au Québec." *Voix et images* 8.2 (1983): 299 – 309.

————. *Surprendre les voix.* Montréal: Boreal, 1986.

————. *Langue et littérature au Québec 1895 – 1914.* Montréal: l'Hexagone, 1991.

Belleau, André, Manon Brunet, and Greg M. Nielsen, eds. *Sociologies de la littérature.* Special issue of *Études françaises* 19.3 (1984).

Belmore, Rebecca. "*Ihkewhak Ka-ayamihwat:* Means Women Who are Speaking." *Parallelogramme* 14.4 (Spring 1989): 10 – 11.

Belsey, Catherine. *Critical Practice.* London: Methuen, 1980.

Benjamin, Andrew. *Translation and the Nature of Philosophy: A New Theory of Words.* London: Routledge, 1989.

Benjamin, Walter. *Illuminations: Essays and Reflections.* Ed. Hannah Arendt. Trans. Harry Zohn. New York: Schocken, 1969.

Benveniste, Emile. *Problems in General Linguistics.* Trans. Mary E. Meek. Coral Gables: U of Miami P, 1971.

Bernabé, Jean, Patrick Chamoiseau, and Raphael Confiant. *Éloge de la créolité/In Praise of Creoleness.* Paris: Gallimard, 1993.

Bernd, Zila. "Brésil/Québec: la difficile inclusion de la parole de l'autre." *Confluences littéraires: Brésil-Québec, les bases d'une comparaison.* Eds. Michel Peterson and Zila Bernd. Montréal: Les Éditions Balzac, 1992. 97 – 109.

Bersianik, Louky. *L'euguélionne.* Montréal: La Presse, 1975.

————. *The Euguélionne.* Trans. Gerry Denis, Alison Hewitt, Donna Murray, and Martha O'Brien. Victoria: Porcépic, 1981.

Bessière, Jean. *Dire le littéraire: points de vue théoriques.* Liège: Ed. Pierre Mardaga, 1990.

Bhabha, Homi, ed. *Nation and Narration.* London: Routledge, 1990.

———. *The Location of Culture.* New York and London: Routledge, 1994.

Birney, Earle. "Can. Lit." *Poetry of Mid-Century.* Ed. Milton Wilson. Toronto: McClelland & Stewart, 1964. 37.

Bishop, Neil. "L'évolution de la critique hébertienne." *Critique et littérature québécoise.* Eds. Annette Hayward and Agnes Whitfield. Montréal: Triptyque, 1990.

Blanchot, Maurice. *L'Espace littéraire.* Paris: Gallimard, 1968.

Blodgett, E.D. "Intertextual Designs in Hugh MacLennan's *The Watch that Ends the Night.*" *Canadian Review of Comparative Literature* 5 (1978): 280–88.

———. *Configurations: Essays on the Canadian Literatures.* Toronto: ECW, 1982.

———. "How Do You Say 'Gabrielle Roy'?" In *Translation in Canadian Literature.* Ed. Camille LaBossière. Ottawa: U of Ottawa P, 1983. 13–34.

Bök, Christian. "Nor the Fun Tension: Steve McCaffery and his Critical 'Paradoxy.'" *Open Letter* 8th ser. 3 (Spring 1992): 90–103.

Bonenfant, Joseph, Janine Boynard-Frot, Richard Giguère, and Antoine Sirois. *A l'ombre de DesRochers: Le mouvement littéraire des cantons de l'est, 1925–1950.* Sherbrooke: La Tribune and PU de Sherbrooke, 1985.

Bonnycastle, Stephen. "The Power of *The Watch that Ends the Night.*" *Journal of Canadian Studies* 14.4 (1979–1980): 76–89.

Borges, Jorge. *Labyrinths.* Eds. D.A. Yates and J.E. Irby. New York: Grove, 1964.

———. *Discussion.* Paris: Gallimard, 1966.

Bosco, Monique. *Babel-Opéra.* Montréal: Éditions Trois, 1989.

Bourdieu, Pierre. "Le marché des biens symboliques." *L'année sociologique* 22 (1971): 49–126.

———. *The Field of Cultural Production.* Ed. Randal Johnson. Oxford: Polity, 1993.

Brand, Dionne. *In Another Place, Not Here.* Toronto: Knopf, 1996.

———. *At the Full and Change of the Moon.* Toronto: Knopf, 1999.

———. *A Map to the Door of No Return.* Toronto: Knopf, 2001.

Brisset, Annie. *Sociocritique de la traduction: théâtre et alterité au Québec 1968–1988.* Montréal: Le Préambule, 1990.

Brochu, André, and Gilles Marcotte. *La littérature et le reste.* Montréal: Quinze, 1980.

Brooks, Cleanth. "The Heresy of Paraphrase." *The Well-Wrought Urn: Studies in the Structure of Poetry.* New York: Perry Yoder Library, University Paperbacks, 1968. 192–214.

Brossard, Nicole. *L'amèr: Ou, le chapitre effrité.* Montréal: Quinze, 1975a.

———. "Préliminaires." *La Nouvelle barre du jour* 50 (1975b): 6–9.

———. "E muet mutant." *La Nouvelle barre du jour* 50 (1975c): 10–27. Trans. M.L. Taylor. *Ellipse* 23–24 (1979): 45–63.

———. *These Our Mothers: Or, The Disintegrating Chapter.* Trans. Barbara Godard. Toronto: Coach House, 1983.

————. *Le désert mauve.* Montréal: l'Hexagone, 1987.

Brown, Russell. "Critic, Culture, Text: Beyond Thematics." *Essays on Canadian Writing* 11 (1978): 151–84.

Brumble, H. David. *American Indian Autobiography.* Berkeley: u of California P, 1988.

Calabrese, Omar. *Caos e bellezza: Immagini del neobarocco.* Milan: Domus Academy, 1991.

Callaghan, Barry. "An Interview with Marie-Claire Blais." *Tamarack* 37 (1965): 29–34.

Cameron, Barry. "Criteria of Evaluation in the Canadian Novel: A Response to Robert Kroetsch." *Essays on Canadian Writing* 20 (1980–1981): 19–31.

————. "English Critical Discourse in/on Canada." *Studies on Canadian Literature: Introductory and Critical Essays.* Ed. Arnold E. Davidson. New York: MLA, 1990. 124–43.

Cameron, Barry, and Michael Dixon. "Mandatory Subversive Manifesto: Canadian Criticism vs. Literary Criticism." *Minus Canadian: Penultimate Essays on Literature.* Eds. Cameron and Dixon. Special issue of *Studies in Canadian Literature* 2 (1977): 137–45.

Canada. *Report of the Royal Commission on National Development in the Arts, Letters, and Sciences.* Ottawa: King's Printer, 1951.

————. *Report of the Royal Commission on Bilingualism and Biculturalism.* I – VI. Ottawa: Queen's Printer, 1967–1972.

Canada Council. *Program Information, Book Publishing Support 1996.* Ottawa: Canada Council, 1996.

Canada in the World/Le Canada dans le monde. Ottawa: Queen's Printer, 1995.

Carroll, Lewis. *Alice's Adventures in Wonderland/Les aventures d'Alice au pays des merveilles.* Trans. Henri Parisot. Paris: Aubier-Flammarion, 1970.

Cartier, Jacques. *A Shorte and briefe narration of the two Nauigations and Discoueries to the Northwest partes calle Newe France* (1580). Trans. Florio. The English Experience No. 718. Amsterdam and Norwood, NJ: Walter J. Johnson and Theatrum Orbis Terrarum, 1975.

————. *Relations: Édition critique.* (1545) Ed. Michel Bideaux. Montréal: P de l'Université de Montréal, 1986.

————. *The Voyages of Jacques Cartier.* Trans. H.P. Biggar. Intro. Ramsay Cook. Toronto: u of Toronto P, 1993.

Castoriadis, Cornelius. *The Imaginary Institution of Society.* Trans. Kathleen Blamey. Cambridge: MIT, 1987.

Chamberland, Roger. *Claude Gauvreau: La libération du regard.* Québec: CRELIQ, 1986.

Cherniak, Leah, Ann-Marie MacDonald, and Martha Ross. *The Attic, The Pearls, and Three Fine Girls.* Toronto: Playwrights Union, 1996.

Cheyfitz, Eric. *The Poetics of Imperialism: Translation and Colonization from The Tempest to Tarzan.* New York: Oxford UP, 1991.

Cixous, Hélène. "Textes de l'imprévisible: Grâce à." *Les nouvelles littéraires* 2534 (26 May 1976): 18–19.

Clark, David L. "Disfiguring the Post-Modern." Rev. of *Reading Canadian Reading* by Frank Davey. *Canadian Poetry* 26 (1990): 75–86.

Cobb, David. "'I have, I think, a grateful heart.'" *The Canadian, Toronto Star*, 1 May 1976: 10–13.

Cohn-Sfetcu, Ofelia. "To Live in Abundance of Life: A Study of Time in Five Canadian Authors." Diss. McMaster u. 1980.

Contemporary Verse 2. (2000). "Edge/wise: Canadian women's writing at century's end." Part 1: 22, 4 (Spring); Part 2: 23.1 (Summer).

Conway, Alison. "Ethnic Writing and Canadian literary Criticism." *Open Letter* 7th ser. no. 5 (Summer 1989): 52–66.

Conway, Sheelagh. "Women Writers in Canada: 'A Bleak Picture'." *The Globe and Mail*, 26 May 1989: A7

Cook, David. *Northrop Frye: A Vision of the New World*. Montreal: New World Perspectives, 1985.

Corriveau, Hugues, and Normand de Bellefeuille. *A double sens: Échanges sur quelques pratiques modernes*. Montréal: Herbes Rouges, 1986.

Creelman, David. "Robert Kroetsch: Criticism in the Middle Ground. " *Studies in Canadian Literature*. 16.1 (1991) : 63–81.

Crémazie, Octave. *Oeuvres*. ed. Odette Condamine 2 vols. Ottawa: P de l'Université d'Ottawa, 1972–1976. 90–91.

Culler, Jonathan. *Structuralist Poetics*. London: Routledge & Kegan Paul, 1975.

Czarnecki, Mark. "Bloody Cloud of Words." *Maclean's*, 24 March 1980: 56.

Dansereau, Estelle. "Convergence/Éclatement: l'immigrant au risque de la perte de soi dans la nouvelle 'Ou iras-tu Sam Lee Wong?' de Gabrielle Roy." *Canadian Literature* 127 (1990): 94–109.

Darling, Michael. "A Hard Twayne's Gonna Fall." Rev. of *John Metcalf* by Barry Cameron. *Essays on Canadian Writing* 37 (Spring 1989): 172–84.

Davey, Frank. "Surviving the Paraphrase." *Canadian Literature* 70 (1976). Rpt. *Surviving the Paraphrase*. Winnipeg: Turnstone, 1983. 1–12.

———. "Canadian Canons." *Critical Inquiry* 16 (1990): 672–81.

———. *Post-National Arguments: The Politics of the Anglophone Canadian Novel Since 1967*. Toronto: u of Toronto P, 1993.

———. "AND Quebec: Canadian Literature and the Quebec Question." *Canadian Poetry* 40 (1997): 6–26.

Deacon, William Arthur. Rev. of *Bonheur d'occasion*. *The Globe and Mail*, 13 December 1947:13.

de Andrade, Mario. *Macunaíma o Herói sem nenhum caráter*. Sao Paulo: Livraria Martins, 1928.

De Andrade, Oswald. "Manifesto antropófago." *Revista de Antropofagia* 1 (1928) 3, 7.

de Campos, Augusto. "Revistas Re-Vistas: Os Antropófagos." *Revista de Antropofagia 1928–1929*. Sao Paulo: Cia Lithographica Ypiranga, 1976. N.p.

———, Decio Pignatari, and Haroldo de Campos. "Plano-Piloto Para Poesia Concreta/

Pilot Plan for Concrete Poetry." *Concrete Poetry: A World View*. Ed. Mary Ellen Solt. Bloomington: Indiana UP, 1968. 70 – 72.

de Campos, Haroldo. "The Open Work of Art." *Dispositio* 6 nos. 17 – 18 (1981): 5 – 8.

———. "Mephistofaustian Transluciferation: Contribution to the semiotics of poetic translation." *Dispositio* 7 nos. 19 – 20 (1982): 181 – 87.

———. *Metalinguagem & Outras Metas: Ensaios de teoria e crítica literária*. 4th ed. Sao Paulo: Editora Perspectiva, 1992.

———. "Barroco-ludisme deleuzien." *Gilles Deleuze: Une vie philosophique*. Ed. Eric Alliez. Trans. Ilda dos Santos. Le Plessis-Robinson: Institut Synthélabo, 1998. 545 – 53.

———. *Junijornado do Sahor Dom Flor: ediçao commemorativa do Bloomsday 2002*. Sao Paulo: Olavobras, 2002.

de Campos, Haroldo, and Octavio Paz. *Transblanco: em torno a Blanco de Octavio Paz*. Sao Paulo: Editora Siciliano, 1994.

de Grandpré, Chantal. "La canadianisation de la littérature québécoise: le cas Aquin." *Liberté* 27, 3 (1985): 50 – 59.

de Lauretis, Teresa. *Technologies of Gender: Essays on Theory, Film and Fiction*. Bloomington: Indiana UP, 1987.

Deleuze, Gilles, and Félix Guattari. *Kafka: Pour une littérature mineure*. Paris: Minuit, 1975.

———. *Kafka: Toward a Minor Literature*. 1975. Trans. Dana Polan. Minneapolis: U of Minnesota P, 1986.

———. *A Thousand Plateaus: Capitalism and Schizophrenia*. Trans. and Foreword Brian Massumi. Minneapolis and London: U of Minnesota P, 1987.

de l'Incarnation, Mère Marie. *Word From New France: The Selected Letters of Marie de l'Incarnation*. Ed. and trans. Joyce Marshall. Toronto: Oxford, 1967.

———. *Correspondance*. (1681) Ed. Dom Guy Oury. Solesmes: Abbaye Saint-Pierre, 1971.

———. "La Relation de 1654." In *Écrits spirituels et historiques*. Vol. ii. Ed. Dom Albert Jamet. Québec: Les Ursulines, 1985.

Delisle, Jean. "Les interprêts sous le régime français." Mémoire de Maîtrise. U de Montréal, 1975.

———. *La traduction au Canada 1534 – 1984*. Ottawa: P de l'Université d'Ottawa, 1987.

de Man, Paul. "The Resistance to Theory." *Yale French Studies* 63 (1982): 3 – 21.

———. *Allegories of Reading: Figural Language in Rousseau, Nietzsche, Rilke, and Proust*. New Haven, CT: Yale UP, 1982.

———. "The Rhetoric of Temporality." *Blindness and Insight: Essays in the Rhetoric of Contemporary Criticism*. 2nd. ed. Minneapolis: U of Minnesota P, 1983. 187 – 228.

Demers, Jeanne, and Line McMurray. *L'enjeu du manifeste/Le manifeste en jeu*. Longeuil: Préambule, 1986.

Derrida, Jacques. "La structure, le signe, et le jeu dans le discours des sciences humaines." *L'Écriture et la différence*. Paris: Seuil, 1967. 409 – 28.

———. "White Mythology: Metaphor in the Text of Philosophy." *Margins of Philosophy*. Trans. Alan Bass. Chicago: U of Chicago P, 1982. 207 – 71.

————. *The Truth in Painting.* Trans. Geoffrey Bennington and Ian McLeod. Chicago: u of Chicago P, 1987.

Deslandres, Dominique. "L'éducation des Amérindiennes d'après la correspondance de Marie Guyart de l'Incarnation." *Studies in Religion/Sciences réligieuses* 16, 1 (1987): 91–110.

Dickason, Olive. *Canada's First Nations: A History of Founding Peoples from Earliest Times.* Toronto: McClelland & Stewart, 1992.

Dickinson, Peter. *Here is Queer: Nationalisms, Sexualities and the Literatures of Canada.* Toronto: u of Toronto P, 1999.

Dirlik, Arif. *The Postcolonial Aura: Third World Criticism in the Age of Global Capitalism.* Boulder: Westview, 1997.

Djwa, Sandra. In conversation. October 1991.

Dorsinville, Max. *Caliban without Prospero: Essay on Quebec and Black Literature.* Erin: Porcépic, 1974.

Dossier comparatiste Québec-Amérique Latine. Special issue of *Voix et images,* 12.1 (1986).

Douglas, Mary. *Purity and Danger: An Analysis of Concepts of Pollution and Taboo.* New York: Praeger, 1966.

Dowling, Kevin. "The Cultural Industries Policy Apparatus." *The Cultural Industries in Canada.* Ed. Michael Dorland. Toronto: Lorimer, 1996. 328–46.

Druick, Zoe. "Narratives of Citizenship: Governmentality and the National Film Board." Unpublished PHD diss., York u, 1999.

Dubois, Jacques. *Institution de la littérature.* Paris: Nathan-Labor, 1978.

————. Introduction. "L'institution littéraire II." *Littérature* 44 (1981): 3–7.

Dudek, Louis. "Anne Hébert Translated: Some Thoughts on Dual Literature in Canada." *The Montreal Gazette,* 29 April 1967: 19.

Dumont, Fernand, and Jean-Charles Falardeau, eds. *Littérature et société canadiennes-françaises.* Quebec: PU Laval, 1985.

Dumont, Marilyn. *A Really Good Brown Girl.* London: Brick, 1996.

Duncan, Dorothy. "Le Triomphe de Gabrielle." *Maclean's,* 15 April 1947: 54.

Dupré, Louise. *La memoria.* Montréal: XYZ, 1996.

Dybikowski, Ann, Victoria Freeman, Daphne Marlatt, Barbara Pulling, and Betsy Warland, eds. *In the Feminine: Women and Words/Les femmes et les mots.* Edmonton: Longspoon, 1985.

Eagleton, Terry. "The Rise of English." *Literary Theory: An Introduction.* Oxford: Basil Blackwell, 1983. 17–53.

Eco, Umberto. *L'oeuvre ouvert.* Paris: Seuil, 1965.

————. *The Role of the Reader.* Bloomington: Indiana UP, 1979.

Elder, Jo-Anne. "An Economy of Words." *Essays in Canadian Writing* 50 (1993): 62–74.

Ellenwood, Ray. "Some Actualities of Literary Translation." *Translation in Canadian Literature.* Ed. Camille LaBossière. Ottawa: u of Ottawa P, 1983. 61–71.

————. "Translating 'québécisme' in Jacques Ferron's *Le Ciel du Québec.*" *Culture in Transit: Translating the Literature of Quebec.* Ed. Sherry Simon. Montréal: Véhicule, 1995. 101–109.

Emond, Maurice. *La femme à la fenêtre:l'univers symbolique d'Anne Hébert dans les* Chambres de Bois, Kamouraska *et les* Enfants du Sabbat. Québec: ᴘ de l'Université Laval, 1984.

Éthier-Blais, Jean. *Signets.* 3 vols. Montréal: Cercle du Livre de France, 1965 – 1973.

———. "Quand on démonte le rouage de la traduction." *Le Devoir,* 17 October 1970: 16.

———. "Our Pioneers in Criticism." *Contemporary Québec Criticism.* Ed. and trans. Larry Shouldice. Toronto: ᴜ of Toronto ᴘ, 1979. 21 – 36.

Evan-Zohar, Itamar. *Papers in Historical Poetics.* Tel Aviv: The Porter Institute for Poetics and Semiotics, 1978.

Fagan, Drew. "It's the Year 2025. There is no U.S. Border. Has Canada Become the 51st state?" *The Globe and Mail.* March 16, 2002. ꜰ1, ꜰ8.

Fanon, Frantz. "Sur la culture nationale." *Les damnés de la terre.* 2nd ed. Paris: Maspero, 1968. 141 – 65.

Fee, Margery. "Canadian Literature and English Studies in the Canadian University." *Essays on Canadian Writing* 48 (1992): 20 – 40.

Feral, Josette. "Performance et théâtralité: le sujet démystifié." *Théâtralité, écriture, mise en scène.* Montréal: ʜᴍʜ, 1985. 126 – 40.

Ferron, Jacques. "Contes du pays incertain." *Contes.* Montréal: ʜᴍʜ, 1968.

Fischman, Sheila. "Blais." *The Montreal Star,* February 1978: ʙ6.

Forsyth, Donald W. "Beginnings of Brazilian Anthropology: Jesuits and Tupinamba Cannibalism." *Journal of Anthropological Research* 39, 2 (1983): 147 – 78.

Forsyth, Louise. "La critique au féminin: Vers de nouveaux lieux communs." *Parlons-en/Talking Together.* Montreal: Simone de Beauvoir Institute, 1981. 95 – 102.

Foucault, Michel. *L'ordre du discours.* Paris: Gallimard, 1971.

———. *Power/Knowledge: Selected Interviews and Other Writings, 1972 – 1977.* Ed. Colin Gordon. Trans. Colin Gordon et al. New York: Pantheon, 1980.

———. "The Subject and Power." *Michel Foucault: Beyond Structuralism and Hermeneutics.* Eds. H.L. Dreyfus and P. Rabinow. Sussex: Harvester, 1982. 208 – 26.

———. "Governmentality." *The Foucault Effect: Studies in Governmentality.* Eds. Graham Burchell, Colin Gordon, and Peter Miller. Chicago: ᴜ of Chicago ᴘ, 1991. 87 – 104.

Freeman, Victoria. "Rights on Paper: An Interview." *Fuse,* March – April 1988: 36 – 38.

French, William. "Quebec Gothic." *The Globe and Mail,* 17 May 1973: 15.

Frye, Northrop. *Anatomy of Criticism.* Princeton: Princeton ᴜᴘ, 1957.

———. "Conclusion." (1965) *Literary History of Canada.* 2nd. ed. Vol. ɪɪ and vol. ɪɪɪ. Ed. Carl F. Klinck. Toronto: ᴜ of Toronto ᴘ, 1976. 333 – 61.

Gagnon, Madeleine. "La femme et le langage: Sa fonction comme parole en son manque." *La Barre du jour* 50 (1975): 45 – 57.

———."La femme et l'écriture." Actes de la rencontre québécoise internationale des Écrivains. *Liberté* 18.4 – 5 (1976): 249 – 54.

Gallays, François. "Gabrielle Roy et ses deux 'soeurs' Marie-Claire Blais et Anne Hébert." *Colloque International Gabrielle Roy.* Ed. André Fauchon. Saint-Boniface: ᴘ Universitaires de Saint-Boniface, 1996. 565 – 74.

Galloway, Priscilla. "Sexism and the Senior English Curriculum in Ontario Secondary – 3 Schools." Unpublished diss., u of Toronto, 1977.

Garebian, Keith. "Exploring the Underbelly of the Soul." *The Montreal Star*, 26 May
1979: E3.

———. "Hybrid Curiosity." *Essays on Canadian Writing* 37 (Spring 1989): 169 – 71.

Gauvin, Lise. *Langagement: L'écrivain et la langue au Québec*. Montréal: Boréal, 2000.

Gauvin, Lise, and Jacques Dubois. "Table ronde: l'Institution littéraire." *Lectures
européennes de la littérature québécoise*. Montréal: Leméac, 1982. 274 – 310.

Gauvin, Lise, and Jean-Marie Klinkenberg. *Trajectoires: Littérature et institutions au
Québec et en Belgique francophone*. Montréal: PU de Montreal, 1985.

Gauvin, Lise, and Laurent Mailhot. *Guide culturel du Québec*. Montréal: Boréal,
1982.

Gellner, Ernest. *Nations and Nationalism*. Oxford: Blackwell, 1983.

Genette, Gérard. "Critique et poetique." *Figures III*. Paris: Seuil, 1972.

Gérin-Lajoie, Antoine. *Jean Rivard*. (1862) Montréal: J.B. Rolland, 1874.

Giroux, Robert, and Hélène Dame, eds. *Sémiotique de la poésie québécoise*. Cahiers d'études littéraires 5. Sherbrooke: Département de français, u de Sherbrooke, 1981.

Giroux, Robert, and Jean-Marc Lemelin. *Le spectacle de la littérature*. Montréal:
Triptyque, 1984.

Glissant, Edouard. *Poétique de la relation*. Paris: Gallimard, 1990.

———. *Introduction à une poétique du Divers*. Montréal: PU de Montréal, 1995.

The Globe and Mail, 19 Nov. 1988: A4, A6.

[Godard], Barbara Thompson. "The City of Montréal in the English and French-
Canadian Novel, 1945 – 1965." Unpublished MA thesis, u de Montréal, 1967.

Godard, Barbara. "God's Country: L'homme et la terre dans le roman des deux
Canada." Diss. of u de Bordeaux, 1971.

———. "Man and the Land in the Novel of the Two Canadas." *Revue de littérature
comparée* 47, 2 (1973): 225 – 42.

———. "The Geography of Separatism." *Laurentian University Review* 9, 1 (1976a): 33 – 50.

———. Review of Anne Hébert's *Poems*. *Waves* 4, 2 (Winter 1976b): 13 – 17.

———. "Between One Cliché and Another: Language in *The Double Hook*." *Studies
in Canadian Literature* 4, 2 (Summer 1978): 114 – 65.

———. "The Avant-garde in Canada: *Open Letter* and *La Barre du jour*." *Ellipse* (1979):
23 – 24, 98 – 113.

———. "The Oral Tradition and National Literatures." *Comparison* 12 (Spring 1981):
15 – 31.

———. "*La nouvelle barre du jour*: Vers une poétique féministe." *Fémininité, subversion écriture*. Eds. Suzanne Lamy and Irene Pages. Montréal: Remue-Ménage,
1983a. 195 – 205.

———. "Tessera, Texere: Feminist Intertextuality." ACUTE Conference, Guelph,
June 1983b.

———. "Other Fictions: Robert Kroetsch's Criticism." *Open Letter* 5th ser. 8 – 9
(May 1984a): 5 – 21.

——. "Translating and Sexual Difference." *Resources for Feminist Research* 13, 3 (1984b): 13–16.

——. "World of Wonders: Robertson Davies' Carnival." *Essays on Canadian Writing* 30 (1984–1985): 239–86.

——. "Flying away with Language." *Lesbian Triptych*. Jovette Marchessault. Toronto: Women's P, 1985a. 9–28.

——. "Reading Difference: Views of/from Québec." *Borderlines* 2 (1985b): 38–41.

——. "Epi(pro)logue: In Pursuit of the Long Poem." *Open Letter* 6th ser. 2–3 (Summer–Fall 1985c): 301–35.

——. "Mapmaking: A Survey of Feminist Criticism." *Gynocritics/Gynocritiques: Feminist Approaches to Canadian and Québec Women's Writing*. Ed. Barbara Godard. Toronto: ECW, 1987a. 1–30.

——. "The Canadian Discourse as the Discourse of the Other. Response to Sherry Simon." *A/part: Papers from the 1984 Ottawa Conference on Language, Culture and Identity in Canada*. Ed. G.M. Bumstead. Supplement No. 1. *Canadian Literature* (I May 1987b): 130–37.

——. "Introduction." *Gynocritics/ Gynocritiques: Feminist Approaches to Canadian and Québec Women's Writing*. Toronto: ECW, 1987c. i–xi.

——. "Translation in the Service of the Nation." Paper presented to the Gerstein Seminar, "Translation Studies in Canada: Institutions, Discourses, Practices, Texts." Glendon College, York u, March 1988.

——. "Ri/post: Postmodernism and Feminism in Québec." *Québec Studies* 9 (Autumn 1989): 131–43.

——. "Critical Discourse in/on Québec." *Studies on Canadian Literature: Essays Introductory and Critical*. Ed. Arnold E. Davidson. New York: MLA, 1990a. 271–95.

——. "Reappropriation as Translation." *Canadian Theatre Review* 64 (1990b): 22–31.

——. "The Discourse of the Other: Canadian Literature and the Question of Ethnicity." *The Massachusetts Review*, XXXI, 1–2 (1990c): 153–84.

——. "New Critical Fictions: Phenomenology, Structuralism, Post-Structuralism, Feminism." *100 Years of Critical Solitudes: Canadian and Québécois Criticism from the 1880s to the 1980s*. Ed. Caroline Bayard. Toronto: ECW, 1992a. 248–83.

——. "Can/Con?" Review of Stephen Scobie's *Signature Event Context*. *Open Letter*, 8th ser. (Spring 1992b): 104–07.

——. "Writing on the Wall." Culture Slash Nation. *Border/lines*. 38/39 (1995): 98–103.

——. "Feminist Speculations on Value: Culture in an Age of Downsizing." *Ghosts in the Machine: Women and Cultural Policy in Canada and Australia*. Eds. Alison Beale and Annette Van Den Bosch. Toronto/Melbourne: Garamond P, 1998. 43–78.

——. "Privatizing the Public: Notes on the Ontario Culture Wars." *Fuse* 22, 3 (1999a): 27–33.

——. "Une littérature en devenir. La ré-écriture textuelle et le dynamisme du champ littéraire: Les écrivaines québécoises au Canada anglais." *Voix et images* 72 (1999b), 495–527.

———. "La traduction comme reception: Les Écrivaines québécois au Canada anglais." TTR 15.1 (2002): 65 – 101.

———. *Translation Studies in Canada: Institutions, Discourses, Practices, Texts.* Ed. Barbara Godard. Toronto: Éditions du GREF. Forthcoming 2008.

Godzich, Wlad. "Introduction." *The Formal Method in Literary Scholarship*, M.M. Bakhtin and P.M. Medvedev. Cambridge: Harvard UP, 1978. XV – XXIX.

———. "Préface: La littérature manifeste." *L'enjeu du manifeste/Le manifeste en jeu.* Jeanne Demers and Line McMurray. Longueuil: Préambule, 1986. 7 – 19.

———. "Brésil-Québec: à la recherche du *tertium comparationis.*" *Confluences littéraires: Brésil-Québec, les bases d'une comparison.* Eds. Michel Peterson and Zila Bernd. Montréal: Les Éditions Balzac, 1992. 41 – 56.

Gooderham, Kent. *I Am an Indian.* Toronto: J. M. Dent, 1969.

Grace, Sherrill. *Regression and Apocalypse: Studies in North American Literary Expressionism.* Toronto: U of Toronto P, 1989.

———. "Structuring Violence: The Ethics of Linguistics in *The Temptations of Big Bear.*" *Canadian Literature* 104 (1985): 7 – 22.

Gramsci, Antonio. "Notes on Language." Trans. Stephen Mansfield. *Telos* 59 (1984): 127 – 50.

Green, Alma/Forbidden Voice. *Tales of the Mohawks.* Toronto: J.M. Dent, 1975.

Green, Mary Jane. "Les romancières québécoises devant la critique universitaire aux États-Unis." *Oeuvres et critiques* 14, 1 (1989): 115 – 21.

Greene, Rayna. "The Pochahantas Perplex: The Image of Indian Women in American Culture." *Sweetgrass* 1 (July/August 1984): 17 – 23.

Hadjukowsi-Ahmed, Maroussia. "Le Carnavalesque dans le roman québécois." Thèse de doctorat 3e cycle. U de Paris-Sorbonne, 1979.

Hakluyt, Richard. *Discourse of Western Planting.* London: 1584.

Hammond, Karen. "Goodbye Hockey Sweater, Hello Casey at the Bat." *Quill & Quire* 66, 10 (2000): 25 – 26, 29.

Harlow, Barbara. *Resistance Literature.* New York and London: Methuen, 1987.

Harman, Lesley. *The Modern Stranger: On Language and Membership.* Berlin: Mouton de Gruyter, 1988.

Hart, Jonathan. *Representing the New World: The English and French Uses of the Example of Spain.* New York: Palgrave, 2001.

Harvey, Carol J. *Le cycle manitobain de Gabrielle Roy.* Saint-Boniface: Les Éditions des Plaines, 1993.

Hébert, Anne. *Dossier de presse, 1942 – 1986.* Sherbrooke: Bibliothèque du Séminaire de Sherbrooke, 1986.

Hébert, Pierre. "Roch Carrier au Canada anglais." *Oeuvres et critiques* 14, 1 (1989): 101 – 13.

———. "La littérature québécoise devant la critique ontarienne, 1867 – 1960." *Cultures du Canada français* 9 (1992): 13 – 34.

Hémon, Louis. *Maria Chapdelaine.* (1914) Paris: Grasset, 1924. Trans. W.H. Blake. Toronto: Macmillan, 1921.

Henderson, Jennifer. "Gender in the Discourse of English-Canadian Literary Criticism." *Open Letter* 8th ser. 3 (Spring 1992): 47 – 57.

Hitakonanu'laxk. *The Grandfathers Speak: Native American Folk Tales of the Lenapi People.* New York: Interlink, 1994.

Hjartarson, Paul. "The Fiction of Progress: Notes on the Composition of *The Master of the Mill.*" Learned Societies Conference, Ottawa, 1982.

Hobsbawm, Eric. *Nations and Nationalism since 1780.* Cambridge: Cambridge UP, 1990.

Hofstadter, Douglas R. *Gödel, Escher, Bach: An Eternal Golden Braid.* New York: Vintage, 1980.

hooks, bell. *Ain't I a Woman? Black Women and Feminism.* Boston: South End P, 1981.

Horne, Dee. *Contemporary American Indian Writing: Unsettling Literature.* New York: Peter Lang, 1999.

Howells, Coral Ann. *Private and Fictional Worlds: Canadian Women Novelists of the 1970s and 1980s.* London: Methuen, 1987.

Hunter, Lynette. *Outsider Notes: Feminist Approaches to Nation State Ideology, Writers/ Readers and Publishing.* Vancouver: Talonbooks, 1996.

Hunter, Lynette, and Shirley Chew, eds. *Borderblur: Essays on Poetry and Politics in Contemporary Canadian Literature.* Edinburgh: Quadriga, 1996.

Hurd, Burton. *Origin, Birthplace, Nationality and Language of the Canadian People.* Ottawa: King's Printer, 1929.

Hutcheon, Linda. *Narcissistic Narrative: The Metafictional Paradox.* Waterloo: Wilfrid Laurier UP, 1980.

———. "Peddling 'Versions of the Word': Cliché and Intertextuality in the Poetry of Leonard Cohen." Lyric Poetry Conference, Toronto, October 1982.

———. *The Canadian Postmodern: A Study of Contemporary English-Canadian Fiction.* Toronto: Oxford UP, 1988.

Innis, Harold. *The Strategy of Culture.* Toronto: U of Toronto P, 1952.

———. *Essays in Canadian Economic History.* Toronto: U of Toronto P, 1956.

Irigaray, Luce. *This Sex Which Is Not One.* Trans. Catherine Porter. Ithaca: Cornell UP, 1985.

Irvine, Lorna. "A Psychological Journey: Mothers and Daughters in English-Canadian Fiction." *The Lost Tradition: Mothers and Daughters in Literature.* Eds. E.M. Bromer and C. Davidson. New York: Frederick Ungar, 1980. 242 – 52.

Iser, Wolfgang. "The Reading Process: A Phenomenological Approach." *The Implied Reader.* Baltimore: John Hopkins UP, 1974. 274 – 94.

Ismail, Jam. "from Diction Air." *Tessera* 4 (CV2: 11, 2 – 3): 37 – 41.

Jakobson, Roman. "Linguistics and Poetics." *Style in Language.* Ed. Thomas A. Sebeok. Cambridge, MA: MIT P, 1960. 350 – 77.

The Jesuit Relations and Allied Documents: Travels and Explorations of the Jesuit Missionaries in New France 1610 – 1791. (Bilingual ed.) Ed. and trans. Reuben G. Thwaites. Vols. XX, XXI. (1640 – 1641) New York: Pageant, 1959.

Jameson, Fredrick. *The Prison-House of Language.* Princeton: Princeton UP, 1972.

————. *The Political Unconscious: Narrative as A Social Symbolic Act.* Ithaca: Cornell UP, 1981.

JanMohammed, Abdul R. "Colonialism and Minority Literature: Toward a Definition of Counter-Hegemonic Discourse." *boundary* 2 (1984): 281–99.

Jones, D.G. *Butterfly on Rock: A Study of Themes and Images in Canadian Literature.* Toronto: U of Toronto P, 1970.

Kamboureli, Smaro. "Theory: Beauty or Beast? Resistance to Theory in the Feminine." *Open Letter* 7th ser., 8 (Summer 1990): 5–26.

————. *Scandalous Bodies: Diasporic Literature in English Canada.* Toronto: Oxford UP, 2000.

————. "Fred Wah: A Poetry of Dialogue." *Line* 4 (1984): 44–62.

Kant, Immanuel. "What is Enlightenment?" *On History.* Ed. and trans. Lewis W. Beck. Indianapolis: Bobbs-Merrill, 1963. 3–10.

Karasick, Adeena. "Tract Marks: Echoes and Traces in the 'Toronto Research Group.'" *Open Letter* 8th ser. 3 (Spring 1992): 76–89.

Kertzer, Jon. "Speaking Out of Turn." Rev. of *The Vernacular Muse* by Dennis Cooley. *Essays on Canadian Writing* 40 (Spring 1990): 179–83.

————. *Worrying the Nation: Imagining a National Literature in English Canada.* Toronto: U of Toronto P, 1998.

Keywan, Zonia. "Straight from the Heart." *The Montreal Gazette*, 10 March 1979: 73.

Kimmel, David. "The Spirit of Canadian Democracy: Margaret Fairley and the Communist Cultural Workers' Responsibility to the People." *Left History* 1, 1 (1993): 34–55.

King, Thomas, Helen Hoy, and Cheryl Calver, eds. *The Native in Literature: Canadian and Comparative Perspectives.* Toronto: ECW, 1987.

Kirchhoff, H.J. "Writers Reject Bid to Study Plight of Minorities in Publishing." *The Globe and Mail*, 30 May 1989a: A19.

————. "Wanted: Native Canadians Who Want to Learn to Write." *The Globe and Mail*, 6 July 1989b: C10.

————. "Second Story Publishes Fiction that Caused Friction." *The Globe and Mail*, 31 July 1989c: C7.

————. "The Obsession that has Chosen Me is Language." *The Globe and Mail*, 4 January 1990: C5.

Koustas, Jane. "Lost from the Canon: The Canada Council and French-English Translation." *Translation Studies in Canada: Institutions, Discourses, Practices, Texts.* Ed. Barbara Godard. Toronto: Editions du GREF, 2008. [Forthcoming.]

Kristeva, Julia. "The Speaking Subject." *On Signs.* Ed. Marshall Blonsky. Baltimore: Johns Hopkins UP, 1985. 210–20.

Kroetsch, Robert. "A Canadian Issue." *boundary* 2, 3, 1 (1974): 1–2.

————. *Field Notes: Collected Poetry.* Toronto: General, 1981.

————. "Unhiding the Hidden: Recent Canadian Fiction." *Open Letter* 5th ser. 4 (Spring 1983): 17–22.

————. *The Lovely Treachery of Words: Essays Selected and New.* Toronto: Oxford UP, 1989.

Krupat, Arnold. *For Those Who Come After: A Study of Native American Autobiography.* Berkeley: u of California P, 1985.

Kurath, Gertrude. *Dance and Song Rituals of Six Nations Reserve, Ontario.* Bulletin 220. Ottawa: National Museum of Canada, 1968.

Lacan, Jacques. *Feminine Sexuality.* Eds. Juliet Mitchell and Jacqueline Rose. Trans. Jacqueline Rose. New York: W.W. Norton, 1982.

LaCapra, Dominick. *History and Criticism.* Ithaca: Cornell UP, 1985.

Lamontagne, André, Annette Hayward, and Réjean Beaudoin. "La réception anglo-canadienne de la littérature québécoise (1867 à 1989)." Ottawa: Colloque de l'APFUCC, May 1998.

Lamy, Suzanne. *d'elles.* Montréal: L'Hexagone, 1979.

———. *Quand je lis, je m'invente.* Montréal: L'Hexagone, 1984.

———. "Les écritures au féminin. Un désir de perversion." Gauvin and Klinkenberg, 1985. 33–44.

Laroche, Maximilien. *Le miracle et la métamorphose; essai sur les littératures du Québec et d'Haiti.* Montréal: Éditions du jour, 1970.

———. "L'américanité: ou l'ambiguïté du 'je'." *Études littéraires* 8, 1 (1975): 103–28.

———. *La découverte de l'Amérique par les Américains.* Quebec: GRELCA/u Laval, 1989.

LaRue, Monique. *Copies conformes.* Montréal: Lacombe, 1989.

Lecker, Robert. "Time and Form in the Contemporary Canadian Novel." Unpublished diss., York u, 1979.

———. "The Canonization of Canadian Literature: An Inquiry into Value." *Critical Inquiry* 16 (1990): 656–71.

———, ed. *Borderlands: Essays in Canadian-American Relations.* Toronto: ECW, 1991.

———. "The Canada Council's Block Grant Program and the Construction of Canadian Literature." *English Studies in Canada* 25 (1999): 439–69.

Lee, Charles. Rev. of *The Tin Flute. Philadelphia Bulletin,* 1947.

Lefevere, André. *Literary Knowledge.* Amsterdam: Van Gorcum, 1977.

———. *Translation, Rewriting and the Manipulation of Literary Fame.* London: Routledge, 1992.

Lejeune, Claire. *Du Point de vue du tiers.* Montréal: NBJ, 1986.

Lemire, Maurice, ed. *L'institution littéraire.* Québec: Institut québécois de recherche sur la culture, 1986.

———. *Le mythe de l'Amerique dans l'imaginaire "canadien."* Québec: Nota Bene, 2003.

Létourneau, Jocelyn. "Penser le Québec (dans le paysage canadien)." *Penser la nation Québécoise.* Ed. Michel Venne. Montréal: Québec-Amérique, 2000. 103–22.

Levinas, Emmanuel. *Totality and Infinity: An Essay on Exteriority.* Trans. Alphonso Lingis. Philadephia: Dusquesne UP, 1961/1998.

Lévi-Strauss, Claude. *The Raw and the Cooked.* Trans. John and Doreen Weightman. New York: Harper & Row, 1969.

Lewis, Paula Gilbert. *The Literary Vision of Gabrielle Roy.* Birmingham: Summa, 1984.

————, ed. *Traditionalism, Nationalism and Feminism: Women Writers of Quebec*. 1985

Littérature canadienne-anglaise. Spec. issue of *Voix et images* 10.1 (1984).

Lotman, Yuri. *Universe of the Mind: A Semiotic Theory of Culture*. Trans. Ann Shukman. Bloomington: Indiana UP, 1990.

Lusignan, Serge. "La Topique de la *translatio studii* et les traductions françaises de textes savants au xiv siècle." *Traduction et traducteurs au Moyen Age*. Paris: Editions du CNRS, 1988. 305–13.

Lyotard, Jean-François. *The Post-Modern Condition: A Report on Knowledge*. Trans.Geoff Bennington and Brian Massumi.Minneapolis: U of Minnesota P, 1984.

MacBeth, R.G. "A Noted Authoress." *Vancouver Star,.* 17 August 1928.

MacKenzie, Sally. "Glimpsing the Native View." *Images: West Kootenay Women's Paper* (Summer 1987) 12.

MacLulich, T.D. "Atwood's Adult Fairy Tale: Lévi-Strauss, Bettelheim and *The Edible Woman*." *Essays on Canadian Writing* 11, 1978. 111–29.

————. "Thematic Criticism, Literary Nationalism and the Critic's New Clothes." *Essays on Canadian Writing* 35 (Winter 1987): 17–36.

McCaffery, Steve. "Narrative." *Open Letter* 2nd ser. 5 (1973): 5–16.

————. "The Death of the Subject." *Open Letter* 3rd ser. 7 (1977): 61–63.

McLaughlin, Paul. "Turbulent Love Triangle Ended in Murder." *The Ottawa Citizen*, 16 June 1973: 37.

McLuhan, Marshall. "The Story of the Man in the Mask." *New York Times Book Review* 17 November 1968: 36, 38.

————. "Canada: The Borderline Case." In *The Canadian Imagination: Dimensions of a Literary Culture*. Ed. David Staines. Cambridge: Harvard UP, 1977: 226–48.

McPherson, Hugo. "The Garden and the Cage: The Achievement of Gabrielle Roy." *Canadian Literature* 1 (1959): 46–57.

McRoberts, Kenneth. "Internal Colonialism: The Case of Quebec." *Ethnic and Racial Studies* 2.3 (July 1979): 293–318.

Madureira, Luis. "Lapses in Taste: 'Cannibal-tropicalist' Cinema and the Brazilian Aesthetic of Underdevelopment." *Cannibalism and the Colonial World*. Eds. Francis Barker, Peter Hulme, and Margaret Iversen. Cambridge: Cambridge UP, 1998. 110–25.

Magder, Ted. "Going Global." *Canadian Forum* (August 1999): 11–16.

Major, André. "Notre Matriarcat." *Le Petit journal*, 25 July 1965: 39.

Mandel, Eli, ed. "Introduction." *Contexts of Canadian Criticism*. Chicago: U of Chicago P, 1971. 3–25.

————. "The Poet as Critic." In Mandel, *Another Time*. Erin: Porcepic, 1977. 11–14.

————. *Criticism: The Silent Speaking Words*. Toronto: CBC, 1966.

Manuel, George, and Michael Posluns. *The Fourth World: An Indian Reality*. Don Mills, ON: Collier-MacMillan, 1974.

Maracle, Lee. *I Am Woman*. Vancouver: Write-on Press, 1988.

Marcel, Jean. "Les forces provisoires de l'intelligence." *Livres et auteurs canadiens*, 1965. 23–32.

Marcotte, Gilles. *Le temps des poètes*. Montréal: ʜᴍʜ-Hurtubise, 1969.

Massey, Doreen. *Space, Place, and Gender*. Minneapolis: u of Minnesota ᴘ, 1994.

Mathews, Lawrence. "The Martian of Estevan." Rev. of *The Family Romance* by Eli Mandel. *Essays on Canadian Writing* 37 (Spring 1989): 155–60.

——. "Future Imperfect." Rev. of *Future Indicative: Literary Theory and Canadian Literature*, ed. John Moss. *Essays on Canadian Writing* 40 (Spring 1990): 162–72.

Mauriac, Claude. "Le génie est là." *Le Figaro*. 4 April 1966. Rpt. *Le Devoir*, 12 April 1966.

Marie Claire Blais: dossier de presse, 1959–1980. Sherbrooke: Bibliothèque du Seminaire de Sherbrooke [1981].

Melançon, Joseph. "The Writing of Difference in Québec." *Yale French Studies* 65 (1983): 21–29.

Merleau-Ponty, Claude. "What Is Phenomenology?" *European Literary Theory and Practice*. Ed. Vernon Gras. New York: Dell, 1973. 69–86.

Merler, Grazia. *Mavis Gallant: Narrative Patterns and Devices*. Ottawa: Tecumseh, 1978.

Merrell, Floyd. "Structuralism and Beyond." *Diogenes* 23 (1975). 67–103.

Mezei, Kathy. "The Scales of Translation: The English-Canadian Poet as Literal-Translator." *Revue de l'Université d'Ottawa* 54, 2 (1984): 63–84.

——. "The Question of Gender in Translation: Examples from Denise Boucher and Anne Hébert." *Tessera* 3/*Canadian Fiction Magazine* 57 (1986): 136–41.

——. "'Speaking White': Literary Translation as a Vehicle of Assimilation in Quebec." *Culture in Transit: Translating the Literature of Quebec*. Ed. Sherry Simon. Montreal: Véhicule, 1995. 133–48.

Michon, Jacques, ed. *Structure, Idéologie et reception du roman québécois de 1940 à 1960*. Sherbrooke: Département d'Etudes Françaises, u de Sherbrooke, 1979.

——. "Les revues littéraires d'avant-garde au Québec de 1940 à 1979." Gauvin and Klinkenberg, 1985. 117–28.

Miller, J. Hillis. "The Critic as Host." *Deconstruction and Criticism*. Harold Bloom, Paul de Man, Jacques Derrida, Geoffrey Hartman, and J. Hillis Miller. New York: Seabury, 1978. 217–53.

Miyoshi, Masao. "A Borderless World? From Colonialism to Transnationalism and the Decline of the Nation-State." *Critical Inquiry* 19 (1993): 726–51.

Moers, Ellen. *Literary Women*. New York: Doubleday, 1977.

Mohanty, Chandra Talpade. "Under Western Eyes." *boundary 2*, 12.3–13.1 (1984): 333–58.

Montpetit, Marie. "La traduction comme moyen de diffusion: le cas de *Bonheur d'occasion*." *Cultures du Canada français* 9 (1992): 137–51.

Mooney, James. *The Ghost Dance Religion and the Sioux Outbreak of 1890* (1896). Chicago: u of Chicago ᴘ, 1965.

Morency, Jean. "Forms of European Disconnection in the Literature of the Americas." Trans. Nicole Santilli. *Topia* 2 (1998): 11–21.

Morriset, Jean. "De la baye de Gouanabara à la Grande Rivière du Canada." *Confluence littéraires: Brésil-Québec, les bases d'une comparaison*. Eds. Michel Peterson and Zila Bernd. Montréal: Les Éditions Balzac, 1992. 203–28.

Moses, Daniel David. *Coyote City*. Stratford: Williams-Wallace, 1990.

———. *Almighty Voice and His Wife*. Stratford: Williams-Wallace, 1992.

———. *Brebeuf's Ghost*. Toronto: Playwrights Union of Canada, 1997.

Moses, Daniel David, and Terry Goldie. "Preface: Two Voices." *An Anthology of Canadian Native Literature in English*. Toronto: Oxford UP, 1992. xii–xxii.

Moss, John. *Patterns of Isolation in English Canadian Fiction*. Toronto: McClelland & Stewart, 1974.

———, ed. *Future Indicative: Literary Theory and Canadian Literature*. Ottawa: U of Ottawa P, 1987.

Moyes, Lianne. "'Canadian Literature Criticism': Between the Poles of the Universal-Particular Antimony." *Open Letter* 8th ser. 3 (Spring 1992): 28–46.

Mundwiler, Leslie. "Heidegger and Poetry." *Open Letter* 2nd ser. 3 (1972): 52–61.

Murray, Heather. "Reading for Contradiction in the Literature of Colonial Space." *Future Indicative: Literary Theory and Canadian Literature*. Ed. John Moss. Ottawa: U of Ottawa P, 1987. 73–84.

———. "Resistance and Reception: Backgrounds to Theory in English-Canada." *Signature* 4 (Winter 1990): 49–67.

———. "English Studies in Canada to 1945: A Bibliographic Essay." *English Studies in Canada* XVII, 4 (December 1991): 437–67.

———. *Working in English: History, Institutions, Resources*. Toronto: U of Toronto P, 1996.

Nepveu, Pierre. *L'Écologie du réel: Mort et naissance de la littérature québécoise contemporaine*. Montréal: Boréal, 1988.

———. *Intérieurs du Nouveau Monde: Essais sur les littératures du Québec et des Amériques*. Montréal: Boréal, 1998.

Neuman, Shirley. "Unearthing Language: An Interview with Rudy Wiebe and Robert Kroetsch." In *A Voice in the Land: Essays by and about Rudy Wiebe*. Ed. W.J. Keith. Edmonton: NeWest, 1981. 226–48

———. "Figuring the Self in Field Notes: Double or Noting." *Open Letter* 5th ser. 8–9 (1984): 176–94.

———, and Robert Wilson. *Labyrinths of Voice: Conversations with Robert Kroetsch*. Edmonton: NeWest, 1982.

New, W.H. *Land Sliding: Imagining Space, Presence and Power in Canadian Writing*. Toronto: U of Toronto P, 1997.

———. *Borderlands: How We Talk about Canada*. Vancouver: UBC P, 1998.

Noël, Francine. *Babel, prise deux ou Nous avons tous découvert l'Amérique*. Montréal: VLB, 1990.

NourbeSe Philip, M. "Notes from the Margin: Social Barbarism and the Spoils of Modernism." *Fuse X* 6 (Spring 1987): 31.

———. *She Tries Her Tongue Her Silence Softly Breaks*. Charlottetown: Ragweed, 1989a.

———. Letter to the Editor. *The Globe and Mail*, 17 June 1989b: D7.

———. "Why Multiculturalism Can't End Racism." *The Toronto Star*, 6 March 1990: A21.

O'Meara, John. *Delaware-English, English-Delaware Dictionary.* Toronto: u of Toronto P, 1996.

O'Neill-Karch, Mariel. "Gabrielle Roy et William Arthur Deacon: une amitié littéraire." *Cultures du Canada français* 9 (1992): 75–96.

Ontario Arts Council. *Annual Report 1963–64.* Toronto: Ontario Arts Council, 1964.

———. *Measuring the Economic Impact of Arts Organizations.* Toronto: Ontario Arts Council, 1998a.

———. *Notepad.* Toronto: Ontario Arts Council, 1998b.

Ouellette-Michalska, Madeleine. *L'Échappée des discours de l'oeil.* Montréal: Nouvelle Optique, 1981.

P.S. "McLuhan à la chaise électrique?" *Parti pris* 3, 7 (1966): 77.

Parker, George L. "Growing Pains in World War II: The Struggle to Build a Real Publishing Trade in Canada with a Little Help from the British." *English Studies in Canada* 25, 3–4 (1999): 369–406.

Parmenius, Stephen. "Letter from Parmenius to Richard Hakluyt" (1583). Trans. Richard Hakluyt. In Hakluyt, *The Principal Navigations, Voiages, Traffiques and Discoveries of the English Nation.* (1589), 697–99. III (1600). 161–63.

Pêcheux, Michel. *Language, Semantics, and Ideology.* Trans. Harbans Nagpal. New York: St. Martin's P, 1982.

Pennee, Donna. "Culture as Security: Canadian Foreign Policy and International Relations from the Cold War to the Market Wars." *International Journal of Canadian Studies* 20 (1999): 191–213.

Perkes, Carolyn. "Les seuils du savoir littéraire canadien: le roman québécois en traduction anglaise, 1960–1990." *Canadian Review of Comparative Literature/Revue canadienne de littérature comparée* 23, 4 (1996): 1195–1211.

Perron, Paul. "Structuralisme/Post-Structuralisme: Québec/Amérique." *Dalhousie French Studies* 10 (1986): 72–90.

Petrone, Penny, ed. *Aboriginal Pre-Twentieth Century Canadian Literature Materials.* Thunder Bay: Faculty of Education, Lakehead u, 1983.

Piggott, G.L., and A. Grafstein. *Ojibwa Lexicon.* Ethnology Dossier No. 90. Ottawa: National Museum of Man, 1983.

Poitras, Edward. "Indian Territory." Power Plant, Toronto. June–10 September 1989.

Pollock, Griselda. *Vision & Difference: Femininity, Feminism and the Histories of Art.* London: Routledge, 1988.

Poronovich, Walter. "CBC to Show Literary View of French Canada's Soul." *The Montreal Star*, 13 February 1979: C3.

Poulet, Georges. *Études sur le temps humain.* 4 vols. Edinburgh: Edinburgh UP, 1949–(65).

———. Introduction. *Littérature et sensation.* By Jean-Pierre Richard. Paris: Seuil, 1954.

———. "Phenomenology of Reading." *Issues in Contemporary Literary Criticism.* Ed. Gregory T. Polleta. Trans. Richard Macksey. Boston: Little, 1973. 103–118.

Poulin, Jacques. *Volkswagen Blues*. Montréal: Québec/Amérique, 1984.

Pratt, Mary Louise. *Imperial Eyes: Travel Writing and Transculturation*. London and New York: Routledge, 1992.

Purchas, Samuel. "A Discourse of the diversity of Letters used by the divers Nations in the World; the antiquity, manifold use and variety thereof, with exemplary descriptions of above threescore severall Alphabets, with other strange Writings." In *Hakluytus Posthumus, or Purchas His Pilgrimes*, 20 vols. Glasgow: James MacLehose & Sons, 1905. Vol. 1.

Purdy, Anthony. *A Certain Difficulty of Being: Essays on the Quebec Novel*. Montreal: McGill-Queen's UP, 1990.

Quinn, David B., and Neil M. Cheshire. *The Newfoundland of Stephen Parmenius*. Toronto: U of Toronto P, 1972.

Radin, Paul. *The Trickster: A Study in American Indian Mythology*. 2nd. ed. New York: Greenwood, 1969.

Randall, Marilyn. "Hubert Aquin: Canadien malgré lui?" *Cultures du Canada français* 9 (1992): 98–114.

Rea, Annabelle. "Le premier jardin d'Anne Hébert comme hommage à Gabrielle Roy." In André Fauchon, ed. *Colloque International Gabrielle Roy*. Saint-Boniface: P Universitaires de Saint-Boniface, 1996. 575–91.

Readings, Bill. *The University in Ruins*. Cambridge: Harvard UP, 1996.

Redekop, Magdalene. "Authority and the Margins of Escape in *Brébeuf and His Brethren*." *Open Letter* 6th ser. 3–4 (1985): 45–60.

Reiss, Timothy. *The Discourse of Modernism*. Ithaca: Cornell UP, 1982.

Riddell, Joseph. "Decentring the Image: The Project of American Verse." *TextualStrategies: Perspectives in Post-Structuralist Criticism*. Ithaca: Cornell UP, 1979. 322–58.

Rièse, Laure. "Christian Poetry in Translation." *Canadian Forum* (December 1962): 210.

Rioux, Michèle, and Christophe Peyron. "Possible ou impossible intégration? Les limites de la logique marchande." *Le Devoir*, 1 November 2003: G3.

Robinson, Douglas. *The Translator's Turn*. Baltimore: Johns Hopkins UP, 1991.

Ross, Malcolm. "Critical Theory: Some Trends." *Literary History of Canada*. Ed. Carl Klinck. 2nd ed. Vol 3. Toronto: U of Toronto P, 1976. 160–75.

Gabrielle Roy: dossier de presse, 1945–1980. Sherbrooke: Bibliothèque du Séminaire de Sherbrooke, 1981.

Roy, Lucille. *Entre la lumiere et l'ombre: l'univers poétique d'Anne Hébert*. Sherbrooke: Naaman, 1984.

Royer, Jean. "Regards sur la littérature québécoise des années 70." *Le Devoir*, cahier 3 (21 Dec. 1981): 1.

Saint-Jacques, Denis. "L'envers de l'institution." *L'Institution littéraire*. Ed. Maurice Lemire. Quebec: IQRC, 1986. 43–48.

Salgado, Plinio. "A Lingua Tupy." *Revista de Antropofagia* 1 (1928): 5–6.

Savard, Felix-Antoine. *Menaud, maitre-draveur*. Montréal: Fides, 1937.

Schechner, Richard. *Performance Theory*. 2nd ed. Rev. New York: Routledge, 1988.

Schmidt, Sarah. "Pay-per-use." *This*, July 1999: 22–23.

Scobie, Stephen. *bpNichol: What History Teaches.* Vancouver: Talonbooks, 1984.

———. *Signature Event Context Essays.* Edmonton: NeWest, 1989.

Scott, David. *Refashioning Futures: Criticism after Postcoloniality.* Princeton: UP, 1999.

Scott, Frank, with Anne Hébert. *Dialogue sur la traduction.* Montréal: HMH, 1970.

Scott, Gail. "A Passionate Heritage at Home in Quebec." *The Globe and Mail,* September 1977.

Sekyi-Otu, Ato. "Three Syntaxes of Particularity." *Ethnicity in a Technological Age.* Ed. Ian Angus. Edmonton: U of Alberta P, 1988. 193–200.

Seminaire de Sherbrooke. *Marie-Claire Blais: dossier de presse, 1959–1980.* Sherbrooke, QC: La Bibliothèque, 1981.

Serafin, Bruce. "Colonial Mentalities." Rev. of *North of Intention* by Steve McCaffery. *Books in Canada* 19.8 (November 1990): 21–23.

Serres, Michel. *Hermes III: La Traduction.* Paris: E de Minuit, 1974.

Shouldice, Larry, ed. *Contemporary Québec Criticism.* Trans. Larry Shouldice. Toronto: U of Toronto P, 1979.

Showalter, Elaine. "Toward a Feminist Poetics." (1979) In *Feminist Criticism: Essays on Women, Literature and Theory.* Ed. Elaine Showalter. New York: Pantheon, 1985. 125–43.

Simon, Sherry. "'*Fous*' a Compelling Tale in Lyrical Language." *The Montreal Gazette,* 27 November 1982: C6.

———. *Le Trafic des langues: Traduction et culture dans la littérature québécoise.* Montréal: Boreal, 1994.

Sirois, Antoine. "Prix littéraires pour les écrivains québécois." *International Perspectives in Comparative Literature.* Ed. Virginia M. Shaddy. Lewiston: Edwin Mellen, 1991. 147–59.

Skelton, Robin. "Canadian Poetry?" *Tamarack* 29 (Autumn 1963): 71–82.

Slemon, Stephen. "Magic Realism as Postcolonial Discourse." *Magic Realism: Theory, History, Community.* Lois Parkinson Zamora and Wendy B. Faris, eds. Durham: Duke UP, 1995. 407–26.

Smart, Patricia. *Écrire dans la maison du père: l'émergence du féminin dans la tradition littéraire du Québec.* Montréal: Québec/Amérique, 1988.

[Smart] Purcell, Patricia. "The Agonizing Solitude." *Canadian Literature* 10 (1961): 51–61.

Smith, Barbara Herrnstein. "Contingencies of Value." *Critical Inquiry.* 10 (1983): 1–35.

Smith, Beverley. "Blood Marriages." *Books in Canada* 2, 2 (1973): 15–16.

Snead, James A. "Repetition as a Figure of Black Culture." *Out There: Marginalization and Contemporary Cultures.* Eds. Russell Ferguson, Martha Gever, Trinh T. Minh-ha, and Cornel West. Cambridge: MIT P, 1990. 213–32.

Sociologies de la littérature. Special issue of *Études françaises* 19.3 (1984).

Spence, Donald P. *Narrative Truth and Historical Truth: Meaning and Interpretation in Psychoanalysis.* New York: W.W. Norton, 1982.

Spivak, Gayatri Chakravorty. *In Other Worlds.* New York: Methuen, 1987.

————. "Can the Subaltern Speak?" *Marxism and the Interpretation of Culture.* Ed. Cary Nelson and Lawrence Grossberg. Chicago: U of Chicago P, 1988. 271–313.

————. "The Politics of Translation." *Outside in the Teaching Machine.* New York: Routledge, 1993. 179–200.

Stallybrass, Peter, and Allon White. *The Politics and Poetics of Transgression.* Ithaca: Cornell UP, 1986.

Stam, Robert. *Tropical Multiculturalism: A Comparative History of Race in Brazilian Cinema and Culture.* Durham and London: Duke UP, 1997.

Steele, Charles. *Taking Stock: The Calgary Conference on the Canadian Novel.* Downsview: ECW, 1982.

Stock, Brian. "Canada's Foreign Policy Vacuum: Cultural Affairs." *Canadian Forum* (May 1973): 21–26.

Stratford, Philip. *Marie-Claire Blais.* Toronto: Forum, 1971.

Symons, T.H.B. *To Know Ourselves: The Report of the Commisssion on Canadian Studies.* Vols. I and II. Ottawa: Association of Universities and Colleges of Canada, 1975.

Tallman, Warren. "Wolf in the Snow: Part I, Four Windows onto Landscape." *Canadian Literature,* 5 (1960): 41–48.

Terdiman, Richard. "Ideological Voyages: Concerning Flaubertian Dis-orientation." In Francis Barker, ed. *Europe and Its Others.* Colchester: U of Essex P, 1985. 28–40.

Tessera 2. October 1986. *La nouvelle barre du jour.*

Tessera 3: Feminist Fiction Theory. Special issue of *Canadian Fiction Magazine* 57 (1986).

The Language of Difference: Writing in Québec(ois). Special issue of *Yale French Studies* 65 (1983).

Thérien, Gilles. "La littérature québécoise, une littérature du tiers-monde?" *Voix et images* 12.1 (1986): 12–20.

Thurston, John. "The Carnival Comes To/From Vancouver Island." Conference on Bakhtin and his Circle. Queen's U. October 1982.

Todorov, Tzvetan. *Introduction à la littérature fantastique.* Paris: Seuil, 1970.

————. *The Poetics of Prose.* Trans. Richard Howard. Ithaca: Cornell UP, 1977.

Valentine, Lisa Philips. *Making It Their Own: Severn Ojibwe Communicative Practices.* Toronto: U of Toronto P, 1995.

van Herk, Aritha. "The Sound and the Fury." *Books in Canada* 13, 2 (1984): 10.

————. *Places Far From Ellesmere: A Geografictione.* Red Deer: Red Deer College P, 1990.

Vastokas, Joan M. "Native Art as Art History: Meaning and Time from Unwritten Sources." *Journal of Canadian Studies* 21.4 (1986–1987). 7–36.

Venuti, Lawrence. *The Translator's Invisibility.* London: Routledge, 1995.

————. *The Scandals of Translation: Towards an Ethics of Difference.* London: Routledge, 1998.

Verduyn, Christl. "Checking the Pulse." *Canadian Issues/Thèmes Canadiens* (Summer 2000): 5.

Vincent, Isabel. "Celebrating Native Spirituality: Writer Feels Society can Learn from Native Ways." *The Globe and Mail,* 10 June 1989: C9.

Vizenor, Gerald. *The Trickster of Liberty: Tribal Heirs to a Wild Baronage.* Minneapolis: u of Minnesota p, 1988.

Volosinov, V.N. *Marxism and the Philosophy of Language.* Trans. I. Matejka and I.R. Titunik. New York: Seminar p, 1973.

Waddington, Miriam. "Afterword." *The Street of Riches.* Toronto: McClelland & Stewart, 1991. 159–65.

Wallace, Keith, and Eugenio Valdès Figueroa. *Stretch.* Toronto: The Power Plant, 2003.

Ware, Tracy. "A Little Self-Consciousness is a Dangerous Thing: A Response to Robert Lecker." *English Studies in Canada* xvii 4 (December 1991): 481–93.

Warkentin, Germaine. "Myth and History: David Thompson's Vision of the New World." Paper presented at the mla, San Francisco, 28 December 1979.

Weinzweig, Helen. *Basic Black with Pearls.* Toronto: Anansi, 1980.

Weir, Lorraine. "Towards a Feminist Hermeneutics: Jay MacPherson's Welcoming Disaster." *Gynocritics/Gynocritiques: Feminist Approaches to Canadian and Québec Women's Writing.* Ed. Barbara Godard. Toronto: ecw, 1986. 59–70.

Wershler-Henry, Darren. "The (W)Hole in the Middle: The Metaphysics of Presence in the Criticism of Robert Kroetsch." *Open Letter,* 8th ser. 3 (Spring 1992): 58–75.

White, Hayden. *Tropics of Discourse.* Baltimore: Johns Hopkins up, 1978.

———. *The Content of Form: Narrative Discourse and Historical Representation.* Baltimore: John Hopkins up, 1987.

Whiteman, Bruce. "Davey on Souster & Dudek." *Canadian Poetry* 8 (1981): 98–99.

Whitfield, Agnes. "La modernité: Des formes qui (s')inquiètent." *Lettres québécoises* 46 (1987): 56–58.

———. "Gabrielle Roy as Feminist: Re-reading the Critical Myth." *Canadian Literature* 126 (1990): 20–31.

Wilden, Anthony. *The Imaginary Canadian.* Vancouver: Pulp Press, 1980.

Williams, Raymond. *Marxism and Literature.* Oxford: Oxford up, 1977.

Wilson, Edmund. *O Canada: An American's Notes on Canadian Culture.* New York: Farrar, Strauss & Giroux, 1965.

Wilson, Edward F. *The Ojebway Language: A Manual for Missionaries and Others Employed among the Ojebway Indians.* Toronto: Rowsell and Hutchison for the Society for Promoting Christian Knowledge, 1874.

Wilson, Robert Rawolon. "Theory/Text/Self: Scobietext." *Open Letter,* 8th ser. (Spring 1992): 108–14

Woolf, Virginia. *A Room of One's Own.* London: Granada, 1977.

Zumthor, Paul. *Babel ou l'inachèvement.* Paris: Seuil, 1997.

INDEX

A

A Border Within National Identity, Cultural Plurality, and Wilderness (Angus) 333–34
À l'ombre de Desrochers (Bonenfant) 86
Ain't I a Woman? (hooks) 133
Allison, Gay 34
Almighty Voice and His Wife (Moses) 206, 219–33
Althusser, L. 112–13, 159
America (Curnoe) 328–29
American Indian Movement (AIM) 133, 134, 229
Amiskouevan, Marie 214–17, 219
Anatomy of Criticism, The (Frye) 59, 63, 240
Anderson, Benedict 262
Andrès, Bernard 322
Angus, Ian 259, 333–34
Anna's World (Blais) 301
Aquash, Anna Mae 140
Aquin, Hubert 289–90
Armstrong, Jeannette 117, 122–23, 132–41, 148–57, 159
Arnold, Matthew 242
Assepanse, Nicole 217
Association des auteurs des Cantons de l'Est 98
Association des professeurs de français des universités canadiens (APFUC) 34
Association for Canadian and Quebec Literatures (ACQL) 30, 32
Association of Canadian Theatre History 32
Association of Canadian University Teachers of English (ACUTE) [now ACCUTE] 28, 30, 37–38
Association of Universities and Colleges of Canada 50

At the Full and Change of the Moon (Brand) 236
Atwood, Margaret 59, 182, 238–39, 243, 274, 304, 346, 348–50

B

Babel (Bendtsen) 327–28
Babel, prise deux (Noel) 351–52
Babel-Opéra (Bosco) 352
Bachelard, Gaston 21, 71
Bakhtin, Mikhail 28, 67–68, 80–82, 91, 126–27, 132
Bal, Mieke 93
Bannerji, Himani 41
Barthes, Roland 22, 23, 68–69, 77–78, 84, 104
Basic Black with Pearls (Weinzweig) 346–48
Beaudet, Marie-Andrée 86, 87–88, 336
Beaudoin, Réjean 274
Belleau, André 86, 90, 91–94, 96
Belmore, Rebecca 109
Belsey, Catherine 241
Bendtsen, Tom 327–28
Benveniste, Emile 158, 239
Berman, Antoine 43
Berque, Jacques 129
Bersianik, Louky 100, 274
Bertelsmann 254
Bessette, Gérard 32
Bhabha, Homi 261, 266
Bibliotheca Canadensis (Morgan) 294
Birney, Earle 238
Bishop, Neil 295
Black, Ayanna 34
Blais, Marie-Claire 274, 278–79, 284, 285–87, 290–93, 298–302
Blanchot, Maurice 87
Blodgett, E.D. 77, 321
Bloom, Harold 79
Bök, Christian 197–98
Bone Bird (Quaife) 119–21

Bonenfant, Joseph 86, 92

Bonheur d'occasion (Roy) 279 – 80, 290 – 91, 296, 297 – 98

Bonnycastle, Stephen 68 – 69

Borderblur: Essays on Poetry and Politics in Contemporary Canadian Literature (Hunter and Chew) 259

Borderlands: How We Talk About Canada (New) 333 – 35

Borges, Jorge Luis 316, 336 – 37

Bosco, Monique 352

Boundas, Constantin 39

Bourdieu, Pierre 84, 97, 239 – 40, 275, 276 – 77

Bouvard et Pécuchet (Flaubert) 23

Bowering, George 58, 194

bpNichol 196 – 97

bpNichol: What History Teaches (Scobie) 77 – 78

Branco (de Campos) 356 – 57

Brand, Dionne 41, 114, 235 – 37, 254, 264, 344

Brebeuf's Ghost (Moses) 233

Brisset, Annie 98

Brochu, André 89

Brooke-Rose, Christine 23

Brossard, Nicole 34, 35, 43, 90, 98, 100, 102 – 103, 274, 312, 350

Brown, Alan 298

Brown, E.K. 242

Butler-Evans, Elliot 39

Butterfly on Rock: A Study of Themes and Images in Canadian Literature (Jones) 243

C

Callaghan, Barry 299

Callaghan, Morley 299

Cameron, Ann 41

Cameron, Barry 60 – 62, 178 – 79, 186, 187

Campbell, Maria 117

Canada in the World/Le Canada dans le monde 256

Canadian Alliance for Trade and Job Opportunities 249

Canadian Association of Translation Studies 43

Canadian Comparative Literature Association 32 – 33, 43

Canadian Research Institute for the Advancement of Women (CRIAW) 41

Canadian University Services Overseas (CUSO) 19 – 20

Canadian Women's Studies Association (CWSA) 30

Carrier, Roch 28

Cartier, Jacques 210 – 11

Caruso, Barbara 197

Chabwekwechich, Agnes 216

Chamberland, Roger 86, 87

Chatterjee, Partha 262 – 63

Cheyfitz, Eric 206 – 208

Child, Philip 20

Children of My Heart (Blais) 286

Cixous, Hélène 23, 35, 101, 103

Claxton, Brooke 247

Cloutier, Cécile 43

Cobley, Evelyn 37

Cohen, Leonard 68

Cohn-Sfetcu, Ofelia 71 – 72

Coldwell, Joan 35

Collaboration in the Feminine: Writing on Women and Culture 36

Collin, Françoise 106

Coltman, Derek 300

Combined Universities Campaign for Nuclear Disarmament (CUCND) 19

Committee to Reestablish the Trickster 110, 226

Como Era Gostoso O Meu Frances (dos Santos) 329 – 31

Configuration: Essays on the Canadian Literatures (Blodgett) 321

Conway, Sheelagh 113
Cook, Ramsay 19
Copies conformes (LaRue) 350 – 51
Correspondance (de l'Incarnation) 212, 213
Corriveau, Hugues 86 – 87
Coyote City (Moses) 224 – 25
Crawford, Isabella Valancy 29
Crémazie, Octave 339
Culler, Jonathan 59, 63
Curnoe, Greg 328 – 29
Cuthand, Beth 117
Czarnecki, Mark 291

D

Darling, Michael 187
Davey, Frank 24, 25, 27, 28, 42, 56 – 59,
    193, 249, 294
Davies, Ioan 39
Davies, Robertson 81
d'elles (Lamy) 35, 104
de Andrade, Joaquim Pedro 341
de Andrade, Mario 340, 342, 353
de Andrade, Oswald 325, 329, 339 – 40,
    341 – 42
de Assis, Machado 342
de Bellefeuille, Normand 86 – 87
de Campos, Augusto 341 – 42, 354 – 56
de Campos, Haroldo 341 – 44, 354 – 56
de Courtivron, Isabelle 37
de l'Incarnation, Marie 201, 204 – 206,
    209, 211 – 19, 221 – 23
de Lauretis, Teresa 39
de Man, Paul 70, 187
de Pisan, Christine 106
de Staël, Madame 106
Deacon, William Arthur 291, 296 – 97
Deep Shit City (Moses) 109
Deleuze, Gilles 23, 39, 79, 178, 239, 269
Delisle, Jean 206 – 207
Demers, Jeanne 94 – 95, 96, 99
Department of Foreign Affairs and
    International Trade (DFAIT) 256

Derrida, Jacques 23, 40, 74, 84
Dewart, E.H. 193
Dialogue sur la traduction (Scott) 306
Dickason, Olive 229
Dickinson, Peter 262 – 64
Dirlik, Arif 254
Dixon, Michael 178 – 79
Djwa, Sandra 32, 182
dos Santos, Nelson Pereira 329 – 31
Double Hook, The (Watson) 20, 29
Douglas, Mary 175
Dry Lips Oughta Go to Kapuskasing
    (Highway) 109
Dubois, Jacques 84, 96 – 97, 277
Dudek, Louis 56, 308 – 309
Dumont, Fernand 86, 97
Duncan, Dorothy 296
Dupré, Louise 312, 350

E

Eagleton, Terry 63
École Publique Gabrielle Roy 284
Edgar, Pelham 242
Eichler, Margaret 30
Ellenwood, Ray 300, 301, 302
Eliot, T.S. 22
Emond, Maurice 87
En'owkin International School of
    Writing 138
Enwhisteetka (Armstrong) 137
Escarpit, Robert 21 – 22
Esthétique et théorie du roman (Belleau) 93
Éthier-Blais, Jean 85, 309
Études sur le temps humain (Poulet) 70
Euclid Cinema 110
Evan-Zohar, Itamar 281, 282

F

Fairley, Margaret 243
Falardeau, Jean-Charles 21, 32, 86
Fanon, Frantz 129 – 30

Farmer, Gary 109
Faulkner, William 304
Fee, Margery 118, 242
Feltes, Norman 38
Feminist Book Fair 41
Femmes de Caughnawaga (Suzor-Côté) 351
Fernie, Lynne 34
Ferron, Jacques 290
Findlay, Len 38
Findley, Timothy 287, 292
Fireweed 29, 34, 35, 41, 117
Fischman, Sheila 301 – 302
Fisette, Jean 93
Flaubert, Gustave 27
Fogel, Stan 54
Foucault, Michel 23, 40, 54, 79, 80,
   124 – 25, 262
Freiwald, Bina 38
French, William 302 – 303
Front de libération du Québec (FLQ) 19
Frye, Northrop 58 – 62, 63 – 64, 178, 182,
   193, 237 – 38, 239, 240 – 42, 247,
   263 – 64, 306

G
Gagnon, Madeleine 101 – 102, 103
Gallant, Mavis 65 – 66
Gallays, François 285
Galloway, Priscilla 63
Garden and the Cage, The (Findley) 287
Garebian, Keith 291, 301
Gauvin, Lise 86, 97, 274, 277 – 78, 285,
   335 – 36
Gauvreau, Claude 86, 87
Gendering the Nation (Armatage) 258
Genette, Gérard 65, 66 – 67, 84, 93
Gibson, Douglas 113, 114 – 15
Gilbert, Sandra 35, 37
Giroux, Robert 85, 88 – 89, 95 – 96
Glissant, Edouard 318, 323
Globe and Mail, The 114, 291, 296, 297,
   328

Godbout, Jacques 290
Godzich, Wlad 317, 318
Goldie, Terry 118 – 19
Goldmann, Lucien 22, 23
Graham, Gwethelyn 296
Gramsci, Antonio 202
Grandpré, Chantal 289 – 90
Green, Alma/Forbidden Voice 391
Green, Mary Jane 274
Greene, Rayna 391
Greimas, A.J. 40, 65
Groupe d'information sur les prisons 23
Grove, F.P. 266
Guattari, Félix 239, 269
Guterson, David 260
Gynesis (Jardine) 38
Gynocritics 37

H
Hajdukowski-Ahmed, Maroussia 92
Hall, Stuart 261
Harriet's Daughter (NourbeSe Philip) 114
Harris, Claire 114
Hakluyt, Richard 207, 210
Hayne, David 32
Hébert, Anne 274, 279, 284, 285 – 87,
   290 – 92, 293, 295, 302
   poetry 305 – 310
Hébert, Pierre 93, 273, 283 – 84, 294
Heidegger, Martin 62 – 63
Heilbrun, Caroline 34
Hémon, Louis 85
Henderson, Jennifer 194 – 96
Herbert, Lucille 30
*Here is Queer: Nationalism, Sexualities and
   the Literature of Canada* (Dickinson)
   262, 264
Heritage Canada 249, 250 – 51
Highway, Tomson 109, 110
Hjartarson, Paul 79 – 80
Hodgins, Jack 81, 260
hooks, bell 133

Horn, Michiel 26
Horne, Dee 261, 264
Howell, Coral Ann 293
Huot, Charles 327
Husserl, Martin 62
Hutcheon, Linda 73 – 74, 80, 150, 267,

I

*I am Woman: A Native Perspective on
    Sociology and Feminism* (Maracle)
    122 – 23, 132 – 38, 141 – 48
Imbert, Patrick 93
In Another Place, Not Here (Brand) 235
*In the Feminine: Women and Words/Les
    femmes et les mots* 106 – 107
In the Shadow of the Wind (Hébert) 291,
    304
Innis, Harold 245
Inter-American Women Writers 34, 35
*Intérieurs du nouveau monde: Essais sur
    les littératures du Québec et des
    Amériques* (Nepveu) 322
International Summer Institute
    in Semiotic and Structuralist
    Studies (ISISSS) 39 – 40
*Inverted Bell: Modernism and the
    Counterpoetics of William Carlos
    Williams, The* (Riddell) 74
Irigaray, Luce 35, 39, 101, 104
Irvine, Lorna 194 – 95
Iser, Wolfgang 73

J

Jackel, Susan 20, 37
Jakobson, Roman 64, 93
Jameson, Fredric 111
JanMohamed, Abdul 128 – 29
Johnson, Barbara 47
Johnson, Pauline 294
Jones, D.G. 243
Joseph, Hannah 297 – 98

K

Kamboureli, Smaro 81, 188, 257,
    264 – 69
Kamouraska (Hébert) 290, 292, 302 – 305
Karasick, Adeena 196 – 97
Keeshig-Tobias, Lenore 110 – 11, 113,
    114 – 15, 116, 123
Kerouac, Jack 107
Kilfoil, Katherine 42
Kingston Conference on the Arts 245
Kirchhoff, H.J. 114 – 16
Klinck, Carl 182
Klinkenberg, Jean-Marie 86
Koch-Grünberg, Theodor 353
Koffler Gallery 327
Kogawa, Joy 266
Koustas, Jane 274
Kristeva, Julia 84, 87 – 88, 101, 159
Kroetsch, Robert 75, 76, 81, 82, 196, 199
Kulyk Keefer, Janice 195
Kurosawa, Fuyuki 47

L

L'Amèr (Brossard) 101
L'Échappée des discours de l'oeil (Ouellette-
    Michalska) 103 – 104
L'Écologie du reel (Nepveu) 336 – 37
L'enjeu du manifeste/Le manifeste en jeu
    (Demers and McMurray) 94 – 95
L'Euguélionne (Bersianik) 101
L'Institution littéraire (Lemire) 86
La Barre du jour 29, 35, 100, 101
La Casa de Las Americas 328
La Nouvelle barre du jour 90
La petit poule d'eau (Roy) 291
La sourd dans la ville (Blais) 291
Lacan, Jacques 23, 158
LaCapra, Dominick 111 – 12
Lamontagne, André 274
Lamy, Suzanne 35, 90, 98 – 99,
    104 – 106
Lapointe, Jeanne 307

Laroche, Maximilien 316 – 17, 321
LaRue, Monique 312, 350 – 51
Laurence, Margaret 274, 293
Layton, Irving 25
Le désert mauve (Brossard) 350
Le romancier fictif (Belleau) 91, 94
Le tombeau des rois 306, see also The Tomb of the Kings
Learneds 30, 34, 37, 38, 56
Lecker, Robert 71 – 72, 184 – 85
Lefevere, André 280, 281, 282
LeGrand, Albert 21
Lejeune, Claire 172
Lemelin, Jean-Marc 95 – 96
Lemire, Maurice 86, 316
Les Chouans (Balzac) 23
Les fous de Bassan (Hébert) 279, 287, 290
Les Relations des Jésuites 215
Les Têtes de pioche 98 – 99
Létourneau, Jocelyn 335
Lévesque, Père Georges-Henri 247
Lévis-Strauss, Claude 64 – 65
Lispector, Clarice 35
Literary History of Canada (Frye) 182, 193, 237, 240 – 41, 247, 252, 264, 332
Littérature et societe canadienne-française (Dumont and Falardeau) 86
Little Boy Lost Meets Mother Tongue (bpNichol) 77 – 78
Lucas, Alec 69
Lukács, Georg 23
Lyotard, Jean-François 83, 84

M
MacBeth, R.G. 294
Mackay, Isabel 294
MacLean, David 110
MacLennan, Hugh 68 – 69, 296
MacLulich, T.D. 187, 188
Macunaíma (de Andrade) 340 – 41, 352 – 54
Mad Shadows (Blais) 292

Mailhot, Laurent 274
Mandel, Ann 36
Mandel, Eli 25, 57, 58, 70, 240
Manheim, Ralph 300
Manuel, George 321
Manuscripts of Pauline Archange (Blais) 300
Maracle, Lee 41, 122 – 23, 132 – 38, 141 – 48, 159
Marcel, Jean 90
Marcotte, Gilles 90
Maria Chapdelaine (Hémon) 85
Marks, Elaine 37
Marlatt, Daphne 36
Massey-Lévesque Royal Commission on National Development in the Arts, Letters, and Sciences 245 – 46, 288
Master of the Mill, The (Grove) 79 – 80
Mathews, Robin 30 – 31, 187
Mauron, Charles 56
Mavis Gallant: Narrative Patterns and Devices (Merler) 65
McCaffery, Steve 75 – 76, 197 – 98
McCullers, Carson 304
McGee, Thomas D'Arcy 247
McLaughlin, Paul 303
McLuhan, Marshall 22, 325, 332 – 34
McMullen, Lorraine 34
McMurray, Line 94 – 95, 96, 99
McPherson, Hugo 287, 288 – 89
Melançon, Joseph 97
memoria, La (Dupré) 350
Menaud, Maître-draveur (Savard) 85
Mercredi, Ovide 196
Merleau-Ponty, Claude 62
Merler, Grazia 65 – 66
Merril, Judith 115
Meschonnic, Henri 43
Mezei, Kathy 36, 301, 310
Michon, Jacques 96 – 97
Miller, J. Hillis 70, 74, 76 – 77
Miller, Peter 305, 309

Miyoshi, Masao 258
Moers, Ellen 304
Mohanty, Chandra 124
Mojica, Monique 110
Molson Prize 292
Montreal Gazette 287
Montreal Star 286, 287
Moodie, Susanna 81
Moore-Ede, Carol 286
Morency, Jean 317–18
Morgan, Henry 294
Morriset, Jean 316
Moses, Daniel David 109–110, 201, 204,
    206, 219–33
Moss, John 243
Moyes, Lianne 193–94, 199
Multiculturalism Act 264–67
Mundwiler, Leslie 58
Munro, Alice 274, 304
Murray, Heather 186

N
Native Earth Performing Arts 229
Neekna and Chemai (Armstrong) 137
Negabmat, Marie 216
Nepveu, Pierre 106, 322, 336–37
Neuman, Shirley 75
New, W.H. 259–60, 333–35
New French Feminisms 37
Newson, Jan 49
Nights in the Underground (Blais) 286,
    291, 301
No Address (Obomsawin) 110
Noël, Francine 351–52
North American Boundary
    Commission 328
North American Free Trade
    Agreement (NAFTA) 318–19
NourbeSe Philip, Marlene 114, 161–73,
    195–96
Nuits de l'Underground (Blais) 299, see
    also *Nights in the Underground*

O
O Canada (Wilson) 299
Obomsawin, Alanis 110
Official Languages Act 42, 279
Olson, Charles 74–75
Ondaatje, Michael 77
Ontario Arts Council (OAC) 251–52
Ontario's Advisory Committee on
    Confederation 18
Open Letter 24, 29, 42, 58, 70, 284
Organization of American States 319
Ouellette-Michalska, Madeleine 90,
    103–104
Oxford Companion to Canadian Literature
    294

P
Panet, Jean-Antoine 327
Panet, Louis-Philippe 327
Parmenius, Stephen 210
*Patterns of Isolation in English Canadian
    Fiction* (Moss) 243
Patterson, Janet 93
Paz, Octavio 356–57
Pêchaux, Michel 125–26
Peirce, C.S. 23
Pemmican Press 138
Pennee, Donna 256
Perkes, Carolyn 281–82, 284, 295, 311
Peyron, Christophe 319
Pickthall, Marjorie 294
Pignatari, Décio 341
Places Far From Ellesmere (van Herk)
    344–46
Pleasure of the Text, The (Barthes) 68,
    77–78, 104
Poetics of Prose, The (Todorov) 67
Poetics of Space, The (Bachelard) 71
Poets of Reality (Miller) 74
Poitras, Ed 109
Pollock, Griselda 131
Polster, Claire 49

Poronovich, Walter 286–87, 289
Poulet, George 70–71
Poulin, Jacques 351
Pour une sociologie du roman (Goldmann) 22
Power Plant 319–20
Powwow Highway 109
Prince, Gerald 93
Princess Pocahontas and the Blue Spots (Mojica) 109
Private and Fictional Words (Howell) 293
Prix David 279
Prix Femina 279, 290
Prix des Libraires 290, 302
Prix Médicis 290, 299

Q
Quaife, Darlene Barry 119–21
Quand je lis, je m'invente (Lamy) 104

R
Radin, Paul 232
Randall, Marilyn 289–90
Rea, Annabelle 286
Records of Early English Drama (REED) 32
Redekop, Magdalene 80
Relations (Cartier) 210
Report of the Royal Commission on Bilingualism and Biculturalism 163–64
Resources for Feminist Research/ Documentation sur la recherche féministe 30
Rez Sisters, The (Highway) 109
Rich, Adrienne 34
Richards, I.A. 22
Ricoeur, Paul 40
Riddell, Joseph 74
Rièse, Laura 307–308
Riffaterre, Michael 67–68

Rioux, Hélène 312
Rioux, Michèle 319
Roberts, Charles G.D. 50
Roper, Gordon 20, 21
Ross, Malcolm 20–21, 269
Roux, Jean-Pierre 83
Roy, Gabrielle 247, 274, 278–80, 284–93, 296–98
Roy, Lucille 87
Royal Commission on National Development in the Arts, Letters, and Sciences 245–46, 288
Royer, Jean 99

S
Sage, the Fool, and the Dancer, The (Highway) 109
Saint-Jacques, Denis 277, 278
Saussure, Ferdinand de 67–68
Savard, Félix-Antoine 85
Scandalous Bodies: Diasporic Literature in English Canada (Kamboureli) 264–69
Scobie, Stephen 37, 77–78, 198–99
Scott, David 258
Scott, F.R. 305–307, 309–310
Scott, Gail 36, 290
Second Story Press 114
Sen, Nebeeneta Dev 39
Serafin, Bruce 197–98
Shapiro, Norman 302
She Tries Her Tongue, Her Silence Softly Breaks (NourbeSe Philip) 162, 166
Sheard, Charlene 34
Signature 37
Signature Event Cantext: Essays (Scobie) 198–99
Silvera, Makeda 41, 113
Silverman, Kaja 39
Sirois, Antoine 98, 273
Sister Vision Press 41, 113
Sitting Bull 228–29

Skelton, Robin 308
Slash (Armstrong) 41, 122–23, 132–41, 148–57
Smart, Patricia Purcell 34, 37, 286, 307–308
Smith, A.J.M. 175, 193
Smith, Beverley 303
Snead, James 167
Social Sciences and Humanities Research Council of Canada (SSHRC) 32, 253
Spivak, Gayatri Chakravorty 122, 131–32, 233, 294
St-Denys Garneau & Anne Hébert: Translations (Scott) 305
St. Louis Blues (Blais) 300
Starobinski, Jean 87
Stock, Brian 255
Stratford, Philip 21
Street of Riches (Roy) 290
Structure, idéologie et reception du roman québécois de 1940 à 1960 (Michon) 86
Summit of the Americas 319
Surfacing (Atwood) 346, 348–50
Survival: A Thematic Guide to Canadian Literature (Atwood) 243
Suzor-Côté, Marc-Aurèle 351
Symon Commission 30–31

T

Tale of Don L'Original, The (Maillet) 42
Tallman, Warren 304
Tardivel, Jules-Paul 20–21
Tel Quel Group 64–65
Temptations of Big Bear, The (Wiebe) 166
Tessera 35–37, 43, 106–107, 284, 310. 311–12
Theatre Passe Muraille 109
Théoret, France 98–99
Thérien, Gilles 107
These Our Mothers (Brossard) 42
Theytus Books 137, 138

This Sex Which Is Not One (Irigaray) 104
Thomas, Audrey 77
Thomas, Clara 25, 30
Threadgold, Terry 39
Tin Flute, The (Roy) 290, 296, 297–98
To Know Ourselves: The Report of the Commission on Canadian Studies 31, 50
Todorov, Tzvetan 59, 65, 66–67
Tomb of the Kings, The (Miller) 305, 309–310
Toronto Area Women's Research Colloquium 29
Toronto International Women's Day Committee 41
Toronto Semiotic Circle 39
Trajectoires (Guavin and Klinkenberg) 86
Trajectoires: Littérature et institutions au Québec et en Belgique francophone (Gauvin and Klinkenberg) 107
Transblanco (em torno a Blanco de Octavio Paz) (de Campos and Paz) 356–57
Trickster, The (Highway) 110, 111, 123
Turgeon Commission 245

U

Une joualonais sa joualonie (Blais) 300
Une saison dans la vie d'Emmanuel (Blais) 279, 286, 290, 299
Urbas, Jeannette 30

V

van Herk, Aritha 291, 304, 344–46
Venuti, Laurence 43, 254
Verduyn, Christl 255
Verthuy, Maïr 34, 37, 41
Vincent, Isabel 119
Vivre! Vivre! (Blais) 300
Vizenor, Gerald 231–32
Volkswagen Blues (Poulin) 351

W

Waddington, Miriam 25
Ware, Tracy 184 – 85
Warland, Betsy 34
Watch that Ends the Night, The
    (MacLennan) 68
Weinzweig, Helen 346 – 48
Weir, Lorraine 72
Welty, Eudora 304
Werschler-Henry, Darren 196, 199
White, Hayden 191, 238
Whitfield, Agnes 86
Wiebe, Rudy 75, 166
Williams, Raymond 89
Williams-Wallace 114
Wilson, Edmond 292, 298 – 99
Wilson, Milton 20
Wilson, Robert Rawdon 199 – 200
Wittig, Monique 101
Women and Words 35, 36
Women Writers in Dialogue 34
Women's Cultural Building 34
Woodcock, George 69
Writers' Union of Canada 113, 292

Z

Zumthor, Paul 337 – 38

BARBARA GODARD, Historica Chair of Canadian Literature and Professor of English, French, Social and Political Thought, and Women's Studies at York University, Toronto, has published widely on Canadian and Quebec cultures and on feminist and literary theory. Through her writings on translation theory and translations of Quebec women writers, most recently Nicole Brossard's *Intimate Journal* (2004), she has contributed to the "cultural turn" in Translation Studies. Her most recent edited volumes include *Re:Generations: Canadian Women Poets in Conversation* (2005) and *Wider Boundaries of Daring: The Modernist Impulse in Canadian Women's Poetry* (2008, both with Di Brandt).

Godard is the recipient of the Gabrielle Roy Prize of the Association for Canadian and Quebec Literatures (1988), the Award of Merit of the Association of Canadian Studies (1995), the Vinay-Darbelnet Prize of the Canadian Association of Translation Studies (2000), and the Teaching Award of the Northeast Association of Graduate Schools (2002). For more information, visit her website at www.yorku.ca/bgodard.

SMARO KAMBOURELI is Professor and Canada Research Chair in Critical Studies in Canadian Literature at the University of Guelph, where she founded and directs TransCanada Institute. Her most recent publication is *Trans.Can.Lit: Resituating the Study of Canadian Literature,* a volume of essays she has co-edited with Roy Miki.

¶ The text face is Cartier Book Pro, Rod McDonald's revival of the distinctively Canadian typeface Cartier, originally designed by Carl Dair in 1967. The sans serif is Priori Sans, designed by Jonathan Barnbrook in 2003.